CRUMLIN VIADUCT

Previous Page – ***Plate 0.1:*** *Ex-GWR pannier tank No. 4678 of Pontypool Road shed heads over Crumlin Viaduct with an eastbound freight on 31st October 1962.* Bill Potter/Kidderminster Railway Museum

This Page – ***Plate 0.2:*** *A circa 1890 panorama showing almost the full extent of the the two bridges making up Crumlin Viaduct, with the longer section spanning the Ebbw Valley and the shorter one across the Kendon Valley to the left. A short westbound freight hauled by a GWR 0-6-0ST working bunker first ventures out onto the Ebbw section on the right.* Neil Parkhouse collection

CRUMLIN VIADUCT

'This singularly graceful and beautiful bridge'

GORDON WOOD
WITH
NEIL PARKHOUSE
& STEPHEN ROWSON

Plate 0.3: *A view looking north-east circa 1880, showing the full extent of the two structures that comprised Crumlin Viaduct, with the two piers holding the spans bridging the Kendon Valley in the foreground, and the six piers of the longer section crossing the Ebbw Valley beyond. The ironwork looks clean and bright, and may in fact have been recently repainted. Note too the clean white fence at the top of the hill between the two sections, which looks new here and was presumably erected as a wind break. In the right distance is Crumlin Junction, where the Llanhilleth Branch met with the NA&HR line.*
Neil Parkhouse collection

The Authors

Gordon Wood is a former member of the Royal Town Planning Institute and during his career in Local Government, he was closely involved with the restoration and refurbishment of historic buildings. One such project was the restoration of Great Malvern station, after an arson attack. Following a significant meeting held at the station, special arrangements were made to permit the study of historic records, then held at Paddington, in order to establish details of the construction of the station. Amongst these documents were found boxes of primary source material relating to the design and construction of Crumlin Viaduct. Additional permission was granted to index and copy the documents, by hand, allowing the completion of a comprehensive private study. This study, based entirely on the primary source material and from which the main text here has been prepared, now questions a number of previously published statements in regards to the viaduct's construction.

Neil Parkhouse is a co-founder (in 1994) and co-director of Lightmoor Press and in 1998 of Black Dwarf Publications, the two imprints joining together in 2003. He has authored numerous books and articles on railway and other related subjects, in particular, a unique and comprehensive series of volumes covering the railways of his home county Gloucestershire, as they appeared prior to the wholesale closures of the 1960s and illustrated entirely in colour. He has compiled the 'A Working Life' and 'A History in Pictures' chapters for this volume and several of the 'Associated Works' sub-sections. For over four decades he dealt in and has collected old postcards and photographs, and has supplied many of the pictures for this book from his extensive archive.

Stephen Rowson has long held an interest in the industrial and transport history of his native Glamorganshire. In conjunction with the late Ian Wright, he co-authored the seminal two volume history of the Glamorganshire & Aberdare Canals, published by Black Dwarf /Lightmoor in 2001-04. He is a member of the Association for Industrial Archaeology, the Railway & Canal Historical Society and the Oxford House Industrial Society. He too has spent decades collecting old postcards and photographs, particularly of South Wales, and many of the most historic pictures in this book are from his personal collection. He has contributed to several chapters, in particular 'Crumlin Viaduct and the Stereoscope', has supplied much additional detail for many of the captions and also the biographical information about Mark Philips.

CONTENTS

Published by LIGHTMOOR PRESS

Designed by Neil Parkhouse

British Library Cataloguing-in-Publication Data. A catalogue record for this book is available from the British Library

ISBN: 9781915069 XX X

LIGHTMOOR PRESS

Unit 144B, Lydney Trading Estate, Harbour Road, Lydney, Gloucestershire GL15 4EJ

www.lightmoor.co.uk / info@lightmoor.co.uk

Lightmoor Press is an imprint of Black Dwarf Lightmoor Publications Ltd

Printed in Poland – www.lfbookservices.co.uk

MONMOUTHSHIRE 1839

A portion of T. Morris's map of the Tramroads, Iron Works, Foundries and Collieries, in the area bounded by Newport, Caerphilly, Ebbw Vale and Abergavenny.
WELSH RAILWAYS RESEARCH CIRCLE

CONCEPT

CHAPTER 1

During the mid-1840s, any group of entrepreneurs looking to promote a railway line in the South Wales region would be confronted with a choice of what gauge of line to use. The Great Western Railway and their allies were constructing lines to Brunel's ambitious 7ft-0¼ inch broad gauge, whereas other promoters, not influenced by Brunel, were constructing lines to a gauge of 4ft 8½ inches, today's standard gauge. The latter was referred to at the time as the narrow gauge but henceforth we shall refer to it as the standard gauge to avoid confusion.

On 4th August 1845, the South Wales Railway Company obtained powers to construct a broad gauge line, laid out by Brunel, from Chepstow to Carmarthen, Fishguard and Pembroke, providing a direct broad gauge link between London and the ferries to Southern Ireland. Sections of the line between Chepstow and Cardiff ran along the South Wales coastline, providing access to, amongst others, the ports at Newport and Cardiff. However, lines serving the Valleys, cut by rivers flowing down to the coast and ports from the Welsh Uplands, were often converted to railways from earlier tramways, and were laid to the standard gauge. Thus any items conveyed on these lines from the valleys and destined for onward transit to locations other than the ports they served, had to be transferred to broad gauge wagons, and possibly further on back to standard gauge wagons for onward transshipment to areas not served by the broad gauge. Similar arrangements were required for incoming goods. Many of the colliery owners and iron masters located in the area preferred the standard gauge and were supportive of any proposal that provided a more accessible route for transporting their goods to the Midlands region.

Why such an impressive engineering structure was constructed across the river valleys of the Ebbw and Kendon at Crumlin can be attributed to the activities of entrepreneurs who favoured and promoted standard gauge lines, particularly those offering the chance to provide an efficient access to new markets for their coal and minerals in the Midlands. In 31st July 1845, the Monmouthshire Railway & Canal Company (MR&CC) obtained an Act of Parliament to construct a standard gauge line from Newport to Coed y Gric, north of Pontypool. The following year the Newport, Abergavenny & Hereford Railway Company (NA&HR) obtained their Act of Parliament to make a line from a junction with the Newport & Pontypool Railway at Coed y Gric to Hereford, where it would make a connection with the Shrewsbury & Hereford Railway, who had obtained their Act of Parliament in 1846, and the proposed Worcester & Hereford Railway.

Recognising the commercial benefits that would accrue by providing a connection between their route with those lines and tramroads serving the coalfields and ironworks of the Taff and Sirhowy valleys to the west, with connections to the Midlands and the agricultural districts of Hereford and Worcester in the east, the NA&HR promoted and obtained an Act of Parliament in 1847, to construct an extension to the Taff Vale Railway – a line that was to run from Coed y Gric to Quakers Yard, south of Merthyr Tydfil. Overcoming the problems of conflict that existed between the supporters of the broad and standard gauges, the line would provide direct access to the high volume of goods traffic, mainly coal, destined for the Midlands, and beyond. With the added possibility of agricultural products being carried on return journeys, a profitable return on investment could be anticipated.

PLATE 1.1: Front page of the NA&HR's 1847 Act.
AUTHOR'S COLLECTION

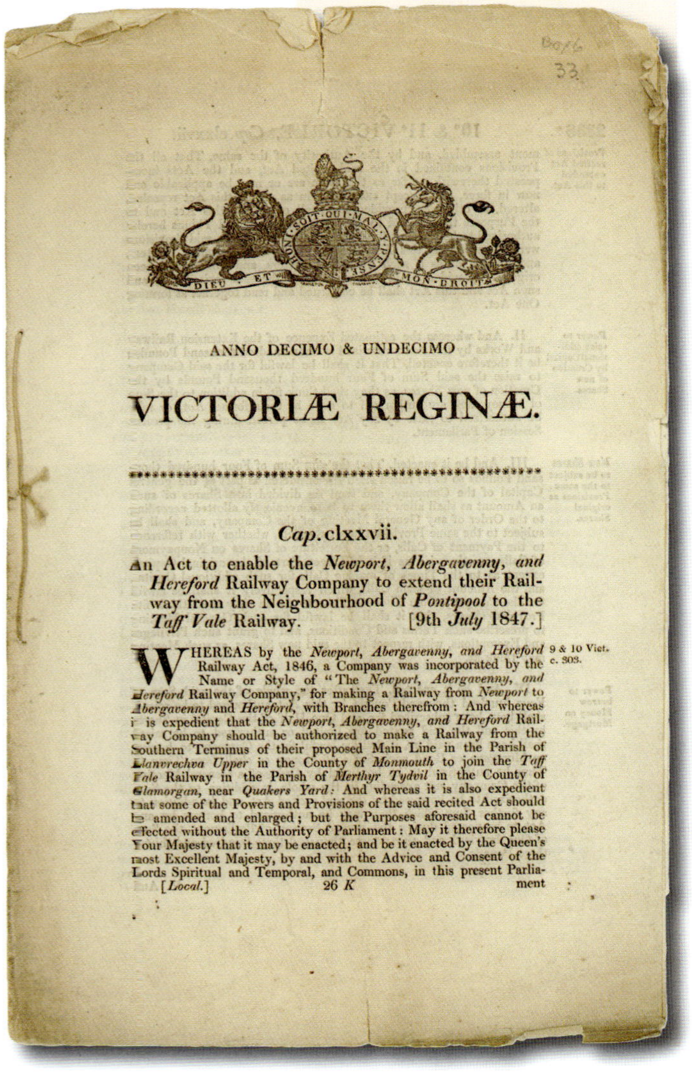

ANNO DECIMO & UNDECIMO

VICTORIÆ REGINÆ.

Cap. clxxvii.

An Act to enable the *Newport, Abergavenny, and Hereford* Railway Company to extend their Railway from the Neighbourhood of *Pontipool* to the *Taff Vale* Railway. [9th *July* 1847.]

WHEREAS by the *Newport, Abergavenny, and Hereford* Railway Act, 1846, a Company was incorporated by the Name or Style of "The *Newport, Abergavenny, and Hereford* Railway Company," for making a Railway from *Newport* to *Abergavenny* and *Hereford*, with Branches therefrom: And whereas it is expedient that the *Newport, Abergavenny, and Hereford* Railway Company should be authorized to make a Railway from the Southern Terminus of their proposed Main Line in the Parish of *Llanvrechva Upper* in the County of *Monmouth* to join the *Taff Vale* Railway in the Parish of *Merthyr Tydvil* in the County of *Glamorgan*, near *Quakers Yard*: And whereas it is also expedient that some of the Powers and Provisions of the said recited Act should be amended and enlarged; but the Purposes aforesaid cannot be effected without the Authority of Parliament: May it therefore please Your Majesty that it may be enacted; and be it enacted by the Queen's most Excellent Majesty, by and with the Advice and Consent of the Lords Spiritual and Temporal, and Commons, in this present Parliament 9 & 10 Vict. c. 303.

[*Local.*] 26 *K*

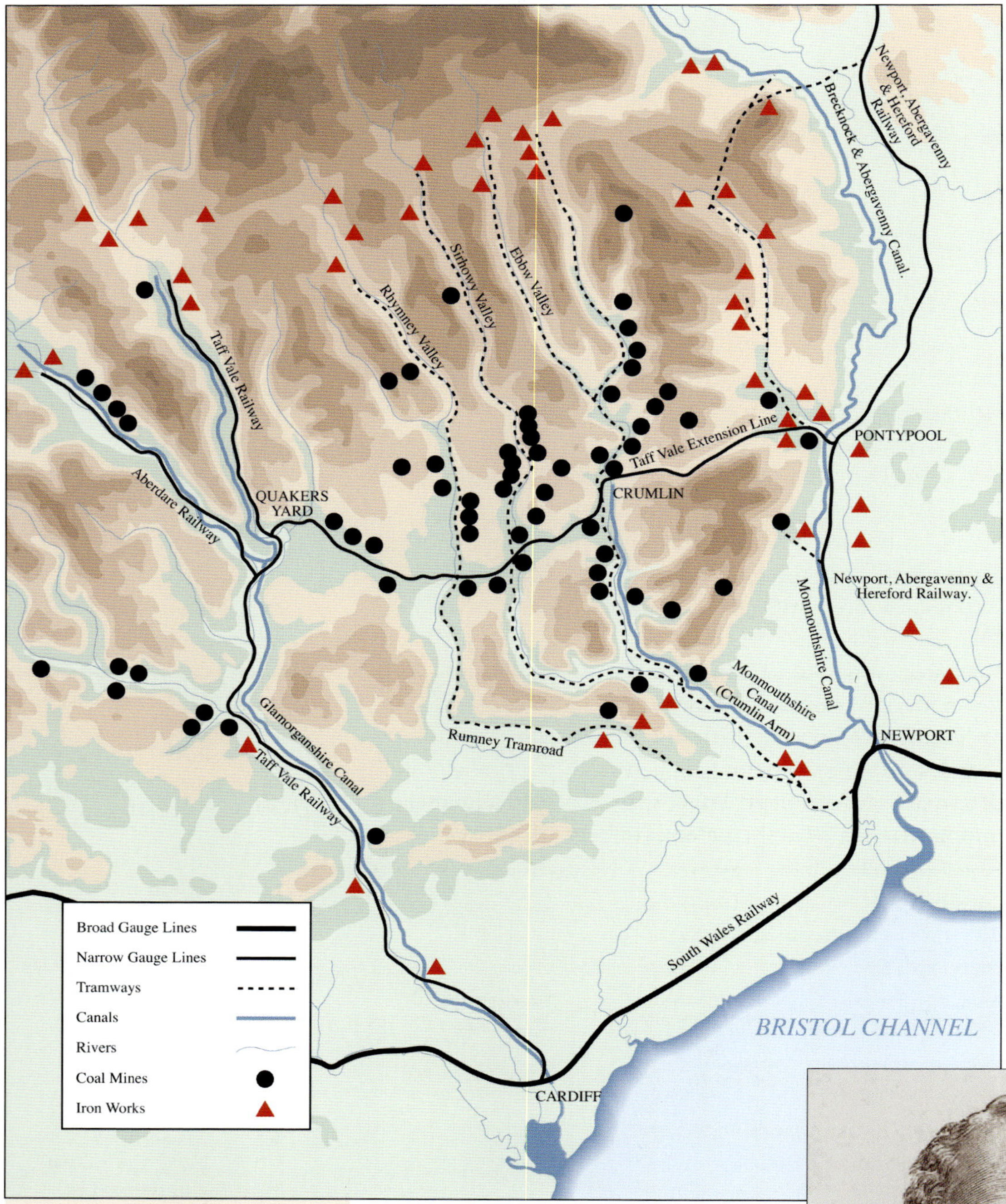

FIG. 1.1: Map showing the railways, tramroads, canals, rivers, coal mines and ironworks in the Western Valleys circa 1850. IAN POPE

However, by running directly across the natural north-south orientation of the Taff, Sirhowy, Kendon and Ebbw valleys, the line was to present any engineer with a number of major engineering challenges, the most significant of which was the crossing of the valleys of the rivers Kendon and Ebbw at or near Crumlin (*Fig. 1.1*). Two engineers were employed by the NA&HR to resolve the problem.

John Miller (1805-1883), then consultant engineer to the NA&HR and better known as an engineer to many of the railway companies in Scotland, surveyed and selected the route of 1847. This was to be one of his final designs, prior to his retirement from railway matters in 1850. Miller chose to cross the Kendon and Ebbw valleys by means of a curved viaduct approximately 540 feet long. At its highest point it would be 117 feet above the valley floor, and approached by severe gradients (*Fig's 1.2 & 1.3*).

Charles Liddell (1813-1894) was a former pupil of George Stephenson and had worked with Robert Stephenson on the North Midland Railway. Outside of railway work he was involved in land drainage and land reclamation, whilst overseas work included laying undersea cables. At a board meeting held on 14th February 1851, it was reported that the secretary had met Mr Liddell to discuss terms for the post of engineer in Chief. At the same time Liddell was given instructions to *'immediately lay out a line from Pontypool to Crumlin, and to provide an estimate of costs for the construction of their Taff Vale Extension line, but only as a single line'*.

As well as being the company's engineer, Liddell also held the same post with the Worcester & Hereford Railway. He was formally appointed as engineer in Chief to the NA&HR on 28th April 1851 but on terms still to be agreed. These were later confirmed in full and reported to a board meeting on 29th May 1851. In partnership with Liddell was Professor Lewis Dunbar Brodie Gordon, who was the first Professor of Engineering at Glasgow University. He resigned from his academic post in 1855 in order to devote more time to his commercial interests.

PLATE 1.2: Portrait of Charles Liddell (1813-1894), which was published with a short obituary in the Illustrated London News of 25th August 1894.

At a board meeting held on 29th April 1852, Liddell recommended a number of amendments that included easing gradients, reducing the length of tunnels and forming better junctions with other compatible lines. Liddell made two amendments in the Crumlin area. The first was a branch that left the main line close to the Ebbw Valley and a proposed viaduct, and ran down a gradient of 1 in 45 to Llanhilleth, where it formed a junction with the MR&CC's lines serving the coalfields and ironworks of Monmouthshire's Western Valleys. The other amendment was to take the route of the line further up the valley of the River Ebbw, and to cross the valley by means of a viaduct reported to be 1,632 feet long and 208 feet above the valley floor (*Fig's 1.2 & 1.4*). The extent of Liddell's amendments required the company to obtain an Amendment Act that received the Royal Assent on 4th August 1853.

Prior to the company obtaining their amended Act of Parliament, Liddell and Gordon had spent time during 1852 analysing the economic constraints associated with the different forms of construction required to complete the viaduct. Their initial reaction was to construct a viaduct using traditional tried and tested methods of brick or masonry piers, bridged with iron trusses. Developing these ideas further, Gordon began to favour a viaduct with arches of either cast or wrought iron resting on masonry piers. Influencing his opinions was the design of the wrought iron arches he and Liddell had produced for the bridge over the River Wye at Hereford. Gordon considered it to be a beautiful and successful design, although he did admit that adopting the same design at Crumlin would present them with a number of challenging problems. However, a consultancy engagement and a chance meeting was to change Gordon's opinion in favour of the recently patented Warren Truss. Commenting on the use of the Warren Patent Truss, Gordon was to state, '*I was down in Norfolk on estuary business where I had been engaged as engineer, and on my return from Norfolk I met the party who were returning from the Newark Dyke Bridge, and it was at that period that the matter was brought prominently before me*'.[1]

The principle feature of the design of the Warren Patent Truss or girder was the use of small quantities of iron, assembled in such a manner as to carry relatively large and heavy loads. James Warren (1802-1870), who patented the design, was not a trained engineer but someone who held an obsession for developing a structurally sound and economic iron truss, to use for carrying railway lines across roads, rivers and valleys.[2]

At that time financiers, ironmasters, engineers, colliery owners, contractors and entrepreneurs all belonged to a very close knit social and business community. These personal contacts and the interaction of business interests are evident during the commissioning and construction of Crumlin Viaduct. Within the Crumlin circle was Charles Heard Wild (1814-1857), an advocate and joint patentee for the Warren Truss, who also held a financial interest in the use of the patent. He began his career as a

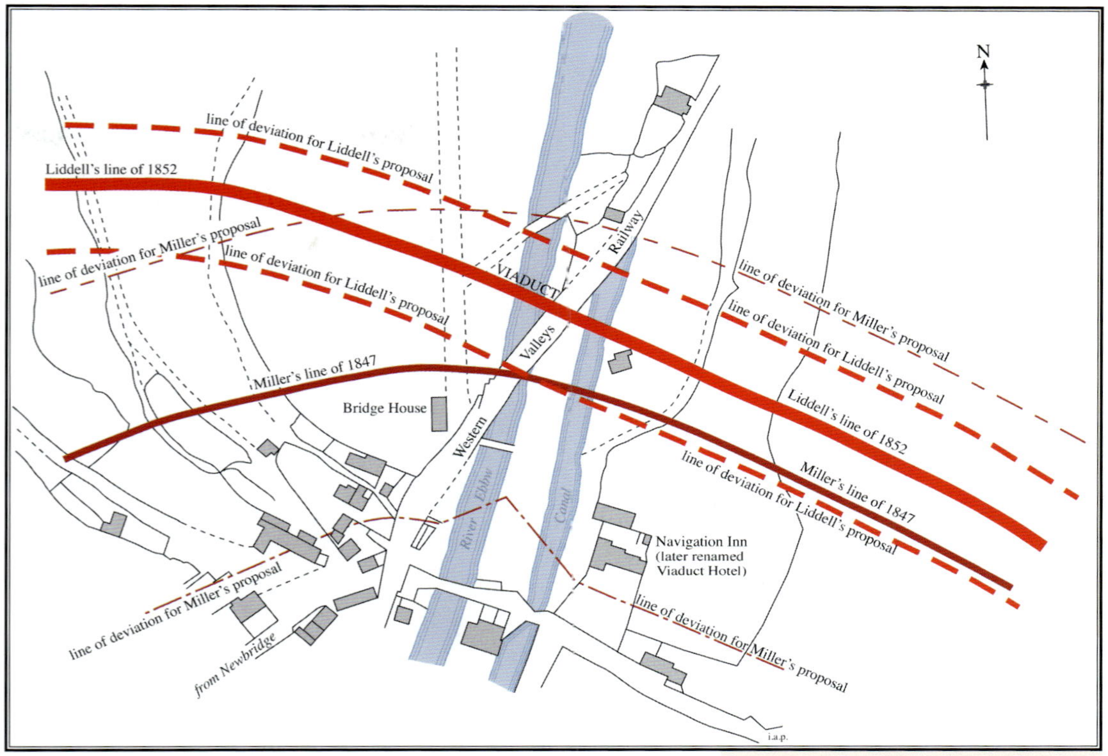

FIG. 1.2: Map illustrating Miller's line of 1847 and Liddell's line of 1852 for crossing the Ebbw and Kendon valleys at Crumlin. IAN POPE

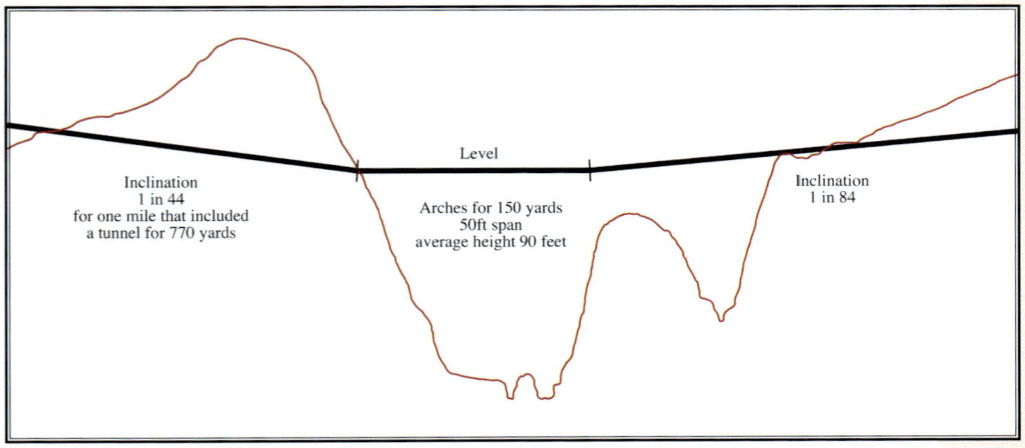

FIG 1.3: Miller's section for the line across the Ebbw and Kendon valleys. IAN POPE

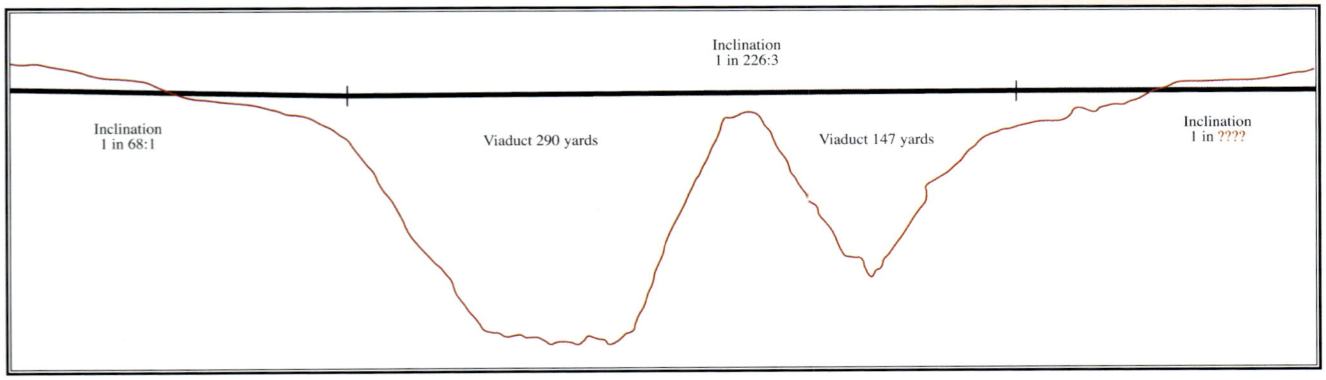

FIG 1.4: Liddell's section for the line across the Ebbw and Kendon valleys. IAN POPE

PLATE 1.3: An engraving of Gordon and Liddell's new viaduct carrying the NA&HR across the River Wye at Hereford, from the ILN of 17th December 1853, looking east towards the cathedral. In fact the line was officially only open to goods at this time, since 30th July 1852 in fact, with formal opening to passengers scheduled for 6th December 1853. However, a slip at Llanvihangel led to Captain Wynne, the board of Trade inspecting officer, refusing this, delaying the start of the passenger service until 2nd January 1854.

draughtsman on the Manchester & Birmingham Railway, before working under Robert Stephenson on the Chester & Holyhead Railway. Here he would have been familiar with the Conwy (Conway) and Menai tubular bridges. Wild was also the resident engineer during the relocation of Paxton's Great Exhibition Hall of 1851 from Hyde Park to Crystal Palace.

An associate of Wild's was Robert William Kennard (1800-1870), a banker and ironmaster, who had made a fortune from investing in railway ventures. Robert Kennard had witnessed the growth in the demand for the use of iron associated with railway construction and had obtained financial interests in ironworks at Falkirk in Scotland, and at Blaenavon and nearby Garnddyrus in South Wales. He also held an interest in warehouses located on the River Thames, where finished iron was stored ready for despatch to construction sites. In 1851, he was investing in railways in India, where he was invited to supply Warren Trusses for the railways then being developed by the East India Company. Acting at that time as Robert Kennard's consultant engineer, Wild probably had an interest in their design.

PLATE 1.4: Portrait of Robert William Kennard (1800-1870) in his later years. Amongst other things, Kennard was a city banker cum iron merchant, owner of the Falkirk Ironworks and a director of the Blaenavon Ironworks. AUTHOR'S COLLECTION

Thomas William Kennard (1825-1893), second son of Robert, had a personal interest in the use of the Warren Truss and its further development. However, statements regarding Thomas Kennard's early engineering activities are contradictory and dubious. The first reference to him being involved with bridges was in 1851, when he was working with the engineer Joseph Cubitt on the Great Northern Railway. Under his direction he gained some experience on the design and construction of bridges using the Warren Patent Truss. By 1852, Kennard was claiming that he had established his own business for the manufacture of bridges.

PLATE 1.5: Robert Kennard's Iron Wharf on the River Thames, photographed looking north-west from Southwark Bridge circa 1860. Far left, leading down to the water, is Queenhithe Stairs and St. Paul's Cathedral looms large in the background.
STEPHEN ROWSON COLLECTION

Amongst the group that Gordon met on his return from Norfolk were Wild and Kennard, who never lost an opportunity to call on him to promote the virtues of the Warren Truss. During a visit to the offices of Gordon and Liddell in June 1852, Kennard '*had a long chat about Crumlin Viaduct*'.[3] Discussions between Gordon and Liddell regarding the design principles of the Warren Truss resulted in both engineers becoming, according to Gordon, '*partisans – as it were – to the Warren system*', and they '*determined on recommending the Newport, Abergavenny & Hereford Company to adopt that system*'.[4] It was then arranged that Liddell should contact Kennard (who claimed to be a close friend of Liddell) and advise him that they (Liddell and Gordon) were preparing a report for presentation to the board, advising them to adopt the Warren Patent Truss for viaducts on their Taff Vale Extension line. Their intention was to inform the board that Kennard had given much attention to the subject and that he was prepared to tender for their construction, and at a lower rate than any other form of bridge Liddell and Gordon had studied. To assist them, when reporting to the board, Liddell asked Kennard to let him have a drawing or tracing of a 200 foot girder, and to accompany it with an estimate as to what rate per foot run he would expect to be able to do the work. Liddell suggested to Kennard that he should state an amount rather above what he would offer to do the work for in a formal tender.[5]

Kennard seized on the opportunity and produced a tracing of a design for the superstructure as Liddell had requested. He

PLATE 1.6: Portrait of Thomas William Kennard (1825-1893), published with his obituary in the ILN of 23rd September 1893.

THE LATE MR. THOMAS WILLIAM KENNARD.

was prepared to undertake the construction for a sum of £15 per foot run. For an additional cost of 20 shillings per ton, he would erect the whole, on the spot, and lift each completed girder into place on each pier.[6] After discussing his estimates, and on Liddell's advice, Kennard increased the sum of £15 per foot run to £17 per foot run.[7] Kennard was examined on these figures by Counsel in a later arbitration hearing, with damning results.

Liddell's and Gordon's report to the board stated that, '*for some months we have been considering the means of constructing viaducts over the valleys at Crumlin, and other deep valleys on the Taff Vale Extension line*'. Liddell provided examples, with comparable costs, of various designs of bridges and had concluded that a braced girder bridge on the Warren Patent was the cheapest that he had assessed. He then provided the board with the design and costs prepared by Kennard who, Liddell explained, had in the past three years erected several bridges on the Warren principle, one of them having a span of 250 feet that had been constructed under the direction of Mr Cubitt on the Great Northern Railway. According to Liddell, the prices stated in Kennard's letter were calculated from experience gained in erecting bridges on this design. Liddell recommended to the board that they take tenders from Kennard for the supply of 250 foot and 200 foot girders for the viaduct at Crumlin and the prices for girders of different spans for crossing other valleys. Liddell was to supply the precise details for these later.[8]

The board, on considering Liddell's report, decided to defer any decision until their next meeting.[9] Robinson, the deputy chairman and an ironmaster from Nantyglo, Monmouthshire, had mentioned to the board details of a bridge of wrought iron across the Taff Vale at Trefas (Treforest), that had been erected by William Doyne. The board requested Robinson to obtain a tender from Doyne for a wrought iron bridge over five openings of 200 feet. Liddell was requested to report on Doyne's and Kennard's structures at a board meeting to be held on 16th September 1852.[10]

Within days, Liddell had forwarded to Kennard and Doyne a letter and copies of a tracing that he had prepared for crossing the Ebbw Valley, with piers shown for two different spans – one of four openings of 250 feet each and one for five openings of 200 feet each but leaving Kennard and Doyne to provide details of their suggested proposals, subject to them meeting certain conditions that Liddell had set out in his letter. Liddell specified that '*the load was to be taken at 1 ton per foot running on each line* (i.e. 400 tons on each opening of 200 feet and 500 tons on each opening of 250 feet) *exclusive of the weight of the girders, platform and roadway themselves. That the strain of the tension beam was not to exceed 5 tons per square inch at least, and that the*

Plate 1.7: In 1851, William Thomas Doyne had designed and built a wrought iron lattice bridge of 200 feet span in the Taff Valley, which carried the Aberdare Iron Company's railway from its rolling mills at Treforest across the River Taff to the Glamorganshire Canal. Doyne had worked for both the Aberdare Company and the Ebbw Vale Company as engineer and geologist. Although Liddell was decided on Kennard, the board conceded to inspecting Doyne's bridge and then allowed him to tender for the viaduct contract too. This circa 1908 postcard view shows (bottom right) Doyne's bridge, now a footbridge and overshadowed by Glyntaff station on the Pontypridd, Caerphilly & Newport Railway. Of additional interest in this picture are the two Barnum & Bailey coaches that the Alexandra (Newport & South Wales) Docks & Railway had acquired from the circus when Buffalo Bill returned to the USA in October 1904. The span of Doyne's bridge was replaced later in the century and remains today, supported on the original stone abutments.
NEIL PARKHOUSE COLLECTION

compression beam was to be in equilibrium with the tension beam. The platform of the roadway was to be of double 4 inch planking laid diagonally upon the upper side of the girders which were to be well braced laterally. Prices quoted were to be made for both sizes of girder fixed complete with platform, hand rail and bed plates'. The masonry piers up to the level of the bottom of the girders would be prepared by the company, the exact height being determined by the depth of the girder either Kennard or Doyne proposed. The depth of the girder shown on the tracings provided by Liddell was 30 feet but he agreed that this could be varied. He also pointed out that only one of the two viaducts would be required to be tendered for but adjoining was another crossing the Kendon Valley, which would have had two spans of about 250 feet each.[11]

Both tenders were considered at the next board meeting but the directors failed to reach a conclusive decision and referred them to Liddell, with instructions '*to supply plans and specification of the ground work and understructure of the Crumlin Bridge to Mr Kennard and Mr Doyne, leaving them to alter the spans to any dimension they considered most economical in terms of cost of construction, but without diminishing the strength and safety of the bridge, and to submit tenders for the whole*'. Liddell then had to report back to the board on 30th September 1852.[12]

Liddell informed Kennard that his tender was the lowest, telling him that Doyne's price was £15 0s for 29 feet deep girders, 25s per foot run for fixing and 2s 6d a foot for roadway. Doyne had suggested that if the whole work was done as one contract, the ironwork in the piers and lifting of the girders would be cheaper, as the scaffolding etc would be useful for both. The board considered that Mr Rennie, the company's contractor for the line, did not have a right to be offered a contract for the masonry work and that the best way would be to request Doyne and Kennard to provide tenders for two bridges, complete with masonry. Liddell also told Kennard that Doyne had got a notion that he could do the work much cheaper by using iron piers with large spans, and '*that now requires me to make half a dozen designs for different spans to provide for all the changes*'. On the design of the piers, Liddell let Kennard know that he had often thought of trying wrought iron, built up and braced with tie rods and ribs, and sent Kennard a rough illustration of his ideas (**Fig. 1.5**). He added: '*You have a fortnight for giving in the tenders and I propose to include the whole length of the double valley which will take some 8 spans of 200 feet each in all.*'. Liddell suggested that if Kennard wanted to continue and to provide a tender, he should visit Crumlin and meet Mr Rennie, then try to assess the size and costs of the works involved for the piers, so as not to provide for too many sizes. He warned Kennard that if the brick or masonry work exceeded 22s or 24s a yard, the bridges would never be built and it would be of no value if he quoted £3 per cubic yard for ashlar work. He also told Kennard that he would not have to do anything more on the ironwork calculations and drawings unless he thought that he could beat brickwork at shillings. Rather than go to any unnecessary expense, Liddell advised him that if he chose to use iron piers they had to be at a price within the shillings limit.[13]

An important document missing from the historical records is a copy of Doyne's letter to Liddell. The contents had obviously set Liddell thinking seriously on the use of iron piers for him to mention the fact in his letter to Kennard. What appears very unprofessional was the fact that he had, by letter, disclosed to Kennard details of Doyne's costs and thoughts, with no reference to having provided Doyne with the contents of Kennard's letter, unless it had been agreed that the deputy chairman, Robinson, should do this. If this was not the case it would appear that there was a strong bias in favour of Kennard and the use of the Warren Patent Truss from the outset.

Kennard was quick to respond to the suggestion that he visit Crumlin when he offered to meet Liddell at Newport on any day agreeable.[14] Casual comments made several months later suggest that Kennard met Gordon and Liddell at Newport, before continuing to Crumlin where he met Rennie. Kennard then submitted a further tender that included a figure for the superstructure and the piers. He and Rennie had visited quarries in the area and had concluded that the cost of constructing masonry piers would be 30s per cubic yard. With regard to the superstructure he submitted a modification of a design for a wrought iron column he claimed he had made previously; however, he failed to provide any details of its design or location.

In calculating the cost of the wrought iron columns, Kennard recommended that the valley be divided into six spans of 150 feet each with girders of 150 feet clear span. For this he provided a number of options:

- If divided into 6 triangles...............£9 0s per foot run
- If divided into 6 triangles but the girder increased in depth ....£9 10s per foot run
- If divided into 8 equilateral triangles..£11 0s per foot run
- The superstructure composed of girders 150 feet clear span ....£12 0s per foot run

Fig. 1.5: *Copy of Liddell's sketch that he sent to Kennard.* Author

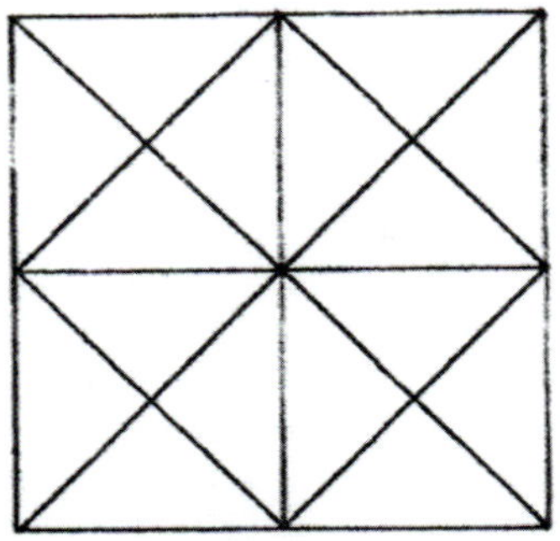

Fig. 1.6: *Suggested layout of the bracing for Kennard's nine columns.* Author

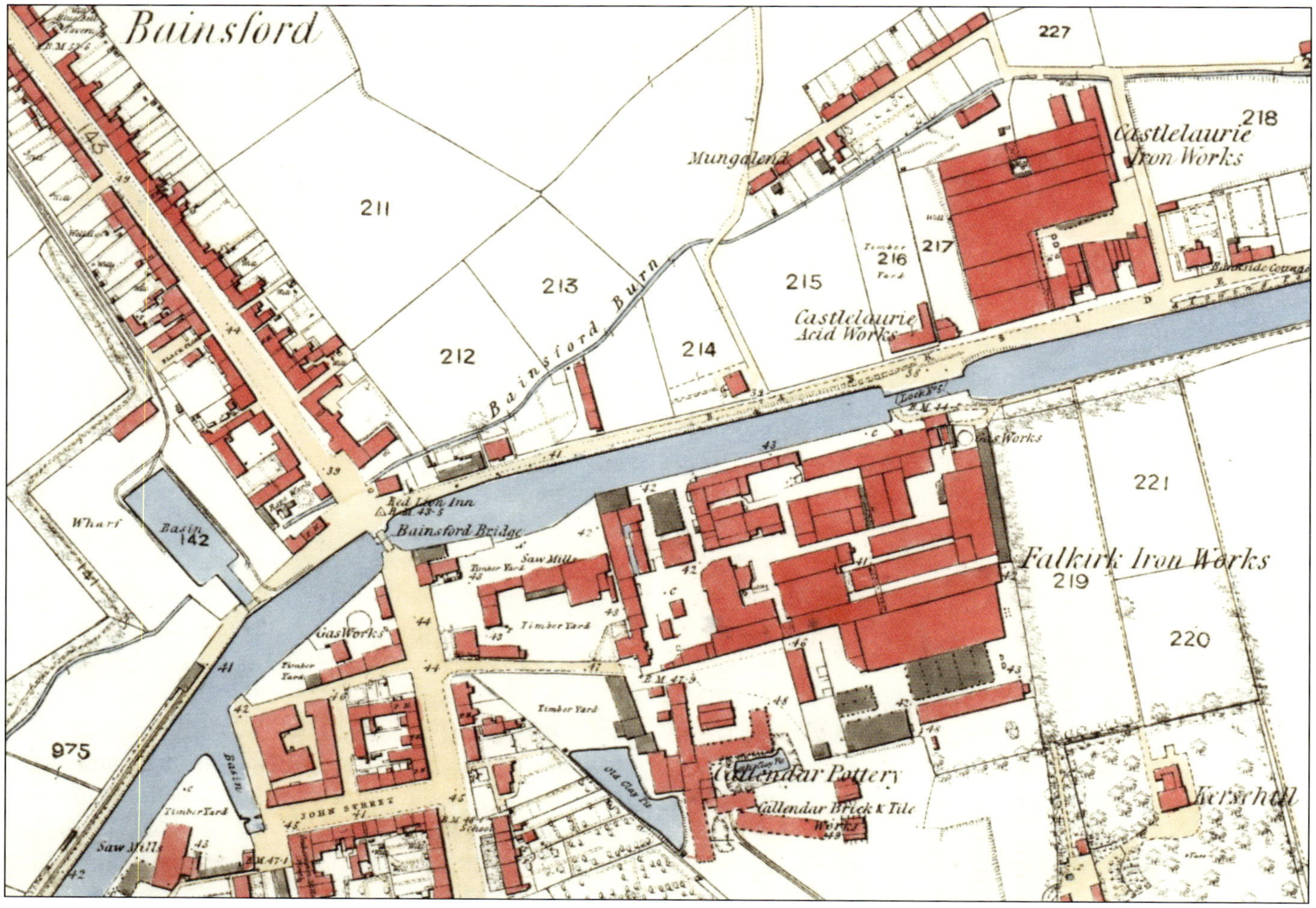

Fig. 1.7: *Falkirk Ironworks, as shown on the 1st Edition 25 inch OS, surveyed in 1859 and published in 1862.*

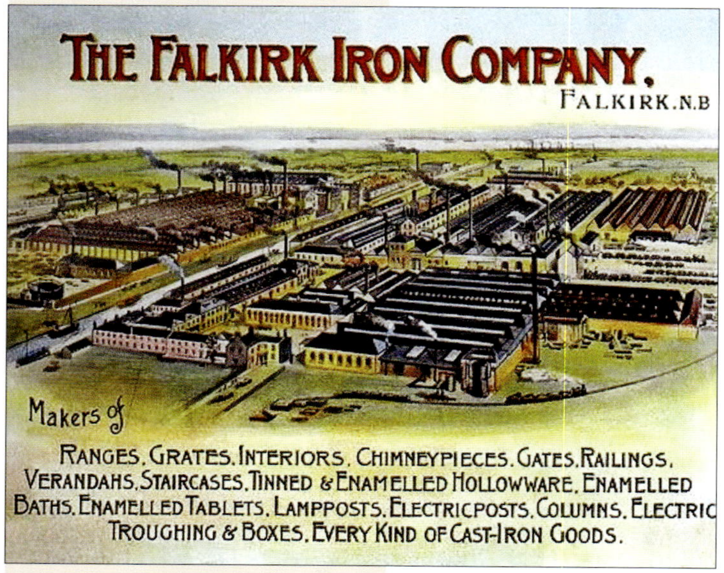

Plate 1.8: *A circa 1900 colour litho advertisement for the Falkirk Iron Company, by which time the works had expanded considerably from that shown on the OS map.*

Kennard's plan for the piers was to use nine columns. The total cost, including foundation plates, cross bracing and fixing, was estimated to be £10 per foot run but this price could vary depending on the amount of strain that was considered safe to place upon them. According to Kennard, his design had been calculated to leave but a slight strain upon the iron and it was possible that he had erred in making it too strong. If Liddell thought that this was the case, then he could erect a similar structure within the limits of safety at £8 per foot run[15] (*Fig. 1.6*).

It would appear that Kennard had completely misread Liddell's specification. Liddell had made it quite clear in the specification that he was seeking a price for two viaducts, one over the Ebbw Valley and the other over the Kendon Valley, as one structure with a total length of 1,600 feet. To clear up the confusion and to obtain a price for the whole structure, Liddell consulted Kennard. In his company, and with Kennard's agreement, the tender figures were amended to cover the 1,600 foot long viaduct and these amended figures were attached to Kennard's submission as a memorandum:

Girders 1,380 feet long at £14 foot per foot run complete........................£19,200
Height of piers including spaces between the girders 1,120 feet at £8, total........................£ 8,960
Abutments........................£ 2,000
Earthwork........................£ 600
Painting etc, etc, etc,........................£ 600
or £19 12s per foot run for 1,602 feet, total......£31,480[16]

When the board next met, they referred the tenders and memorandum from Kennard and Doyne to Liddell, to prepare a report that he was to present the following day to an appointed committee, which included Mr Robinson. The Committee were instructed to decide on which bridge was to be erected.[17] A report prepared by

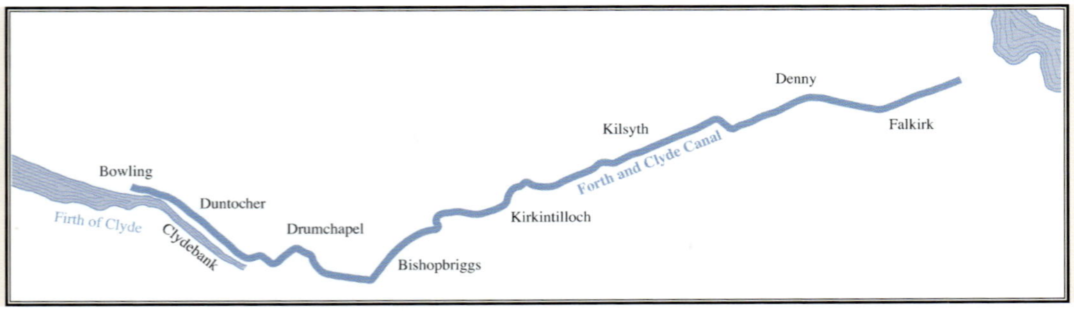

Fig. 1.8: Route of the Forth & Clyde Canal from Kennard's Falkirk Ironworks to the wharf at Bowling. Ian Pope

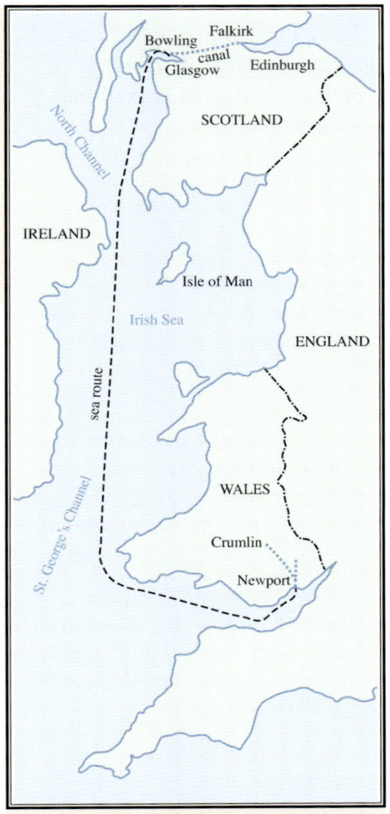

Fig. 1.9: Short sea route from Bowling Wharf to Newport via the Irish Sea. Ian Pope

Fig. 1.10: Route from Newport, via the Crumlin Arm of the Monmouthshire Canal. Ian Pope

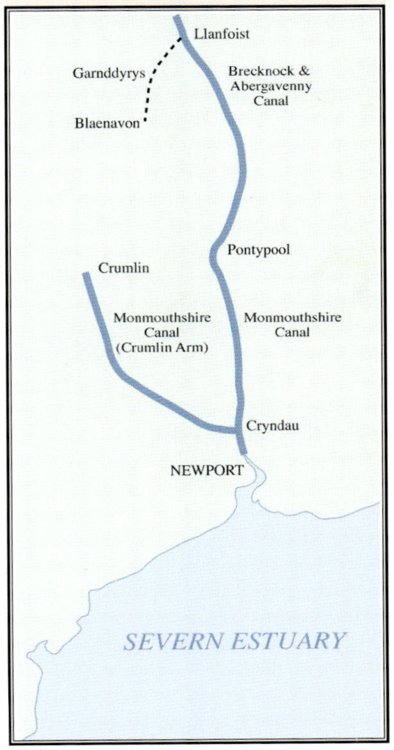

Gordon and presented to them by Liddell read as follows:

'Report on designs sent in by Messrs T.W. Kennard and W.T. Doyne

30th September 1852

Having carefully examined the designs of Messrs Kennard and Doyne for the Crumlin Viaduct I am of the opinion,

1) That Mr Kennard's design for the superstructure affords the necessary assurance of sufficiency of strength and stiffness and facility of examining all the parts from time to time required in so important a structure.

2) That the construction of cast iron piers proposed by Mr Kennard does not perfectly fulfil all the conditions required for stability, but the design may be altered in this respect so as to secure all that is wanted without adding to its cost.

3) That the cost of the viaduct proposed in one design submitted by Mr Kennard including every detail of permanent way, except the rails, is per tender £19 12 0 per foot run for the whole length of 1,602 feet £31,480. Whilst for another design in which spans of 120 feet are proposed instead of 150 feet the cost would be only £17 per foot run, or for the whole length of 1,602 feet £27,234.

4) That Mr Doyne's design for the superstructure is chiefly a lattice bridge of malleable iron latticing and does not afford the necessary assurance of sufficiency of strength and stiffness of facility of maintenance. The lattice framings of Mr Doyne's bridge are of unprecedented breadth and no apparent precaution has been taken to prevent the buckling to which the sides of these structures are notoriously and necessarily liable. The roadway superstructure is quite insufficient even if the distance of only 22 feet between the parapets could be admitted which it should never be. Mr Doyne's drawings contain extremely few details of the construction or dimensions of the parts and I cannot therefore enter into a determination of its absolute strength.

5) That the piers of Mr Doyne's bridge have sufficient strength (supposing the pipes to be 1 inch thick metal) as mere columns, but they are deficient in lateral stability and would require to be essentially modified, though perhaps not much increased in weight to answer the purpose for which they are intended.

6) That according to the tender the cost of Mr Doyne's bridge complete is £24 per foot run or for the total length of 1,602 feet, £38,448.

7) That on the score of engineering merit and also of economy, Mr Kennard's tender should be accepted. In accepting the tender however, it will be necessary to stipulate that the contract be drawn up on the principle of a lump sum contract for the work completed, (according to my specification), which is not to be exceeded and at the same time on a schedule of prices so that any economy of weight that may result in working out the details, may accrue to the advantage of the Railway Company.

8) Since I suggested the use of iron piers the division of the valley into spans of 150 feet proves more economical than the division into greater spans, and the calculations I have made enable me to state that the design for malleable iron arched girders could be carried across the 1,602 feet for less than the sum of £38,000 and such a design is unquestionably preferable to any lattice bridge as far as I have knowledge of the construction. It is only because I am satisfied of the means of determining the strength of every part of Warren's bridge and decided economy of it, that I withdraw that design in favour of Mr Kennard's.[18]

Following a considerable time spent in discussion, the Committee agreed to accept the tender submitted by T.W. Kennard.

However, Kennard was soon to face the problem of accepting a fixed price tender when, in a letter to Liddell in early October 1852, he identified the first of the financial problems that were to follow him throughout the period of the contract. He was concerned about the fact that iron had already risen in price, adding a further £1,000 to his estimated cost of the piers.[19]

The acceptance of his tender was to benefit other members of Kennard's family then involved in the production of iron. The columns would be cast at their Falkirk Works before being transported along the Forth & Clyde Canal by barge to Bowling (*Fig. 1.8*), from there by sailing barge to Newport (*Fig. 1.9*) and then by canal to Crumlin (*Fig. 1.10*). Cast iron produced at the Blaenavon Works was taken by tramroad to Garnddyrys,

Plate 1.9: The Monmouthshire Canal opened in February 1796, with the 11-mile long Crumlin Arm following in 1799. This left the main line at Malpas Junction, now spanned by the M4 Motorway immediately west of Junction 26, just to the north of Newport. Whilst the main line carried on northwards to meet with the Brecknock & Abergavenny Canal at Pontymoile, the Crumlin Arm headed off due west, gradually turning north as it passed Rogerstone, Risca and Crosskeys. The flight of three locks at Allt-yr-yn lay just a quarter of a mile on from the junction but two other locks had to be navigated before boats reached this point. This sylvan view, from circa 1908, illustrates the route that the columns cast at Falkirk followed to the viaduct site from Newport Docks. Although traffic declined dramatically with the opening of the railways, the Crumlin Arm was not finally abandoned as a commercial waterway until 1930, although traffic had ended in 1915, when the twice weekly general cargo boat ceased running.
Neil Parkhouse collection

where facilities were developed to enrich the cast iron and produce wrought iron. The wrought iron was then transported by tramroad to the basin at Llanfoist on the Brecknock & Abergavenny Canal, from where it would be taken to the Monmouthshire Canal at Pontymoile, where canal access was then available to Crumlin.

When the company accepted Kennard's tender in early October 1852, the known facts relating to the Crumlin Viaduct were less than positive. The company had not yet deposited their Amendment Bill for the re-alignment of the approach roads to the viaduct with the necessary authorities, the closing date being 30th November. Liddell's amended line had positioned the viaduct marginally further up the valley but within the line of deviation shown on Miller's authorised plans of 1848 (*Fig. 1.2*). Gordon and Liddell had dismissed the use of masonry piers because stone from local quarries was sub-standard and too expensive. As an alternative they were investigating the use of iron piers. The span of each truss was to be 150 feet with five piers across the Ebbw Valley and two across the Kendon Valley. No one had produced any working drawings for the use of Warren Patent Trusses on which to accurately base Kennard's fixed price tender for £31,480. On a broader picture, there had been no further indication that Gordon and Liddell had abandoned the use of the Warren Patent Truss for bridges and viaducts elsewhere along the Taff Vale Extension line.

References

1. Evidence of Gordon given at arbitration hearing, 1861
2. Patent No. 12242, 1848
3. Evidence of Gordon at arbitration hearing 1861
4. Evidence of Gordon at arbitration hearing 1861
5. Letter, Gordon and Liddell to Kennard, 3rd Aug. 1852
6. Letter, Kennard to Gordon and Liddell, 4th Aug. 1852
7. Letter, Kennard to Gordon and Liddell, 6th Aug. 1852
8. Liddell's report to the directors, 4th Aug. 1852
9. Board of directors meeting, 9th Aug. 1852, minute No. 767
10. Board of directors meeting, 28th Aug. 1852, minute No. 779
11. Letter, Liddell to Kennard, 28th Aug. 1852
12. Board of directors meeting, 16th Sept. 1852
13. Letter, Liddell to Kennard, 16th Sept. 1852
14. Letter, Kennard to Liddell, 18th Sept. 1852
15. Letter, Kennard to Liddell, 28th Sept. 1852
16. Letter, Kennard to Liddell, 29th Sept. 1852
17. Liddell's report to the directors, 30th Sept. 1852
18. Board of directors meeting, 1st Oct. 1852, minute No. 825
19. Letter, Kennard to Liddell, 5th Oct. 1852

CONTRACT

CHAPTER 2

In today's litigious world, the legal representatives of any company proposing to undertake major constructional work would have serious concerns about allowing anyone to commence operations without having the legal powers to carry this out unless they had a signed and sealed contract document. In October 1852, the Newport, Abergavenny & Hereford Railway Company had accepted a tender of £31,480 from Thomas Kennard for the construction of the viaduct at Crumlin.[1] In May 1853, following a number of alterations to the design, an amended tender figure of £38,740 was agreed between the company and Kennard.[2] Powers for the amended route of the line were obtained in August and not until October 1853 was a contract prepared and signed by Kennard, and then under duress. The terms of the contract were to form the basis of the primary arguments in an arbitration hearing brought by T.W. Kennard against the NA&HR that started in 1861.

At the end of 1852, Liddell wrote to Kennard requesting a set of working drawings, the quantities of iron in the viaduct and particulars of the weights of it, and that a contract and specification ought to be arranged as soon as possible.[3] At a subsequent meeting, Kennard attempted to set up an arrangement that would be to his financial advantage. He wanted any payments made to be based on a schedule of prices of goods supplied, and work undertaken and completed. This approach was not acceptable to Liddell, who pointed out to Kennard that from the outset he had been made fully aware that any submitted tender was to be a lump sum tender not to be exceeded.[4]

In 1853, following a series of amendments to the design of the piers, Liddell contacted Kennard informing him that he considered it to be essential that they should have all of the contractual business finalised.[5] Kennard agreed with Liddell that he would calculate the revised total weight and a price for all of the required iron work. Liddell accepted that he would have to report back to the directors and explain that the modifications to the design of the viaduct, as agreed with Kennard, would result in an increase in the contract price over and above that previously accepted.

Joining Kennard's office with the specific role of preparing the working drawings for the viaduct was a young engineer, Stanley Baldwin. Sometime later, Kennard visited Gordon and left him with a set of calculations showing the cost of the original design and the cost of the revised design that had been extracted from the then almost completed working drawings. Kennard estimated the revised figure to be £39,854, whilst Baldwin estimated the cost from the completed working drawings to be £39,254; however, Kennard later revised and reduced his estimate to £39,105. Gordon disagreed with all of these calculations and requested a set of the working drawings for his own use, making arrangements for his assistant Mr Rumble to visit Kennard's office who, along with Baldwin, would rework the figures. According to Gordon's calculations, he could not arrive at a sum above £37,740. Kennard persisted with his figure of £39,105, a difference of £1,365. Part of the difference in the figures turned out to be for work that Kennard would no longer have to do. However, Gordon did allow an increase in the valuation for cast iron and wrought iron in the piers, concluding that the contract price should be no more than £38,740.[6] Liddell's report to the directors in May provided full details of the amendments and revised prices, and concluded with a statement that '*working drawings with detailed quantities and costs of all parts have been made and agreed upon by Mr Kennard and me, copies of which I send herewith to be appended to the contract*'.[7]

Having concluded their deliberations in May 1853, with all sides having agreed to the revised tender figure of £38,740, the preparation and execution of the formal contract was again overlooked. It was not until October 1853, when Kennard applied for a large payment of £10,000 for goods delivered to the viaduct site and with work on the foundations having commenced, that the company secretary raised the question of a contract not having being signed. At this point, the directors refused to consider any further payments until such time as a contract, made between the two parties, had been signed and sealed with the NA&HR Co's seal.[8] At

Thomas William Kennard shall ... perform execute and complete the said works with materials of the best quality and in a substantial and workmanlike manner under the direction and to the satisfaction of the said Charles Liddell ...

Also that ... Thomas William Kennard ... at his ... own proper costs and charges find furnish and provide all and all manner of Tools Scaffolding and every description of elements and utensils and also all the labor workmanship freight carriage wages and lodgings for workmen sheds coverings and all other matters and things whatsoever which shall or may be required or necessary for constructing performing fixing and finishing the said Works ...

... and in case any difference of opinion shall arise between the said parties hereto or their respective engineers as to the part or portion of such works so to be measured or the quantity thereof to be charged or allowed in respect thereof or as to the extent amount or value of such works as are included in this contract but which may be omitted to be done and executed as hereintobefore mentioned then and in any such case the same shall be ascertained settled and determined by two engineers one to be appointed by each of the said parties hereto respectively and in the event of their disagreeing by a third party to be nominated by two Referees in writing under their hands before they proceed in such arbitration and the estimate of such arbitrators or any two of them shall be final and conclusive as to both parties ...

a meeting between Kennard, Gordon and Liddell, it was agreed that Kennard's solicitor should prepare the legal documents, with Kennard preparing the specification.[9] Kennard's solicitors were Morris, Stone & Company and John Morris, son of the senior partner and a junior clerk in the practice, was assigned to the task of preparing the contract documents. He had been approached by Kennard previously but was concerned that it was the duty of a solicitor from the railway company to prepare them. He suggested to Kennard that he should approach the company with the view that they should complete the documents. The response from the company's solicitors, however, was that they could not entertain the preparation of contract documents for at least a month and they would '*raise no objection to the documents being prepared by Morris, Stone & Company*'.[10]

Morris agreed to prepare the contract '*if it is on an understanding that it is an accommodation for those gentlemen, I shall be happy to do the best I can*'.[11] However, at that time he was very busy with other cases so, in order to accommodate Kennard (the partnership were also solicitors to his father R.W. Kennard), John Morris senior prepared the contract in draft in one evening.[12] The only instructions they had received from Kennard was '*prepare me a contract for Crumlin Viaduct*'. The draft was copied by a clerk in their office the next morning and sent to the company's solicitors for their perusal. When returned, it was sent to Morris's stationers with instructions to prepare two documents by 10.00 the following morning, 19th October, so that they would be ready by 20th October. The initial agreement between Kennard and his solicitors was that, on delivery of a signed contract, they would receive '*£6,000 in debenture stock from the Newport, Abergavenny & Hereford Railway Company guaranteed by the London & North Western Railway Company on which they could raise money in payment for their services and for Kennard's business*'.[13] Unfortunately for Kennard, the money market was depressed and everyone who was approached to take up an option to convert the debentures into a loan declined to do so.

When Kennard was questioned on the preparation of the contract at the arbitration hearing, he had to admit that it was his assistant Baldwin who contacted his solicitor with instructions to prepare a draft contract. He could not recollect giving his solicitor instructions and he was unable to recollect seeing him about getting a contract prepared. He admitted that he could never remember his solicitor preparing the contract nor leaving any spaces blank for figures, prior to their being filled in, he believed, by the company's solicitor. He could never remember seeing the contract. He could not remember instructing Baldwin to prepare the contract but thought that he must have done so as he was unquestionably trustworthy. Kennard never had any discussions with Baldwin on what to include and what not to include in the contract. He did not prepare the specification, as he thought Gordon prepared one and Baldwin also prepared one. Which one was included in the contract documents he did not know. He never had an interview with his attorney and never read through a draft contract, although just before he signed the contract, Gordon went through the specification with him. He could not remember who had filled in the blank spaces left in the contract for someone to insert the agreed contract price.[14]

According to Morris, the specification attached to the contract was the one prepared by Kennard or Baldwin and that Kennard went to his office to discuss and agreed the final draft '*because he was too busy to run after him*'.[15] The contract was signed at the offices of the General & Medical & Invalid Insurance Company in October and the company seal was affixed by the chairman five days later.[16] Kennard confirmed that he signed the contract on Gordon's recommendation and not that of his attorney.[17]

At the arbitration hearing, Morris was questioned in depth on who had filled in the figures on the contract. He could recognise some of his own figures but not others. He was unable to remember where he obtained the figures from but could remember filling in the list of drawings. When shown a copy of the contract executed by Kennard, he confirmed that he was familiar with Kennard's writing, but not his figures. He could not recollect whether Kennard gave him the figures to put in. According to Morris, everything was done in a hurry in the clerk's office at Charing Cross. He believed that when the contract was prepared all references to figures were left blank. He was asked a series of questions about who had instructed him on the preparation of the contract, Kennard or Baldwin, but he could not remember. He did not read the specification but agreed that the two versions shown were different, that on one draft being different from the one signed on the contract. Morris confirmed that he was not an engineer and therefore he would not have looked at the specification. He did not provide Kennard with a copy because he thought he would have one – Morris was working from a copy and he expected Kennard to have one too. The signed copy of the contract was retained by Morris.[18]

Kennard was then examined and after being reminded that he was under oath, a pertinent question was put to him by the Arbitrator:

'Arbitrator: Did you or did you not read the contract?

Kennard: Well I should think I did – I will say I did – I do not recollect it but of course I must have done so – I do not recollect reading it, but I must have read it.'

A close study of the hearing records indicate that the Arbitrator was not impressed with Kennard when he admitted to him that he never possessed a copy of the contract and had never seen it until the arbitration hearing commenced. He never looked at the specification or had a copy of it; he never thought of the contract, working only from what he knew and from the drawings.

Further questions were then put to Kennard on the terms of the contract:

'Arbitrator, Had you a copy of the specification?

Kennard: I do not believe that I looked at the specification or had a copy of it from the day the thing was signed, I had the drawings and knew what was required. I knew the sum of money that was involved. I set to work to make the bridge. From the time the contract was signed until I got into difficulties I never thought of the contract.

A: The question I wish to put to you is what you had to guide you in the performance of the work. We all know that people who execute works of this kind ought to have the specifications in their pocket ready to refer to at all times. Had you any separate copy of the specification or anything except that which was upon the Parchment itself?

K: No.'

The salient points of the contract, which was signed on 20th October 1853, are included here as illustrations in the margins. Payments were to be made to Kennard on the last day of every month as certified by Liddell. He was to be paid £11 per ton for all wrought iron delivered to the site and £8 per ton for all castings in the piers, each as certified by Liddell. As soon as any iron was delivered to the workshops or on site, it was to became the property of the company. The company were authorised under the terms of the contract to a retention figure of 10% of the contract price until three months after the completion of the works. The Second Schedule, illustrated below, went into more detail in regards to the viaduct's construction, including the type of iron to be used and the foundations for the piers.

References

1. Board of directors meeting, 1st Oct. 1852, minute No. 825
2. Liddell's report to board of directors meeting, 14th May 1853
3. Letter, Liddell to Kennard, 31st Dec. 1852
4. Letter, Liddell to Kennard, 5th Feb. 1853
5. Letter to Kennard, 5th Feb. 1853
6. Transcript of evidence given at arbitration hearing, 1861
7. Liddell's report read to board of directors 14th May 1853
8. Letter, Liddell to Kennard, 7th Oct. 1853
9. From transcript of evidence given at arbitration hearing, 1861
10. Evidence of John Morris given at arbitration hearing, 1861
11. Evidence of John Morris given at arbitration hearing, 1861
12. Evidence of John Morris given at arbitration hearing, 1861
13. Evidence of T.W. Kennard given at arbitration hearing, 1861
14. Evidence of T.W. Kennard given at arbitration hearing, 1861
15. Evidence of John Morris given at arbitration hearing, 1861
16. Board of directors meeting, 3rd Nov. 1853, minute No. 1172
17. Board of directors meeting, 3rd Nov. 1853 minute No. 1172
18. Evidence of John Morris given at arbitration hearing, 1861

And Also that he the said Thomas William Kennard his executors or administrators shall and will erect finish fix and complete the viaduct and works hereby agreed to be constructed made done and performed on or before the thirty first day of August one thousand eight hundred and fifty four ...

And it is declared and agreed that in case the said Thomas William Kennard shall make default in erecting constructing completing and finishing the said viaduct works and buildings hereby contracted to be erected within the time hereinbefore covenanted ... and in that case ... shall forfeit and pay to the said Company the sum of two hundred pounds per week for every week subsequent to such default until the said works shall be finished and completed ...

The Second Schedule referred to in the foregoing contract

The viaduct has ten spans of 150 feet clear span each.

The girders are upon what is termed 'Warrens Patent' principle. They are composed entirely of wrought iron and arranged so that the platform for the railway is laid on the top kerb of the girders. The girders rest on piers of cast iron columns braced by wrought iron cross braces as shown on the drawings. The exact position of the viaduct to be set out ... by the engineer to the Company who shall exercise absolute control over every part of the work during its progress ... The foundations of the piers and abutments shall ... be laid on the solid rock. Where the rock lies at a great inclination one half of the space for foundations is to be worked out of the rock and the other half is to be built up with tooled ashlar work. Where the rock is not met with the foundation must be formed with a bed of concrete six feet thick ... The cast iron foundation pieces to be accurately bedded on three feet thickness of ashlar masonry set on the face of the concrete after it has set ...

The masonry of the abutments to be the best description of rubble work with rough scrabbled quoins and well bonded.

The columns and horizontal bracing girders of the piers to be of the best Scotch iron. The castings to be perfectly sound and straight.

The gulls of the columns to be faced on the lathe. The horizontal bracing girders to be accurately fitted and bolted in their places.

The horizontal and vertical cross bracing bars to be Blaenavon iron of quality approved by the engineer ... and all the cross bracing to be firmly tightened with keys and gibs respectively after the horizontal bracing girders are fitted and bolted in their places.

The bridge girders are to be plain Blaenavon wrought iron excepting the joint plates which must be of Staffordshire boiler plate iron.

These girders before being raised on to the piers are to be tested in the presence of the engineer with a load of 150 tons uniformly distributed over a pair of the girders and when put up in their places on the piers provision is to be made for expansion and contraction to the satisfaction of the Company's engineer.

The first pair of girders and any other pair the engineer may select in the progress of the work to be tested of a load of 225 tons or $1\frac{1}{2}$ tons per foot run uniformly distributed. When the pair of girders is loaded with one ton per foot run in addition to the weight of the platform and rails the deflection shall not exceed 3 inches otherwise the engineer shall have power to reject these girders.

The platform to consist of yellow pine 6 inches in thickness securely bolted down to the compression bars of the girders, each piece of timber to be creosoted before erection.

The handrailing to be of cast iron bolted down to the timber at such a distance from the edge as to leave a clear roadway on the top of the viaduct of twenty five feet.

The whole of the ironwork bolts in girders and piers to be painted with three coats of oil paint.

Plate 3.1: Etching of the completed Crumlin Viaduct which was included as a frontispiece in Humber's book A Practical Treatise on Cast and Wrought Iron Bridges and Girders as Applied to Railway Structures (1857). *The view is looking west, across Crumlin Low Level goods yard – the wooden structure to the right is almost certainly the original MR&CC goods shed, which was later replaced by the GWR with a much larger building. In the background Mark Philips' tramroad incline is clearly shown, which brought coal from Trinant Colliery down to a wharf alongside the railway.*

PIERS AND GIRDERS

CHAPTER 3

First hand information on the construction and design of the viaduct was lost with its demolition in 1965-66. The details of this now rely on an analysis of contemporary descriptions and drawings, photographs and a series of recently discovered contract drawings.

First to put pen to paper was John Clayton (1820-1861), architect to the NA&HR Co. In May 1857 he gave a presentation to the Royal Institute of British Architects that included a description of the methods used in the construction of the viaduct.

Also in 1857, William A. Humber (1821-1881), civil engineer, had two works published on the use of cast and wrought iron in bridges and girders that included, amongst others, a detailed description and drawings of the viaduct at Crumlin. A close scrutiny in the use of the language used in Clayton's and Humber's descriptions suggests that they were prepared as a joint authorship or, subject to a few alterations, one description was copied from the other.

In 1855, Henry Maynard was appointed manager at the Viaduct Works by Kennard, remaining in that position following the purchase of the works by Kennard's brothers in 1859. Later, he was a major shareholder in the company that purchased the works from the Kennard Brothers in 1865, remaining as manager until it went in to liquidation in 1871. In 1865, he published a handbook that included drawings and extensive details on the background to the construction of the viaduct. In 1868, he published a further handbook giving detailed descriptions of bridges made in the Viaduct Works and erected in Australia, India, South Africa, South America, Portugal and Spain. Both resemble a publicity document aimed at promoting the Viaduct Works and over the years, the handbook of 1865 has come to be seen as a standard reference publication on the design and construction of Crumlin Viaduct. However, a careful study of its contents highlights a number of contradictory and misleading statements and drawings, particularly when these are compared with the works of Clayton and Humber, who also include contradictory information in their detailed descriptions. Unfortunately, all three published works lack precise details of a number of the significant features of the viaduct's construction.

By way of illustration, one of the more identifiable inconsistencies is the figure given for the height of the viaduct. Many sources refer to this being 200 feet but do not state from what level the height is taken. Pier No. 4 is generally quoted as being the tallest but calculating this from the details and measurements given in Maynard's handbook indicates that it was 194 feet 4 inches to the top of the handrail taken from the top of the foundations, shown as being at ground level. In the text, Maynard states that the height was 200 feet but does not specify where it was taken from. He also quotes a figure of 208 feet to the top of the handrail, measured from the underside of the foundations, which he states were 14 feet deep (194ft 4ins + 14ft = 208ft 4ins). Clayton also states that the height of the viaduct was 200 feet but he quotes it as being taken to rail level. Details taken from Maynard's handbook indicates the rail level to be 191 feet 3 inches above the top of the foundations shown at ground level. Fortunately, Clayton qualifies his measurement by stating that his height of 200 feet had been taken from the bed of the River Ebbw but Humber stated that it was taken from water level.

Also, when comparing Humber's and Maynard's outline drawings of the main viaduct, be aware that they are illustrated from different directions. Humber's illustration is taken from east to west, whereas Maynard's is from west to east. Working from east to west on the large viaduct, Humber's drawing indicates that Piers No's 1 and 6 have five tiers, Piers No's 2, 3 and 4 have ten tiers, and Pier No. 5 has nine tiers. Maynard's drawing indicates that Piers No's 1 and 6 have five tiers, Pier No. 2 has nine tiers, and Piers No's 3, 4, and 5 have ten tiers (*Fig. 2.1*). Maynard was the only one to indicate on his drawings that there were six tiers to each pier in the small viaduct. The final height of each pier, and number of tiers, was determined by using a theodolite, and

Fig. 3.7: Elevation of tallest piers. Author (after Maynard and Humber)

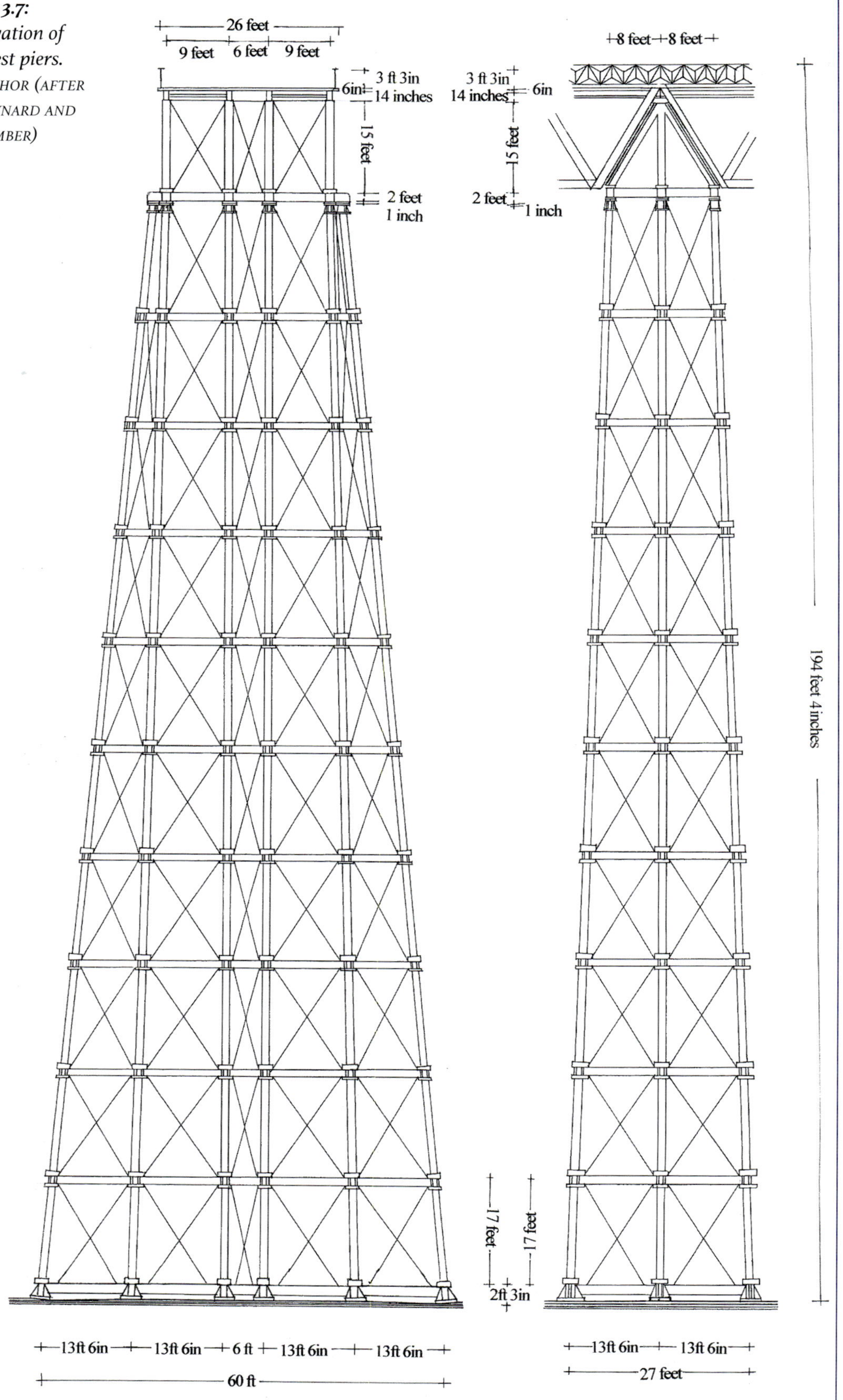

considered it, however, because Wild was impressed by the calculations he agreed that wind pressure should be taken into account'. He accepted Kennard's calculations and the solution put forward, although it would cost the company more money, because he considered Wild to be '*a man of considerable experience and especially he was a man of very considerable scientific attainments to whose opinion one looked with respect*'.[7] Liddell believed that Wild's suggestion of raking columns presented a more elegant appearance to the piers[8] (***Fig. 3.7***).

When constructed each cast iron column had an external diameter of 12 inches, the raking columns were 1 inch thick and the remainder were 3/4 of an inch thick. The original drawings had shown the fourteen columns to be 1 inch thick. On Kennard's recommendation, these had been reduced to 5/8 of an inch but the foundry at Falkirk were experiencing difficulties in completing a casting to this thickness. Following strong representation from the Kennard family, Gordon agreed to increase the thickness to 3/4 of an inch. In so doing, Gordon accepted that it was agreed to '*against his better judgement, because any increase in the size of the casting would result in an increased cost to the Company*'.[9] Maynard in his handbook states that the two outer bracing columns were 1 inch thick.

The two inner columns placed 6 feet apart from centre to centre and being a consistent 17 feet long, they were the only columns that remained in a vertical position throughout a pier's height. The junction of each vertical column would be maintained in a horizontal plane. The other columns were inclined inwards and therefore being the hypotenuse of a triangle were marginally longer than the 17 feet (***Fig. 3.8***). The greatest inclination was about 1 in 12 for the raking columns that were approximately 1 3/4 inches longer (***Fig. 3.9***) and with an inclination of about 1 in 46 for the others, they were around 3/4 inch longer (***Fig. 3.10***). Each column was planed to an appropriate angle in order to maintain a consistent downward force throughout the height of the pier. Humber indicates these facts on one of his drawings. On the contract drawing of the piers, it states that the 17 feet was taken to the triangle (***Fig. 3.11***). The inward inclination was seen as a further aid in providing resistance to the force of the wind and any sideways thrust created by moving railway traffic.

To join each of the columns, lugs had been cast at the ends with bolt holes for securing them together (***Fig. 3.12***); they would have been cast oversize to allow for the necessary machining to size prior to fixing. Records itemising the purchase of machinery for use within the works confirms Clayton's statement that '*the joints to the*

FIG. 3.8

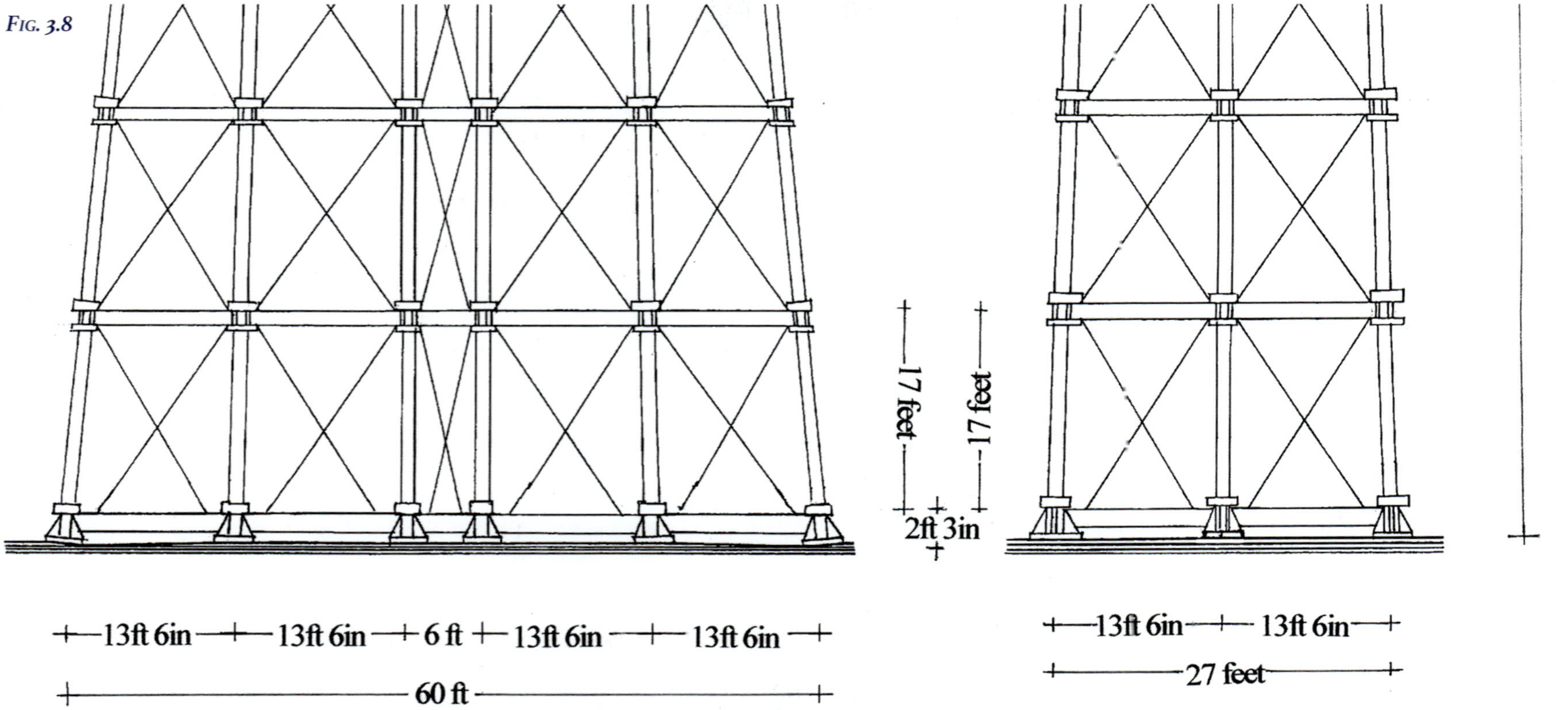

columns were planed and fitted together with the greatest nicety to ensure a perfect bearing'. Modern engineers have suggested that the machining to size was undertaken in two separate operations. To ensure a close fit at the junction of the columns, a socket joint with a projection of ½ an inch was turned on a lathe for the upper column, which then sat in a corresponding ½ an inch turned recess in the lower column (***Fig. 3.13***). The flange on the upper column would have been faced off in the lathe. The lower column would then have been positioned in a jig set out on a long bench, where a horizontal planning machine planed them to size, making an allowance for their angle of inclination – these were detailed on the contract drawing as of 9/16 an inch in 18 inches and 1½ inches in 18 inches. The final operation would be to offer up adjoining columns, to ensure that they made an accurate fit, before

FIG. 3.9

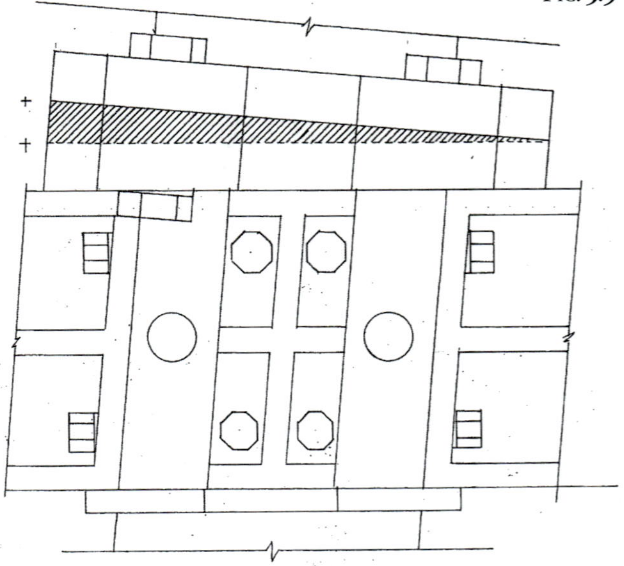

FIG. 3.10

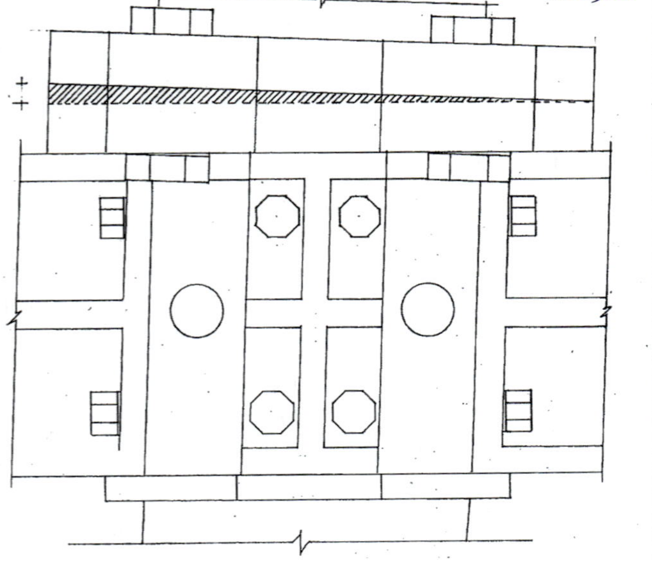

*FIG. 3.8: An enlargement of the bottom section of **Fig. 3.7**, illustrating the angles of columns in the piers.*
AUTHOR (AFTER MAYNARD AND HUMBER)

FIG. 3.9: Diagram illustrating the angle of the junction of the 1 in 46 columns in each pier. AUTHOR

FIG. 3.10: Diagram illustrating the angle of the junction of the 1 in 12 columns in each pier. AUTHOR

Plate 3.2: This 1856 photograph taken at the base of pier 4 shows the cast iron plates at the feet of the columns and the plates on which they rested. At the moment we can only speculate who these men are, posing with Tom Kennard, centre – Charles Liddell and Professor Lewis Gordon were the line's engineers, with Mark Carr, the resident engineer; Henry Martyn Kennard (then aged 23) and Henry Maynard were managers of the Viaduct Works. Carr was often at Hereford and so had an assistant site engineer at Crumlin named McDonnell. Our best guess is that we are looking at here, from left to right, Professor Lewis Gordon, possibly McDonnell, Tom Kennard, Charles Liddell and, on the end, perhaps Henry Maynard.
Stephen Rowson collection

Plate 3.3 (Page Opposite): Alfred Pumphrey really knew about 3D composition and the stereo effect in his photography is generally superb. This is No. 15, taken in the late 1850s and one of the best to show the engineering detail of the structure as built. The 1873 London Gazette *notes that there were two concurrent partnerships between Josiah and Alfred Pumphrey: J. & A. Pumphrey, india rubber manufacturers, which was probably their original business, and Pumphrey Brothers, photographic publishers. On dissolution of these partnerships, Josiah continued the rubber manufacture while Alfred ran the photographic business. They were Quakers, born in Birmingham, Alfred in 1830 and where he then also died in 1913.*
Stephen Rowson collection

marking and recording their exact junction points. All of these joints were turned and planed accurately by skilled men in the viaduct workshops in order to ensure a controlled and accurate fit. An alternative but unlikely arrangement in making allowances for the different angles would have been to make use of suitably shaped wedges.

Once placed in position, the columns were bolted together, the amount of bolts used depending on the number of bolt holes available at any given position – the least number would have been four at the junction of the cross girders. The first column of each pier was attached to a specifically designed cast iron base that had been fixed to the foundations. According to Maynard, these were 3 feet square and 2 feet 3 inches high, with strong 1 inch feathers cast on the outside that helped

15

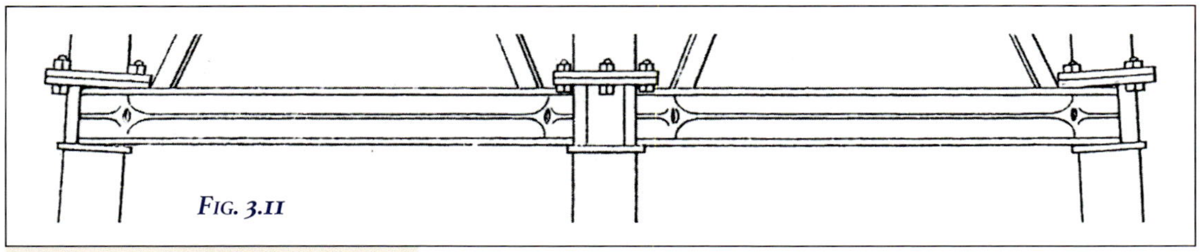

FIG. 3.11

FIG. 3.11: Section indicating the junction of each tier. HUMBER

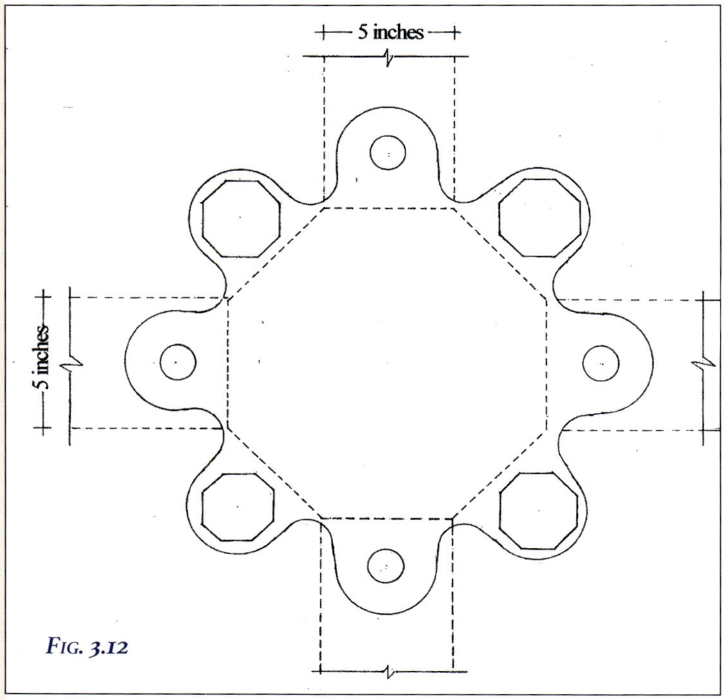

FIG. 3.12

FIG. 3.12: Drawing to illustrate method of fixing columns together. AUTHOR (AFTER MAYNARD)

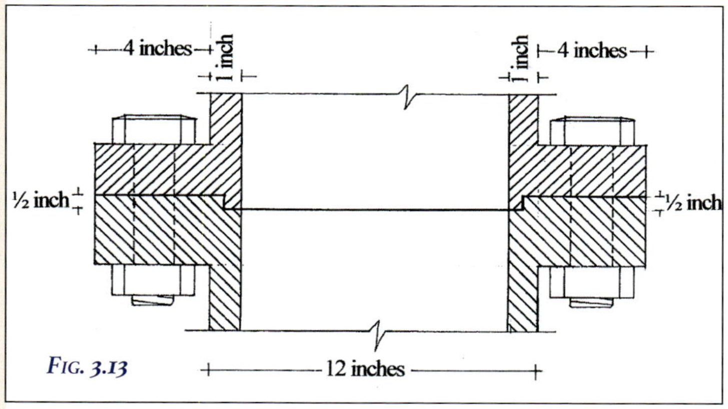

FIG. 3.13

FIG. 3.13: Diagram to illustrate recess at junction of columns. AUTHOR (AFTER MAYNARD)

distribute the loading of each column onto the base and to the foundations. Humber's and Clayton's descriptions suggest that the feet (base) upon which the columns rested were from 3 feet to 5 feet in height, making up any small differences between the finished ground level and the bottom of each column. Humber states that the plate on which they rested was 8 feet square, on a bed of masonry 3 feet to 5 feet deep. Maynard's drawing suggests a depth of 5 feet, whilst Clayton mentions that the plate was 3 feet square but gives no details on the depth of the masonry. Baldwin, in his calculations, suggests that the height of the feet ranged from 2 feet 6 inches to 6 feet. All three mention that the base plate was secured to existing excavated rock or built-up masonry foundations by 12 inch rag bolts, let into the foundations and fixed in position by pouring molten brimstone into the joints (*Fig. 3.14*). The contract drawings show the differences in height were taken up by alternative heights of the feet, 2 feet 4 inches or 6 feet for column 1 and 2 feet 3½ inches or 6 feet 3½ for columns A and B. At the completion of the contract, the foundations and their method of construction was to become a central issue at the start of the litigation proceedings that Kennard brought against the company in 1861.

Humber's drawings indicate that the heads of the columns were finished with a capital in the classical style (*Fig. 3.15*). Plans and elevations of the capitals on the contract drawings provide more precise details of their unique decoration. In contrast to the fixing of the feet square on to the foundations, the capitals for each column were cast at their bases to match the angle of inclination at the top of each column and flat at the top to provide a level platform to support the trusses. On top of each capital was an iron plate, 2 feet square and 1 inch thick, that again provided a means for creating a level platform for the positioning of cast iron girders. Cast iron girders 2 feet in depth rested on the tops of the columns in a lengthways direction, the centre ones protruding beyond the columns to which the bracing column was attached. Eight shorter girders fitted inside them in order to join and hold them in place (*Fig. 3.16*). An important feature at the top of the piers was their mode of construction to support the weight of the girder. Humber merely stated

PLATE 3.4: A large group of workmen gathered together at the base of one of the piers, probably in the summer of 1856. STEPHEN ROWSON COLLECTION

FIG. 3.14

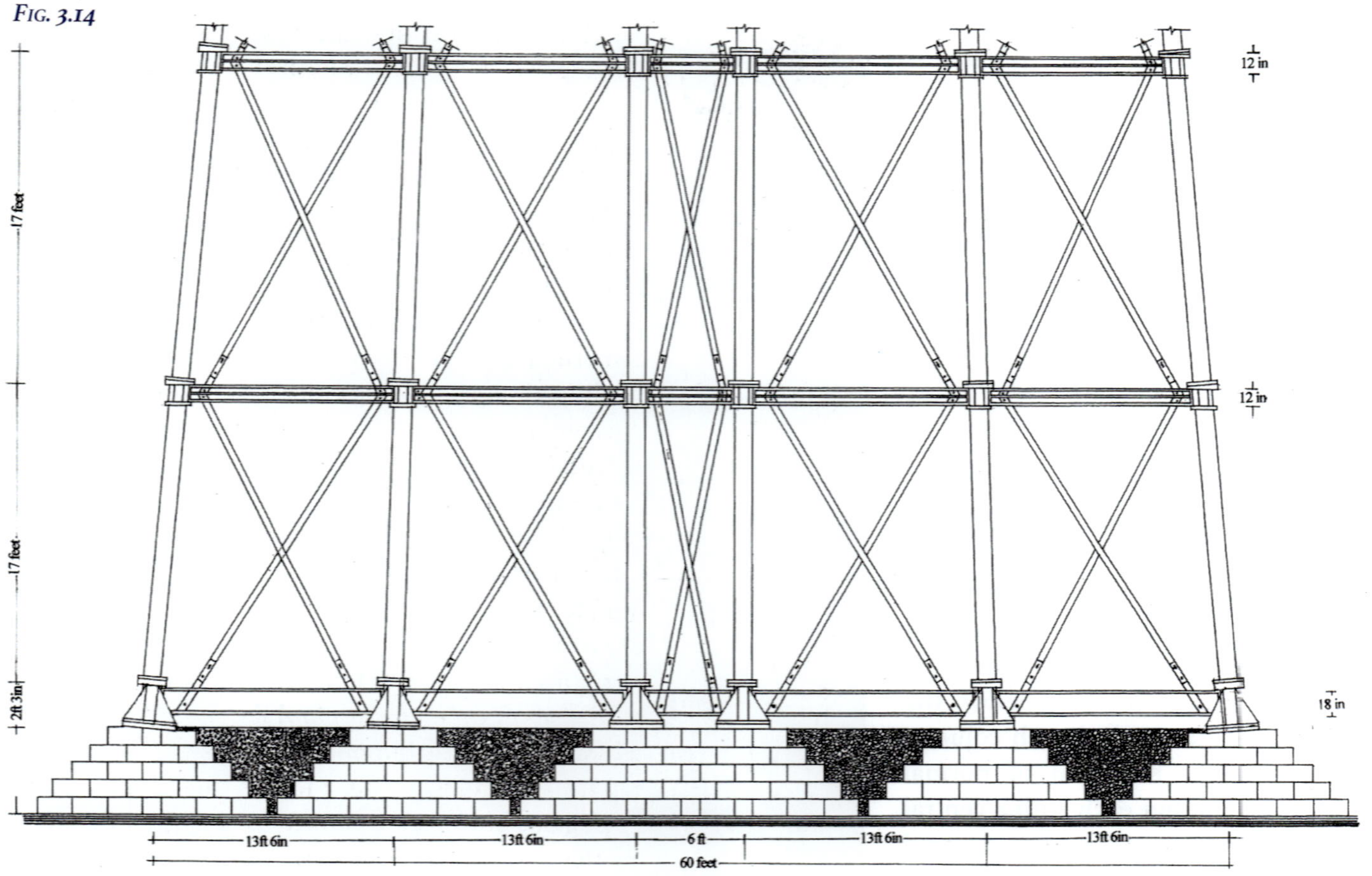

FIG. 3.14: Diagram to illustrate how columns and piers were positioned on foundations. AUTHOR (AFTER MAYNARD AND HUMBER)

that each pier was surmounted by a triangular truss upon which the girders rested. Clayton commented that the upper stages of the columns were connected together at the top by stronger horizontal girders than those below and that they were finished with 'A' shaped or triangular trusses placed over each row of columns below, upon which the girders rest. Maynard, meanwhile provided a more detailed description, explaining that resting on the girders and above each set of three columns was a 14 foot high 'A' frame made of cast iron (***Fig. 3.17***). The sides of these frames were of a similar shape and angle to those of the main girders. A vertical strut passed from the apex of the triangle to its base, coinciding with the middle column and thereby helping to distribute the pressure of the superstructure evenly over the whole of the columns. The four 'A' frames of each set were linked together by wrought iron bracing bars, 4 inches wide and 1/2 an inch thick. A plan and elevation of the 'A' frames forming part of the contract drawings (page 307), '*described as triangle at summit of piers*', provides further details of its construction.

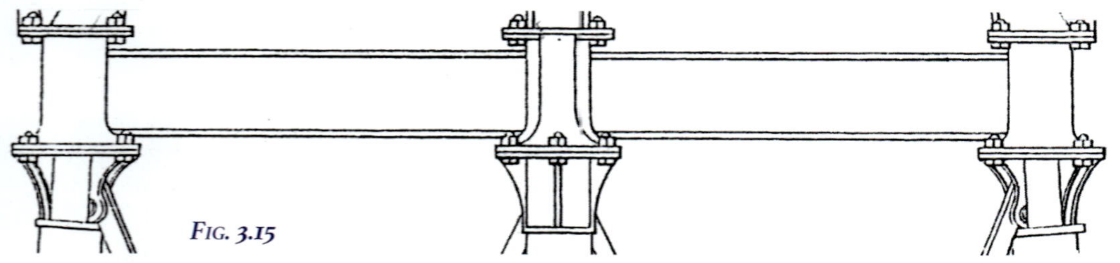

FIG. 3.15

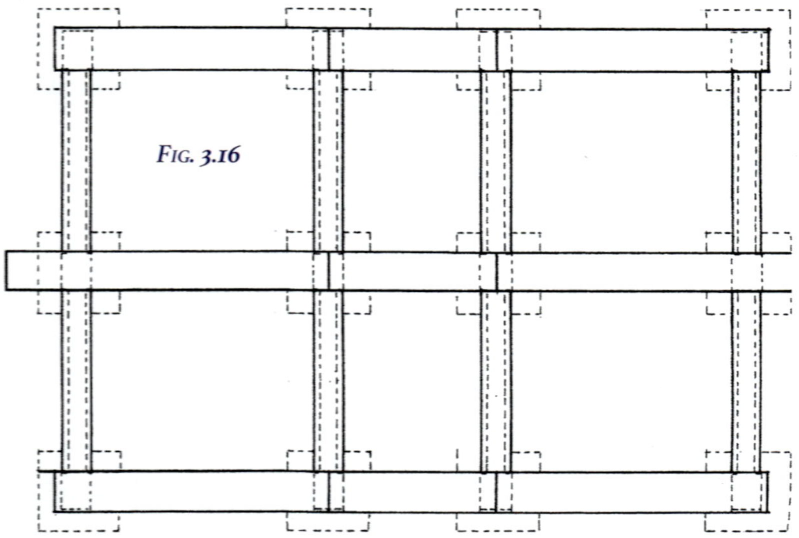

FIG. 3.16

FIG. 3.15: Treatment of columns at top of piers. AUTHOR (AFTER HUMBER)

FIG. 3.16: Suggested layout of girders at top of columns. AUTHOR

PLATE 3.6: A detail study of a truss on the Ebbw section, photograpghed in February 1926. *JOHN MANN COLLECTION*

accepted length of 150 feet. Against this, Kennard had chosen to connect the compression beams together at their junction with a 9 inch plate fixed to the top flange, thus forming a continuous rectangular tube over the whole length of the viaduct of 1,050 feet. Photographs and drawings indicate that the ends of each girder butted up to one another.

An innovative design feature of the whole structure referred to by Humber and Clayton, as being '*worthy of particular notice*' was the method chosen to connect the $3^1/_4$ inch diameter pins with the saddle casting. Maynard provides no centre to centre distance between the end pins of the compression beam; however, he does include, when describing the construction of the tension beam, that the length of the iron bars making up the beam were 16 feet 4 inches at the base of each equilateral triangle. Taking this measurement for the base of the triangle on the compression beam, and assuming that this distance is consistent throughout, we arrive at a distance between centres of 147 feet. Humber, on his drawings, indicates a similar distance of 16 feet 4 inches for the centre to centre distance of the pins at the base of each triangle. Making the same assumption as in Maynard's description, this also results in a distance of 147 feet. Clayton in his description, however, specifies a centre to centre distance of 148 feet for the end pins in the compression beam, a measurement that neither Humber nor Maynard refer to.

Taking the two men's centre to centre assumed distance of 147 feet, the centre of the $3^1/_4$ inch pin had a bearing of 3 inches from the end of the saddle casting, whereas Clayton's centre to centre distance of 148 feet would provide a bearing of 9 inches from the end of the casting (***Fig. 3.33***). If this was considered to be a more realistic distance, it would mean that the end outside tie would not form part of an equilateral triangle when attached to the compression beam. In the absence of any dimensions in Maynard's description for the size of the casting at the top of the 'A' frame, it is not possible to suggest any bearing figures for the supporting pin and therefore the only clue was his comment that the cast iron saddle was of a '*suitable shape and dimension to fit the end of the girder*'.

The junction the tension beam made with the stone abutment during the periods when the girder was in a state of expansion proved to be very troublesome (***Fig's 3.34 & 3.35***). One solution, dealt with by Kennard, was to place rollers under the girders where they met the abutment, but this caused damage to the stonework.[12] When this was reported to Gordon he wrote to Carr, '*The provision for expansion and contraction is very defective, this is principally owing to Kennard's absurd junction plate put on top to join all the girders together – get these removed at once*'.[13] Following a meeting between Gordon and Carr, at Crumlin, the junction plates were removed and an improved system of rollers were placed on the abutments to allow each truss to move along the rollers and not the rollers along the abutment.[14]

The pins which passed through the compression and tension beams, holding the ties and struts in position, protruded for a distance of 1 inch on the inner face of the beams. A cast iron cap with a flange covered the end of each pin, which was fixed to the centre of the pin by a 1 inch bolt, the aim being to stop the pin from working loose. In the early years of traffic crossing the viaduct, engineers noticed that these pins gradually came undone through vibration but as was stated at the time, '*this was easily rectified*'. Each pair of girders were connected, top and bottom, by hollow cast iron distance tubes of 6 inches external diameter by ½ inch thick, although Clayton states that the external diameter was 5 inches. Flanges had been cast on the ends of the distance tubes in such a manner that they could be fastened to the flanges on the cap covering the projecting ends of the pins. Diagonal bracing bars, 3 inches by ½ inch, were attached to the distance tubes by gib and cotter, in a similar manner as that used in attaching the vertical bracing bars to the distance girders of the piers (*Figs 3.36, 3.37 & 3.38*).

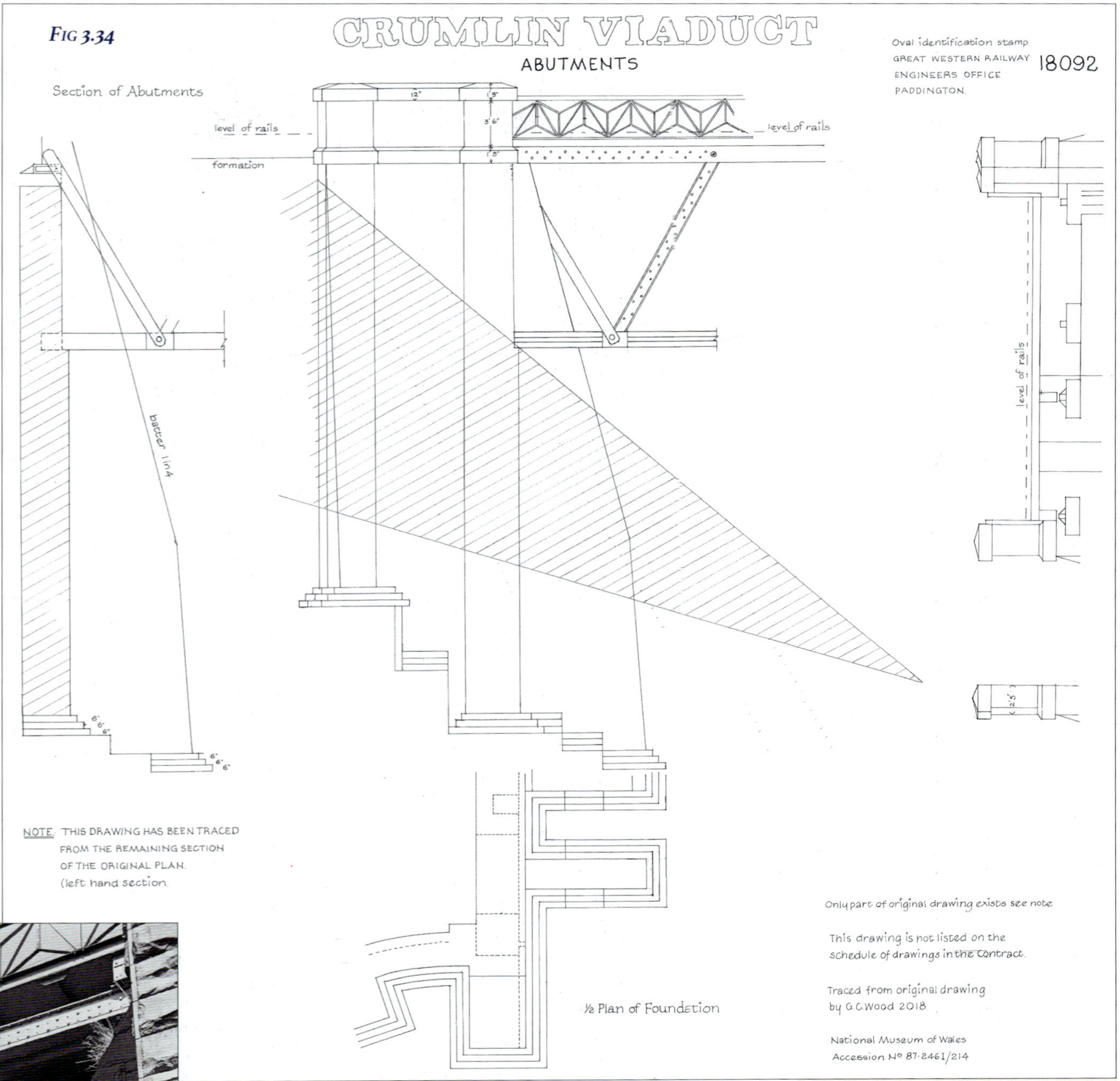

FIG. 3.34: *Cross section showing embankment built up from the natural slope for the abutment. Traced from the original drawing.* AUTHOR

PLATE 3.7: *The junction between an abutment and the tension beam, photographed in the summer of 1955 for the National Buildings Record.* ERIC DE MARE/COFLEIN

Never successfully resolved by successive engineers was the constant failure and breaking of the distance tubes throughout the life span of the viaduct.

Riveting on the compression and tension beams and elsewhere on the viaduct was, wherever practicable, performed by a riveting machine that had been developed in the works, which was found to be more economical and efficient than hand riveting. It was discovered that the pressure exerted on a rivet by the machine filled the hole better than by hand riveting.[15]

At an early stage in the construction of the trusses, Gordon had given instructions to Mark Carr that across each girder of the main viaduct there should be

FIG. 3.35: Detail of horizontal bracing at top and bottom of the girders. MAYNARD

FIG. 3.36: Detail of horizontal bracing at top and bottom of the girders. HUMBER

FIG. 3.37: Suggested detail of horizontal bracing at top and bottom of the girders following study of a photograph. AUTHOR

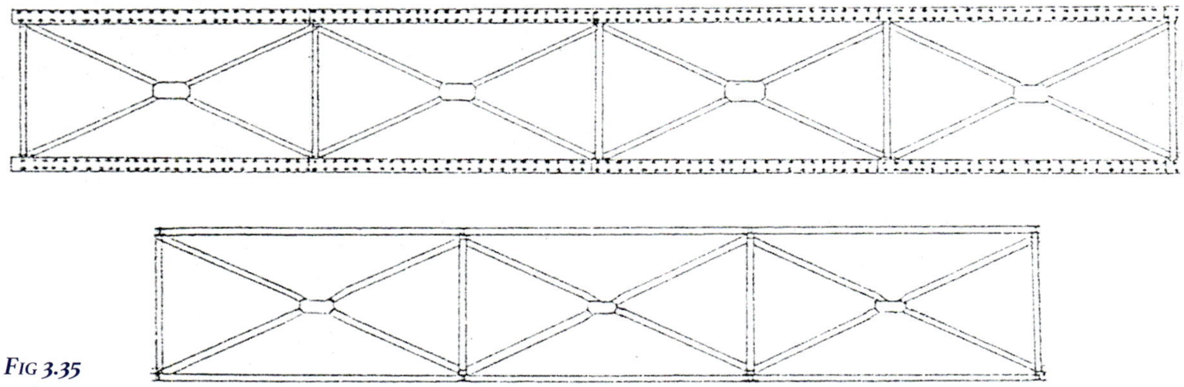

FIG 3.35

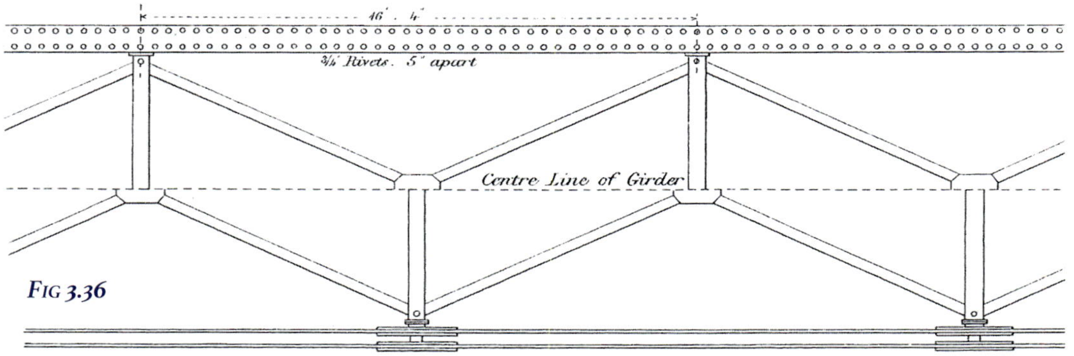

FIG 3.36

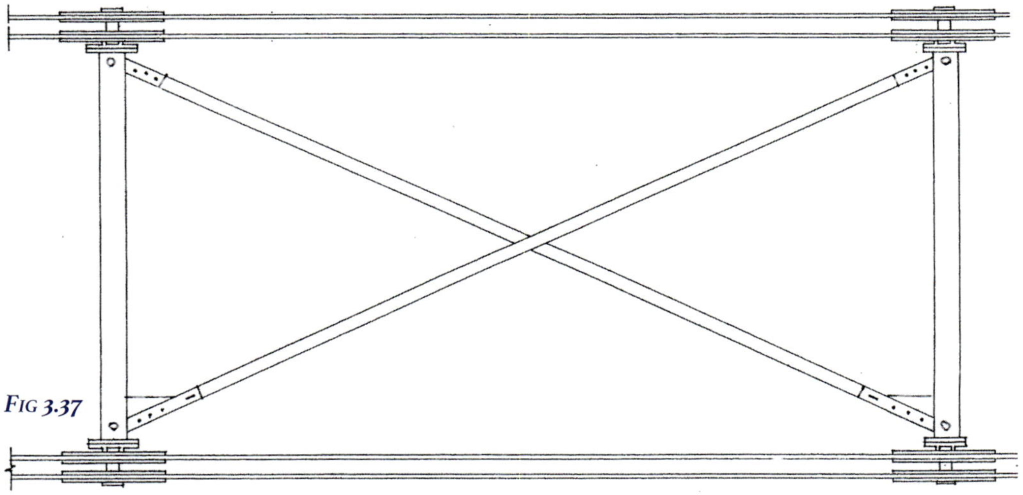

FIG 3.37

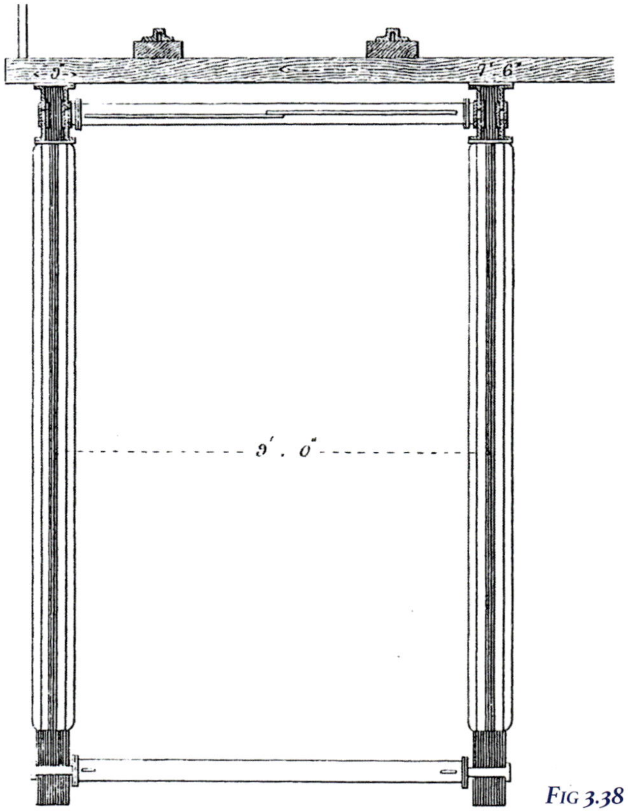

FIG 3.38

FIG. 3.38: Elevation of girders and horizontal bracing with details of fixing of platform and the permanent way. HUMBER

a camber of 4 inches, to counter any deflection created when traffic was passing over and thus provide a more level permanent way.[16]

References

1. Maynard's *Handbook to the Crumlin Viaduct*, 1862, Clayton's talk to the Royal Institution of British Architects, 1857, and Humber's publication *A Practical Treatise on Cast and Wrought Iron Bridges and Girders as Applied to Railway Structures*, 1857
2. Board of directors meeting, 1st Oct. 1852
3. Gordon's evidence to arbitration hearing
4. Liddell's report to the directors, May 1853, and Kennard's evidence to arbitration hearing
5. Gordon's evidence to arbitration hearing
6. Gordon's evidence to arbitration hearing
7. Liddell's report to board of directors, 12th Oct. 1853
8. Kennard's evidence to arbitration hearing
9. Liddell's report to board of directors, 14th May 1853
10. Letter, Kennard to Liddell, 17th May 1854
11. Letter, Liddell to Carr, 18th May 1854
12. Letter, Kennard to Liddell, 17th May 1853
13. Letter, Gordon to Carr, 21st July 1858
14. Meeting held 23rd July 1858
15. Maynard's *Handbook on the Crumlin Viaduct*
16. Letter, Gordon to Carr, 13th July 1854

UNDER CONSTRUCTION

CHAPTER 4

Work started in earnest on the construction of the viaduct in November 1852, with Kennard asking Liddell to meet him to discuss the position of the abutments.[1] Although he had never met Mark Carr, the company's site engineer, Kennard's next request was to send him a drawing showing a section taken across the valley, with the position of the proposed piers marked on it. He asked Carr to '*cause these spots to be thoroughly bored, at my expense, in order that the exact position can be ascertained*'.[2] A week later, Kennard informed Carr that he was visiting Crumlin and was anxious to know how he was getting on with the borings.[3] After a further two weeks, Kennard was again pressing Carr for information on the foundations, hoping that he had found rock on both sides of the valley. Enclosing a sum of £25, Kennard presumed it would be as much as Carr required for completing the survey.[4]

PLATE 4.1: This spring 1856 bird's eye view from the viaduct takes in practically the whole of Crumlin village at that time, with a terrace of three-story buildings nearing completion centre left. The MR&CC Tramroad through Crumlin had been upgraded and reopened for passengers on 23rd December 1850 but was still a 4ft 2ins gauge combined plateway and edge railway. Captain Simmons, the board of Trade Inspector, had recommended fencing the entire route, providing signals, gates at road crossings, and improving the track. Conversion of the line to a standard gauge railway was finally completed in May 1855. The gates and the disc & crossbar signal seen here were therefore relatively new. Crumlin station platforms were on the south side of the level crossing, whilst the road then carries on over the Ebbw River and the Crumlin Arm of the Monmouthshire Canal on stone-built bridges. Between the two bridges the towpath gate lies open and a length of railway leads from the tipping wharf off picture right. Just upstream of the river bridge is the canal feeder pipe from the reservoir at Pen y Fan. In the foreground is the rear of the substantial and newly renamed Viaduct Hotel, previously the Navigation Inn that stood at the canal head. The 1871 sale catalogue lists ten bedrooms and a large billiard room; the outbuildings to the right comprised a six-stall stable and coach house.
DAVID DICKINSON COLLECTION

Plate 4.2: *The first column of the first pier – No. 4, the 'Isabella Pier' – was raised in December 1853. In August 1854, the site was visited by an amateur photographer and member of the Photographic Society, W.H. Nicholl. His portrait from alongside the Ebbw River of the by then almost complete 'Isabella Pier' was published in the* Photographic Album for the Year 1855. *The picture is looking upstream, with the river bridge in the foreground carrying Mark Philips' tramroad to its coal wharf on the canal (off right). The tramroad's route from Trinant Colliery ran along the top of the escarpment behind, on its way to the incline down to the wharf, off picture to the left. In the background is the bridge carrying the Western Valleys line, which marked the 1829 continuation from canal head of the MR&CC's tramroad across the river and further down the valley towards Newport. The foundations of this pier blocked off the old canal basin and so truncated the canal by a short length. Only a year before this photograph, the main line tramroads had been converted to a proper standard gauge (4ft 8½ins) edge railway. On top of the pier is the crane used for bringing up components for its construction and ready to be used for raising the transverse girders.* Stephen Rowson collection

Carr wrote to Liddell in January 1853, providing him with details of his work in the valley. Progress had been delayed because of bad weather and poor light, which had restricted him to working outdoors for seven hours a day, making levelling virtually impossible. In a warning to Liddell, Carr mentioned that '*the Great Western people were prowling around between Pontypool and Crumlin and making diligent enquiries for dissentients to our line*';[5] the company's amended Taff Vale Extension line was then before Parliament. In the event, the work that Carr had put in to complete the survey for the borings and levels across the main valley was to prove of little value. He had been working from a drawing that Liddell had supplied to Kennard, for submitting an estimate for a girder of

200 feet that had been reduced to 150 feet by the former. Kennard was aware of the amendment but had failed to pass the information on to Carr.

Whilst work was continuing in setting out and excavating the foundations to the revised distances, a number of major alterations were being made to details of the viaduct's construction. At this early stage, Liddell had found it necessary to make further amendments. Lengthening the viaduct by 153 feet, for instance, resulted in a reduction in the length of hill between the Ebbw and Kendon valleys.[6]

During March, Carr was surveying and levelling in the Kendon Valley prior to the preparation of a sectional drawing. Kennard was requesting this in order to complete detailed drawings for the small viaduct.[7] In one of Carr's regular reports to Liddell he mentions that the '*foundations for several of the piers at Crumlin were well opened*'. He had foreseen a drainage problem on the hill to the east side of the valley but putting in a deep drain that was outside of the company's property would be expensive; Carr was asking for Liddell's opinion. He also mentioned that the stone coming out of the foundations had even natural beds but '*unfortunately it could not be dressed for an ashlar finish*'.[8]

Liddell visited Crumlin in early August and Kennard had asked him, by letter and prior to his visit, to examine the foundations for the abutment '*on the top of the hill*'. Solid rock had been reached and, consequently, Kennard considered that there was no need to excavate any deeper.[9] In August 1853, Carr calls Liddell's attention to the fact that the base plates for the columns in the piers were only 3 feet square. Carr considered that it would not be necessary to make the whole base in masonry but instead to build a substantial masonry pier under each column or cluster of columns and then fill in between with concrete.[10] Carr had discussed this with Kennard, who wanted to use rubble instead of concrete, possibly because he had a good supply of rubble left over from laying out his works.[11]

Towards the end of August, the foundations for No. 1 pier had been excavated to a depth of 5 feet, where '*a very firm and even bed of dirty gravel had been opened*'. Carr was seeking instructions as to the type of flooring he should request the contractor to put under the base plates at this particular excavation.[12] At this stage, Kennard was full of optimism, giving instructions to his staff '*to push on with the foundations as fast as possible*'. He anticipated within the next month to have excavated all of the foundations and have all of the piers erected by Christmas 1853, weather permitting.[13]

Reporting to Liddell in September, Carr had observed that the rubble in the foundations of pier No. 5 was progressing satisfactorily, though at first '*it was short of the mark*'. Apparently the importance of establishing a sound foundation had not been appreciated by '*those in immediate responsibility*', until Carr had instructed them of the function the foundation had to perform. He noted that '*the lime was very first rate and so is the sand*'.[14]

Kennard was manufacturing other railway components at Crumlin for the company, as well as those required for the viaduct. His problems in the supply of switches (points) and crossings, in readiness for the opening to passengers of the main line from Coed y Gric to Hereford on 6th December, overshadowed reports on the progress of the works at Crumlin. However, work had continued

PLATE 4.3: *An enlargement from the previous photograph, showing the Viaduct Works yard. Note the wooden-jibbed cranes and also the disc & crossbar signal in the centre background on the MR&CC line. The trestles on the right are thought to have been used to erect the transverse girders on site, prior to then being raised, one side at a time, into position.*
STEPHEN ROWSON COLLECTION

PLATE 4.6: There are two London Stereoscopic Company versions of this view (see also page 111), one showing more of the portable steam engine than the other. They are evidence of how the photographer had control over the workforce to get them into the picture. This contrasts with the later impersonal attempt by Francis Bedford to take the same view of the works' yard. In the left background is the cupola remelting furnace whilst in the right foreground is an example of the iron travelling cranes that the Kennards were constructing for the market.
STEPHEN ROWSON COLLECTION

In respect to the design of the viaduct, Kennard accused Liddell of not doing him justice: '*I have never on any occasion claimed the invention of any new system either with respect to the superstructure or of the piers ... If arrangement can be called design I should say that he* [Wild] *designed the Newark Dyke Bridge and I the Crumlin, both are on the same system and the same calculations apply ... You have omitted the chief feature in the Crumlin girders namely the absence of the boiler plate work and forging (pray excuse the bull) by which I was enabled to construct them much cheaper than they had been before, keeping within the limit laid down by Mr Gordon ... With reference to the piers I claim no new system, none is employed. It is a singular fact that we all had the same idea almost at the same time*'.[20]

These exchanges do little to answer the question on who designed the piers and trusses for the viaduct. It is obvious that several people were involved, each contributing a different facet that eventually came together to form the design as constructed. The girders were Warren's Patent, with all details and modifications submitted to and agreed by Wild, who was in Kennard's office every day that the drawings and calculations were being prepared by Baldwin. The drawings were then sent to Gordon to check and oversee the calculations.

However, the design of the piers continued to rankle with Liddell throughout the period of the contract. It was Doyne who first suggested using iron, Liddell who developed the idea into a design using tubular sectioned columns that he then referred to Gordon, who suggested angle iron bolted together, and Kennard who recommended square sectioned columns. This was after Kennard had calculated the force of the wind at the top of the pier and raised his calculations with Wild and Gordon. Liddell added the details and strengthened the cross and vertical bracing, whilst it was Wild who suggested the raking columns that eventually finalised the layout and form of the piers as constructed. However, Gordon was to comment later that, along with Liddell, '*we had put up one set of cast iron piers on the Usk Bridge at Pempercwm* [sic – Penpergwm Viaduct, near Abergavenny, rebuilt in 1866] *on the main line of the Newport, Abergavenny & Hereford Railway pretty much in the same way, and the gigantic nature of this was a perfectly new case, although when one sees the drawing of one and the other to an unintentianated* [sic] *person they would appear to be alike*'.[22]

Over the two weeks that Liddell and Kennard were having this 'spat' with one another, the erection of the remaining columns on pier No. 4 (which was to become known as the 'Isabella Pier') continued, as did the columns for other piers in the main valley but with little publicity. Once a tier had been completed, planks were laid across the distance girders to form a good platform. Materials for the next tier were drawn up by common windlass and because the heaviest piece did not exceed 1 ton in weight, it could be bolted in place by using sheer legs and pulleys. Reports suggested that a pier with ten tiers could be completed in ten or eleven weeks.

At the end of January 1854, Carr had identified a problem with Kennard's setting out of the foundations and received instructions from Liddell to '*shift all of the foundations slightly, it will only make two or three inches difference in the foundations, and I see nothing to prevent it, the stones must be quite wide enough*'.[22]

Whilst the piers were being erected, it was discovered that the thickness of the metal in some of the castings was not always as consistent as it should have been. The 17 foot long columns were specified in the contract to be a consistent 3/4 inch or 1 inch thick throughout their length.

Kennard had previously told Carr that he did not expect the castings to be too large regularly from top to bottom of the viaduct. However, from Carr's observations he wanted Kennard to carry out a systematic examination of all of the castings and in his presence.[23]

The foundry at Falkirk was experiencing difficulties in maintaining the required consistency and following the rejection of some columns – because the castings were too thin – the foundry management, without referring it to the engineers, decided to cast the columns thicker. Similar problems arose over the casting of the base plates and in the girders. Carr wrote to Gordon with a more specific request regarding an acceptable average thickness for metal in the base plates and girder flanges taken at the bolt holes and whether this would be a sufficient guide to judge their effective strength. If so he requested Gordon to determine the minimum for such an average.

Carr suggested that, for those cases in which the least thickness is specified to be over 5/8 inch, the minimum average should be 3/4 inch; for a case in which the least thickness is 5/8 inch or under, the minimum average should be 5/8 inch; and any base or girder where the minimum thickness of metal is 1/2 inch or under must be condemned.[24] Gordon agreed with Carr and considered that the rules set out would '*be safe and unobjectionable*'.[25]

Kennard was finishing the foundations for the piers in the Ebbw Valley during March 1854 (six months behind schedule) and he wanted a set of drawings of the abutments for the smaller viaduct across the Kendon Valley.[26] Work was being held up because drawings for the purchase of land from Sir Benjamin Hall had not been completed, although no difficulties were foreseen.[27]

In April 1854, Kennard was in one of his optimistic moods, asking Carr to write to Liddell and let him know, '*that he is making much better progress with the viaduct now than hitherto*'. Carr, in his letter to Liddell, adds '*I really do begin to be satisfied with the progress. If he goes on improving a little longer I shall soon be proud of him*'.[28]

Liddell at that time was having second thoughts on the method for crossing the smaller Kendon Valley. He was thinking seriously of abandoning that section of the viaduct and sinking two more shafts on an unspecified tunnel so that they could bring the earth through a cutting at Hayford, in order to tip and fill the valley. Along with earth from other existing cuttings, creating an embankment would, he believed, be cheaper than a viaduct. In the back of his mind he could have been thinking of increasing the radius of a proposed curve at this point, making the line a more convenient access point for an unpublished line from Ebbw Vale to Crumlin, suggested by Mr Brown, one of the company's directors. At the same time, Liddell was pushing Kennard to let him have a report on '*the state of the work and preparation of parts for the Crumlin Viaduct*'. The report was to contain information on the length of time

PLATE 4.7: *The* Illustrated London News *published its first view of the viaduct in December 1854, when the girders were starting to be placed in position. All of the piers had to have been completed for this to commence. To commemorate the event, the managing director of the works, Tom Kennard's brother Henry Martyn, persuaded the workforce to forgo a day's pay as a contribution to a fund for troops fighting in the Crimea. At that time the family's Falkirk Ironworks was doing very well working night and day to supply armaments to the war with Russia. This view, looking south, shows the line of the former Blaencuffin Tramroad running between the fences, parallel to the railway on its right, which runs into the newly established Viaduct Works on the site of the old canal wharf. The main line continues over the river towards Newport, with a branch siding on the right to the coal wharf.*
COURTESY OXFORD HOUSE INDUSTRIAL HISTORY SOCIETY

THE CRUMLIN VIADUCT, ON THE WESTERN VALLEY RAILWAY.

PLATE 4.11: An intimate portrait of someone thought to be one of the Viaduct Company's directors and (presumably) his wife posing on and by a travelling crane in the yard. They appear elderly but mid-Victorian sensibilities were clearly drawn to buying such a photograph. The wooden framework behind them was used in prefabricating the cross-members prior to raising them to the top of the piers. This photograph also shows the structure of a typical pier tier. STEPHEN ROWSON COLLECTION

been tested; in Carr's opinion, '*anyone other than Kennard would have done so*'.[45] Liddell's reaction was to tell Carr that '*Kennard must not be allowed to play such tom foolery with the work – order Rumble to have everything tested to insure the work being done without accident*'.[46] Kennard went defensive claiming there was nothing wrong with the ropes, they were brand new and specially made for the job and they should have carried five times the weight.[47]

What was seen as a simple solution to the problem at that time was a pair of safety slings at each end of the girder, consisting of two bars of 6 inch by ½ inch flat iron, with holes 1½ inches in diameter, punched 2 inches apart throughout. These were to be suspended in such a position that a man could use two bars alternately, putting them in the holes one above the other and following the girder from bottom to top of the pier. These bars would receive the girder in the event of any mishap to the lifting tackle. Maynard describes the use of sheer legs in raising the girders within the gap left by not installing the distance girders. The main girders were drawn up by horses pulling on ropes or chains fixed to a common windlass attached to sheer legs.[48] Once a girder had reached the top of a pier it was necessary to move it sideways into its final position. A timber frame was constructed that formed a crosshead on top of the pier, upon which an upper pulley block was suspended on a roller frame, which could pass along the crosshead. When the girder had reached its intended position, it was lowered into place on the A-frame fixed at the top of the pier.

At the beginning of December 1854, Carr informed Gordon that one girder was in place and that it looked well.[49] However, this was a long way behind Kennard's prediction at the ceremony of erecting the first column on 8th December 1853, when he had forecast that the viaduct would be completed within twelve months. A report in the *Illustrated London News* stated that '*when the girder was planted at about half past three in the afternoon, a loud and hearty cheer burst from the lips of the workmen, who were some of them in most perilous postions, while one, more courageous than the rest, actually walked across the girder*'. Given its 9 inch width and the fact that it was about 200 feet above ground level, this was courageous indeed. Henry Martyn Kennard mounted a platform to speak to the men and afterwards supplied them with '*food and drink to celebrate the achievement*'.[50]

Throughout this period, work had been progressing on the preparation of plans for crossing the Kendon Valley. Land had been purchased from Sir Benjamin Hall and Liddell had discarded his plans to tip soil and create an embankment. The position of the piers had been set out by Mr Curley, a surveyor who had been working on the company's main line and who later became surveyor to Hereford Town Council.[51] This particular section of the viaduct lay on a curve. Baldwin, when preparing the initial plans, questioned the proposed 18 chain radius of the curve but Carr confirmed that, as then laid out, the radius had been increased to 20 chains. The girders as constructed were straight, so Kennard devised a plan to shorten the inner girders. His proposals were forwarded to Liddell but how the problem was eventually overcome was never specified.[52]

Whilst raising the second girder between piers No's 1 and 2 in December 1854, a tragic accident occurred but the precise dates are confusing. Kennard informed Fitzmaurice, NA&HR chairman, '*we have had a sad accident at Crumlin, by which I fear one or more men will be killed, my brother* [H.M. Kennard] *has come up expressly to fetch me down and although I hardly know what to do without seeing it I must go*'.[53] Then, in January 1855, Kennard's brother informed Carr that they had a very serious accident the previous day whilst lifting a girder, by which '*a man was very badly hurt, but is a little better today*'.[54] H.M. Kennard left the girder where it was when it broke free and proposed to retain it in the position that it had come to rest until Kennard had arrived and inspected it. The latter reported that he could not understand the cause of the accident but needed to see Liddell and Gordon to discuss a new arrangement for lifting the girders; '*pray come down if you can*' he wrote.[55] During the lifting operation, the girder had buckled and turned on its side, throwing the man off the pier, who fell about 40 feet to the ground. As Kennard was writing the note he commented that '*a messenger had just informed him that the man was dead, and the man's brother was with him crying like a child*'.[56] The fatality brought progress in raising any further girders to an end until such time as a solution to the buckling could be found.

After a number of experiments, the system adopted was to stiffen the top chord of the girder with temporary bracing. Pieces of timber 6 by 9 inches in section, were bolted together using iron plates, to form two lengths almost as long as the girder. These were laid 6 feet apart and connected with each other every 5 feet by pieces of timber of the same section laid across the girder. These pieces were bolted to the longer pieces and to the main girder. Braces of round iron, tightened with keys, formed a complete girder of wood about 120 feet long and 6 feet wide. Who devised the system is not clear; years later, Maynard claims it for Kennard but Carr writing to Gordon comments '*I was delighted to hear you have put Kennard right for lifting the girders – I hope we may now get him on faster*'.[57] Liddell also refers to Gordon having designed it.[58] Carr was not impressed with progress at that time, suggesting to Gordon that at the current pace of lifting it would take at least 30 months (to mid-1857) to complete the viaduct.[59] Kennard was also delighted with the bracing, writing to Carr and suggesting '*I may now say we are out of all our difficulties the girder is up and nothing could succeed better than the plan proposed. I have had another set made*'. With another of his predictions he stated '*I will now show what can be done*'.[60]

Work on lifting the girders was progressing as Kennard had predicted and, by April, two girders were being raised a week and it could have been quicker but for another accident and poor weather.[61] Subject to good weather, Kennard was predicting that he would then complete the viaduct in less than three months (by July 1855).[62] However, later that same day (18th April), four girders in the sixth opening had been erected into their places but had not been permanently fixed and they toppled and fell. One man was killed instantly and another died later due to his injuries, whilst three others were injured but not seriously. Kennard was present at the site when the accident happened and in a letter to NA&HR company secretary Pritchard he wrote: '*I assure you I had lost almost all energy seeing the fearful accident that took place on Wednesday, having only just left the platform myself seeing as it were the men smashed at my feet*'.

Plate 4.12: Henry Martyn Kennard 1833-1911. This is the only known image of Tom Kennard's younger brother, taken from a portrait executed in 1891 by the artist W.W. Ouless. HMK became joint manager with Maynard of the Viaduct Works in 1855 and later made quite a name ofr himself in the world of archaeology.

PLATE 4.13: The LSC issued this stereograph which they simply entitled 'Welsh Workmen' and we know little else about it. They might be part of the Crumlin workforce, perhaps from the factory where they were assured of keeping their feet on the ground considering their apparent old age. However, the LSC also published a number of views of the Ebbw Vale Ironworks in the late 1850s and this may be one from that series. Notwithstanding, it provides us with another fascinating study of industrial workmen of the period, a time when photography was still very much in its infancy.
STEPHEN ROWSON COLLECTION

Kennard, though, appeared to be more concerned over the damage that occurred to the pier and the girder: '*not knowing the damage done quite upset me. I am happy to say however, that it is not serious as first contemplated. £5 will cover the expense of damage to the pier and a few hundreds will repair the girders that have come down*'.[63]

A rapidly arranged inquest was held at the Navigation Inn, Crumlin, in front of a coroner and jury on Saturday, 21st April 1855. The first witness called was John Ives, who was referred to as '*the superintendent of the west department of the bridge*'. He explained that, at about half past five on Wednesday evening, he was on the west abutment. He had spoken to George Ives, one of the deceased, about three distance columns that had to be placed between the south side girder and the adjoining, which was missing. They had also discussed the cross bracing for the whole of the girders before asking him to return the sheer leg poles to the yard. Ives had given him strict instructions not to remove the scaffolding or raking struts until the girders were secured. The girders were apparently resting on the pier and on plumber blocks or saddles on the abutment and not fixed. The four girders were connected together by a chain and a cross beam above them.

William Ives, brother of the deceased, when giving evidence told how, at about seven o'clock, when he was on top of the stage, he saw Bannister (the second man killed) knocking the prop away from the north side girder. They had been trying to get the transverse crossings in that morning but could not as they were not straight. According to the witness none of them had the least fear of insecurity. He explained that when Bannister struck the prop he commented '*that there was a great weight on it*'. The prop was inside the girder, resting on the platform, and was fixed against the top of the girder to keep it in its place. The north girder then having no support fell against the other three girders and all four fell off the scaffolding.

Kennard, in his evidence, confirmed that he was the contractor and at the time of the accident the west side girders were complete, with the exception of three distance columns which were used as a gauge to keep the girders at their proper centres and to secure them. The wrought iron cross bracing was to be put in immediately. Kennard did not know what could have induced Ives to have the props removed until that was done but he presumed he thought that the girders were perfectly safe. Until the cross bracing was attached, Kennard remarked that it was a well known fact that the girders would have no lateral stability and whilst the removal of the props might take place a hundred times without an accident occurring, it would be imprudent to do it. Kennard thought that Ives would not have removed the prop had he known the amount of weight being thrust upon it. Kennard suggested that Bannister, in removing the prop, was the cause of the accident. The jury returned a verdict of accidental death.[64]

Carr, when forwarding the results of his investigation into the accident, concluded: '*Such facts as I have been able to collect show that the man who disobeyed orders in striking the props was guilty of gross carelessness in the manner in which he did it*'.[65] A report in the *Merlin* newspaper sheds a little more light on the incident, explaining that the last span of the larger viaduct, as well as three spans of the smaller one, had to be arranged so as to accommodate the curvature of the track. The westward ends of the four girders of the last span were slewed to the south, which meant that there was slightly less space between them. All morning men had been trying to fit the horizontal bracings but had been unable to do so. According to the report, it was suggested that the foreman was attempting to move the outer girder to make room for the stays.[66]

During May 1855, Kennard ran into trouble with the MR&CC. Their engineer, Robert Sayce, refused to allow the Kennard's workmen access and facilities to erect a stage over the Western Valley lines for the purpose of lifting the girders between piers No's 4 and 5. Maynard had made an application to Sayce requesting permission to erect the stage and received a notice by return not to proceed with any works of the viaduct '*under pain of action by the Monmouthshire Company by destroying appliances*' and intimating that any letters from Kennard '*would not be the subject of a reply*'. Maynard requested assistance from Gordon, who at the next board meeting obtained a resolution from the directors '*that the notice referred to especially when taken in connection with the proceedings of the Monmouthshire Company at Llanhilleth appears to be at variance with the frequently expressed desire on the part of the Monmouthshire Company to be on the most friendly terms with this Company, and in excess of the legal powers granted to the Company*'.[67] Kennard was then to face another problem when a further rope broke during the lifting of a girder. He reported that no one was hurt '*owing to the great precautions I had taken*' but it was then arranged to lift all subsequent girders by using chains that he had at the works.[68]

Although the iron work was nearing completion by the end of June 1855, Kennard was being chased by Carr to get a coat of paint on the structure before winter set in.[69] Plans were then being prepared for the opening of the line from Pontypool to Crumlin and he was also being chased by Pritchard, who added as a footnote to one of his letters to Kennard: '*we are working up to the grand opening on the 1st June. It will be well for your cause that the viaduct is then complete*'. As part of the opening ceremony, Carr was expecting a creosoting tank to be removed from the site of a proposed station to be located at the end of the small viaduct (Crumlin High Level). Maynard promised that everything would be done as far as was within their power to comply.[70] Carr must have been using threatening language towards Kennard at this time, because he wrote to Carr with regard to his comments, '*that he was not satisfied with the progress being made with painting the viaduct*' and that he had mentioned taking '*strong measures*': '*If by this you mean assisting in getting some good men who will work on the bridge the sooner you take strong measures the more I shall be obliged to you*'.[71] Carr responded curtly, telling Kennard that such strong measures as his company would have to take would '*doubtless take the turn you seem to expect*' but that the expense would be greater than the Kennard's could do the work for.[72] Kennard then informed Carr that the painting was now alright, the men taken on were first rate hands and promised that the whole work would be finished with one coat in three weeks[73] but this turned out to be yet another of his promises that failed to materialise.

Liddell then called a halt to any further work on fixing of the handrail during August. According to him, it was a very unsatisfactory job and '*an eyesore of a wriggling line that needed getting rid of*'. He also wanted to be informed of the dates when Kennard intended to lift the last six girders in the Ebbw Valley.[74] Around this period the struts came into question again. Liddell wrote to Kennard expressing his opinion that he '*could not see any good effect from the keys you proposed for the struts*'. However, he promised to look in to Kennard's suggestion, along with Gordon. In his opinion, the principle of the joint adopted in the girders was perfectly understood at the time of the intended design and the purpose of the struts was first calculated. After a lengthy analysis of stresses and strains, and the effectiveness and practicality of Kennard's suggestion, Gordon considered that it would serve no purpose but added '*you know that I am open to conviction and so pray demonstrate to me that I am wrong, if you can*'. The effectiveness of the struts as originally designed was tested by Kennard, who found that they would support the equivalent of trains of five engines on each line. No records have been identified to indicate that any further action was taken.[75]

There was another ceremony during September 1855, when the last girder of the main viaduct was placed in position. It was reported that an 'Ensign of England' had been raised at either end of the bridge, accompanied by a series of cheers from workmen. A procession left from the Viaduct Works, walked through the village and on up the Kendon Valley, then up the steep sides of the hill to the viaduct. A narrow footway of loose planks had been laid down across the girders to the Pontypool side. As the procession reached the centre of the viaduct, a number of cannon located on the hillside were fired. Continuing to the Pontypool side of the viaduct, the procession descended the incline and, on reaching the Navigation Inn, two barrels of beer were struck, with singing, dancing and music bringing the event to a conclusion.[76]

The relationship between Kennard and Liddell became an issue once again when the former, in a '*private*' letter to Gordon, made a formal complaint about Liddell. In response, Gordon refuted most of Kennard's complaints, pointing out that in business they held nothing '*private*'. He agreed with Liddell's comments that losses or expenditure above Kennard's original

Plate 4.14: *This view from spring 1856, taken from across the Ebbw Valley, shows the Kendon portion but with the decking not yet complete, whilst to the right, the ground had not yet been made up on the island between the two viaducts. The photograph provides a clear illustration of what was required in building up the land between the two sections. The quarry, bottom right, may have supplied stone for the abutments and waste for the infill but, equally, it could well have been longer established, providing the stone for building Crumlin village. The recently moved tramroad (made necessary by the building of the TVE) from Cefn Coch and Kendon collieries to Newbridge, can be seen passing under the left-hand span – the Kendon Road was the original route to the canal for tramroads from the collieries round the corner, futher up the valley.*
Stephen Rowson collection

calculations were due not from the work done but from the manner in going about it. The problems now being faced were of Kennard's own making;[77] this is detailed more fully in the chapter on payments.

In November, problems had been identified with the abutments, which needed alterations. Maynard was asking for instructions on how to make these because he had masons spare.[78] What the alterations amounted to were not specified but Carr made arrangements to visit Crumlin in order to resolve the problem.[79]

On a more eventful note, Carr had informed Liddell that there remained only four girders to be lifted into position, five having been lifted in November, commenting '*the sooner we get it finished the better*'. Carr was hoping to get an engine over the first span during Christmas week but the rails would have to be released from Pontypool wharf, whilst in a sarcastic aside he added, '*Kennard will doubtless have his timber to order for the permanent way yet*'.[80] Carr also wrote to Kennard suggesting to him that, with his current rate of progress, he could have the last girder raised before Christmas week. He also gave notice to Kennard that he was attempting, with Liddell's agreement, to arrange for an engine to pass over the first span during Christmas week.[81] All that Liddell needed to do was determine what guide rail to use, whilst Carr had also ordered the planking for the smaller viaduct.

Carr was confronted with yet another problem in early December. Maynard asked to be allowed to use, in the trusses, some 9 inches by $^1/_2$ inch iron, with $^3/_4$ inch holes punched in them 12 inches apart, 3 inches from the edge and in line with the nuts at the ends of their fixing points, thereby not injuring the use of the bars as ties. Mr Price, a company inspector, thought that they should not be used, supported by Kennard, who had given instructions that they should not be used; contrary to his instructions, however, Maynard had used them for '*experimental*' purposes, claiming that if the bars could not be used, more would have to be cast as there were

PLATE 4.15: Interestingly, the decking in this second view is more complete, which suggests that the photographic assignment took more than just a few days.
STEPHEN ROWSON COLLECTION

PLATE 4.16: This coloured stereo view is captioned 'Quarries Newport - Mon' but gives no clue otherwise as to where it was taken. The stone-built hut on the left looks a match for the one seen in the stereo slide captioned 'Quarries, Newport, Monmouthshire', which appears on page 229. There is a railway line to the right and a river on the far side of that, so it could well be somewhere along the MR&CC/Western Valleys line but it does not quite match with any quarry in the vicinity of Crumlin. However, as an early photograph of a mid-19th century Monmouthshire quarry it is invaluable.
STEPHEN ROWSON COLLECTION

no 9 inch bars left on site. To overcome any objections to their visual appearance, Maynard suggested that the open holes could be filled up with nuts and bolts.[82] Carr contacted Liddell, emphasising the fact that he had always applied a rule for any alterations to items specified on drawings forming part of the contract – he would not authorise them without Gordon's or Liddell's authority.[83] Gordon responded '*you need not hesitate to allow the bars to be used*'.[84] In mid-December, H.M. Kennard informed Carr that the last girder had been raised into position.[85]

A problem that had surfaced regularly throughout the contract came to the fore in January. Liddell asked Kennard to supply him with sketches of the foundations in order to compare them with the contract, as he had information that the piers were not as deep as they were shown on the drawings. Liddell wanted the situation '*cleared up as soon as possible*'.[86] Kennard disputed Liddell's comments, claiming that the foundations never formed part of a contract drawing and that the general elevation showed the style proposed but did not form part of any quantities and were shown merely to make the drawings look well; '*the question was not considered in the estimates*'.[87] Liddell accused Kennard of '*not taking the drawings seriously*'.[88]

Further problems and misunderstandings surfaced in February 1856, concerning the laying of the planking over the small viaduct. Kennard was proposing, according to Carr, to lay diagonal planking across the viaduct, with a 4 inch bottom layer and a 2 inch upper layer, using lengths of timber to suit him. Kennard had informed Carr that this method had been arranged with Liddell.[89] However, in the absence of any written instructions from Liddell, Carr would not sanction the laying of any further timber on the smaller viaduct. Liddell informed Kennard that the subject of diagonal planking had never been discussed with Carr,[90] the laying of which, in two layers, had been Kennard's proposition as he considered it to be superior to straight planking. Liddell gave instructions to Carr to ensure that the work, as proposed by Kennard, was carried out '*to his entire satisfaction as to the lengths of planks and as to their spiking and pitching*'.[91] However, the cost of laying two layers was not to exceed the cost for laying one thickness. Carr sent Kennard a drawing illustrating how the joints between the timbers should be made. Kennard, irrespective of being told by Liddell that the cost of supplying and fixing the planking in two layers should not exceed one layer, immediately applied for an '*extras payment*'.

Liddell was not impressed and told Kennard that if he

PLATE 4.17: This photograph's publisher is not certain but it was taken shortly after 1856, looking north-east at the finished viaducts, with the land between them now made up to complete the route across. The lower part of the incline to the upper works on the eastern side of the Ebbw Valley can just be made out far right, as it drops down behind the works buildings. Crumlin High Level station was opened a year later, above and behind where the photographer was standing.
STEPHEN ROWSON COLLECTION

had expected further payments for laying the planking diagonally, he should have said so at the outset. All along, Liddell had been under the impression that Kennard had specifically asked for diagonal planking in order to make use of timber then in his possession.[92] Liddell then instructed Carr to send him details for the laying of the timber, because he had been informed that Kennard's workmen had told him that they were allowed to lay it at any length that suited you and that you had settled it with me: '*To this I entirely object as well as paying extra*'. Carr wrote to H.M. Kennard reinforcing what Liddell had specified. Kennard had permission to '*lay diagonally in two layers the bottom in 4 inch timber the upper in 2 inch timber. The bottom layer was to be composed entirely of whole lengths of planking, roughly creosoted. The upper layer could be laid in shorter lengths that were to be jointed alternatively on the two middle girders and had to be spiked to the lower especially at the joints and were to be thoroughly tarred and pitched*'.[93]

The next mention of planking was in June 1856. John Rennie was ready to commence tipping over the small viaduct, in order to raise the height of the intermediate hill and Liddell had therefore asked Kennard to complete the planking on it so that Rennie could lay a temporary road for the purpose.[94] As soon as Kennard had completed the planking and Rennie was tipping soil, Carr was asking Liddell to prepare a drawing showing details of what arrangements he had made for facing off and providing fencing at the foot of the embankment.

Both Liddell's and Carr's relationship with Kennard was at a low ebb at this time, as witnessed from a letter from Liddell to Carr telling him that he had given Kennard a '*blowing up*' about his bad work and he says '*you have just taken me to see some of the worst I told him you would show him plenty of it if he wished for the truth ... you had better offer him facilities for doing so*'.[95]

Towards the end of any contract, one of the problems encountered is to get contractors to carry out repairs or finish specified items to the satisfaction of the client and Kennard and the viaduct contract was no exception. Not for the first time, at the end of November 1856, Carr was asking Kennard to complete repairs to an abutment and No. 4 pier, the ones damaged as a result of the girder falling, and to alter and finish the handrail. In a note to Liddell he comments '*he has never shown the slightest disposition to commence with it*'.[96]

PLATE 4.18: Arguably the most iconic photograph of the viaduct is this view of a top-hatted Tom Kennard standing on the completed bridge deck of the Ebbw Valley section in the summer of 1856. Along with the pictures on the next two pages, they may have been taken on the occasion of the public open day before track laying commenced. As the text indicates, the trials and tribulations endured by all concerned in reaching this stage had been considerable, many of them caused by Kennard himself but his sense of pride and satisfaction in this moment must have been immense, even for a man of his undoubted enormous ego. More was to come, however, with Kennard initiating legal proceedings against the NA&HR for payment of monies he felt that he was due.
STEPHEN ROWSON COLLECTION

PLATE 4.19: Top-hatted gents and ladies with parasols pose on the viaduct, lending credence to this being the occasion of the public open day. The chance to stroll across would have been quite a thrill for all concerned, an experience which at this date would have been difficult to replicate anywhere else. Meanwhile, a pair of workmen, no doubt long used to the height, sit nonchalantly on one of the abutments, feet dangling over the drop. The gangway below the level of the railway was intended for inspection and maintenance but as noted in the text, became a popular attraction with the general public too.
STEPHEN ROWSON COLLECTION

Thinking years ahead, Carr suggested to Liddell, in April 1857, that an easy access for future maintenance and inspection of the viaduct should be provided.[97] His idea was to lay a footpath along the entire length of the viaduct between the two centre girders, not necessarily the whole width but wide enough to be safe, say two or three planks, with two access points on the large viaduct and one on the small viaduct. Liddell reported the suggestion to the board and obtained their approval to the footway at an estimated cost of £387.[98] Although the footpath was intended for ease of inspection and maintenance once the viaduct had been completed, it became a local attraction for tourists to walk across and admire the details of the viaduct's construction and the landscape of the valleys.[99] Having succeeded with his footpath suggestion, however, Carr was still having no success with Kennard, who he continued chasing to complete a number of small jobs.

The laying of the permanent way that was started in 1856 was run as a separate contract but as this work was progressing, work on the viaduct had not been completed. During May 1857, whilst Gordon was at Crumlin checking on the testing of the viaduct, Carr took the opportunity to discuss with him several jobs remaining to be completed. These included repairs to some damaged 'A' frames at the top of a pier, completion of the handrail and the application of a final coat of paint. In a letter of the following day's date, Carr asked Gordon to issue an order to Kennard to complete the work with regard to the handrail: '*it has been many months in its present incomplete condition and I cannot get them to finish it*'.[100]

With the date approaching for the inspection of the viaduct by a Board of Trade inspector, Carr wrote to Kennard giving instructions to ensure that he had all the tension bars clear of the 'A' frame struts when the weight is on: '*make good the deficiencies in wrought iron wedges on top of the 'A' frames and under saddles, and also the coffers to piers*'; and also to fit the gusset pieces on the broken 'A' frame.[101] Even after the line had been opened, Carr was still having a tussle with Kennard to complete the works – he had not finished fixing of the handrail and portions of the ironwork had received only two coats of paint, which in some places had already scaled off from the lack of perfect cleaning and rubbing down.[102]

Liddell forwarded these defects to Pritchard to report to the board. He requested the directors authorise an expenditure, estimated to be £214, to complete the works, by either deducting it from Kennard's balance or allowing it to him as part of any sum beyond what he was entitled to be paid under the terms of the contract, and what the directors may decide to pay him. However, Liddell thought that it would be a much better idea for the company to complete the work than continuing to try to get Kennard to do it. The directors resolved to authorise the engineer to finish the painting and to put the hand rail straight if Kennard refused to complete the works.[103] Liddell forwarded a copy of particulars of work required to be done to complete everything, along with a copy of the board's resolution, with a request for Kennard to inform him whether he would complete the work. If the company did it there would be a charge of £214 to the contract. Particulars of the work required to be done and sent to Kennard were as follows:

'*To open out clean and paint the bottoms* [i.e. the bases] *and bottom set of cross girders of piers No's 1, 2 and 6 with three coats of paint as per the specification.*

To clean and paint the bottoms of piers No's 3, 4 and 5 with one coat of paint.

To clean and paint all of the Warren Girders [forty in number] *one coat of paint.*

To properly set the handrail upright, with an even top and in regular line-straight where the line is straight and properly curved to suit the curvature of the line where the latter is curved.

To complete the painting of the handrail in accordance with the specification [about half of it required one coat and the remainder two coats].'[104]

Plate 4.20: *A similar view but from the other side and hand-coloured.*
Stephen Rowson collection

However, Kennard continued to ignore all attempts and threats to get him to complete the works. Carr again writes to him: '*as you do not inform me that you will complete the viaduct yourself it is necessary that I should in accordance with Mr Liddell's instructions at once make the necessary preparations on behalf of the Company – if I do not hear from you thereupon by the 7th* [September] *inst. I will put the matter in hand*'.[105] Responding after the deadline issued by Carr, Maynard informs him that Kennard would complete his contractual arrangements. According to Maynard, Kennard had visited Crumlin and was surprised to find that the main girders had not been painted.[106] Carr was not impressed and let Kennard know that he had made all of the necessary arrangements for the company's workforce to complete the works on Monday of the following week. His final comment to Kennard was understandable: '*I hope you will have the work commenced at once and carried out thoroughly*'.[107]

PLATE 4.21: Tom Kennard surveys his masterpiece whilst leaning on the railings which at one time had caused disagreement. Below, looking down the valley from left to right, are the Monmouthshire Canal, the River Ebbw and the MR& CC railway line to Newport.
STEPHEN ROWSON COLLECTION

References

1. Letter, Kennard to Liddell, 19th Nov. 1852
2. Letter, Kennard to Carr, 22nd Nov. 1852
3. Letter, Kennard to Carr, 1st Dec. 1852
4. Letter, Kennard to Carr, 14th Dec. 1852
5. Letter, Carr to Liddell, 9th Jan. 1853
6. Liddell's report read to board of directors, 14th May 1853
7. Letter, Kennard to Carr, 16th Mar. 1853
8. Letter, Carr to Liddell, 28th July 1853
9. Letter, Kennard to Liddell, 4th May 1853
10. Letter, Carr to Liddell, 15th May 1853
11. Letter, Carr to Liddell, 18th Aug. 1853
12. Letter, Kennard to Carr, 26th Aug. 1853
13. Letter, Kennard to Carr, 26th Aug. 1853
14. Letter, Carr to Liddell, 23rd Sept. 1853
15. Maynard's *Handbook on Crumlin Viaduct*
16. *Monmouthshire Merlin*
17. Letter, Liddell to Kennard, 23rd Dec. 1853
18. Letter, Kennard to Liddell, 24th Dec. 1853
19. Letter, from Scott, journalist to *The Monmouthshire Merlin*, 1854
20. Letter, Kennard to Liddell, 9th Jan. 1854
21. Evidence of Gordon given to arbitration hearing
22. Letter, Liddell to Carr, 30th Jan. 1854
23. Letter, Carr to Liddell, 2nd Feb. 1854
24. Letter, Carr to Gordon, 4th Feb. 1854
25. Letter, Gordon to Carr, 6th Feb. 1854
26. Letter, Kennard to Carr, 31st Mar. 1854
27. Letter, Carr to Liddell, 9th Mar. 1854
28. Letter, Carr to Liddell, 24th Mar. 1854
29. Letter, Liddell to Carr, 28th April 1854
30. Letter, Liddell to Carr, 18th May 1854
31. Letter, R.W. Kennard to Kennard, 27th June 1854
32. Letter, Gordon to Liddell, 13th July 1854
33. Letters, Kennard to Gordon, 1st Aug. 1854 and Kennard to Liddell, 2nd Aug. 1854
34. Letter, Carr to Gordon, 9th Aug. 1854
35. Letters, Kennard to Gordon, 22nd July 1854 & 2nd Aug. 1854
36. Letters, Carr to Kennard, 22nd Aug. 1854, Kennard to Carr 24th Aug. 1854, Carr to Liddell, 25th Aug. 1854, Liddell to Carr, 4th Dec. 1854
37. Letters, Kennard to Carr, 15th Sept. 1854 & 18th Sept. 1854
38. Letter, Kennard to Liddell, 8th Nov. 1854
39. Letter, Kennard to Liddell, 15th Oct. 1854
40. Letter, Kennard to Carr, 13th Sept. 1854
41. Letter, Kennard to Carr, 18th Sept. 1854
42. Letter, Kennard to Liddell, 15th Oct. 1854
43. Letter, Kennard to Liddell, 8th Nov. 1854
44. Letter, H.M. Kennard to Liddell, 22nd Nov. 1854
45. Letter, Carr to Liddell, 26th Nov. 1854
46. Letter, Liddell to Carr, 27th Nov. 1854
47. Letter, Kennard to Gordon, 28th Nov. 1854
48. Maynard's *Handbook on Crumlin Viaduct*
49. Letter, Carr to Gordon, 8th Dec. 1854
50. *Illustrated London News*
51. Letter, Rumble to J.N. Jones, 8th Dec. 1854
52. Letter, Carr to Liddell, 15th Dec. 1854
53. Letter, Kennard to Farquehar, 17th Dec. 1854
54. Letter, H.M. Kennard to Carr, 2nd Jan. 1855
55. Letter, Kennard to Liddell, 3rd Jan. 1855
56. Maynard's *Handbook on Crumlin Viaduct*
57. Letter, Carr to Gordon, 22nd Mar. 1855
58. Letter, Liddell to Carr, 23rd Mar. 1855
59. Letter, Carr to Gordon, 22nd Mar. 1855
60. Letter, Kennard to Carr, 25th Mar. 1855
61. Letter, Kennard to Carr, 2nd April 1855
62. Letter, Kennard to Pritchard, 18th April 1855
63. Letter, Kennard to Pritchard, 20th April 1855
64. Report in *Monmouthshire Merlin*
65. Letter, Carr to Gordon ,22nd April 1855
66. Report in *Monmouthshire Merlin*

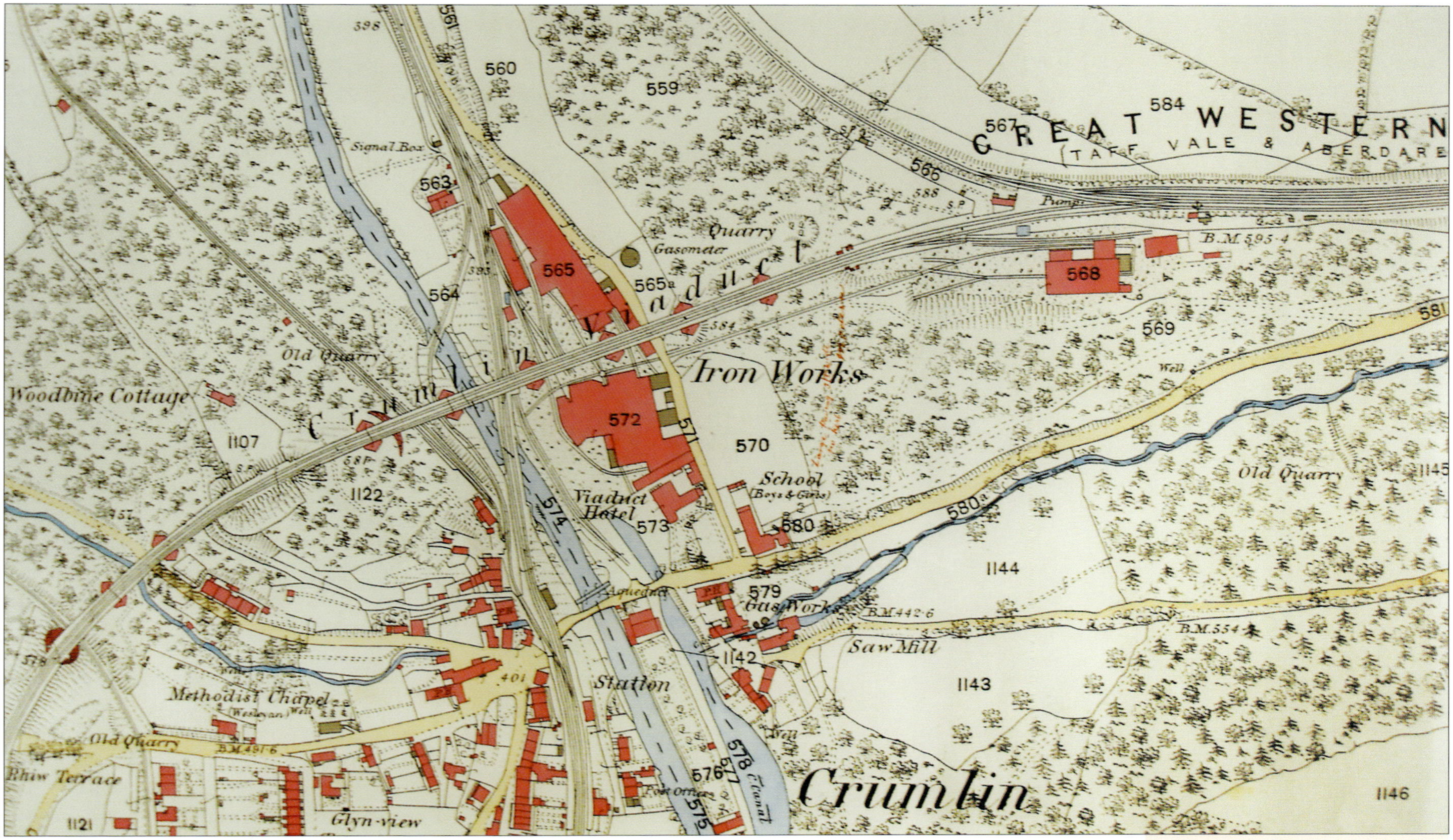

Fig. 4.1: Crumlin Works, Low Level station, Junction and viaduct as shown on the 1st edition 25 inch OS, which was surveyed in 1878-79.

67. Board of directors meeting, 4th June 1855, minute No. 1857
68. Letter, Kennard to Carr, 13th June 1855
69. Letter, Carr to Maynard, 28th June 1855
70. Letter, Maynard to Carr, 30th June 1855
71. Letter, Kennard to Carr, 18th July 1855
72. Letter, Carr to Kennard, 20th July 1855
73. Letter, Kennard to Carr, 21st July 1855
74. Letter, Liddell to Kennard, 23rd Aug. 1855
75. Letter, Liddell to Kennard, 28th Aug. 1855
76. Report in *The Monmouthshire Merlin*
77. Letter, Gordon to Kennard, 16th Sept. 1855
78. Letter, Maynard to Liddell, 5th Nov. 1855
79. Letter, Carr to Kennard, 7th Nov. 1855
80. Letter, Carr to Liddell, 26th Nov. 1855
81. Letter, Carr to Kennard, 26th Nov. 1855
82. Letter, Kennard to Carr, 10th Dec. 1855
83. Letter, Carr to Liddell, 12th Dec. 1855
84. Letter, Gordon to Carr, 17th Dec. 1855
85. Letter, H.M. Kennard to Carr, 17th Dec. 1855
86. Letter, Liddell to Kennard, 28th Jan. 1856
87. Letter, Kennard to Liddell, 28th Jan. 1856
88. Letter, Liddell to Kennard, 30th Jan. 1856
89. Letter, Carr to Liddell, 2nd Feb. 1856
90. Letter, Liddell to Kennard, 4th Feb. 1856
91. Letter, Carr to Kennard, 5th Feb. 1856
92. Letter, Liddell to Kennard, 6th Feb. 1856
93. Letter, Carr to H.M. Kennard, 8th Feb. 1856
94. Letter, Liddell to Kennard, 18th June 1856
95. Letter, Liddell to Carr, 26th May 1856
96. Letter, Carr to Kennard, 7th Nov. 1856
97. Letter, Carr to Liddell, 15th April 1857
98. Liddell's report to the board of directors, 26th April 1857
99. *Murray's Handbook for Travellers in South Wales, and Its Borders, Including the River Wye*
100. Letter, Carr to Gordon, 8th May 1857
101. Letter, Carr to Kennard Brothers, 13th May 1857
102. Letter, Carr to Liddell, 27th July 1857
103. Letter, Liddell to Pritchard, 28th July 1857
104. Letter, Liddell to Kennard, 17th Aug. 1857
105. Letter, Carr to Kennard, 27th Aug. 1857
106. Letter, Maynard to Carr, 11th Sept. 1857
107. Letter, Carr to Kennard, 12th Sept. 1857

Plate 5.1: *Francis Bedford's somewhat sterile view (No. 171) of the Viaduct Works' yard with not a workman in sight. It is thought that Bedford probably visited Crumlin in 1861. In the picture, it can be seen that the truncated canal had been walled off to create a new canal head within the Works. In the foreground, erected over the canal, there is a sawing platform and timber logs lie on the bank awaiting the sawyers. On the opposite bank is the original tip for tramroad waggons coming down from Trinant Colliery, coming across the river from the foot of the incline. Here it looks now to be in use for the works' internal narrow gauge trolleyway. The wooden bodied, railway wagons are on the Works branch from the main line, while those in the right distance, across the river, are on the siding leading to the tramroad incline wharf and which also serviced Crumlin village.*
Stephen Rowson collection

PAYMENTS

CHAPTER 5

According to the terms of the contract, the company had covenanted to make payments to Kennard on the last day of each month, provided Liddell had issued a certificate authorising such a payment. Certificates had to be confined to work completed, along with payments of £11 per ton for wrought iron delivered and standing on site; payments of £8 per ton for all castings delivered and standing on site; and a sum, to be paid at Liddell's discretion, for iron delivered and work completed on the girders but not fixed. All payments were subject to a 10% retention to be held by the company until three months after the completion of the contract. Kennard agreed to complete it by 31st August 1854, paying to the company £200 per week for each week that the works remained in an unfinished state. On delivery of iron to the site it became the property of the company.

Kennard made his first application for a payment to the directors in June 1853, almost eight months after the acceptance of his first tender in October 1852. No specific sum of money was requested; as a result of him making several large outlays on iron, he was, as he explained, '*able to make considerable progress with the viaduct*'. He mentioned that he was not desperate for a large sum, £1,000 or £2,000 would be sufficient to meet his demands.[1] Liddell certified a payment of £1,000 on account of work prepared, and at the next board meeting a cheque for that amount was drawn in favour of Kennard.[2] However, such an indecisive and open request did not spur the company's directors or management to react fully to it, nor did it instil in them confidence when dealing with applications for future payments. Kennard asked for the cheque to be crossed to Messrs Haywoods, Kennard & Company.[3]

When making his next application in July 1853, Kennard again bypassed Liddell and wrote to the directors, something that was to be the forerunner of many such letters and requests for payments. At this early stage he was disclosing his financial difficulties, and pleading for payments over and above that to which he was entitled to under the terms of the contract. By then the tone of his requests had changed. He claimed that 900 feet of the estimated 1,500 feet of iron for the superstructure had been delivered, with a net value of £6,000. He mentioned that the cost of the iron excluded the cost of the workshops and tools, and an outlay for the castings for the piers were in a forward state, and that he had already laid out on this account £4,500. Kennard explained that the entire quantity of iron work in the viaduct amounted to about 2,300 tons and expected this to be delivered within the following two months, involving him in a further and expensive outlay. This time he requested an advance of £4,000, with future payments made at a rate of £4,000 per month until all of the material had been delivered. Acting within the terms of the contract, Liddell recommended a payment of £2,000 on account of the iron delivered and a cheque for that sum was sent to Kennard the same day.[4]

At the end of July, Kennard's next request for payment was sent direct to Liddell, as required under the terms of the contract. He explained to Liddell that 900 feet of iron had been delivered for the superstructure and that this, together with the £4,500 on account for castings, some of which had been delivered, was involving him in a very large outlay. The whole of the material, amounting to £23,000, would be on the ground before he could obtain another payment on account. Kennard was asking Liddell for a certificate for £7,000[5] and Liddell recommended a payment for that amount on account of cast and wrought iron delivered for the viaduct.[6] No record has been discovered to show that the 900 feet of iron was actually on the ground but Thomas Pritchard, secretary to the company, wrote to Kennard stating that he had been authorised to pay him £4,000 in debenture stock, as had been arranged with him, and for the remaining £3,000 he would get a cheque drawn at the next board meeting in early August.[7]

Communications from Kennard over the next weeks illustrate an irrational state of mind. Since receiving his last payment in August, Kennard was claiming that he had paid out a further £6,000 for materials and had to pay a further £3,000 within weeks, placing him in a financial situation of '*considerable inconvenience*'. At this early stage, Kennard was beginning to realise the financial implications of taking a contract that involved him in the initial and heavy expenditure of his own money. As he explained to Liddell, '*old Pritchard stuck £4,000 of Debentures into me in my last and though I don't object to hold £4,000 as an investment, they will not pay for iron and wages*'. Although he was purchasing iron and cast iron from his father's works at Blaenavon and Falkirk, he had to pay on invoice by cash and was pressing Liddell for a certificate of £5,000 or £6,000. He admitted that the contract was one where there was not much to show in the way of erection but the material alone far more than outweighed in cost the sum of all of Liddell's previous certificates. He also pointed out that, since his last communication, he had received the castings for a large portion of all columns for the piers.[8] Before Liddell had taken any action on this request, Kennard had contacted him again expressing a fear that if Carr was to make a report on the material on the ground, he would not get a certificate in time for any payment. It becomes obvious that Kennard had submitted an inflated claim because, in an attached schedule he admits to the following:

'900ft superstructure delivered, value, say	*£10,000*
Wrought iron for piers invoiced and believed to be on the ground	*£ 2,000*
Castings for which I have paid, not all on the ground	*£ 5,000*
Cast iron bought by me to secure the rise, paid for	*£ 2,480*
Foundations, labour, plant for the viaduct and expenses	*£ 3,000*
Total	*£22,480'*

What gives his claim away was an admission in an added note stating that '*all of the castings are not delivered some are at Newport, others on the road and some in Scotland*'. Of the cast iron bought, this item will never be defined but '*it is an outlay that I was obliged to incur*'.[9] Up until that time Kennard had received £6,000 by cheque and £4,000 in debenture stock. To meet the residue of £12,480 Kennard told Liddell that he only needed £6,000 in cash and requested a certificate for no more than £2,500 to £3,000 adding that he would really like it before the end of the month. In a separate appeal to Pritchard, he asked for £3,000.[10] Appealing to the board he mentions an even greater sum of money, proposing that they pay him £4,000 in cash and £6,000 in debentures, having six months to run. He added a rash statement that, '*upon this advance being made I agree to deliver the whole of the material and to complete the principal viaduct without a further payment on account*'.[11] In a note to Carr he asks for a certificate as large as possible and although he wrote that he had asked Liddell for £5,000-£6,000 (previously stated as £2,500-£3,000), he was suggesting to Carr that he made it £10,000. He was complaining that Pritchard had '*stuck £4,000 worth of debentures in to him against his wishes*'.[12] Carr forwarded Kennard's request to Liddell as it contained matters for the latter's consideration and not his, adding '*I doubt poor fellow if he has had to pay £23,000 already, he is not going to put up the viaduct for his contract sum*'.[13]

Kennard continued to plead for money with a further letter to Liddell asking him to send as large a certificate as possible, suggesting a payment of £2,000-£3,000 or £4,000 in cash and the balance in 5% debenture bonds, such debentures to be redeemable in six months in cash. Against the debenture bonds Kennard expected to raise half of their value, which would be sufficient, as he thought, to allow him to continue with his intention of completing the viaduct within six months.[14]

Whilst Kennard was pleading for money, Carr went to Crumlin to take stock of the actual amount of iron that had been delivered. Carr found 420 tons of iron for the superstructure. Kennard, having claimed that he had paid for 750 tons, explained that the balance was somewhere between Newport and Crumlin – Newport being the point at which Kennard took delivery, and where the iron people considered that their contract had been completed. As a result of Carr's findings, Kennard admitted that he did not expect to receive a certificate until he had seen Liddell.[15]

As events begin to unfurl, it gradually becomes obvious how lax Kennard was – in many respects a situation that was endemic throughout the contract. He failed to check invoices against deliveries and failed to check that deliveries were made within the timescales that he had stipulated. Liddell did not pull any punches at this time; apologising for not agreeing to issue a certificate, he tells Kennard, '*really it is your own fault. In the first place it is not admissible to make a certificate upon anything that is not actually on the ground or at the works*' and this was followed by a lecture on how he should administer his record keeping. Liddell told Kennard that '*had he spent more time at the works and taken more care in having the materials which he claimed were lying about the Kingdom delivered to the works then without much difficulty he would have given him a proper return*'.[16] Kennard thanked Liddell and appreciated that he should not have expected a certificate under the circumstances but he was down to his last £10,000.[17] At the beginning of October, the board resolved to pay Kennard £2,000, with the remainder to be paid at the end of October, '*provided the Falkirk Company and the Blaenavon Company shall certify that the material is held by them for the Newport, Abergavenny & Hereford Company*'.[18] Liddell notified Kennard of the board's decision, adding '*Before going further however, it will be necessary to have your contract completed which I believe has never been done yet, will you put this in train*'. Liddell also mentioned that he had directed Carr to visit Crumlin and check the extent of work done and the amount of iron delivered.[19]

Unable to be present during Carr's visit, Kennard forwarded details of his costs in the hope of getting as large a certificate as possible. A large certificate was needed to cover Kennard's costs for 508 tons of wrought iron from Blaenavon, 35 tons of boiler plate from Stafford and 420 tons of iron castings. Other costs included £5,000-£6,000 in wages, plus small cash accounts, of which about £2,000 was spent on foundations, stone getting, etc, £1,000 connected with the viaduct, and about £2,500 on tools and plant.

Matters did not improve for Kennard when Pritchard discovered that iron and other goods had been delivered to the works in Kennard's name and not in the name of the company. In an effort to resolve the situation, Pritchard referred the matter to Liddell and the company's solicitor. At the same time, Pritchard invited Kennard to attend the next board meeting armed with a figure agreed by Carr and Liddell for work completed, along with letters that had been approved by the company's solicitor from the Falkirk and Blaenavon companies, confirming that the iron delivered to the works had been accredited to the Newport, Abergavenny & Hereford Company.[20]

Accepting Pritchard's invitation, Kennard again stressed the financial problems that he was encountering and withdrew his suggestion of taking £10,000 in debenture bonds as part payment. He explained that he had arranged a loan of £10,000 using the bonds as security but delays in providing the company with the required evidence of the delivery of goods and in whose name they were delivered to, led to the loan arrangement being withdrawn. Kennard felt that there was then no longer any justification for accepting the debenture bonds as suggested, as the state of the money market at that time would leave him with unconvertible stock. He pointed out to the board that the amount he was already involved in, including the material delivered, the securities offered and engineer's certificates, amounted to more than £25,000. To meet this need he had received only £6,000 in cash and £4,000 in 4% debenture bonds that were unconvertible stock, because of the depressed money market.

Having set out his financial position, Kennard then immediately undermined his reasoning and placed himself in the hands of the company directors. He agreed to take debenture bonds on account of material delivered to site and if during the course of the next month he was able to negotiate a loan against the security of the bonds, he promised not to press for any further payment on account of work done.[21]

After considering the implications of Kennard's address, the directors accepted his financial problems but stipulated that any further payments would be

PLATE 5.2: Alfred Pumphrey's view No. 14, taken shortly after the railway had opened and showing the full length of the viaduct, gave an impressive stereo effect. In the bottom left corner, the tramway incline down to the Viaduct Works can just be made out. The man posed gazing at the structure may be Pumphrey himself or an assistant.
STEPHEN ROWSON COLLECTION

conditional upon him accepting that materials delivered to site were made legally to the company, as stated in the contract. Accepting this proposition, the directors issued a cheque for £2,000, in accordance with the terms agreed to, with a further cheque for £2,000 being issued at the next board meeting. Pritchard was also instructed to prepare debenture bonds in Kennard's favour for £6,000 with interest at 5% over a period of two years '*in compliance of the said agreement, and that the agreement with Mr Kennard be sealed*'.[22] The agreement referred to related to the signing of the contract at that time under preparation.

Needing to raise additional cash, Kennard had made attempts to dispose of his debenture bonds but, due mainly to the short periods that they had to run he had experienced major problems in obtaining investors. At that time he was holding bonds worth £4,500 at 5% interest with eighteen months to run and £3,500 of bonds at 4% with two and a half years to run. To make the bonds more acceptable to investors, Kennard asked the board to convert the whole of his holdings into three year bonds at 5% interest.[23] However, the minute books contain no further reference to this request, so it is assumed that this was not done.

Asking for a further payment for the balance of his account in late June 1854, Kennard stated '*I am quite ashamed at being so pressing, but really, at the present moment I am most uncomfortably short of ready money*', begging Liddell for a certificate, and then to go to the board to sanction a further payment. According to Kennard, '*Crumlin Viaduct had absorbed a much larger sum than I anticipated and in which account I am at present time greatly crippled in my exertions for its completion*'.[24] In support of his request he pointed out that, with the exception of 120 tons of iron which he anticipated would be delivered immediately, the whole of the iron both cast and wrought was either at Crumlin or on its way from Falkirk. According to Kennard, he had estimated that the cost to him of material calculated at the prices stated in the contract and other works then amounted to £32,500, comprised of:

'Wrought iron 1,000 tons at 11/-	*£11,000*
Cast iron 1,200 tons at 8/-	*£ 9,600*
Labour and masonry	*£ 7,500*
Plant and tools	*£ 3,000*
Personal expenses	*£ 1,500*
Total	*£32,600'*

Against this amount of outlay he had received in cash and debentures £22,000. As he explained '*with this sum, in addition to capital of my own, I had intended to complete the viaduct or at least to make great progress towards it, however, I have experienced great disappointment in many quarters, both as to money and men, and I am therefore compelled to solicit a further payment*'.[25] However, before Liddell could finalise a report to the directors, Kennard had sent him another request for cash, pleading with him to issue a certificate: '*It is exceedingly painful for me to ask favours of the directors, I must do so for to go on any longer without cash I cannot*'. Kennard insisted that he was out of pocket by more than £14,000, a figure he claimed he was unable to stand. News of his cash problems had reached many financial institutions and consequently he was unable to borrow money and his creditors were pressing for payment without giving him any grace. He commented at the time '*the world thought that the viaduct would ruin anybody who touched it*'.[26]

At this time, Kennard was searching for a partner in the hope that this would inject money into the business and help overcome his financial problems but, in the meantime these did not go away. In early July 1854, he was again pressing Liddell to support him by recommending to the board a payment of £4,000 in July and £3,000 or £4,000 a month after, or at least for August and September, revealing that '*without it I shall positively suffer to a fearful event*'. At the same time, Kennard admitted that the work was running well behind schedule but he attempted to assure Liddell of his intentions to complete the viaduct contract by being permanently based at Crumlin and for the first time take personal control of its supervision, once his money problems were settled. A solution Liddell had discussed with Pritchard was one of persuading Kennard to offer his workshops and plant as security by entering into a mortgage agreement with the company, who would then advance him a figure of £5,000.

Reporting to the board, Liddell suggested that the value of the work, if it had been completed as determined by the schedule of prices included in the contract, would stand at £27,815 and with an estimated cost for completing the work of £9,060, the total cost of the viaduct would amount to £36,875. The margin between this estimated cost and the contract price showed a saving of £1,675. Liddell was unable to issue a certificate but recommended to the board that if the company were to hold the security of materials delivered to the works and the use of the workshops and plant, they might safely advance a sum to Kennard of up to £27,815, adding that he was asking for a further £5,000.[27]

At their next meeting the directors agreed, following advice from their solicitor, that if Kennard executed a conveyance to the company for the workshops and plant, giving security for the delivery of the remainder of the material, £2,000 could be advanced immediately and a further £3,000 on Liddell's certificate in the course of the following week.[28]

Kennard was then confronted with another problem, which again was one of his own making. He had failed to obtain a lease on the land on which the workshops were erected and he was therefore not entitled to enter into a valid mortgage deed in favour of the company. The problem was overcome initially by Kennard endorsing a 'Bill of Sale', conveying the engines, machinery and tools in Kennard's workshops to the company by a deed endorsed on the contract. Further delays in making any payment to Kennard forced him to write a letter to Gordon, complaining about Pritchard not forwarding a cheque as agreed by the board. In addition to not receiving a cheque, Kennard was aggrieved that, '*they have made me hand over my works and still refuse to pay me the small sum I ask. I do assure you that I cannot go on any longer in this way. It is not to the interest of the Company that I should be ruined over this job*'.[29]

Before the land on which the workshops were erected had been conveyed to the company, their solicitors had obtained a written undertaking, from Kennard's solicitors, that they would forward the lease of the land then being granted to him as soon as it had been endorsed. With these assurances, combined with the information contained in a statement from Liddell, it appeared to the company's solicitor sufficient grounds to authorise making an advance to Kennard. At the following board meeting, a cheque to the value of £2,000 was signed and delivered to Kennard.[30]

In early September, after taking stock, Kennard wrote to Carr that he could not account for 130 tons of iron delivered to Crumlin, whilst about 100 ton of castings came out short on invoices of materials delivered to Crumlin.[31] Carr wrote to Liddell that the stocktaking at Kennard's had been very troublesome, with an unsatisfactory result. Kennard had paid for the delivery of 1,030 tons but after repeated examinations, only about 900 tons of iron was on site. Carr expressed his feelings by adding, '*Kennard and I have been hammering at various views for several hours this morning and has left me to report to you my impression that the cost of the viaduct to him will be £46,000.*' In a second analysis, Carr suggests that £8,000 should be sufficient to enable Kennard to complete the work and that it would be safe to let him have up to £35,700. According to Carr, Kennard appeared to be distressed for the want of money and at his request, because he thought it would be an advantage to him, Carr sent Liddell the results of their discussions, adding '*as well as I am able*'.[32]

Kennard's father R.W. Kennard now enters the fray and becomes financially committed to seeing that the contract is completed. R.W.K., in a communication with the directors, on condition that Kennard was paid immediately a sum of £9,530 10s (the amount outstanding on the contract), guaranteed the outstanding balance of the delivery of the 250 tons of cast iron on its way from Falkirk, 123 tons of wrought iron then at Llanfoist and 22,000 feet of timber at Newport Docks. R.W.K. felt that the work ought not to be impeded for lack of financial assistance and had thus resolved to assist his son. In providing financial aid, R.W.K. was anticipating that the company would make all certified payments promptly. He saw these as being essential for maintaining progress on the viaduct and that it would reflect credit on all parties concerned.[33]

PLATE 5.3 *A London Stereoscopic Company carte-de-visite portrait of Robert W. Kennard when an old man.*
STEPHEN ROWSON COLLECTION

the meantime had shown the designs for the viaduct to other contractors and informed Kennard that they had estimated a realistic figure of £40,000.

On being informed of Liddell's action, Kennard wrote to Gordon making a complaint against him but the forthright reply must have come as a shock. He told Kennard, '*With the single exception of the foundations my deliberate opinion is that you had a fair price for the work done and I think myself fully to say that you have yourself alone to blame in the first place*'. Gordon reminded Kennard that both he and Liddell had urged him to put in a price that would pay for '*the ingenuity and cheapness of the structure as well as for the work done*'. He also pointed out that he had urged Kennard, '*as strongly as a friend of so short standing could do that without more direct personal superintendence you would lose time and money*'. There was one section of Kennard's letter that Gordon took particular exception to. Kennard had objected to the fact that Liddell had '*placed my drawings in the hands of other contractors*' but Gordon pointed out that he had shown the general designs of similar work to English and foreign contractors in order to gain a sample all round sum that a similar viaduct could be erected for and that figure turned out to be £40,000. However, the real issue was Kennard's reference to '*my drawings*'. Gordon's response to this comment was frank: '*If you put stress on these words and use them in the sense of designs – engineering designs – then I mean to say that you use them quite erroneously. For after Mr Liddell had settled the general design it was in consultation with myself that you and Mr Wild in reference to the piers and you and Baldwin and I in reference to the girders settled the details. Convenience alone determined that the working drawings should be made in your office instead of ours*'. He wanted Kennard to very much consider this point, '*for various facts have indicated from time to time that there is confusion of ideas abroad as to the engineers and contractors for the work being the work of one person*'.[54]

The next move came from R.W.K., who approached Liddell in an attempt to obtain a further payment on certificate. The latter pointed out that Kennard was not to receive any more than the £36,000 until work had been completed. He reminded R.W.K. that the company was entitled to withhold 10% of the contract price until such time as the work had been completed and that there was still a good deal to do. Liddell had previously advised Kennard not to ask for any further payments until the whole bridge was complete but he did promise to prepare an up to date account for the viaduct, a copy of which he would forward to R.W.K.[55]

Liddell instructed Carr to prepare an account for the viaduct as it stood, valuing the whole as per the contract price of £38,740, plus the additional work ordered, such as the extra iron in the struts, etc. However, it did not include the additional work to the foundations and allowed from the total a deduction for the work remaining to be done. Liddell also asked for a valuation of the foundations and abutments, and the quantities of rubble and ashlar as it then stood, supposing them to be finished and without any reference to what was allowed in the contract.[56]

Mark Carr's figures and the fact that Kennard had admitted receiving £36,000 on account were reported to the board by Liddell. To the contract sum of £38,740 was added £1,104 16s 4d for extras, giving a total of £39,884 16s 4d. Carr had estimated work still to be done as £1,500, leaving a figure of £38,344 16s 4d. With a 10% retention of £3,834, the total value as it stood, according to Carr's figures, was £34,510 10s 8d, indicating that Kennard had been overpaid to the sum of £1,489 13s 4d.[57] However, Liddell suggested to the board that if the company continued to hold sufficient securities from Kennard, they could release the greater part of the 10% retention or give up the securities.[58]

Ignoring all of the previous advice that had been given to Kennard, he was so desperate for cash that he continued to apply to the company for additional money. At the end of October 1855, for instance, he was so short that he did not have sufficient cash in hand to pay his men their wages. R.W.K. was refusing to provide him with any more than the £25,000 he had already advanced, whilst Kennard could not dispose of his debenture bonds. He therefore turned to Pritchard with a request for him to make arrangements with the board to pay him £300 a week in order to cover his wages bill.[59]

At the beginning of 1856, there began a difference of opinion over the prices allowed for the abutments and for the foundations, a dispute that was to remain unresolved until Kennard filed for a court judgement against the company. Liddell was anxious to settle all matters regarding the viaduct and was seeking from Kennard sketches for the foundations to compare with the contract drawings, because he had been informed that the piers were not as deep as was shown on these.[60] Kennard maintained that there were no sketches and that details of the foundations were only put on the drawings '*to make them look pretty*'. They did not, in his opinion, form part of the contract.[61] Kennard's response obviously upset Liddell, who accused him of '*treating the drawings lightly*'; he told Kennard that, '*the difference between the foundations shown and executed could be the only grounds for making a claim for extra payment*'.[62]

During February 1856, Kennard was broadcasting the fact that the viaduct had cost him £54,000 without anything for his personal time and expenses. Approaching Carr, he requested from him a copy of the details of the amount of extras that they had agreed upon. At the same time, he accused Carr of walking onto his land without permission and that he would look into it when he next visited Crumlin.[63]

That R.W.K. never refrained from asking for more money for Kennard is evidenced from a note sent to him by Liddell. The latter explained that if Kennard would bring his accounts in full for all of his work with the viaduct, switches (points), etc., then he would examine them and settle the amounts payable. Liddell promised to sign any necessary certificate for the balance but added that there was no chance of getting any money at present – '*the till is long ago exhausted. No money was available until new stock could be raised*'.[64] Mark Carr's reaction to Kennard's plight was more philosophic than helpful, suggesting that, '*you must learn to look on Crumlin Viaduct as a rare and beautiful seed purchased by much money and trouble but cheap at the price when compared with the fruit which will spring from it*'.[65]

Liddell wrote to Carr at the end of May requesting an exact account of the works to be completed, made out and agreed with Kennard. If Kennard would not settle and was only expecting evidence to use against Liddell, then he would have to wait until Carr had discussed it with him. He informed Carr that he had given Kennard a '*blowing up*' over bad work and that Carr could show Kennard more examples.[66]

Kennard submitted his account to Liddell in July 1856 and admitted that the sum exceeded that which they had previously agreed. He claimed that he was not trying to obtain a single shilling of profit but merely to realise a return on the money he had actually spent. Kennard was

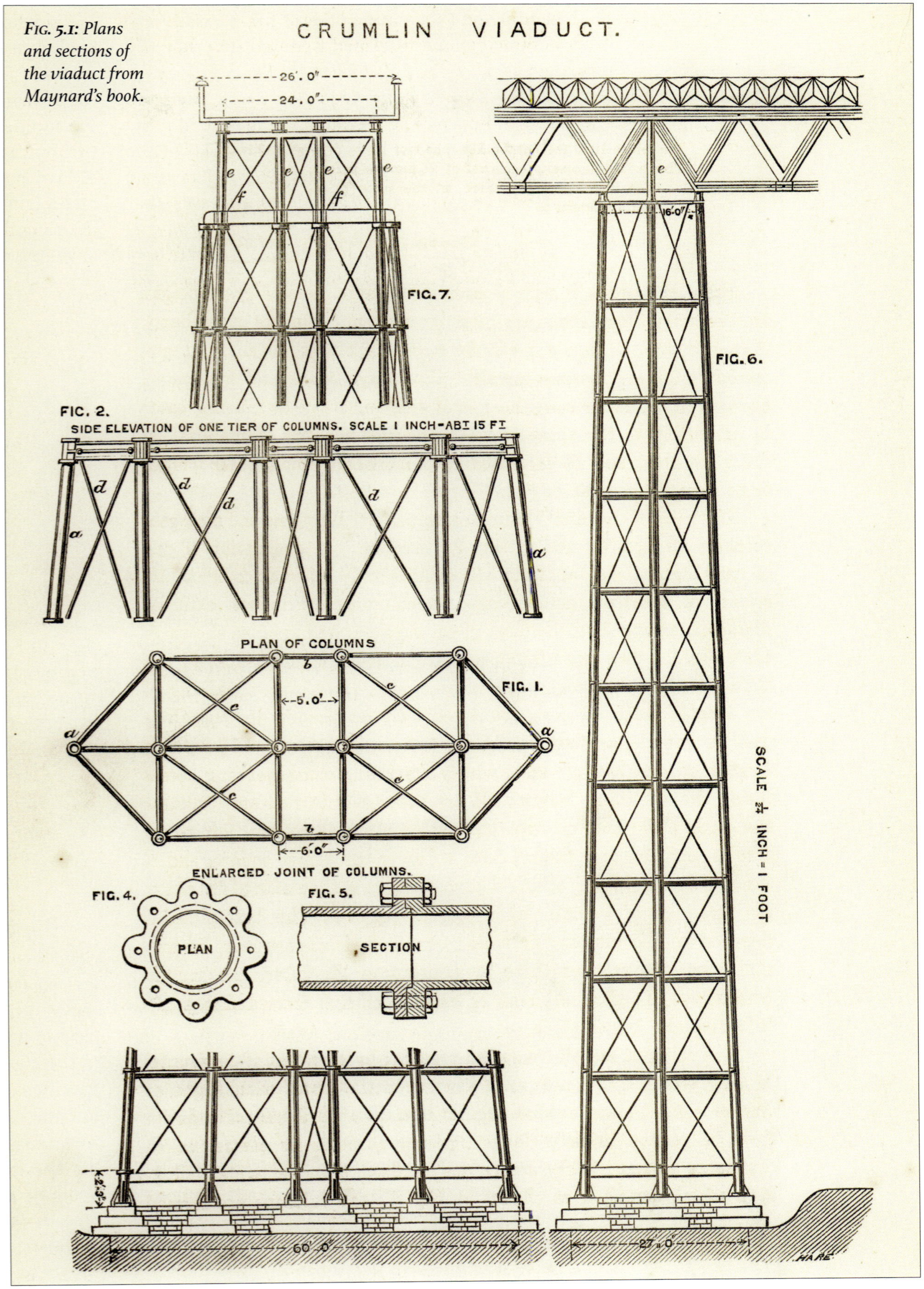

Fig. 5.1: Plans and sections of the viaduct from Maynard's book.

Plate 5.5: *The reference to the West Midland Railway dates this early print to between July 1860 and July 1863, the short period when the company was in existence. An Up TVE train can be seen proceeding across the viaduct top left, whilst a Down MR&CC train heads south bottom left.*
Oxford House Industrial History Society collection

bemoaning the fact that such a great work as the viaduct ought to have been a source of large profit but he had experienced a loss. He was appealing to Liddell's sense of justice not to advise the directors to adopt a course that would involve him in a loss that would be ruinous in its consequences. What Kennard was pleading for was for the company to pay him gratuities significantly greater than the sum contracted for.[67]

Kennard next approached the directors complaining that he had made frequent requests to the company's solicitors for the return of the deeds to his workshops, pointing out that the '*bridge has now been finished a year and in addition to the bonds in question I consider there is a balance due to me of about £72,000*'. How this figure was arrived at was never reported.[68] Liddell was preparing a report on Kennard's account in February 1857 and after examining with Gordon all of the documents relating to the contract, it was realised that it had been signed specifying iron pillars in the abutments. It had been intended to substitute masonry for iron but the drawings were never prepared, and when the contract was signed the attached drawings showed iron abutments. Liddell made an offer to Kennard to substitute drawings showing masonry abutments if he thought that it would improve his financial position but he never responded.[69]

Whilst on a visit to Crumlin in June 1857, Kennard

presented an account to Liddell for a sum of £60,289 10s 3d. On his return to London, Liddell went through the figures with Carr only to discover that Kennard, without any further discussions, had altered the figures previously agreed with the latter and to his advantage. Liddell wrote to Kennard '*wanting an explanation*'. Prior to the next board meeting, Pritchard had an interview with Howard J. Kennard (banker and Falkirk Ironworks board member, and Thomas Kennard's brother), who submitted an account for £58,182 10s.[70] From this time on, all communications in writing to Liddell or the board were signed Kennard Brothers. When Liddell reported to the board they instructed him to take legal advice on the appropriate terms specified in the contract and gave their General Purposes Committee authorisation to settle and clarify the account for final payment.[71]

Liddell's report to the General Purposes Committee pointed out that the amount for the contract of £38,740 was correct but he contested two charges that were to prove contentious right through to a final settlement. Kennard was claiming large additional payments for the abutments and for the foundations. Disputing these claims, Liddell maintained that the charges for the abutments were too high and were greatly in excess of the same work done by the company. He explained that, under the terms of the first tender, the abutments were to be built in iron but in making the working drawings, the viaduct was lengthened in its span and the abutments reduced in height and built in masonry. The reason for this substitution was due to an objection to the ironwork being buried in the embankment. This, according to Liddell, reduced the overall cost of the abutments from £2,600 to £1,100 – a figure that was later altered to £1,700. The charges for the foundations he did not recognise as admissible, as there was very little difference from what was anticipated when the contract was signed.

Of more concern to Liddell was the fact that Kennard had altered several items previously agreed, without orders and without Liddell's knowledge. According to him, by working to the terms of the contract the amount due to Kennard, including extras, was £42,068 19s 8d, a difference of £18,021 10s 7d. Liddell pointed out to the committee that he feared that the contractor had lost heavily and if Kennard would accept this account, the directors might fairly make up payments to him of £46,000,[72] a figure that Carr had suggested the works could be completed for in September 1854. The committee instructed Pritchard to write to Kennard and obtain an explanation on the items on his account which were then not agreed upon.[73]

Pritchard's letter to Kennard was very curt, asking for an explanation on what authority had the charge of £3,694 for foundations to the piers been made? On what authority and with whose knowledge was the alleged extra weight in the superstructure and piers amounting to £5,500 made? On the charge for delay of the works amounting to £5,000, any delay was incidental to the contractors department, and on the alleged loss of £1,500 on debentures, the directors required an explanation. Both parties must have gauged the atmosphere and eventual outcome to the situation, because Pritchard added that Kennard's explanation would be considered without prejudice to any legal questions if it became necessary for either side to settle any dispute.[74]

Kennard's response failed to cover all of the points. With reference to the charge of £3,694 for foundations, he stated that it was a prime cost for that portion of the work. The £5,500 for extra weight in the superstructure and piers was incurred due to a need to increase the weight of the scantlings, and £4,000 was for extra iron in the piers. When casting the piers the founders refused to proceed, as they found the specification too slight, and increasing it added £4,500. Further costs of £2,000 were due to the difficulty in lifting the girders and there was a £1,500 loss on debenture bonds. Kennard then reasoned that, by simple justice, the directors should take a liberal view and meet his claims.[75]

Pritchard, on the instructions of the directors, wrote to Kennard expressing their views that they failed to understand his reasoning for the extra money for the foundations, and the claim for another £5,500 for extra work in the superstructure and piers.[76] Kennard claimed that it was the cheapest bridge ever erected and that another (unidentified) bridge, which according to him was of similar design and construction, had been let by open tender for more than double the amount, and on testing had shown a deflection of 20% more than the bridge at Crumlin.[77] He again raised the issue of the foundations and claimed that the prices for the work had been completed in a hurry, and that consequently

Plate 5.6: Howard John Kennard, 1839-96. During his lifetime he was a director of the Falkirk Iron Company, chairman of the Blaenavon Iron Company, a director of the Great Eastern Railway, joint chairman of the Rail Makers' Association, president of the Royal Metal Trades' Pension Society, a Past Master of the Carpenters' Company, a Justice of the Peace for Stirlingshire and one of Her Majesty's Lieutenants for the City of London. With George Nottage, he also founded the London Stereoscopic Company.
Stephen Rowson collection

mistakes had been made. In an attempt to get the account finally settled, Kennard and Liddell were invited to attend the next board meeting.[78]

Prior to the meeting, Liddell sent to Pritchard a number of significant remarks that started with Kennard's acceptance of the original tender of £31,480. On the extra costs of iron in the superstructure and piers, Liddell stressed that if it was done, it was done without his authority and without any knowledge of Kennard's intention to raise a claim. On the claim for thickening the columns, it was Kennard who had calculated the section of the original columns that turned out to be thinner than the founders were willing to undertake. Liddell claimed that he knew nothing of the actual quantity of iron in the columns but as far as he was concerned the weight that had been allowed in the contract was sufficient to ensure that they could be easily cast, and any additional metal in the foundations could on no account be required under a plea of difficulty of casting. On the topic of lifting the girders, Liddell considered that the problems encountered were of Kennard's own making. Once the ropes for lifting had been obtained from a reputable manufacturer, there were no further problems. According to Liddell, the real cost of lifting the girders, to Kennard, were the accidents and delays he had created by '*mal-arrangement and want of proper attention to the work*'. As regards the foundations, Liddell stated that it was not a fact as Kennard suggested that it was anticipated that nothing had to be done. Referring to the drawings, Liddell pointed out that the price being charged by Kennard was at least twice the value of the work. The actual contract was finally settled at £38,740 and Liddell had calculated that extras amounted to no more than £1,500. Whilst not wishing to prejudice any offer that the directors might wish to make, Liddell suggested that a sum of £46,000 could be offered to Kennard as a full settlement. Liddell concluded his report by stating that '*if the work had to be done again at so largely an increased cost, I should certainly have limited the work to be done in iron to about half the present length i.e. it would be cheaper to build a great part of it in stone*'.[79] On the subject of the debenture bonds, Pritchard had prepared a comprehensive report on their date of issue to Kennard and details of their disposal, which showed that his loss was £44 7s 11d.[80]

Letters passed to and fro between Kennard, Pritchard, R.W.K. and Liddell for the remainder of 1857. Many of the letters from Kennard contained personal remarks against Liddell and Professor Gordon. At one stage, Liddell found Kennard's notes so rambling and unintelligible that he was unable to make sensible comments.[81] The General Purposes Committee had agreed to invite Liddell and the Kennards to attend and the company's solicitors were instructed to draft a letter on the subject of Kennard's account in order to guard the company from being committed by any interview or consultation. They later passed a significant resolution in the outcome of the intensifying dispute between the two parties: '*That the Committee having had several meetings on this subject and having devoted much time and attention to it and having seen Mr Kennard senior and junior with Messrs Liddell and Gordon thereon find that Mr Kennard is willing to accept £50,000 in full of all claims but see no reason why the Company should exceed the sum recommended by the engineer viz. £46,000 and this they believe to be a liberal offer*'.[82]

In May 1858, Kennard wrote direct to the board. He had been advised that his claim did not rest on his contract but was then an open question for work and labour done. He now claimed that the actual cost had been £62,000, which did not include any sum for profit and his time. Kennard then proposed that he should be paid £14,000 in discharge of his claim but there were no figures produced to substantiate this. If the company refused to pay the sum Kennard suggested, his claim was to be settled by friendly arbitration but if that action was agreed to, he considered himself at liberty to make his claim '*in such a manner and such amount as advised*'.[83] However, the General Purposes Committee saw no reason for them to change their resolution which offered Kennard £46,000 in full settlement.[84]

In a serious attempt to settle their differences, the board appointed two of their members to negotiate with R.W.K. and Kennard,[85] the objective being to reach a settlement on all matters relating to Kennard's account. Terms could not be agreed and no further positive action took place until April 1859, when the company received a notice from Kennard's solicitors requiring a payment of £20,777 18 7d.[86] This was the notice that initiated the start of the legal action of Kennard versus the Newport, Abergavenny & Hereford Railway Company.

References

1. Letter, Kennard to board of directors, endorsed by Liddell 9th June 1853
2. Board of directors meeting, 10th June 1853, minute No. 1061
3. Undated letter, Kennard to Pritchard
4. Kennard to board of directors, 7th July 1853
5. Letter, Kennard to Liddell, 26th July 1853
6. Liddell's report to directors, 27th July 1853

7. Letter, Pritchard to Kennard, 28th July 1853, and meeting of directors, 4th Aug. 1853, minute No. 1091
8. Letter, Kennard to Liddell, 19th Sept. 1853
9. Letter, Kennard to Liddell, 23rd Sept. 1853
10. Letter, Kennard to Pritchard, 23rd Sept. 1853
11. Undated letter, Kennard to board of directors
12. Letter, Kennard to Carr, 24th Sept. 1853
13. Letter, Carr to Liddell, 26th Sept. 1853
14. Letter, Kennard to Liddell, 26th Sept. 1853
15. Letter, Kennard to Liddell, 27th Sept. 1853
16. Letter, Liddell to Kennard, 29th Sept. 1853
17. Letter, Kennard to Liddell, 1st Oct. 1853
18. Board of directors meeting, 6th Oct. 1853, minute No. 1148
19. Letter, Liddell to Kennard, 7th Oct. 1853
20. Letter, Pritchard to Kennard, 10th Oct. 1853
21. Letter, Kennard to board of directors, 19th Oct. 1853
22. Board of directors meeting, 20th Oct. 1853, minute No. 1167
23. Letter, Kennard to board of directors, 23rd Mar. 1854
24. Letter, Kennard to Newell (Finance Dept.), 23rd June 1854
25. Letter, Kennard to Liddell, 29th June 1854
26. Letter, Kennard to Liddell, 5th July 1854
27. Liddell's report to board of directors, 6th July 1854
28. Board of directors meeting, 13th July 1854
29. Letter, Kennard to Gordon, 22nd July 1854
30. Letter, company solicitor to Pritchard 31st July 1854
31. Letter, Kennard to Carr, 6th Sept. 1854
32. Letter, Carr to Liddell, 11th Sept. 1854
33. Letter, R.W. Kennard to board of directors, 27th Sept. 1854
34. Letter, Liddell to Kennard, 2nd Oct. 1854
35. Liddell's report to board of directors, 5th Oct. 1854
36. Chairman's report to board of directors, 5th Oct. 1854
37. Board of directors meeting, 5th Oct. 1854, minute No. 1565
38. Letter, company solicitor to Pritchard, 12th Oct. 1854
39. Letter, R.W. Kennard to chairman, 13th Oct. 1854
40. Undated letter, Carr to R.W. Kennard
41. Letter, R.W. Kennard to chairman, 18th Oct. 1854
42. Letter, R.W. Kennard to board of directors, 19th Oct. 1854
43. Board of directors meeting, 26th Oct. 1854, minute No. 1562
44. Letter, Kennard to Pritchard, 2nd Nov. 1854
45. Board of directors meeting, 23rd Nov. 1854, minute No. 1605
46. Letter, Kennard to Pritchard, 17th Dec. 1854
47. Letter, Kennard to company solicitor, 18th Dec. 1854
48. Board of directors meeting, 21st Dec. 1854, minute No. 1649
49. Letter, Liddell to Kennard, 21st Feb. 1855
50. Letter, Kennard to Pritchard, 14th Mar. 1855
51. Letter, Kennard to Pritchard 21st Mar. 1855
52. Board of directors meeting, 22nd Mar. 1855, minute No. 1808
53. Letter, Pritchard to Kennard, 26th Mar. 1855
54. Letter, Gordon to Kennard, 16th Sept. 1855
55. Letter, Liddell to R.W. Kennard, 13th Oct. 1855
56. Letter, Liddell to Carr, 15th Oct. 1855
57. Letter, Carr to Liddell, 18th Oct. 1855
58. Liddell's report to board of directors, 19th Oct. 1855
59. Letter, Kennard to Pritchard, 27th Oct. 1855
60. Letter, Liddell to Kennard, 28th Jan. 1856
61. Letter, Kennard to Liddell, 28th Jan. 1856
62. Letter, Liddell to Kennard, 30th Jan. 1856
63. Letter, Kennard to Carr, 28th Feb. 1856
64. Letter, Liddell to R.W. Kennard, 4th Mar. 1856
65. Letter, Carr to Kennard, 7th Mar. 1856
66. Letter, Liddell to Carr, 25th May 1856
67. Letter, Kennard to Liddell, 18th July 1856
68. Letter, Kennard to board of directors, 4th Nov. 1856
69. Letter, Liddell to Kennard, 17th Feb. 1857
70. Letter, Liddell to Kennard, 18th June 1857
71. Board of directors meeting, 20th July 1857, minute No. 2285
72. Liddell's report to board of directors, 10th July 1857
73. Meeting of General Purposes Committee, 18th July 1857 minute No. 2098
74. Letter, Pritchard to Kennard, 18th July 1857
75. Letter, Kennard to Pritchard, 13th Aug. 1857
76. Letter, Pritchard to Kennard, 31st Aug. 1857
77. Letter, Kennard to board of directors, 30th Sept. 1857
78. Meeting of General Purpose Committee, 9th Sept. 1857
79. Liddell's report to board of directors, 12th Oct. 1857
80. Pritchard's report to board of directors, 20th Oct. 1857
81. Letter, Liddell to Pritchard, 26th Oct. 1857
82. Meeting of General Purposes Committee, 26th Oct. 1857, minute No. 62
83. Letter, Kennard to board of directors, 1st May 1858
84. Board of directors meeting, 8th May 1858 and letter, Pritchard to Kennard, 28th May 1858
85. Board of directors meeting, 6th Nov. 1858
86. Notice dated 8th April 1859

Plate 5.7: *In the 1860s, the Cardiff photographer Alfred Dunmore published as a carte-de-visite this photograph of an artist's interpretation of the scene.* STEPHEN ROWSON COLLECTION

Plate 6.1: *This would have been an unusual scene for the LSC photographer, so might in fact have been taken by Pumphrey. The foreground is dominated by the wagon loaded with Trinant Colliery coal, whilst a young girl looks on no doubt with some curiosity. Both stand at the village wharf and the wagon's end tipping mechanism indicates how the load was deposited on the shipping tip at Newport. The viaduct looms over the scene and the incline that took goods and materials from the valley floor to the upper works can be seen on the right. The stereo effect is created nicely from three levels – the coal wagon in the foreground, the works buildings on the middle ground and the viaduct as the backdrop.* Neil Parkhouse collection

PERMANENT WAY

CHAPTER 6

The year 1856 opened with Thomas Pritchard writing to Kennard asking him to *'drop in and tell me when your viaduct will be ready to receive the permanent way'*. Pritchard was requesting this information because there was concern over an agreement the company had to carry coal from a '*Mr Turquant's Colliery*' (it is not known to which colliery this refers – Turquant may have been an agent or solicitor) over the viaduct to Hereford and Newport via Pontypool. This had been entered into in order to save the colliery owners the expense of having to travel '*over the inclines*'.[1]

Around the same time, discussions were being held between Liddell, Kennard and his brothers regarding the laying of the permanent way over the viaduct. During the course of a meeting with Kennard's brothers in May, Liddell agreed that Mark Carr would forward to Martyn Kennard copies of a specification and estimates of quantities required. Amongst the main items contained in the specification was the use of common chairs for holding the rails, which would be made available from the company's stock. The length of the permanent way was to run continuously over the two viaducts and 20 yards onto the embankment at each end. The longitudinal timbers (sleepers) should not be cut of equal thickness for the curve but made in order to give the rails a cant to suit the particular curvature. Plates originally designed to run continuously along the underside of the platform when fixing the sleepers would be replaced by small plates that would act as washers to each of the platform bolts. When forwarding copies of the specification to Kennard, Carr added, in a special note, that Liddell was anxious that he should lose no time in submitting a tender price.[2]

Being pressurised by the board of directors to open the line, within a week of Carr sending the specification, Liddell was asking Kennard whether he was serious about taking the contract to lay the permanent way, because he had repeatedly asked for a response but had not met with any success.[3] In the week that followed, the contents of the contract were settled between Liddell and Martyn Kennard, who suggested that '*work would begin directly*'.[4] This proved to be wishful thinking, because by the middle of June, Liddell was chasing Kennard to agree to the specification, confirm his prices and sign a contract.[5]

If the construction of the viaduct raises doubts on the effectiveness of Kennard's supervisory and management skills, then the laying of the permanent way over the viaduct can only reinforce those views. According to Kennard the contract should take no more than five weeks to complete but in the event it took almost twelve months and only then was it completed after a number of threats from Carr, Liddell, Pritchard and the board of directors.

The first of a number of problems that were to be pointed out by Kennard related to a drawing, supplied by Carr, for the casting of chairs for use on particular sections of the permanent way. The chairs for the check rails had to be slid individually along the rail prior to it being fixed. It was pointed out that the problem could be easily remedied with only a slight modification that was accepted by Carr.[6] An amended drawing and specification was settled quickly and sent to Kennard for his signature.[7]

Little or no progress was being made visually on laying the permanent way and at the end of August 1856, Mark Carr wrote to Kennard warning him that Liddell intended to place the laying of the permanent way in the hands of the company, unless he managed to get timber delivered to the site within a short time. Carr had identified a source of timber for immediate supply at a price of one shilling per lineal yard. Liddell would need to agree to any change in the type of timber specified in the contract. Carr believed that the whole concern was being brought into ridicule by the delay and privately suggested to Kennard that he stirred himself into action or say that he could not undertake the contract.[8]

Carr's warning to Kennard bore little result. Liddell contacted Kennard with an ultimatum that the company could not wait any longer for him to supply the timber and if he was not in a position to start work on the permanent way within a fortnight, the company would carry out the work themselves.[9] However, none of Liddell's threats proved to have any effect on Kennard.

At the end of October, Carr was informing Liddell that he could find no evidence that Kennard was doing anything towards providing the necessary timber, although there was evidence of other materials on site.[10] This prompted Liddell to contact Kennard for information to include in a report he was preparing to present to the directors in November.[11] Liddell wanted positive answers from Kennard as to whether he had any serious intention of providing the timber for laying the permanent way. If this was forthcoming, he asked for authority to then include a statement to the effect that the work would be completed by the end of November but if not, that the opening of the line would be delayed to an unknown date.

Sending Carr a copy of his note, Liddell discloses the fact that Kennard's credit was so low that no one will supply him and this being the case, if the situation did not improve the company would have to take over the work.[12] By the end of October, Liddell was reminding Kennard of the urgency in completing the job. He made a request for a positive response to his letters and warned him that there was so little time to complete the work that he had no alternative than to recommend that someone else take on the work, unless he was prepared to satisfy the board of his intentions at their next meeting in November. However, if Kennard intended to supply the timber, Liddell wanted to know where he was going to obtain it from, as it would have to be examined and approved before cutting up and fixing.[13]

Getting nowhere, Liddell let Pritchard know that he had been unable to move Kennard to complete the viaduct and could not get a response as to whether he intended to supply the necessary timber for the permanent way. So exasperated was Liddell that he sent a formal notice to Kennard for him to attend the next board meeting, adding a footnote that he should be there in person in order to answer for himself the reasons for the delay in commencing work on the permanent way.[14] At the meeting, Kennard reported that he had made arrangements for timber to be delivered within three weeks and that the permanent way would take a further two weeks to complete.[15] The board resolved that if he could report to Liddell by the following day that his arrangements were complete, then he should proceed with laying the permanent way but if such confirmation was not forthcoming, then Liddell was to make other arrangements. Keeping the pressure on Kennard, Liddell asked for details, in writing, as to when and where the timber would be delivered.[16] Having received no reply within three days, Liddell sent a reminder and warned Kennard that if he could not supply the information requested, he must consider that he was doing nothing to take the requests and threats seriously.[17]

At a subsequent board meeting, Liddell reported that the timber for the permanent way had been purchased and sawn up, and within two weeks it would be creosoted. It would then take a further three weeks to lay the permanent way.[18] However, five weeks after this meeting no timber had arrived on site and when it did arrive, it was reported to be so wet that neither Carr nor Liddell would sanction its use.[19] Kennard was given instructions by Liddell to stack the timber for a fortnight and he would then inspect it further.[20] Becoming more and more agitated with him, Liddell discovered, during a visit to the works on Christmas Eve, that against his implicit instructions, Kennard had already had the greater part of the timber creosoted.[21] Liddell had previously given distinct and direct instructions that no creosoting was to be done until either Carr or he were satisfied that the timber had been seasoned satisfactorily. If they were not satisfied that the creosoting had been done efficiently, they would reject it and give instructions for the timber to be placed in the tanks for further treatment.[22] Returning to the site a week later, Liddell had all of the timber examined only to find that it was exceedingly wet and badly creosoted. He noticed that there were a few pieces that had not been prepared and stated he would like to have those done under close scrutiny. If, after twenty-four hours, they were to prove satisfactory, then he was prepared to give instructions to have the remainder creosoted again but if not, the timber would have to be dried properly and then placed in the creosote tanks for further treatment.

At his next inspection Liddell found the timber to be as acceptable as sawn timber could be and gave instructions to Kennard to start laying the permanent way with greater speed.[23] In a note to Carr, Liddell asked him to look after the works and drive Kennard on as fast as possible but further delays meant that work did not commence in earnest until March 1857. Even then, Kennard's assistant Maynard was trying to borrow a track gauge from Carr so that a copy could be made and work commence.[24]

Throughout March and April, Kennard was being pressurised by Carr, Liddell and Pritchard, and the board of directors, to complete laying of the permanent way as soon as possible. The whole process appeared to be one of start, stop, start and stop. Carr, at the beginning of March, had reported to Liddell that the permanent way was being laid with such gusto that it would be completed within a month but work then began to slow down.[25] At first the

Plate 6.2: *Alfred Pumphrey's Crumlin masterpiece, his view No. 13, showing sawyers cutting timber into planks at the canal bank. Across the canal and river at the railway wharf, wagons loaded with coal from Trinant Colliery wait at the foot of Mark Philips' incline. The history of the tramroad is detailed in Chapter 12.* Stephen Rowson collection

Train after train continued to arrive, each laden with about a thousand passengers, and on reaching the platform they were welcomed by firing from nine cannons, placed on the brow hill, the roar from which, as they were successively discharged, danced from pier to pier of the viaduct, producing seven distinct echoes, then thundered down the valley, and ended in a singular sound, somewhat resembling the sound of shot thrown against strained canvas. The simile may not be very *apropos*, but it is the nearest to the sound that we could imagine. The firing continued at intervals throughout the day, and was responded to from other cannons planted near the mansion, in the course of completion, belonging to Mr. Kennard, on the opposite side of the valley.

This picturesque building was designed by Mr. Owen Jones, and is built in the pointed style, with a spire in the centre, and is embosomed in a grove of beautiful trees, on the slope of a hill, looking towards the viaduct. At the first glance from the bridge, it had much the appearance of a Gothic church, but on a nearer view the outline became more distinct, and the beauty of the building was seen.

During the early part of the day visitors were debarred from setting foot upon the wonderful structure which all had come to admire, the passage to it being guarded with sedulous care by Lieut. Gordon, one of the newly-appointed superintendents of the Monmouthshire Constabulary, and ten men of the force placed under his command.

Finding we could not, for the present, view the beauties of the valley from the viaduct, we descended the rugged path to the village. Here, on our way, we met with motley groups carousing in booths – others congregated round one of these profuse dealers in ginger-bread, who at intervals shouted "robbery, robbery," when any fortunate thrower of the shilalah succeeded in striking the peg and capsizing the three cakes of ginger-bread, which was the reward of his dexterity – then we passed stall after stall of ginger nuts and comfits, until our course was arrested by a host assembled round a couple of ballad singers, whose discordant notes, in giving vent to a song in commemoration of the opening of the great Crumlin viaduct, distracted our nerves. However, we had to submit to the affliction for a time, and the following doggerel fell upon our ears:

Hurrah! That glorious day has come
Lads and lasses all in bloom,
Link'd arm in arm, away they run.
On the glorious first of June.
So finely drest all in their best,
Each heart is light and gay,
O'er hill and dale to Crumlin Vale,
To spend their holiday.

CHORUS.

Thousands have come from far and near,
So full of youth and bloom,
To open the great Crumlin bridge,
On the glorious first of June.

This first verse was suffient for us, and probably is *quantum sufficit* for our readers.

We then struggled on through dust and heat, and at length reached the entrance to the Viaduct Hotel. Here, alas!, we were doomed to disappointment, for the passage was thronged with customers, and on peering through the windows, we found every room crowded to excess. It seemed a hopeless case to attempt to get a draught of refreshing beverage at this hostelry, so we took our departure, and climbed the mountain on the opposite side of the valley. Here a green and sheltered walk presented itself – we struck into it and pursued a devious tract over green fields and through shady woods, until we reached the brow of the mountain, which looks down upon a beautifully wooded valley towards Abercarne. After an hour's contemplation on a delightful spot, we retraced our steps, and on arriving at the viaduct we found admission

Plate 6.6: *No photograph showing the rails being laid on the deck of the viaduct has been seen and so this undated amateur stereograph is the earliest picture we have showing the line crossing the Ebbw and Kendon valleys. Whilst the (tresspass?) notice on the left also appears in the early picture on page 63, the wooden pole does not and nor does it feature in any other view. It may be the flag pole that was erected as part of the 1st June 1857 opening day celebrations and if so, would suggest thererfore that this photograph was taken not long after that event.* Stephen Rowson Collection

had been given to the public. Hundreds had assembled upon this admirable piece of workmanship, watching the trains arrive and depart along the line beneath, and looking down from a dizzy height upon the multitude two hundred feet beneath them, whose pigmy size almost reminded us of ants running to and from their hill. Above the centre pier an evergreen arch spanned the bridge, suspended from which was a blue strip, with "Long life and prosperity to T.W. Kennard," and "Success to the firm of Kennard Brothers" painted thereon. Immediately beneath the bridge were the workshops and sheds of the company, and the waters of the Ebbw, with the canal by its side, pursued its course along the vale, the steep sides of which were clothed with beautiful trees in undulating lines, backed up by the cloud-capped mountains in the vicinity of Newport.

THE VIADUCT

On the first sight of this structure, the beholder is struck with wonder and admiration at its airy lightness, combined with elegance and solidity; surrounded within its valleys, mountains and "many coloured woods." To be fully appreciated it must be seen, for no artistic effort can impart to the mind anything but a faint idea of this wonderful and admirable viaduct of Crumlin. This singularly graceful and beautiful bridge, so light and fairy-like, springing up in such a wild and rugged mountain pass, one almost expects to see tottering down into the valley from which its fairy columns spring, before a gale of wind; yet from the support it has given to several hundred tons placed upon it at one time, it has been proved to be a most substantial erection. This stupendous viaduct crosses the valley of Crumlin, extending from the summit of one mountain to that of another, a height of 210 feet over the Western Valleys' Railway, the trains along which may be seen for a considerable distance, taking their serpentine course along that sharply curved line.

The completion of the viaduct, from a variety of unforeseen circumstances, extended over a period of three years. It has been executed by Mr. Kennard and it must be a source of great gratification and pride to that eminent contractor, to find his work, on being tested before the government inspector, capable of standing at least double the working load the viaduct will be required to bear, and to find his labour so far crowned with success, as to call forth the admiration of the inspector, and every person who has had an opportunity of seeing it.

THE DEPARTURE

Towards evening the trains began to reload and return to the different towns, but we cannot say much for the official arrangements. None of the trains had on them any notification of their destination, and the rush to gain seats was terrific – men, boys, and girls, and even women with children in their arms, simultaneously rushed on the stopping of the train, and clambered some yards high over the sides into the trucks, and on more occasions than one, we observed the mother loose the infant at her breast to save herself – fortunately the children were saved by falling on the heads and shoulders of those beneath, and restored after a time to their mothers. About a thousand persons filled each train in less than two minutes, and many, for want of information as to the route of the trains, were taken far from their homes.

Several times, on the arrival of trains from Blackwood, the bridge was obliged to be cleared, which was no easy task. Mr Gordon and his men, comprising first-class constables Ward and Major, and constables, Phillips, Williams, Price, Pritchard, Preece, Hopkins, Harding and R. Jones, were indefatigable in their duties in preserving order and preventing accidents. This was the first occasion on which the new force had been called into requisition, and we gladly give them credit for the firmness they exhibited, which was nevertheless free from harshness and incivility. Throughout the whole day, from ten in the morning until ten at night, the contsables kept watch and ward over the immense crowds, without taking a mouthful of food, and to their vigilance we may, in a great measure, attribute the safety of many lives, and fortunately no accident of any moment occurred.

The numbers present were estimated at 15,000, 20,000, and even 30,000; but from a careful estimation at four o'clock, when the crowds appeared most dense, we believe about 12,000 were congregated, but no doubt upwards of 20,000 paid a visit to the scene during the day.

Most of the trains were unable to start until two or three hours after their appointed time. As for our friends from Usk, they had to remain on the platform and on the road from half-past seven until nearly ten o'clock, before a train arrived to take them off. The rush was then great; the strongest secured the first-class carriages, and many who had taken first-class tickets were obliged to return, hundled together with smashed hats or bonnets, in third class carriages and open trucks as far as Pontypool-road station.

A sumptuous dinner was spread at Mr. Kennard's house, of which about 160 partook; but as for the great majority of the excursionisers, they had to fast the whole day, it being impossible to get anything to eat besides ginger-bread. So ended the *day's pleasure?*

References

1. Letter, Pritchard to Kennard, 14th Jan. 1856
2. Letter, Carr to Kennard, 9th May 1856
3. Letter, Liddell to Kennard, 10th May 1856
4. Letter, H.M. Kennard to Carr, 17th May 1856
5. Letter, Liddell to Kennard 17th May 1856
6. Letter, H.M. Kennard, (pp Kennard) to Carr, 26th June 1856
7. Letter, Carr to Kennard, 3rd July 1856
8. Letter, Carr to Kennard, 29th Aug. 1856
9. Letter, Liddell to Kennard, 3rd Sept. 1856
10. Letter, Carr to Liddell, 25th Oct. 1856
11. Letter, Liddell to Kennard, 27th Oct. 1856
12. Letter, Liddell to Carr, 27th Oct. 1856
13. Letter, Liddell to Kennard, 31st Oct. 1856
14. Letter, Liddell to Kennard, 4th Nov. 1856
15. Board meeting, 6th Nov. 1856, minute No. 2164
16. Letter, Liddell to Kennard, 8th Nov. 1856
17. Letter, Liddell to Kennard, 11th Nov. 1856
18. Board meeting, 20th Nov. 1856, minute No. 2173
19. Letter, Carr to Liddell, 27th Nov. 1856
20. Letter, Liddell to Carr, 27th Nov. 1856
21. Letter, Liddell to Kennard, 24th Dec. 1856
22. Letter, Liddell to Kennard, 31st Dec. 1856
23. Letter, Liddell to Kennard, 14th Jan. 1857
24. Letter, H.N. Maynard to Carr, 3rd Mar. 1857
25. Letter, Carr to Liddell, 9th Mar. 1857
26. Letter, H.N. Kennard to Carr, 11th Mar. 1857
27. Board meeting, 26th Mar. 1857, minute No. 1092
28. Letter, Henry Cooke to Carr, 26th Mar. 1857
29. Letter, Carr to Kennard brothers, 6th April 1857
30. Liddell's report to the directors, 7th April 1857
31. Letter, Pritchard to Kennard, 11th April 1857
32. Letter, Carr to Liddell, 15th April 1857
33. Letter, Liddell to Kennard, 16th April 1857
34. Letter, Liddell to Pritchard, 16th April 1857
35. Letter, Pritchard to Kennard, 17th April 1857
36. Letter, Kennard to Pritchard, 17th April 1857
37. Letter, Liddell to Pritchard, 21st April 1857
38. Letter, Kennard to Pritchard, 21st April 1857
39. Letter, Pritchard to Kennard, 22nd April 1857
40. Letter, Carr to Liddell, 22nd April 1857
41. Board meeting, 23rd April 1857, minute No. 2017
42. Letter, Carr to Liddell, 25th April 1857
43. Letter, Carr to Liddell, 29th April 1857
44. Liddell's report to the directors, 29th April 1857
45. Letter, Pritchard to Kennard, 30th April 1857
46. Letter, Carr to Liddell, 30th April 1857
47. Letter, Kennard to Pritchard, 1st May 1857
48. Letter, Liddell to Pritchard, 2nd May 1857
49. Letter, Carr to Liddell, 1st May 1857
50. Letter, Carr to Kennard brothers, 20th May 1857
51. Letter, Carr to Kennard brothers, 17th Aug. 1857
52. Letter, Maynard to Carr, 21st Aug. 1857
53. Letter, Carr to Liddell, 22nd Aug. 1857

PLATE 6.7: Looking north from the towpath of the Crumlin Arm of the Monmouthshire Canal circa 1890. The canal widened on the right at this point, providing a winding hole for turning boats.
NEIL PARKHOUSE COLLECTION

LITIGATION

CHAPTER 7

The full text of the letter that started the legal action between T.W. Kennard and the Newport, Abergavenny & Hereford Railway Company Ltd, read as follows:

'We hereby on behalf of Mr Thomas William Kennard, Civil engineer, require from you payment of the sum of £20,777 18s 7d due to him, and we give you notice on his behalf, without prejudice to any previous demand for interest or any right theretofore existing, that interest on the sum of £20,777 18s 7d will be claimed from the date of this demand until payment.

Dated this 8th Day of April 1859,

Meyrick & Gedge,

4 Storeys Gate, Great George St, Westminster,

Solicitors'

This was endorsed *'received a copy of the above notice on the 9th Day of April 1859, signed Gordon Graham, secretary.'* (Graham had been appointed secretary to the company on the retirement of Thomas Pritchard).

The demand was discussed at a board meeting in May 1859, when the matter was referred to directors Mr Price and M. Moxon, with instructions for them to report back.[1] In the meantime, Kennard's attorneys, Meyrick & Gedge, served a Special Writ of Summons on the railway company, commanding them to appear within eight days in a Court of the Queen's Bench in an action brought by Kennard.[2] This was acknowledged with a note that the company undertook to appear *'in due time'*.

Meyrick & Gedge next sent a notice to the company's attorneys stating that, of the action being taken by Kennard in the Court of the Queen's Bench to sue the company, it was his intention to continue with his claims without prejudice to his filing a Bill in Equity to reform the contract. It was his contention that mutual mistakes had been made between himself and the officers of the company in reaching the cost of the viaduct, thereby increasing the original contract price. In the event of the contract being reformed, and the amount of the contract price being corrected in the Court of Equity, Kennard also gave notice that he would continue with the action to recover any amount awarded to him beyond that awarded in the proceedings to sue the company, scheduled to take place in the Court of the Queens Bench.[3]

In a further notice of the same date, Kennard itemised the points where he claimed the Newport, Abergavenny & Hereford Company had breached the contract. Following a detailed account of its terms, which Kennard maintained he had fulfilled, the notice specified where he claimed that they had been breached.

The first breach alleged that the company had failed to make payments certified by the engineer, as specified under the terms of the contract, or had failed to make any payments at all.

On a second breach, Kennard claimed that he had completed the works according to the terms but the company had not paid him, after three months of completing the contract, the 10% retention monies.

On a third breach, the company had instructed Kennard to make specific alterations and additions whilst works were in progress, and although the price and value were fixed by measurement and valuation, they had not been paid for.

On the fourth breach, Kennard claimed that the company had impeded and delayed the progress of the work, the resulting additional time taken to complete it compelling him to pay a larger sum for labour, workmanship, freight carriage and lodgings for workmen.

On a fifth breach, certain payments had been made by transferable debentures or bonds. According to Kennard there was an understanding that if they failed to realise their nominal value when transferred, the company would indemnify him against any loss. It was claimed, however, that they had failed to comply with this understanding, resulting in Kennard suffering a loss of £1,500.

On the sixth and final breach, he claimed that he had completed the work, provided materials and made specific payments at the request of the company. In all, Kennard claimed outstanding accounts and interest on the cash expended totalling £40,000. No details of how this figure was reached were provided but in an undated schedule of prices prepared later and headed *'In the Queens Bench'*, a sum of £31,750 7s 8d was quoted as the balance due to him.

The next stage in the litigation process came from the NA&HR Company, who requested their attorneys to prepare the necessary formal statement in their defence. The company forwarded to them copies of the notice and copies of the contract on which Kennard's action was based, along with Pritchard's report to the directors on debentures issued to Kennard, together with details of their transfer to him and a copy of Liddell's report to the directors on his submitted account. It was pointed out that the contract price was £38,740 but with alterations and additions agreed by Liddell, the total amount then to be paid to Kennard was stated to be £42,068 19s 1d. The amount claimed, however, was £69,754 10s 3d. It was mentioned that one of the principal items in dispute was the cost of the bases of the piers, Kennard contending that they were not included in the contract. This was countered by the NA&HR who explained that details had been included within the second schedule of the contract and on the drawings attached to it. Their attention was also brought to the secretary's report to the directors on his findings into Kennard's alleged loss on debentures.[4] There were so many different sets of figures being quoted at that time that it is difficult to reconcile which set Kennard was talking about.

Whilst these events were proceeding, Kennard was out of the country, supposedly in Paris. In his absence, and in order to allow the action to progress, an affidavit was sworn by Mr Dowdall, a clerk from Meyrick & Gedge. Dowdall swore that he had been instructed by Kennard, who had made him aware of all of the principal documents and accounts relating to the viaduct contract, and that the demand arose mainly from work done and materials supplied by him in the construction of the viaduct. Dowdall swore that, up to March 1855, Kennard had received in cash or otherwise £37,062 10s 0d, subject to certain deductions claimed on losses on debenture stock. That the calculations and estimates had, in the first instance, been made by Mr Gordon and not Mr Liddell, and that mutual errors had been made between Kennard and Gordon in the calculations, and if corrected would increase the contract price to £46,000, exclusive of certain errors. This figure it was claimed, due to unspecified mutual errors, should be increased by a further £8,000.

The affidavit advised Kennard to provide evidence to show that the contract had been entirely or in part superseded by Gordon's valid agreement, and that the principal question to be tried in the action was whether the prices to be paid to Kennard were to be based on the estimates initially prepared by Kennard and Gordon, or on measure and value. In addition, there were the prices to be paid for certain admitted extra earthworks and masonry, and for the loss sustained due to delays to the works allegedly caused by the company. Completing the affidavit, Dowdall swore that he had been informed by Kennard that the company would endeavour, if possible, to delay the trial, in order to delay the payment of any money admitted by them due to him. This would be on the grounds of not having sufficient money to meet any costs and that during the progress of the works Kennard was paid large amounts in debentures instead of cash, because the company then had insufficient cash available to pay him.[5]

Towards the end of July, Judge Samuel Martin called Counsel for both sides to his Chambers, the first of a series of requests that he made.[6] At this meeting he ordered Kennard's attorneys to provide particulars of the alterations and additions mentioned in their demand, the hindrances mentioned, and to state which items were included in the contract, and to divorce them from items wholly unconnected with the contract. In default of delivering the information within a specified time, Judge Martin threatened that any further proceedings would be 'stayed' until such particulars had been supplied. Kennard's attorneys were called on the same date to answer why the company should not be at liberty to plead the several matters specified in their demand. The following day, the company's attorneys were ordered to show why they should not within two days deliver to Kennard's attorneys a detailed account, in writing, of their set-off.

Kennard's attorneys made the next move when they served a notice on the company's attorneys stating that it was Kennard's intention in the action to sue the company, to have the case tried by Special Jury at Croydon in the County of Surrey. The first part of the notice was a repeat of one served on the company previously, with the addition of a number of pleas entered by their attorney. They denied all of the charges accusing them of owing money, claiming that they had paid Kennard the sums certified by Liddell, subject to deductions or retentions as set out in the contract. They denied that they had impeded or delayed Kennard in completing the works and claimed that at the commencement of the lawsuit, he was in debt to them for goods supplied, work done and materials provided, and for goods carried at his request. This amount the company were willing to set off against Kennard's claim. On these pleas Kennard took issue, with the notice ending '*Therefore let the Jury come etc*'.[7]

After giving notice that the case should be heard in

PLATE 7.1: This tinted lithograph was used as the frontispiece for Maynard's 1862 book on the viaduct. Looking north, a train approaches Crumlin station (it was renamed Crumlin Low Level in 1881) on the MR&CC's line, whilst a Down train heads west across the viaduct. The Ebbw River flows south through the centre of the view, with the canal to its right.
NEIL PARKHOUSE COLLECTION

front of a special jury, Kennard's attorneys suggested to the company that the case should be referred to *'friendly arbitration.'*[8] To this the company agreed and immediately proposed the terms of reference, including all matters in difference claimed by Kennard, except to any question of reforming the contract. The case was to be referred to a barrister to be agreed upon and the company were to be at liberty to apply for a commission to examine witnesses abroad. They would also be at liberty to pay money into court and make any necessary amendments due to the absence of witnesses. Liddell was working abroad during that period but the power to apply for a commission arose because Carr, who, as they explained, was the resident engineer at the time and under whose superintendence the works were executed, was then working in India.[9]

The judge on various occasions continued to summon the attorneys representing both parties to visit his chambers, either separately or together. The company's attorneys were called to explain why they could not answer an affidavit to produce documents by their officers, on what documents remained in their possession relating to the case and whether the company objected to such documents being produced. He also ordered the company's attorney to illustrate what Kennard's attorneys could not inspect in the presence of witnesses and take copies of material relating to the case, and why they should not be able to amend certain particulars without prejudice to the proceedings. The further particulars included details of all the switches, crossings, turntables, tanks, water cranes and the Clarence Road Bridge made by Kennard. The attorneys for Kennard were ordered to show why the company should have less than one month to provide details of the set off.[10]

From this point on the case becomes even more involved. Kennard was allowed to introduce costs relating to items manufactured for the company other than the work on the viaduct, the financial figures therefore becoming inflated and at times difficult to separate.

At the beginning of August 1859, Judge Samuel Martin issued an Order of Reference, instructing that all of the matters in difference between the parties be referred to arbitration. He named Mr Barstow QC as arbitrator,

examining Kennard, Lloyd would need to skilfully move any questioning to alternative topics as soon as he showed any signs of discomfort. However, he could not save him from the questions he would have to face during his cross examination by Clarke and Mellor. This was evident from the outset. Lloyd's first objective and line of questioning was to establish Kennard's engineering background and expertise but under cross examination by Clarke, he was shown up to be not all that he had claimed to be. For example:

'*Lloyd: I believe that at that time* [summer 1852] *you were interested in a new kind of girder which had been patented – the Warren Girder?*
Kennard: I was
L: You, yourself are a partner in a firm of great iron masters I believe?
K: I was
L: You were at that time?
K: Yes
L: Your own business as a contractor I believe rather in the construction of iron structures?
K: Yes
L: Did you undertake any masonry structures at that time?
K: No
L: This Warren Girder at that time I believe was a novelty?
K: To a certain extent
L: Had it been tried at that time in any other work on a large scale?
K: Oh yes
L: Where?
K: The largest example of it at that time was at Newark Dyke'

In contrast the responses obtained by Clarke in his opening cross examination suggest a different picture:

'*Clarke: Are you a partner in any firm of iron masters?*
Kennard: At the present moment?
C: Yes
K: No
C: Were you at the time the contract was made – at the time of the tender?
K: No – I was myself in business
C: As an iron master?
K: Yes as a contractor for iron bridges – it all depends on what you call an iron master – on what is the meaning of the term
C: The question put to you the other day was you (yourself) a partner in a firm of great iron masters?
K: I mean that I was engaged in business in that I saw myself as a manufacturer of bridges
C: What did you understand then by that question, a firm of great iron masters?
K: The business connected with the construction of bridges and iron masters
C: What firm was that?
K: It was T.W. Kennard
C: Yourself only?
K: Yes, myself
C: No-one but yourself?
K: No
C: Then you were the firm – you were not a partner in a firm?
K: The firm
C: Have you had at any time any interest in the manufacture of iron itself?
K: No – not during the time that the contract was settled
C: When had you first an interest in the manufacture of iron?
K: I have not now – but it was previous to it – I was engaged in a firm previous to this contract being signed but I retired from that firm a little time previous to this contract being signed – I had retired from a manufacturing firm in Manchester
C: What firm was that?
K: That firm was called Ellis & Co.
C: When did you retire from that firm?
K: 1851'

After establishing the engineering background and how he was introduced to Gordon and Liddell, Lloyd's examination started in earnest with details of Kennard's submission of the first tender of £31,000 and his second tender of £38,740. Through the process of question and answer, Kennard explained the principle of the Warren Truss and how the cost of the structure had been worked out with Gordon and Liddell. According to Kennard it had been agreed that the weight of iron in each span would be 80 tons and that he would be allowed £20 per ton for wrought iron in the girders, £15 per ton for wrought iron in the piers and £10 for the cast iron in the piers, girders and columns. A span weighing 80 tons would cost £1,620 and dividing that by the span width of 150 feet gave a figure of £10 16s per foot run. A further £2 5s 6d was added for the timber decking and sums of 13s 4d and 10s 0d for the patentee's royalty, giving a total of £14 4s 10d per foot run. Gordon would not allow the 10s 0d royalty, striking it out, saying that, '*the viaduct would be a great advertisement for the patent, and the patentees ought not to think of getting any advantage out of an affair of that sort*'. Kennard then said that a compromise was reached that allowed him £14 per foot run.

The examination then turned to the consideration of the piers. Kennard explained that the original proposal was to have nine columns, the cost being based on a design put forward by Gordon. The cost for each pier was based on £15 for wrought iron and £10 for cast iron. Having established the price of iron in the piers, Lloyd next turned to the abutments and the original specification to construct them in open iron work, with no masonry. Kennard and Gordon had added a sum of £2,000 for this work, with £600 for earthworks. Lastly, Kennard explained that £600 had been included for painting which, when added up, brought the total cost to £31,480 or £19 12s 0d per foot run for the whole length of the viaduct, and that the sum was written and signed.

Lloyd then went into details on a number of specific points. Kennard confirmed that he had ordered iron immediately on hearing that his tender had been accepted in October 1852. He then detailed the preparation of drawings that, by an arrangement between the two parties, had been prepared in his office by his new assistant Mr Baldwin. He confirmed that they were prepared on the basis of his original skeleton drawing that was used to calculate the prices. Gordon, in his evidence, was to dispute this, saying that it was based on a drawing of the Newark Dyke bridge. Kennard also confirmed that it had been agreed by the patentees, of which he was one, that Wild should check all designs and drawings, and that each was to bear his signature. Gordon and Liddell were aware of Wild's involvement, and Gordon was always advised of everything. Kennard was questioned on his involvement in the preparation of the drawings and the design of the piers and girders, confirming that he did not prepare any of the drawings but simply took an interest. There then followed questions on the drawings, the sizes of iron and the calculations to establish stresses and strains, and figures for compression. Kennard himself did not admit to going through the working drawings to check various aspects of the design but left it to Wild. He could not say the quantity of iron in each 150 foot span but now believed it to be 100 tons, explaining that this figure was not determined until the end of the contract.

The next series of questions from Lloyd returned to the evolution of the design for the piers, Kennard taking full credit for the final result. He could not recall when the drawing for the first column was made but did confirm that the new design of the pier involved additional iron and expense. Kennard was then questioned on the changes made by Liddell to the number and location of the piers; after a site visit the number of piers had been increased and the earthwork in the middle reduced. Any alterations to what had been agreed to in the £31,000 Kennard was not concerned about, as a column added here or a bar there must be paid for within his agreed £20, £15, or £10 figures. This response immediately raised questions on the lack of a signed contract. Kennard explained how he had applied for money and that the directors had refused to pay him until a contract was signed. This was not followed up by Lloyd, who returned to the question of the £600 included in the tender for earthwork eventually completed by the company.

On the next series of questions, Kennard gave the impression of becoming confused, particularly in regard to the amount of iron required in the piers. He confirmed that he had made a calculation he could not remember, although he could remember Gordon wanting more details, sending his assistant Mr Rumble to his office. Kennard admitted that he was not present when Baldwin and Rumble worked out the figures, and did not know the result. He later confirmed the figure was £15,715 and in his handwriting. He had added a figure of 38 tons but could not explain what that represented but at a meeting with Gordon, a figure of £16,375 had been agreed. Lloyd then raised the question of that figure being altered by Liddell, reducing it to £14,960.

'Lloyd: Do I understand you to say that that was not done with your assent?

Kennard: Yes – that is an error – I might have seen it – I do not say that I did not see it, but no other sum was acquiesced in by myself. I should like to make a statement here – That I might have had a certain number of figures shown me without reference to detail and it may have been said "This is how the thing works out" and I might have said yes.'

The arbitrator was not impressed and warned him that he would be asked about his statement minutely later – a very relevant warning when, minutes earlier, during his examination by Lloyd, he had professed at '*having a very good memory*'.

In the remaining period of his questioning, Kennard was to refuse to answer a question, could not bring his brain to recollect a fact, or could not remember a situation on no less than 152 occasions. Only once did Mellor challenge such responses, by informing him that he had '*a very good memory, at times*'. Clarke, after a series of questions was obviously getting nowhere, told Kennard that if he had no recollection to say so. The arbitrator also instructed him to tax his recollection. Why Clarke and Mellor did

PLATE 7.3: Professor Lewis Dunbar Brodie Gordon FRSE (1815–1876), Charles Liddell's partner. AUTHOR'S COLLECTION

not behave more aggressively towards Kennard when, on many occasions, it was obvious that he was being obstructive, may be put down to the original agreement between the parties that '*it would be a friendly arbitration hearing*'.

In his opening address to the hearing, Lloyd had called the arbitrator's attention to the reduction of the figure from £16,375 to £14,900 for the piers, referring to it as a material consideration. He explained that after Wild and Baldwin had agreed an amended design for the piers, and worked out a revised cost, Rumble, from Liddell and Gordon's office, worked out a revised figure with Baldwin of £15,715. Kennard amended this sum by adding certain allowances which brought it out at £16,375, a figure that Kennard claimed was agreed by Gordon. Lloyd pointed out that when Liddell presented his report to the Committee on the revised tender price, the figure had been altered to £14,900. Lloyd claimed that Liddell had fallen into various errors and that this figure was included without Kennard's knowledge.

Kennard, in his examination by Lloyd, agreed that the revised design of the piers had involved him in a very considerable addition to the quantity of cast iron required. He mentioned that, on a working drawing, the figure of £15,715 was indicated and pointed out that an allowance for nuts and bolts, along with other items, had been omitted from Baldwin and Rumble's calculations. He claimed that the whole revised design, eventually worked out with Gordon, came to £16,375.

Kennard confirmed, under examination, that he had never agreed at any time to take any different figure for the piers. Gordon had witnessed, in detail, the whole calculations and agreed afterwards to the figure of £16,375, had seen Kennard writing it down and later copied it down for himself. When questioned by Clarke as to whether the figure of £14,960 was put in with his assent, Kennard responded that it was an error. He stated that he had never discussed the £14,960 with Gordon and the figure had never been submitted to him.

Kennard went on to explain that he had obtained and copied from Carr's book and papers information regarding the piers, and other papers in Gordon's own handwriting. He went on to admit that when discussing the figure of £16,375 with Gordon he did put a pencil line through the figure but this had been produced by the company's side and not his. Kennard dismissed the whole experience leading up to the reduced amount as a simple mistake of putting in the wrong figures.

The company's submission presented to the arbitrator at the start of the hearing stated that there was no written evidence of the change in the price of the piers. They claimed that there had been long discussions that preceded the figure of £14,960, and that there could be no doubt that Kennard was fully aware of it and acquiesced. It did not appear he ever insisted on further investigation into actual weights in the piers as shown by the working drawings, notwithstanding the difference between Baldwin and Rumble's figures. As regards the piers, Gordon was positive that he never for one moment acquiesced to Kennard's demand for £16,375. In early July 1853, he had written to Kennard expressing his doubts in the amount of cast iron calculated and requested drawings so that he could work the quantities out for himself. Gordon eventually allowed a figure of 1,100 tons, which in his opinion was ample and took into account the thickening of the column castings.

Professor Gordon, when being examined by Clarke, provided opposing facts to those of Kennard. Explaining the situation at the Falkirk Works and their reported difficulty in casting the columns to the specified sizes, Gordon indicated how he had allowed them to increase the thickness by $^1/_8$th inch to $^3/_4$ inch, instead of $^5/_8$th inch. He stated that, after a series of calculations, he had allowed an additional weight of 100 tons for the increase in the thickness. It provided no additional benefit to the company though, his main objective being to keep them as thin as possible. He admitted that '*he only consented to an increase in the thickness after a great deal of argument*'. In his opinion the iron founder would send them solid if allowed to and if he increased the weight, he should then have diminished the price and if a founder puts in more thickness than specified it should be at his own risk – '*we do not pay for the iron we pay for the column. If an iron founder cast a column half a ton extra that is his business*'.

Gordon went on to explain that as soon as Kennard had presented him with a revised figure of 1,250 tons for the piers, he objected most strongly and wrote to him saying '*I cannot make out your weights at all*'. Looking at Rumble's figure of 1,130 tons, he removed 30 tons stating that he was there for the company and had no right to give it to Kennard. Just because Falkirk could not cast pipes as specified, he did not think that he should allow him all of the increased price. Kennard he believed '*gratefully accepted it*'.

The company's QC then asked Gordon, in his own words and without having to lead him, to explain as nearly as he could his recollection as to how the matter was ultimately determined. Gordon stated that, in the original tender, an allowance of 700 tons at £10 per ton made out a figure of so much a foot run. For the revised tender, Kennard had persuaded Gordon to allow him an increase in the thickness in the pipes adding 100 tons, whilst for the additional number of pipes he added a further 100 tons. At that time he was going to allow a figure of 1,000 tons but Kennard maintained the figure should be 1,250 tons. After further representations, he had allowed a figure of 1,100 tons, adding that these sums were included in the report to the directors, and had been shown to Kennard on many occasions, evidenced by entries in his diary and presented to the arbitrator. He pointed out that at the end of the report there was a note: '*working drawings with detailed quantities and costs of all parts have been made, and agreed upon by Mr Kennard with me*'.

Reference was made to the details Kennard had copied from the papers belonging to Carr. Kennard claimed these were in Gordon's handwriting, showing figures of 1,130 tons and 45 tons, and that on his copy it had a sum of £16,375. There was though doubt passed on how Kennard had obtained the information that he claimed had been loaned to him by Carr to copy. Although not making any direct accusations, doubt was cast by the introduction of a letter to Kennard from Carr, wherein he requested the return of his books and papers inadvertently left on Kennard's table.[17] There was a feeling that he had perused the books and noted some of Carr's preliminary observations, not necessarily the finalised totals.

Gordon, under examination could remember the figure of £16,375 and the fact that he had crossed it out. Rumble and Baldwin had agreed a figure of 1,130 tons but Kennard believed that they had used the wrong decimal point. This was a figure added to the estimated total weight of iron in recognition of its specific gravity. The actual figure was determined by multiplying the total weight of the iron by a decimal point. There were different sets of tables to aid this calculation, Rumble and Baldwin had used Penn's, whilst Kennard used Thompson's. Gordon was an acknowledged expert in the use of the decimal point and had spent many years researching the subject. That used by Rumble and Baldwin was one not normally used in Gordon and Liddell's office, whilst the one used by Kennard was more favourable to him. That used in Gordon's office would have given a figure 1% lower and that in Kennard's office 2% or 3% higher. Gordon explained that the extra 45 tons wanted by Kennard equates to the use of his decimal point, stating that all along he had accepted Rumble's and Baldwin's figures '*as the basis of my ultimate decision as to what Kennard was to have, although these were higher than my estimate.*'.

Gordon finished this part of his examination by stating that: '*never on any occasion had he asserted to the sum of £16,375 as the price to be paid, nor did he ever write any memorandum as stated by Kennard in his evidence of adding 45 tons for the difference between Kennard's calculations and Rumble's, and also agreeing to an allowance of 14 tons for the bolts and nuts, as stated by him.*'.

Lloyd next made reference to the fact that nothing was said about any masonry foundations for the piers or any excavation for preparing the foundations for them. As in his opening statement regarding the piers, Lloyd referred to the foundations as a material consideration and one that needed to be treated as a separate item from the piers. He stated that nothing had been discussed in respect of the use of masonry for the foundations in the first tender but it was discovered that it was necessary prior to the contract being signed. No further estimate was included for the construction of foundations in that contract, whilst Liddell did not allow for a charge for the foundations at 'measure and value', stating that it was included in the contract. Kennard was claiming that the work to the foundations had involved him in a very considerable cost.

Lloyd then referred to contract drawing No. 26, explaining that it was prepared originally for the purpose of being submitted to a Parliamentary Committee, which was sitting upon the extension of the South Wales Railway and was in order to show them the exact thing, whereas in their initial drawing only foundation plates were shown.

Examining Kennard, Lloyd established that following the acceptance of his first tender, and at his request, Carr had completed a set of borings for each pier along the line of the viaduct. When Liddell added a further pier, a further set of borings should have been taken. When work commenced on excavating the foundations in their re-arranged position, Kennard paid little heed to the cost because as far as he was concerned no sum had been agreed for the work, assuming that he would be paid according to what was actually completed. Kennard stated '*it does not matter, it must have been done so as to give a solid and substantial foundation it will be paid for according to work done*', adding that '*the foundations had cost a considerably much larger sum than had been roughly estimated*'.

Lloyd asked Kennard why, when he had discovered that he had to do the foundations, he did not raise the subject with the board or the engineers to have it reconsidered and adjusted. Kennard responded by explaining that he was on exceedingly friendly terms with Liddell and Carr, and had done all of the masonry work to please Liddell.

It never occurred to him for a single moment '*that they would deliberately oppose my receiving payment for the work done*'. He believed that he would receive a fair price.

When Kennard discovered, in late 1854, that no reference to the cost of foundations had been included in the contract documents, he considered that a mistake had been made. Immediately, he said, he discussed this with Carr, Liddell and Gordon but they all said that he would have to wait until the end of the contract and the viaduct finished. Kennard confirmed that he undertook the work without applying to Liddell or Gordon for a certificate, because he considered that would be paid for differently from the ironworks. He was aware that measurements had been taken as the works progressed but could not confirm who by; he stated that Carr used to say '*of course the Company will pay for these foundations*' but it does not affect the question because he considered Carr '*was only a subordinate*'. Earlier, Kennard had mentioned that all of the work on site was done under the instructions and directions of his foreman, Mr Sinclair, and each complete excavation was examined by Carr, with the foundation for each pier being settled as soon as excavating was completed. Baldwin kept Kennard informed of quantities in the excavation but he never kept a copy. Mr Waite, for the company, kept the records of excavation and quantities of materials used – '*he could always tell what they were, but he has now passed away*'.

Under cross examination by Mellor, Kennard claimed that the foundations were an extra and that he had an equitable right for the work to be considered as such. He had no idea whether he had been paid for any work on the foundations as an extra but did not think that he had ever made a specific claim because he did not think that he ever had the quantities measured. It was not until at least a year after the completion of the viaduct that he had applied for cash for any foundation work. Kennard then changed his mind and said that it was as work was progressing and could remember being there and saying, '*of course it never can be understood that I am doing this work for nothing*'. It was at this point that Mellor suggested to him that '*he had a very good memory at times*'. At this point, Kennard had a relapse and could not remember if he ever did write to Pritchard stating that he had made a large outlay in respect of the bases to the piers. It had never been considered by Kennard as being contained in the contract.

Baldwin, when examined by Mellor, explained that where they expected to find rock there was none but they then found rock where they did not expect to. He had prepared a set of drawings to show how the foundations were constructed, according to the 2nd schedule. The only result of this was greater excavation, which did not add to the cost of the masonry or iron. Liddell had allowed for any extra iron required in the price of the piers, whilst Baldwin confirmed that he had always understood from Kennard that the cost of the foundations was to be paid for by measure. He had often pointed out to him the foolishness of taking a lump sum for foundations: '*I always objected to it, but Kennard said that it would be alright. It was something he always did*'.

Kennard's responses to questions put to him by Counsel require some clarification. Correspondence had been exchanged between the company, Kennard and Maynard from the start of 1856. Liddell had requested that he supply him with '*sketches of foundations to compare with the contract ... as I have information that the piers are not so deep as they are on the drawings for the contract*'. Kennard replied explaining that he did not understand Liddell's letter as to foundations and that there never was a contract drawing. The general elevation shows the style proposed but it was put in without regard to quantities, the question not, according to Kennard, being considered in the estimates. Liddell responded, '*you treat the drawing somewhat lightly*', reminding him that the difference between the foundations shown and executed could be the only grounds for Kennard to claim extra payments. Liddell wanted clarification, pointing out that under the contract he was to '*fill up the valley for a lump sum*', yet he was now asking for consideration for extra on his account. As early as October 1853, Carr had forwarded to Liddell his estimate for work on the foundations in the large valley, which was £1,198 and made up as follows:

'Excavations 6,000 cu. ft at 1/6 per cu. ft.	£	*480*
Rubble 350 cu. ft at 11/6 per cu. ft.	£	*200*
Planking 680 cu. ft at 2/- per cu.ft.	£	*136*
Dressed Ashlar estimated	£	*382'*[18]

Nothing more appears to have passed between them until 1857, when Liddell wrote to Kennard wanting to know why he had altered the figures previously agreed with Carr on his final account. Liddell's report to the directors was the first occasion that any figures for the foundations had been submitted by Kennard. In his report, he states that the charge for the foundations of the piers was not admissible under the terms of the contract. He quoted the second schedule, which specified that the foundations were, where practicable, to be laid on the solid rock and also gave minute instructions as to the thickness of concrete to replace the masonry, and the extent of rubble and ashlar work. He pointed out that the foundations for the piers were '*very little different from what was anticipated when the contract was signed*'.

On the instructions of the board, Pritchard wrote to Kennard asking him to justify his claim – '*on what authority was the charge of £3,694 for foundations for piers made*'.[19] Kennard responded, '*In reference to the charge of £3,694 in my account for foundations, I have to explain that this is a prime cost for that portion of the work. In the original estimate it was altogether omitted, the valley, being of rock it was supposed there would be no outlay sufficient to include*'.[20]

The board's reaction was to instruct Pritchard to write to Kennard explaining that they failed to understand his explanation and requested further comment.[21] His reasoning was that the valley was supposed to be entirely made up of rock, which would provide a suitable foundation with little need to level it. No charge was included for completing the foundations, which Kennard believed was an error.[22] Liddell, in his next report to the directors, concluded '*It is not the fact that Mr Kennard states that it was anticipated that nothing had to be done as may be seen by reference to the drawings and specifications, and price charged by him is in my opinion at least double the value of the work*'. A comparison of the figures Kennard had agreed with Carr and those submitted by him to Liddell were grossly inflated in terms of quantity and cost. For example: Dressed ashlar – Carr 2,182 cu. yds at 3s 6d per cu. yd, Kennard 6,000 cu. yds. at 3s 6d; rubble – Carr 350 cu. yds at 11s 6d, Kennard 1,535 cu. yds at 20s per cu. yd.

Although they had not been included in Lloyd's demands for reforming the contract, the next item he examined were the abutments, Kennard explaining that he thought that it would be cheaper for the company not to have ironwork for the buttresses but to have stone. He claimed that it was his suggestion and that he had prepared a drawing to illustrate his suggested improvement. Instead of the £2,000 estimated for their construction by Gordon and Liddell, he estimated that it would cost £1,100. Liddell then prepared a drawing and after discussing it with Kennard, he explained that the figure therein had been increased to £1,700.

Questions relating to the contract were then put to Kennard. He confirmed that it was signed and sent to the engineers Gordon and Liddell, where the blanks were filled in and they also signed.

When asked when he first became aware the contract sum of £38,740 was the right one or not, Kennard admitted that it was when the viaduct was costing him more money than he thought, getting into debt and having to go to his father for money. This was not until he had obtained, from Carr, a copy of how the contract money was made up; he thought this was a year after signing the contract. Kennard said he realised that there had been a mistake made about the piers and the foundations. He stated that he had made Carr aware of this, as well as Gordon and Liddell, and they all had said that I must wait until the end of the contract and that '*no unfair advantage should be taken of you*'.

Lloyd then pressed Kennard on the weight of iron in the girders. He responded by confirming that anomalies were discovered after the viaduct had been finished, when all of the invoices were gone over and it was found that there was more iron in them than anticipated. Kennard then admitted that the increase in weight had never been discussed with Gordon and Liddell. When he sent in his final account of £62,000 to Liddell, he had included as extra work £4,000 for the superstructure and £1,500 for additional iron in the piers. Liddell would not allow him extras for the foundations to the piers but Carr always told me that '*the Company would pay for the foundations*'; however, it did not answer the question because Carr was only a subordinate. Kennard added that Gordon had agreed a price of £20 a ton for the girders and on a great many occasions.

Plate 7.4: This portrait of Mark Carr, the resident (site) engineer for the construction of the viaduct, is from a carte-de-visite by the London Stereograph Company.
Alastair Warrington collection

Clarke then started to question Kennard on the first tender document and the basis for establishing the prices per foot run. At this point Kennard became very evasive; very rarely did he answer a question directly and at times he gave the impression that he did not understand the most basic of questions. For example, when being questioned on early correspondence with Gordon and Liddell, Clarke asked a series of fairly simple questions:

'Clarke: I think it desirable that we should see the letter book perhaps you will bring it with you when you come again?
Kennard: I will
C: What is the date of the first letter or memorandum that you have found in that letter book – I am speaking of you yourself – not your solicitor – but you yourself – tell me the date of the earliest letter you have found in your letter book?
K:, I cannot answer that question
C: You have not looked?
K: No, I have not
C: Here is a letter dated August 1852 but

without a day of the month – you must have a copy of this letter in your letter book I should think?
K: Does it look as if it had been copied through the press?
C: I think not
K: If it was not copied through the press naturally it will not be there
C: Have you a letter book in which you copy letters which have not gone through the press?
K: No, I have not
C: That, I suppose is your handwriting?
K: Yes, this is my handwriting
Mellor: Perhaps you will read it?
K: I think that this has been copied through the press – it looks like it
M: Was that your first communication?
K: I am not aware'

Kennard was then questioned on his first tender for the superstructure and a letter where he quoted a price of £15 per foot run. He then played at being confused over a 200 foot or 150 foot span and what he was pricing for. A number of questions were put to him on Liddell's specification and the strains that would be put on the compression and tension beams, along with his understanding of the meaning '*being in equilibrium*'. Also included was the sequence of events leading up to the tender being submitted to the company. Completing his questioning on the first tender, Clarke turned next to the second and his calculations when submitting his tender documents. Kennard was not doing himself any favours when he started to ramble rather than answer direct, so much so, that at one stage the arbitrator instructed him to confine himself to answering the questions put to him. Again this had little effect and, becoming evasive, Clarke sometimes asked the same question three or more times before he obtained a positive reply. For example, his cross examination on taking a set of drawings to Gordon:

'Clarke: Do you mean you left them there?
Kennard: Yes
C: With whom did you leave them?
K: I left them in the office of Messrs Liddell & Gordon
C: With whom did you leave them?
K: With Mr Gordon
C: You are sure about that?
K: Yes
C: Are you stating that positively and distinctly?
K: Emphatically'

Soon after this bout of questioning, Kennard received another dressing down from the arbitrator but, as before, it had little effect.

When Kennard was shown a skeleton drawing of a girder, he claimed he could not remember which were his calculations, and which were Gordon's, whilst when working out the figures, he could not remember how they arrived at their weight, nor how they had arrived at a figure of £14 per foot run. After further exhaustive questioning, he had to admit that a large part of the figures on the skeleton drawing were his own. Having explained Wild's role in overseeing the preparation of the drawings and figures, Kennard was examined on how he had calculated the weight of iron in the girders and how he arrived at a sum of £14 per foot run. He had to admit that he had never carried out such a calculation and that, along with Gordon, they had assumed 80 tons as the weight of four girders in one span, pointing out 80 tons in his writing on the skeleton drawing referred to earlier. No matter how many questions Clarke asked Kennard, he had to keep admitting that the figure of 80 tons, along with others, was in his handwriting. He then had to admit that he did not realise that the girders in a span were more than 80 tons. He found it a difficult question to answer but was inclined to think that he did not discover the discrepancy until he had to order more iron from Blaenavon and that was not until near the completion of the contract. However, he was unable to produce invoices for deliveries of iron because the gentleman who kept the accounts died part way through the contract and no-one else kept the records, with many being lost.

The next topic for cross examination was the method and process for lifting the girders. Kennard accepted that he had not made any calculation of their weight for lifting, although the operation caused a good deal of trouble and that he had taken personal control. He had to resort to many experiments and again became evasive but eventually admitted that his mind might have drifted into thinking the weight being about 100 tons. He kept no account of the iron being used, there was no weighing of the materials out of the workshop and he did not weigh a completed girder, although he could have done so.

Another series of questions gave Clarke the opportunity to further illustrate Kennard's ill-conceived responses. Questioning him on the figure of £20 per ton for wrought iron in a girder, which was to include work undertaken on the iron and the extent of Liddell's or Gordon's knowledge of the £20 he claimed had been agreed, Kennard stated that he had a distinct recollection that £20 was the price agreed by Gordon and that he had admitted it to him on fifty occasions since. Clarke then asked him to provide details of one of those occasions but he could only remember two, both at the end of the contract; however, he refused to withdraw his number of fifty occasions.

Kennard was then asked a series of questions in which he, Liddell and Gordon had discussed the price of girders before the tender was accepted. A figure of £16 had been put in and Liddell had substituted this for £17 per ton. Kennard would not undertake to any recollection of the conversation but, bearing in mind the topic being discussed, the questioning continued:

'Clarke: I am speaking of that £16 or £17 with reference to the wrought iron in the girders; will you undertake that there was none?
Kennard: I do not recollect any
C: Will you undertake to say there was none?
K: No, if Mr Liddell says he said it, I do not want to say he states an untruth
C: Will you undertake to say that you did not name £16 per ton?
K: I have no recollection of it
C: Will you undertake to say that you never did?
K: I cannot tell what you refer to
C: I am speaking of the wrought iron girders
K: What girders?
C: For Crumlin Viaduct
K: No, I have no recollection of doing it'

The evasive answers to questions continued until Clarke gave Kennard notice because he did not want to surprise him, that he would be contradicted upon this subject. He then gave him the opportunity to undertake to swear positively that he did not have the conversation or simply swear that he did not recollect it but the only response Clarke could obtain was that Kennard had no recollection.

The cross examination was then taken up by Mellor, who immediately obtained from Kennard an admission that he knew in July 1852 that the directors of the company required a fixed price tender. Mellor also obtained a confession that Kennard did not personally make the Newark Dyke bridge and he was not the contractor. He did claim that he had made calculations for the use of the Warren Truss on other occasions but then could not provide Mellor with any details. On the difference in price between the first and second tender, Kennard explained that it was the result of changes to the design of the piers, that the girders would remain the same. Calculations for all of the additional works were not completed by Kennard – he admitted that they were made for him by Baldwin – the total working out to be £39,854 but he could not recollect, after repeated questions on this, it being reduced to £38,740.

Mellor's next series of questions then began to get Kennard to contradict the response he had given to Lloyd's examination. He turned to the foundations and Kennard's belief that he could claim for the extra work involved as an equitable claim. After discussing the method Kennard had for obtaining money by certificate, authorised by Liddell, he disclosed that he did not claim work on the foundations as an extra until the contract had been completed for a year, and then he could not make a specific claim because he had not kept a record of the quantity of soil excavated; but he had mentioned the works during the construction of the viaduct. It was then put to Kennard that when the matter of his claim was being discussed with the directors, he admitted that he had no legal claim against the company that could be enforced but thought he was entitled to consideration from an equitable point of view. He did remember most distinctly that he told a director that he had no legal claim for what he had put down in his account but that was all, and that he had no legal claim for all he asked – which served to confirm that he had no legal claim upon the company for all of the money that the bridge had cost him. At this point the arbitrator intervened and asked Kennard what he expected. He started to ramble and the arbitrator interrupted again to tell him that he was speaking about the foundations. Mellor then asked Kennard if it had been suggested to him at any time that he was cutting away more rock than was necessary, while the foundations for the piers were being prepared and that the rock he was cutting away would have been better than any of the materials he was then putting in. Kennard recollected something having been said about it very soon after the contract had commenced but before the contract was signed and before the meeting to arrange the alteration to the figures.

In an effort to retrieve parity following Kennard's damaging cross examination, Lloyd re-examined him, going through the events leading up to the signing of the contract. He led Kennard skilfully, providing him with the chance to be more positive in his responses. Lloyd gave him the opportunity to repeat that he was unaware how certain figures were arrived at, and that he did not see any figures put down for the foundations and bases of the piers but he did not comment at the time because everything was being done in a hurry. He failed to raise the matter until the viaduct was finished because he was on extremely friendly terms with Liddell and Gordon, and it never occurred to him that they would deliberately oppose his receiving payment for that work. Then out of the blue, Kennard made an amazing statement to the effect that Gordon was perfectly aware of his desire to make the viaduct as cheap as possible, and as a friend he continually asked Kennard if he was asking enough, begging him that although he might not have wished to make a low offer, he should not make one that would turn out to be prejudicial to him. Prior to Kennard being released, the arbitrator asked him a number of questions regarding the contract that were discussed earlier in Chapter 2.

Baldwin was the next witness called by Lloyd. He was now carrying on a business as a worsted spinner at Stourport in Worcestershire, having given up the practice of civil engineer. He had entered the employment of Thomas Kennard in October 1852 and was his general assistant in the execution of works connected with the viaduct. His role was to prepare the working drawings and to consult with Wild about the various stresses and strains of the design, to obtain his sanction to the drawings, which he then signed before passing them to Liddell and Gordon. He was shown various drawings by Lloyd and, under questioning, went to great lengths in explaining the technicalities of the construction of the girders, their strengths both in compression and in tension. His attention was then directed towards the piers, the number of columns having been agreed as fourteen by the time that he was preparing the drawings. By February 1853, along with Rumble from the office of Liddell and Gordon, he had calculated the amount of iron in the piers and they had arrived at a figure of £15,715. One particular item picked out was a note by Baldwin adding 38 feet for an extra length in the foundations. He explained that certain foundations might require extra long feet to the columns – some needed to be 6 feet long instead of 2 feet 6 inches – but as a result, there would be a saving of 3 feet 6 inches on stone for building up under the piers. All drawings had been completed during April 1853 the final one being a general elevation of the viaduct, made as a show drawing.

Fig. 7.1: Diagram showing amongst other façets of the viaduct's construction, the wooden decking. Note that the 6 inch wood planking is shown running horizontally, and not diagonally as Kennard had wished to do. Author

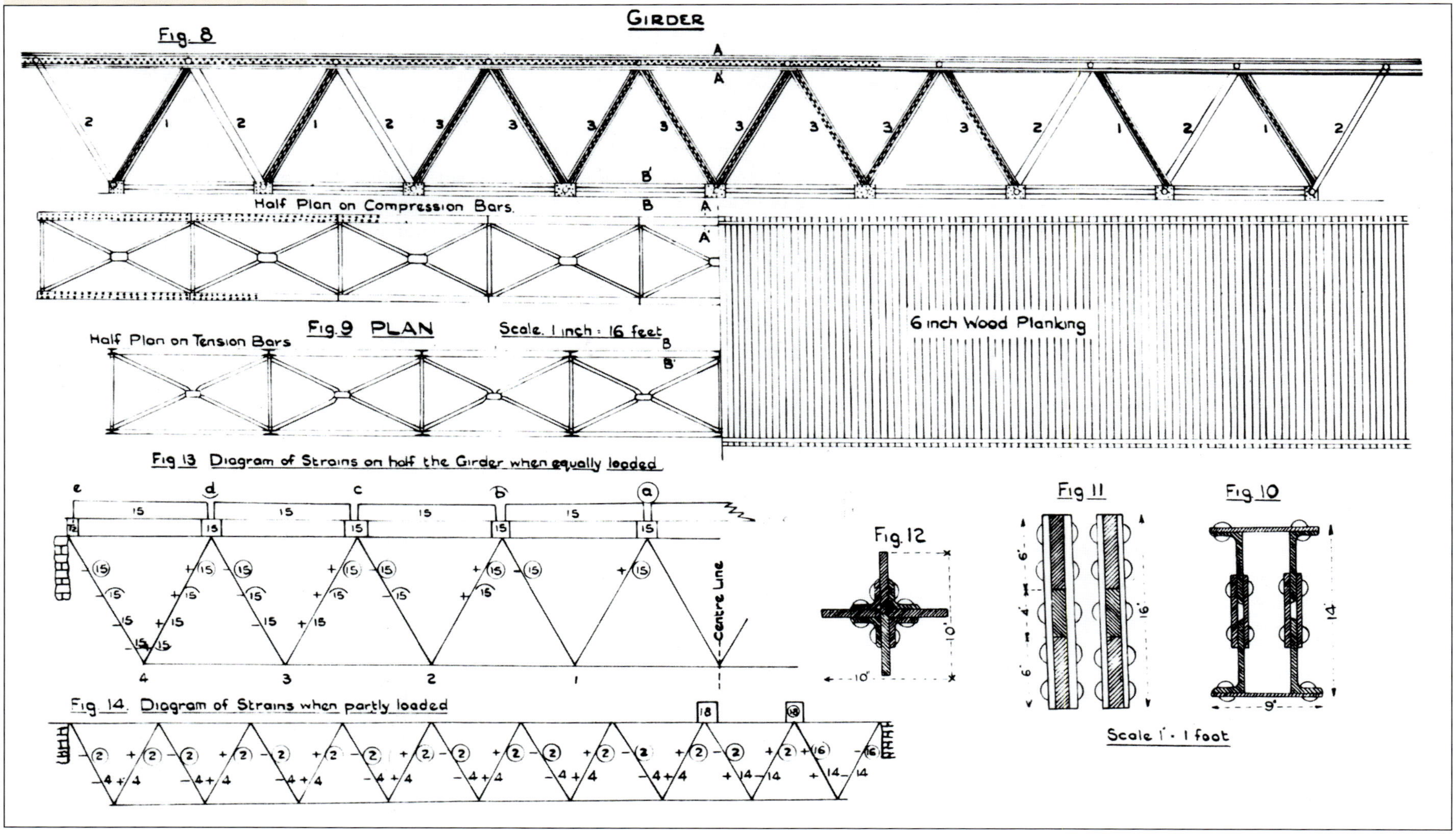

Baldwin was then examined by Lloyd on the changes to the abutments from iron to masonry, admitting that he did not prepare any of the drawings. Questioning then returned to the foundations, Baldwin stating that his only involvement was in pier No. 4. There was a bed of cement at the bottom, followed by a layer of planking, then rubble, large stones and then four courses of ashlar. The ashlar was built up under the feet of the columns and the intermediate part was filled with rubble again, till it was all a level bed at the bottom of the iron. The pier was located in a canal bed and Liddell was afraid of the bottom being of a boggy nature, which was why they put in the timber.

At this point, Mellor intervened and asked Baldwin if the orders for the foundations were given to him, or were they in writing? Baldwin thought they were, in a letter from Liddell and Gordon's office sent direct to Crumlin, but he himself had not seen such a letter. His impression was that he was told by Kennard but could not say when he was given those directions. Mellor asked him to look in his letter book, because they had a different impression; they thought it was a suggestion of Kennard's. Baldwin went on to explain that the profile of the valley was taken from information sent by Carr but in every case they had to excavate deeper to find rock. In the case of No. 4 pier, there were no borings done because of the canal, where they expected to find gravel. When excavating for the foundations, where they found rock it was split and had to be cut away in order to get to solid rock, which was done under the direction of Sinclair. Mellor observed that he had been dismissed shortly afterwards but Baldwin commented that Sinclair left after he did.

Lloyd then returned to the examination of Baldwin, who confirmed that work on the remaining foundations began in March 1853 and continued during that summer. Detailed records were kept by a person from the company named Mr Waite. Baldwin confirmed that he had called Kennard's attention to the extent of the excavations on several occasions. In reference to costs, Baldwin stated that the main increase was in the excavation of materials.

Baldwin was then cross-examined by Mellor, who asked him when he first saw the profile drawing prepared by Carr. He confirmed that it was one of the first things he saw regarding the viaduct in October 1852 and at that time Kennard had not been down to Crumlin to see the works but it had been arranged for him do so when the borings for the foundations had been sufficiently advanced. The questions that followed concerned the foundations and who kept the records of quantities of work undertaken, before returning to the amount of time Kennard spent at Crumlin. Baldwin estimated two or three times a month and sometimes two or three days at the Viaduct Works. Mellor also questioned him on the first pier and its foundation. Baldwin visited Crumlin only when a foundation had been fully excavated and believed that quantities were never taken unless it was to pay the men; no records were ever sent to London. Mellor then turned to the calculations he and Rumble had made on the weight of the piers, and that no copy had been kept, the calculations being made in 1853. Baldwin stated that he never made any calculations regarding the girders. He was then asked what other works Kennard was involved in, replying that during his time in his office, he did not think Kennard was carrying on any other works other than an occupation bridge on the Eastern Counties Railway, and switches and other railway apparatus. Due to a long and severe illness, Baldwin left Kennard in March 1855.

Re-examined by Lloyd, Baldwin accepted that the borings were made before the number of piers had been increased and agreed that any boring for the foundations stopped when they came to rock. When they excavated, they discovered that the rock was split and not suitable for resting the piers on. No sum had been put in the specification, as Baldwin stated he had always understood from Kennard that the foundations were to be paid for by measure but he always thought it foolish of him to include foundations as a lump sum. Baldwin was then questioned on invoices from Blaenavon that degenerated into arguments between the legal representatives.

Next to take the stand was Mr Haynes, Kennard's assistant, who had joined him during 1854. He was first

PLATE 7.5: The only view showing the construction of the abutments is this one, an enlargement from the photograph on page 52. Taken in the spring of 1856, before the gap was infilled to rail level, the twin stone abutments of the Ebbw and Kendon portions face each other across the top of the promontory where the two valleys meet
STEPHEN ROWSON COLLECTION

many of the questions that had been put to him previously regarding the weight of the girders but only succeeded in eliciting contradictory responses. It was similar when asked about payments to his workmen. He agreed that payments for piece work were made on weights, though these were estimated roughly, but then could not recollect – he thought so but had forgotten whether it was piecework or by day work. When piecework was done there was no way to weigh it. Kennard then stated that the girders were 150 feet long and the men would have a certain sum paid in sovereigns for riveting them, and whether they weighed a ton more or less the men would not care one rap, they worked to rivets not weight.

The hearing was adjourned to 12th February 1861, when Haynes was recalled and cross-examined by Clarke on the various calculations he had produced. Confining himself to sets of red and black ink figures on the skeleton drawing, he had calculated a figure of 47 tons per span on four girders but on a previous occasion had calculated a weight of 52 tons per span. Taking the pencil figures on the skeleton drawing, he had calculated a figure of 82 tons per span. None of this information, according to Haynes was sufficiently detailed to provide a figure of 82½ tons, assuming that it all to be in wrought iron. In a calculation prepared specifically for the hearing, Haynes stated that he had reached a figure of 80½ tons per span, which included cast iron, but taking the whole working drawings he had arrived at a figure of 102 tons.

The issue then becomes very involved in a series of different figures and totals for wrought iron and cast iron used. At one point, whilst the different figures were being examined, the arbitrator made a material point when he reminded Counsel that what was being examined was the issue as to what the two parties intended at the time when they made the contract. The next series of questions were aimed at determining how much work was completed beyond that intended under the terms of the contract.

When re-examined by Lloyd, more figures and tonnages were introduced, muddying a confused situation even more. It became more and more obvious that Lloyd was getting nowhere when Mellor interrupted him and asked '*if that was his case*'. Mellor then addressed the arbitrator and requested permission to reserve his summing up and observations that he had to make on the case. His request was granted and he proceeded to examine Gordon.

Mellor opened his examination of Gordon by questioning him on his Proof of Evidence, submitted with the company's deposited documents at the outset of the hearing. The Proof of Evidence was an important document setting out the facts as he was to swear to them. Gordon outlined how he and Liddell had chosen the design of the viaduct and the materials to be used; how Kennard had become involved in 1852, and events leading up to the acceptance of Kennard's tender. He confirmed that, on 29th October 1852, he had met with Kennard and Wild on the design, agreeing to increase the number of columns in the piers from nine to fourteen. In December, Gordon met Kennard and Carr at Newport to discuss the foundations for the piers, and the borings to be undertaken by Carr. When asked for working drawings during December 1852, Kennard visited Gordon and Liddell and endeavoured to make it appear that there was no necessity for a contract or specification, and that he should be paid for the quantity of iron used in the structure upon a schedule of prices. Neither Gordon nor Liddell would accede to this request.

Several discussions were held with Kennard between February and May 1853 to establish a fixed price for the viaduct. At one of the meetings, Kennard asked for £39,854 but said he would accept £39,005. After further calculations, Gordon and Liddell arrived at a figure of £38,740, which was accepted by Kennard prior to Liddell preparing his report to the directors. Gordon denied ever offering £16,375 as the price to be paid for the piers and he did not write a memorandum as claimed by Kennard in his evidence. Gordon agreed that a price of £10 per ton was allowed for a definite quantity of cast iron and if Kennard had fixed a price without limitation of quantity he would have displayed great carelessness on his part. Gordon stated that Kennard had never complained before the action had commenced, about the mistakes he now claimed had been made in estimating the quantity of iron in the girders and piers.

When the case was opened on behalf of the defendants, of significant interest was the fact that during the initial stages of the hearing, it was planned by Kennard's legal team that Gordon would be a material witness in support of the plaintiff. Gordon, in giving evidence on behalf of the defendants, was a formidable material witness. He was able to produce, from the records he had kept and from his diaries, accurate dates and records of meetings, unlike the witnesses who had preceded him.

Mellor, in examination of Gordon, established that he was in partnership with Liddell, that they were engineers to the Taff Vale Extension Railway and that they had been considering how they were going to carry the railway line over the valley at Crumlin since early 1852. Gordon explained how he had made the acquaintance of Wild and other engineers. Knowing that he had to construct a viaduct at Crumlin, they had made him aware of the Warren Truss. On 22nd June 1852, Kennard had called at Gordon's office and, according to the entry in his diary, they had a long chat about Crumlin Viaduct. After discussing the various means of crossing the valley, they agreed to recommend the company to adopt the use of the Warren girders at Crumlin. Kennard was asked to supply the company with a design for a girder of 200 feet span resting on masonry piers. It was appreciated that this would be costly and therefore, the larger the span the better. The principle Gordon and Liddell were aiming for was to make the piers and the superstructure something like equal cost. Kennard's price was reported to the directors in August 1852, who, on considering the quote, instructed Liddell to obtain a tender from Kennard and Doyne based on a specification prepared by Liddell. Mellor then questioned Gordon on how the calculations to meet the terms of the specification were made.

Mellor raises briefly the skeleton drawing that Gordon had seen throughout the hearing. When asked whether it was ever the subject of a discussion with Kennard, as far as he could remember, or as far as anything had been said and after all of the discussion upon it, he could not remember ever having seen the drawing until he had seen it at the hearing; it was never in his office. Gordon went on to state that neither the skeleton drawing nor any other drawing had been discussed in reference to the weights of the girders or in any references to the question which Kennard claimed were discussed upon it. He had received a skeleton drawing from Wild that referred to the Newark Dyke bridge and they used that drawing when discussing the strains; this drawing had Wild's initials in one corner.

Mellor then turned his attention to the piers. Gordon confirmed that, at about the end of August 1852, Liddell wrote to him asking his opinion on whether or not they could design a cast iron pier and provided a rough

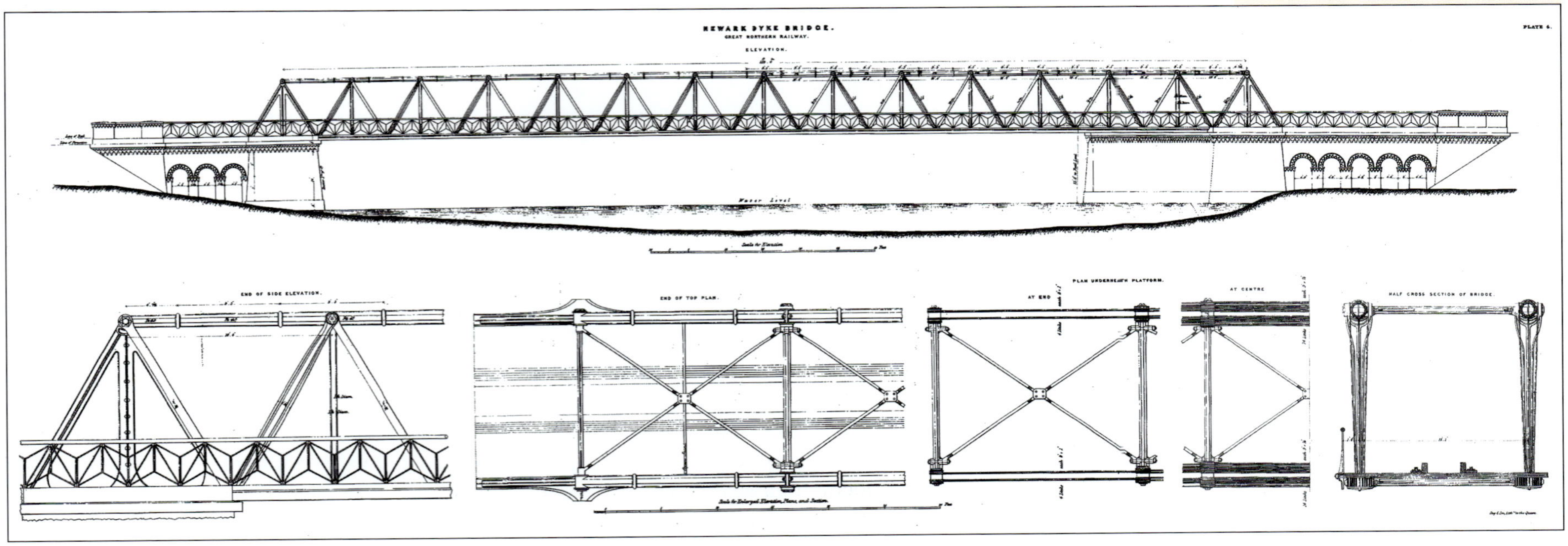

PLATE 7.6 AND FIG. 7.2: Newark Dyke Bridge, a Warren Truss viaduct designed by Charles Wild for the Great Northern Railway and completed in 1852. Its twin spans carried the Up and Down lines separately across the navigable River Trent near Newark. It was rebuilt in 1889, Wild's Warren Trusses being replaced by a pair of bowstring girders but this bridge has in turn since been replaced, by a new twin-track bowstring girder span in 2000. The bridge, which is sited around 100 yards to the north of the famous Newark flat crossing – where the Midland Railway's Nottingham to Lincoln line crosses over the GNR line on the level – is on a sharp skew, so although the river is only 97ft wide at this point, the span was 240ft in length. Note the design of the railings, identical to those later made for Crumlin Viaduct. NEIL PARKHOUSE COLLECTION

sketch in support, to which Gordon responded in September considering it to be a good idea.

That line of questioning was then dropped and Mellor introduced the fact that the board were requesting a tender for the whole work, with iron for the girders and brick or stone for the piers. At first, Kennard's tender was priced at £12 per foot run but was later amended to £14 per foot run, as it had been pointed out to him that he had failed to read the instructions in the specification, and had not provided a price for the bridge complete. Kennard's tender price after making the amendments was £31,480, and had been signed by him '*this is correct*'.

Mellor then asked Gordon if at any time calculations were prepared as to the weight of the girders. He was emphatic in his reply stating '*none whatsoever*'. He pointed out that Kennard was in constant communication with Wild and that every time he went to Kennard's office, Wild was there. When the arbitrator asked him whether he was clear that no calculations had been prepared, Gordon responded, '*yes – none whatsoever was gone into*'; the price given to him was £12. He stated that it was his impression that the weight of a single pair of girders was about 50 tons, which had been his constant impression and Kennard was fully aware that the weight was 50 tons. Gordon could never recall the weight being referred to as anything other than about 100 tons and also confirmed that no mention was ever made regarding the price per ton of iron.

Mellor then returned his line of questioning to the piers and the use of iron instead of brick or masonry. Gordon provided a summary of the development of their design and the eventual acceptance of Wild's suggestion of raking columns, leading up to Liddell having to report to the board a resultant increase in price. Gordon disagreed with Kennard's calculations and the amount of the increase in price, and sent Rumble to check the figures with Baldwin.

The next problem that Gordon faced was the difficulty the works at Falkirk were experiencing in casting the columns for the piers. Gordon and Kennard had a number of arguments over increasing the thickness of the casting and the resultant additional cost the latter was claiming. Gordon's point was if he had increased the weight he should have a diminished price. He was questioned in depth on the calculations leading up to the revised cost for the erection of the viaduct. He had agreed an allowance for the increased thickness in the columns, for the increase in the number of columns and for the use of extra iron in the foundations.

In the meantime, Kennard had reduced his demand to £39,105, whilst Gordon had calculated that the allowances he had agreed increased his final figure to £38,740. From a record in his diary, Gordon could confirm that Kennard visited his office on at least two occasions to discuss their respective calculations. The arbitrator asked Gordon if the draft of the report he was preparing for the board meeting was, as claimed by Kennard, '*never shown to Kennard until sometime after the meeting*'. Gordon replied that '*it had been shown to him many times, and the figures ultimately agreed were the figures mentioned in the contract ... Kennard never made any objection to these figures*'. He confirmed there had been a great deal of deliberation and thought over the figures, because it would have been neither his duty to Kennard nor to the directors if they had done it in a hurry. He thought that the deliberations took two or three months.

Before leaving the subject of the estimates, Mellor wanted to summarise the figures as nearly as he could but only succeeded in opening up the whole debate again, with accusations and counter accusations.

Attention then turned to the returns for the amount of iron actually brought to the viaduct site. Although the arbitrator considered it would not have much bearing on the present issue, Clarke considered it important in that it would appear that Kennard had not used more than his own estimate of the quantity of wrought iron. There was to be 260 tons in the piers and upon his own theory 800 tons in the girders, making a total of 1,060 tons but Gordon could never account for more than 992 tons. Kennard had previously accepted that he had not accounted for more than 600 tons on the site. After a series of statements from the arbitrator and the respective learned counsel, it was finally accepted that, in view of Gordon's statement that he had gone through all of the returns of other people, his evidence of 992 tons was allowed to stand.

This concluded the evidence presented by Gordon but Lloyd informed the arbitrator that he would like a little more time to consider whether he was able to continue to cross-examine Gordon in Kennard's absence. He had returned to America to continue his work as chief engineer of the Atlantic & Great Western Railroad. R.W. Kennard, his father, was to represent him whilst he was out of the country. The hearing was adjourned *sine die*.

A significant feature of the hearing was that none of the witnesses called by the plaintiff were familiar with the whole story. Baldwin was employed from the outset to prepare the drawing but was taken ill part way through the contract and had resigned; Wild, who had to check the drawings and calculations, was dead; Haynes, who replaced Baldwin and checked figures for the hearing, was not a qualified engineer and had little direct involvement with Crumlin; Hamilton, who had kept records of iron delivered, was dead; Sinclair was in Ceylon, whilst Maynard, who was on-site manager at Crumlin, was not called and nor were Kennard's brothers or father. Kennard had sworn an affidavit that Gordon was a material witness on his behalf but he appeared for the defence. Carr could not be cross-examined because he was working in India.

The details of meetings, actions and agreements, that went on behind the scenes after the hearing had been adjourned, were not made available to the public.

It was a notice from Kennard's solicitors in April 1859 that started the legal action against the West Midland Railway as successors of the NA&HR, and it may be considered appropriate that a letter from the company's solicitors to the chairman of the company was to bring the proceedings to a conclusion.[23] The letter, from Farquhar & Leech and dated 19th March 1861, was reported to the board of directors on 21st March 1861:

'Newport, Abergavenny & Hereford v Kennard
You will recollect that authority was given by the West Midland board to settle this matter for £46,000 being the amount we offered to Mr Kennard before the proceedings were commenced. The enquiry before the Arbitrator has been adjourned (after examining Gordon) until the return of Mr Kennard from America – meantime Mr Gordon has had some communication with Mr Kennard Sen. The result of which is that we find the whole matters in dispute may be settled for payment of £47,250, each party paying their own costs. Mr Kennard says he was put to an expense of £1,200 by raising money on the Company's Debentures and he insists that this sum should be added to the £46,000. Upon the whole we are inclined to think a settlement on these terms would be preferable to carrying on a protracted and expensive litigation the costs of which we think it probable would ultimately be cast upon the Company. The enclosed statement of figures will show you that the sum still to be paid to Mr Kennard on such settlement as before mentioned would be £4,362 7s 4d and which he would no doubt look for payment of on our early day.'

The board resolved *'that £47,000 be offered in full settlement of these claims'*.[24] Discussing the matter again in April, they resolved that *'the account in dispute between Messrs Kennard and the Company be referred to the chairman and Deputy chairman and Mr. Sherriff.'*.[25]

Reporting back in May, the board resolved that *'the sum of £5,592 3s 7d be paid to Messrs Kennard in settlement and full discharge of their claims upon the Company'*.[26]

The whole affair was brought to a conclusion on 5th June 1861, when Judge Charles Crompton determined that *'on hearing the Attornies and Agents on both sides and by Consent I do order all further proceedings in this action stayed'*.

References

1. Board meeting, 14th May 1859, minute No. 2592
2. Notice, 13th June 1859
3. Notice, 14th July 1859
4. Pritchard's report to the directors of 20th Oct. 1857
5. Dowdall's affidavit, 21st July 1857
6. Notice, 22nd July 1859
7. Notice, 25th July 1859
8. Letter, Meyrick & Gedge to Johnston, Farquhar & Leech, 27th July 1859
9. Letter, Johnston, Farquhar & Leech to Meyrick & Gedge, 28th July 1859
10. Judge's notice, 25th July 1859
11. Judge Martin Samuels Order of Reference, 2nd Aug. 1859
12. Letter, Johnston, Farquhar & Leech to Meyrick & Gedge, 12th Sept. 1859
13. Letter, Meyrick & Gedge to Gordon, 19th Sept. 1859
14. Letter, Gordon to Meyrick and Gedge, 20th Sept. 1859
15. Notice, 26th Oct. 1860
16. Notices, 11th Dec. 1860 and 4th Jan. 1861
17. Letter, 18th Oct. 1860, books and papers left on Kennard's table
18. Letter, Carr to Liddell, 13th Oct. 1853
19. Letter, Pritchard to Kennard, 17th July 1857
20. Letter, Kennard to Pritchard, 13th Aug. 1857
21. Letter, Pritchard to Kennard, 31st Aug. 1857
22. Letter, Kennard to Pritchard, 5th Sept. 1857
23. Notice, Meyrick & Gedge to Johnston, Farquhar & Leech 13th June 1859
24. Board meeting, 21st Mar. 1861, minute No. 388
25. Board meeting 18th Apr. 1861, minute No. 409
26. Board meeting 16th May 1861, minute No. 434 – this figure includes the £1,200 claimed by Kennard for loss on debenture stock and a small amount of interest. No mention is made of the £5,801 3s 0d set off

Plate 8.1: Standing on the siding into the works in this circa 1860 view are a pair of loaded, end-tipping, dumb-buffered, short wheelbase wagons belonging to the Brithdir Coal & Coke Company, which are coupled to an empty wagon of indecipherable provenance. Perhaps the works' steam engine used coke from this colliery. The MR&CC main line crosses the river in the foreground on its way down to Newport from Ebbw Vale. The route of the incline that had connected the works to the Upper Yard can just be seen climbing the valley side on the right, following the line of the works' roof to the drum house. The 1878 sale catalogue describes the dimensions of the incline winding drum as 5ft diameter and 4ft in width. The incline was probably little used or not at all by the time of this picture.
NEIL PARKHOUSE COLLECTION

THE VIADUCT WORKS

CHAPTER 8

From the time that the Viaduct Works had become operational, two separate and distinct manufacturing processes took place. The primary process was the preparation of ironwork for construction of the piers and girders, which were assembled at the site of the viaduct. The second process was the manufacture of switches, crossings, turntables and other railway apparatus. Analysis of the correspondence that flowed between the company, its engineers and Kennard reveals many of the problems faced and the friction that arose between the parties. Additional evidence of their fractious relationship is evident when considering exchanges over Kennard's other manufacturing processes, which involved making, assembling and delivering finished railway apparatus to the company.

Having secured the contract for constructing the viaduct, Kennard's first and essential requirement was the acquisition of land on which to construct workshops and to store iron. As early as December 1852, he was discussing his land needs with Carr. There was some urgency in identifying a suitable location, because Kennard had ordered for delivery within the next six months all of the iron he estimated would be required to fulfil the contract. Immediately after he had been notified that he had been awarded the contract, and ordered the iron, he discovered that the price of it had increased overnight. Delivery of the first 500 tons of his order was promised for January 1853, and fearful of further increases in the price, he was negotiating for a further 40,000 foot run in anticipation of securing other similar contracts.[1]

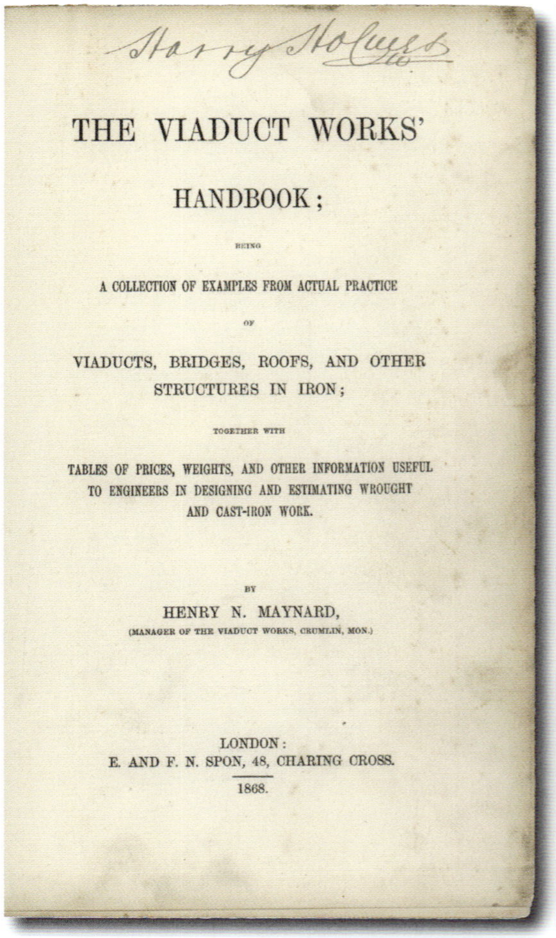

Harry Holmes

THE VIADUCT WORKS'

HANDBOOK;

BEING

A COLLECTION OF EXAMPLES FROM ACTUAL PRACTICE

OF

VIADUCTS, BRIDGES, ROOFS, AND OTHER STRUCTURES IN IRON;

TOGETHER WITH

TABLES OF PRICES, WEIGHTS, AND OTHER INFORMATION USEFUL TO ENGINEERS IN DESIGNING AND ESTIMATING WROUGHT AND CAST-IRON WORK.

BY

HENRY N. MAYNARD,

(MANAGER OF THE VIADUCT WORKS, CRUMLIN, MON.)

LONDON:
E. AND F. N. SPON, 48, CHARING CROSS.
1868.

PLATE 8.2: In 1868, Maynard published a profusely illustrated marketing book that celebrated the variety of work his business undertook. This is the title page.
STEPHEN ROWSON COLLECTION

PLATE 8.3: Alfred Pumphrey's view No. 1402, from the top of the eastern embankment, is by far the best seen to date showing the railway incline that connected the lower works to the upper works. The drum house can be seen in the lower works yard. The 1878 sale catalogue notes that the [horizontal] sheath [wheel] at the top of the incline for the wire rope was 8ft in diameter by 4ins in width, with double wrought iron arms [spokes]; also there were 59 sheaves [wheels] on the incline. The railway branch from Crumlin Junction down to Llanhilleth was opened on 3rd September 1855, serving an NA&HR goods depot. The connection to the Monmouthshire Railway's Western Valleys line at Llanhilleth opened just over six weeks later, on 20th October 1855, which then provided a direct rail connection into the Works' yard and it seems that the incline seen here began to fall out of use soon after that.
STEPHEN ROWSON COLLECTION

PLATES 8.4 & 8.5: Illustrations of trackwork that could be supplied by the Viaduct Works, from Maynard's book. The use of the term 'Switches' is interesting, as this is now considered an Americanism, with the term 'Points' being in general use in the UK.

Kennard had identified a suitable piece of land of about half of an acre from a local map. Ideally, he was looking for a piece of level ground 200 feet by 100 feet, which would accommodate a workshop 200 feet by 40 feet and costing about £280, along with an outside storage area 200 feet by 60 feet. If available, he anticipated asking John Rennie, the company's contractor, to prepare the ground and to lay rubble at 8 shillings per cubic yard.[2] The piece of land Kennard had identified was Blaencuffin Wharf at Canal Head, owned by Edward Kendall of Packingham Hall, Staffordshire. By February, he was negotiating the terms of a lease for this land with Kendall and for a portion of farmland occupied by a Mr Richards.[3]

However, this land also formed part of an area required by the NA&HR, who were, at that time, in an advanced stage of negotiations with Kendall for its purchase. Whether they met Kendall together is not clear but their assessment of him was that '*he was an astute and experienced negotiator*'. Kennard felt that Kendall was gloating over the prospect of him taking a short term lease, so that on completion of the contract the viaduct workshops and ground would revert to him. During his discussions with Liddell, Kennard suggested he erected the workshops on railway company land and use '*old Kendall's land*' for storage. Outwardly, Kennard was giving the impression at this stage, that he did not anticipate continuing with his business at this location on completion of the viaduct contract. He had also suggested that, at the conclusion of the contract, his workshops could be let to the Monmouthshire Railway & Canal Company, as an engine house (locomotive sheds).[4] Negotiations for the purchase of the land by the company had been completed at the beginning of April 1853, with Kendall having no objection to Kennard using the land for his purposes, as soon as '*money has been paid*'.[5]

With Kennard's activities not being confined to producing iron work for the viaduct, and operating from the workshops by mid-1853, he had been approached

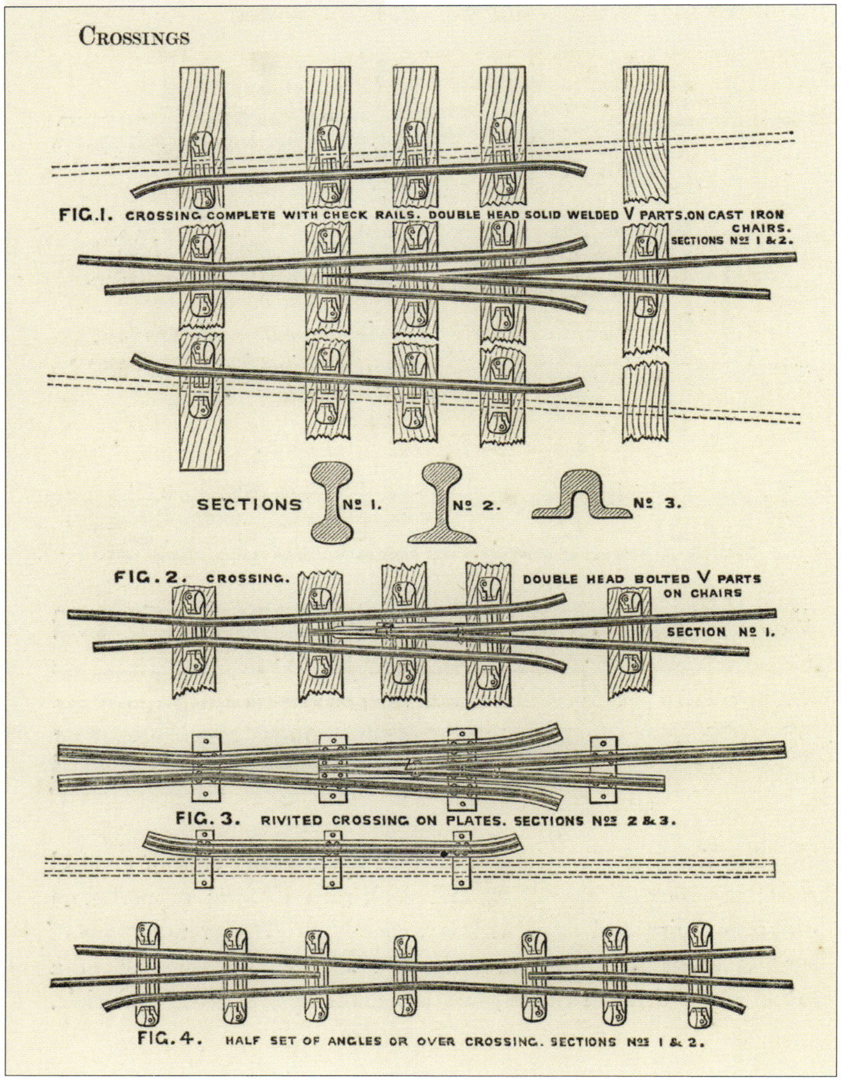

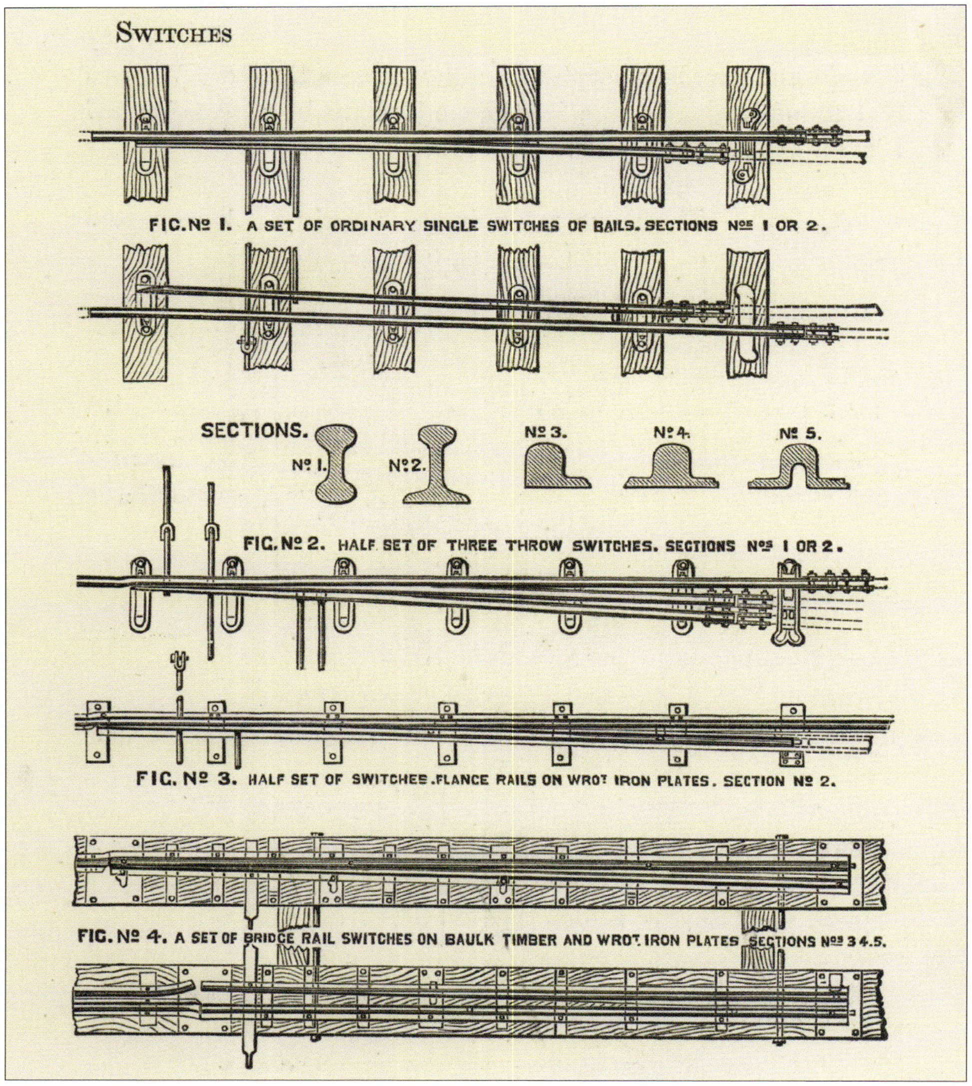

to provide a price for supplying railway apparatus for installation on the NA&HR's main line between Pontypool and Hereford.[6] Days later, Liddell confirmed an order in writing that included the delivery of:[7]

'10 no. ....12 foot turntables at £85 each
2 no. ....40 foot turntables in wrought iron at £380 each
6 no. ....water cranes 8 inch pipes at £30 each
3 no. ....tanks at £9 per tank
20 no.........switches main line at £20 17s per ton
20 no.........crossings main line at £20 17s per ton
30 no.........switches sidings at £18 17s per ton
30 no.........crossings sidings at £12 17s per ton

These items were close to the type of processes undertaken when Kennard was working for an iron foundry and manufacturing company in Manchester, and before he became involved with the Newark Dyke bridge in 1851.

Over the next five months, Kennard was being pressurised by Liddell and Pritchard to complete and deliver the ordered goods. It was during this period that he was shown to be poor at organisation, administration and management, leaving control of jobs to others and not accepting blame when things went wrong. The tone of letters and records of meetings held with Kennard illustrate how infuriated the board, Liddell, Pritchard and Carr were with him and they should have realised at this time the problems that they were likely to encounter during the construction of the viaduct.

Nothing had arrived by September and Liddell was getting nervous as to whether there would ever be any delivery. The management of the NA&HR had been making arrangements to open their main line by the end of October, with the Board of Trade inspection due to take place in the middle of the month. Liddell pointed out to Kennard that, without the items ordered, they would have to cancel all arrangements. He was also in trouble with Liddell over the supply of drums to be delivered to Plymouth and fixed by the beginning of August. At mid-September they were no further forward and delivery could not be expected for a further two weeks. Liddell was vexed because having introduced Kennard for the work on the Plymouth line, managers and engineers were all complaining

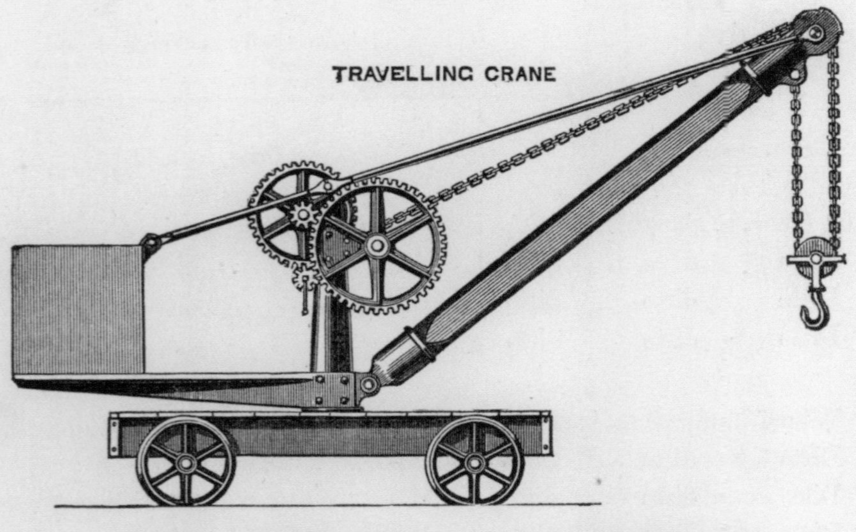

A crane, as above, to lift 2 tons, price about £40.
Ditto ditto 3 ditto £75.
Ditto ditto 5 ditto £110.

PLATES 8.6 & 8.7: *This stereo slide of the works is almost identical to that on page 44 but, with fewer workmen in the picture, more of the portable steam engine around which they are gathered can be seen. The canal was in an untidy state, possibly in use as a timber pond, for seasoning the timber before use. The crane can be compared with the drawing in Maynard's book of 1862,* LEFT, *although the one in the photograph has the wheels inside the frames.*
DAVID DICKINSON COLLECTION

PLATE 8.8: A fascinating study of workmen and boys posing around the remelting cupola furnace. This LSC photograph, taken in the summer of 1856, would have required those involved to remain still whilst the plate was exposed, hence the rather stiff poses and the slight blurring of the man sitting above left. From discovering these LSC stereographs in over some forty years of collecting, it seems fair to conclude that this was the most popular study for Victorian collectors.
STEPHEN ROWSON COLLECTION

to him, particularly with regard to the amount of evasive answers coming from the management at the Viaduct Works. Liddell expressed his feelings by stressing that '*it was not right that there should be so much delay about such a trifling job*' and it made him anxious regarding the delivery of items for the NA&HR's main line.[8] If the ordered items remained undelivered, there would be serious consequences if everything was not ready in time for the opening of their line, as large contracts had been entered into for transporting coal, coke and limestone. As far as Liddell could establish, the items had been promised for a September delivery but nothing had progressed beyond the purchase of materials, some still awaited.[9] Kennard blamed the late delivery of a planing machine, which had been damaged in transit.[10]

In the midst of all of the pressure being placed on him, Kennard wrote to Liddell asking for his assistance in the purchase of a further three acres of land that he wished to acquire, which was owned by Sir Benjamin Hall, a major landowner in the area. Kennard valued the land at £50 per acre to Hall but much more to himself, suggesting £250 per acre.[11]

During October, Pritchard started chasing Kennard, reminding him of the proposed opening date for the Pontypool to Hereford section of their line and the need to deliver their ordered goods. Pritchard was urging him to pay prompt attention to the order[12] but achieving, no reaction, in November Pritchard was chasing both Liddell and Kennard. To Liddell he requested immediate action. For the next board meeting, he proposed to report that none of the apparatus contracted to Kennard, due by September, had been delivered. The opening of the main line had been rearranged for 6th December 1853, with the Board of Trade inspection due on 10th November or soon after, and there would be serious consequences if by negligence or any other issue, the inspector's report delayed the opening of the line.[13] Pritchard wrote to Kennard reminding him that he had promised to let him know, from the Viaduct Works at Crumlin, the current situation on expected delivery of goods in July, and he was still waiting. He suggested to Kennard that it would be in his best interests at almost any cost to provide the items ordered without further delay. If not, he would be held personally responsible for any delay in the opening of their line on 6th December. Pritchard also pointed out that, '*every day's delay was estimated to amount to a £40 loss in revenue and subsequently would affect dividends that would place the directors in an awkward position*'.[14]

Liddell was getting even more forthright with his demands and complaints and at one stage he was '*wanting to know*' what arrangements had been made for the supply of his ordered water cranes, as he had been told that '*those at Crumlin were being manufactured for someone else*'. At Abergavenny he had seen '*a villainous fixed ring turntable of the most commonest possible construction*'. It was the first that had been delivered from the Viaduct Works and Liddell was '*really vexed to have such a thing on the line*', pointing out that he could have done much better by '*borrowing old tables from Euston for temporary use*'. He finished by reminding Kennard that '*in spite of promises the switches and crossings had not been delivered*'.[15]

Pritchard was getting nowhere, and in his next communication told Kennard that '*the Station Committee were surprised at the delay in the delivery of the goods ordered and those items having been sent were not of sufficient quantity to meet their needs. If the Government Inspector, when going over the line refuses a certificate, the blame and responsibility will rest with you*'.[16] Kennard's response was to blame all of the delay on the difficulties he had experienced in the supply of iron.[17] A week later, Pritchard was to contact Kennard whilst he was on holiday and, apologising for doing so, he then pointed out that nothing had been delivered and events had become a serious matter: '*Permit me to call you from your retreat back to Crumlin works to remedy this grievance to greatest authority in your power*'. He pointed out that nothing would prevent them from opening their line on 6th December but if afterwards the London & North Western Railway refused to work the line because of the lack of the necessary apparatus, officially or unofficially, then the blame would be Kennard's – '*for your own sake if not ours I beseech you to be at your post doing all that under the circumstances can be done*'.[18] Pritchard was to follow this with a further threat: '*It is my duty to warn you that if the opening is delayed by breach of your contract the directors will hold you responsible for the damage they will sustain*'. He also mentions that '*only two sets of switches and crossings had been delivered to site and that these were incomplete and consequently useless*'.[19]

At the same time, Kennard was suggesting that information being received by Liddell and Pritchard was incorrect. He claimed that '*with my own eyes I have seen the material in question leave the works*'. He promised to deliver what was outstanding, '*if even at the eleventh hour it is not my fault*'. He blamed his difficulties on obtaining rails but from his own information claimed that the switches and crossings may not be fixed, although '*a considerable number were on the ground*'.[20]

Liddell was furious and contradicted Kennard's claims, his own observations and reports from Carr and contractor Rennie confirming that the switches and crossings had not been delivered. Liddell suggested that '*if the statements made by you are from reports from your people at Crumlin I can only say that you are grossly deceived*'.[21] After all of the complaints and threats, Kennard finally admitted that he had made a number of mistakes resulting in constant delays and unfulfilled promises. His first was accepting the order for the Plymouth drums and the second was taking the contract for the switches and crossings at the Viaduct Works. Kennard admitted that the Plymouth drums were dreadful but blamed the workmen. He reasoned that he had used the same superintendent and tools that he had employed for years and '*felt that I was in a position to do again what I had done before, I was wrong*', his excuse being delays in the supply of materials, and difficulties in finding men to work the machines. Kennard was to declare that '*he was often in a position where the tools were lying idle because of a difficulty in finding the labour force*'. Besides doing the engineering work, wagons for Kennard's own contractual use were being produced at the works. At one stage he blamed a delay in the delivery of goods on the neglect of his superintendents to provide carts, to the extent that in the end he was forced to hire in farmers' carts.[22]

Whilst Kennard continued to fulfil existing and new contracts to supply apparatus to the NA&HR, he was developing the Viaduct Works at Crumlin. During 1853, three large workshops had been built on land below the proposed viaduct and Kennard's '*intelligent and scientific manager Mr Archibald Sinclair, had received instructions, to proceed – as rapidly as possible – with still more extensive works to make this place the chief depot for the manufacture*

Plate 8.9: Something of a strange choice of view again, to be offered for sale by the LSC, showing an untidy works yard, depicting the Pooley table weighing machine and the lever testing apparatus, both of which were still present in the 1878 auction sale catalogue. Stephen Rowson collection

PLATE 8.10: Taken in summer 1856, we cannot be sure who these people are, posing for the photographer across the canal but close study of the gent sat with the little girl on his knee – and comparison with the photograph on page 26 – suggests that it could be Tom Kennard. He had married Octavia Smale in 1847 and they had three children, all girls, the last, Evelyn, born in December 1855; she could be the very young child seated on his knee, with the two older girls and his wife on either side. The Monmouthshire Railway & Canal Company board is headed Public Notice but is otherwise indecipherable and behind it is the railway company's timber-built goods shed. Crumlin station is off to the left, whilst the wagons in the right background are alongside the tramroad wharf, where they have been loaded with coal brought down from Trinant Colliery.
STEPHEN ROWSON COLLECTION

of machinery etc, necessary for other speculations'[23] – a complete change from earlier statements.

In spite of all of the delays, the NA&HR opened their line with due ceremony on Tuesday 6th December 1853, with a special train from Newport that arrived at Hereford at 1.00 pm. It consisted of thirty coaches hauled by three locomotives and carried 640 passengers, whilst an estimated crowd of 20,000 awaited their arrival.

A week after the opening, Liddell was still chasing the delivery of switches and crossings. As he pointed out, '*delivery was still slow and it was prohibiting the opening of the line*'. He had written to Kennard: '*The whole blame must be thrown on your delay. How you mean to justify this to the Company I don't know, but myself I can fairly say that I have never known promises so entirely disregarded*'.[24] In the meantime, the NA&HR were forced to delay the opening of their line for public use until Monday, 2nd January 1854. Much to Kennard's relief, it is generally accepted that this was due to an extensive land slip at Llanvihangel Crucorny, twenty miles south of Hereford. To what extent the delay was also due to the late supply of switches and crossings for completing turnouts from the main line is not possible to quantify but during this period and after, Liddell was still chasing their delivery. Many of them were required for the station and sidings at Barton, Hereford. Again Kennard was blaming his workforce, this time

Sinclair, who he suspended for, as he put it, '*telling lies*'. On discovering that Sinclair had left the area, Kennard then admitted that he should have, '*dismissed him*'. In Sinclair's place, he had appointed a new manager, Henry Nathan Maynard, '*a first rate man*', although in the *Monmouthshire Merlin* newspaper, he was described as a draughtsman.[25]

Whilst the relationship between the two men was strained over the delivery of switches and crossings for the company's main line, as well as the publicity he was getting in the local press, Kennard had also upset Liddell over the reports covering the erection of the first column in pier No. 4 in December. This was followed by a report in the *Monmouthshire Merlin*, describing the development of the works, their activities and prospects for enticing the further development of the area. It was reported that three large buildings had been erected immediately below the line of the viaduct and that other works had been planned to establish them as Kennard's main manufacturing base. One of the workshops contained a large steam engine, which provided the energy to drive the lathes and other machinery. The reporter anticipated that there would be a large influx of population, forecasting that this could total to 300-400 workmen and their families. Such an increase would, in his opinion, develop Crumlin from a small hamlet into a town. It was rumoured that Kennard was planning to provide comfortable cottages and residences for the workmen and their families.

Weeks later, the *Monmouthshire Merlin* included a report on a Christmas treat that Kennard had provided for his workmen and invited guests at the works. The gathering was held in the assembly room at the new foundry which housed the large steam engine. At a long table sat 200 men, and a decorated dais was positioned at one end for invited guests and works managers. They were all served '*roast beef of old England*' with all of the necessary accompaniments and plum pudding swilled down with

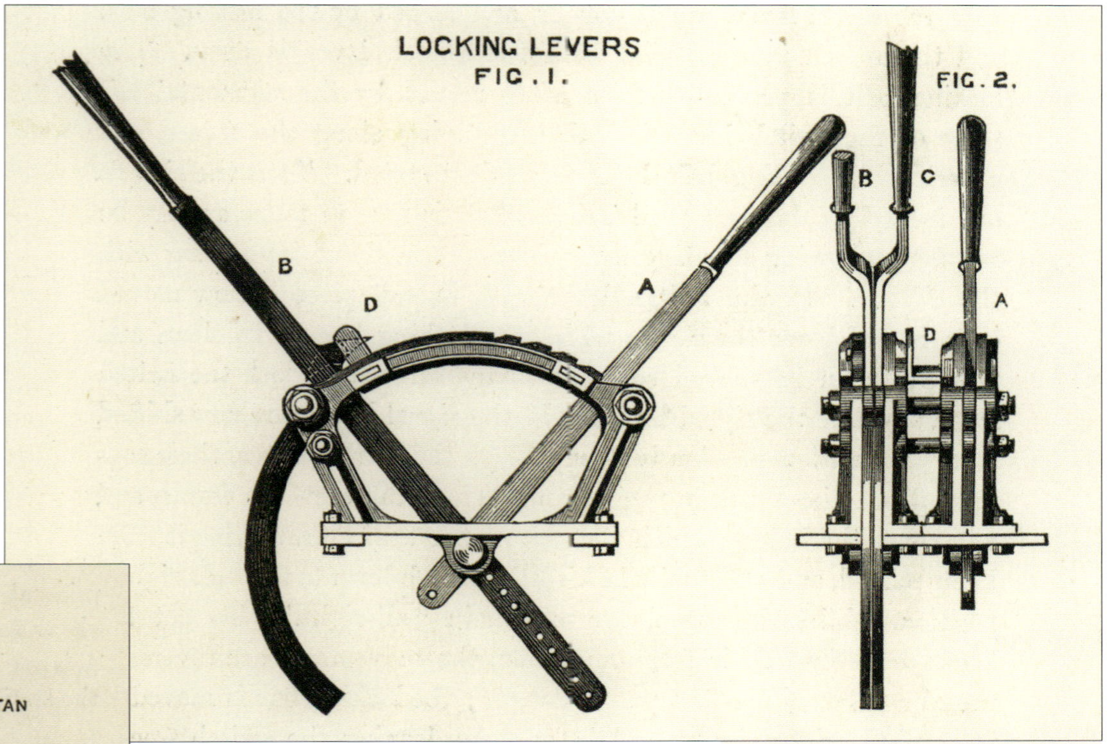

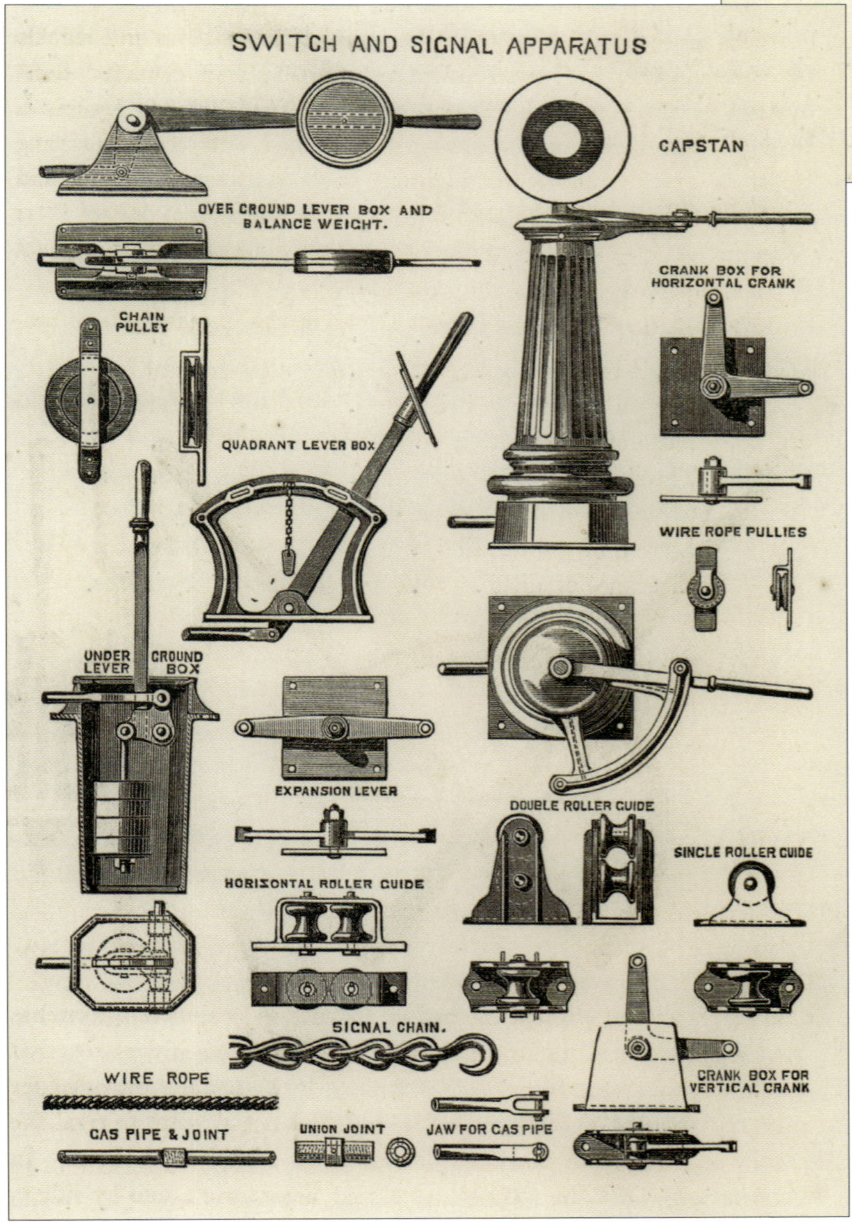

PLATES 8.11 & 8.12: Examples of further railway related products from the Viaduct Works, all for use with signals and switches (points). The manufacture of these items was almost certainly a result of the Works' 1873 agreement to produce signalling levers and locking apparatus based on the patents of Easterbrook & Co. Walter John Easterbrook (1841-1914) was an innovative signalling engineer who worked for Saxby & Farmer but left in 1867 to set up his own business. Easterbrook never had a factory, using various firms to manufacture his equipment, hence his 1873 agreement with the Viaduct Works. His company failed in 1885 after he lost a test case implying patent infringement against the GWR, who were awarded substantial damages.

PLATES 8.13 & 8.14: *The Viaduct Works design for a standard railway water crane,* TOP, *and one mounted on a water tower,* BOTTOM.

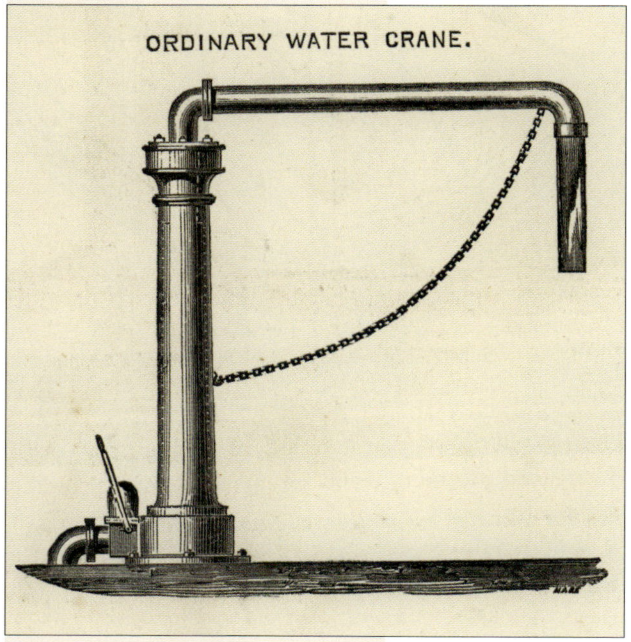

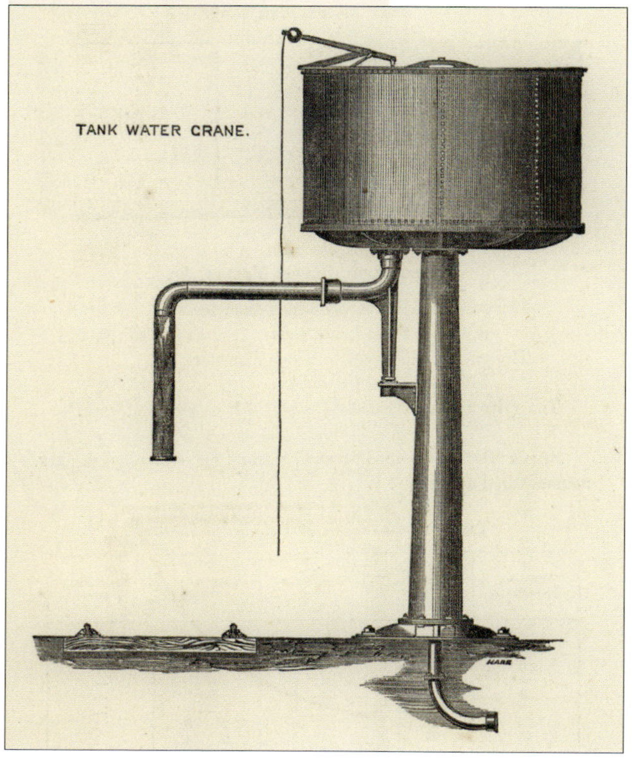

tankards full of '*cwrw da*' (good beer). During his address to the workmen, Kennard announced that, '*any workman then engaged on the viaduct works on 1st January 1854 and remaining until work had been completed would be presented with a commemorative silver medal bearing the workman's name*'.[26] However, no evidence has been found to indicate that this was ever carried out.

Whilst the relationship between Kennard and Liddell had been at a low ebb at the end of 1853, during 1854 Carr was being forced into continual conflict with him over poor workmanship, the late deliveries of iron and castings and other ordered apparatus, and the issue of certificates. Kennard was continually asking for the latter for switches and crossings above the value that Carr was prepared to authorise; he often allowed only 50% of what Kennard was requesting, due mainly to the late deliveries. In January, Carr had reported that Kennard had made a mistake in setting out the masonry in the foundations to the piers. He next discovered, in February, that there was a problem in the casting of the columns from top to bottom of the viaduct,[27] writing to Kennard to press on him to undertake a systematic examination of all castings and to report on the problem. This appears to have been a lack of consistency in the thickness of the flanges at the base and top of each column. On the advice of Professor Gordon, Carr was to condemn any column with a flange thickness of $^1/_2$ an inch or under – they should have had a minimum average of $^7/_8$th inch.[28]

From April, orders were still being placed by the company and Kennard appeared to be spending more time and paying more attention to the manufacturing processes at the Viaduct Works. Carr, writing to Liddell, suggested that if Kennard continued '*to improve a little longer I shall be proud of him*'.[29] Recognising the situation, Liddell wanted Kennard to provide a report on the state of the work, preparation of parts and an estimated time for completion, adding '*We wish very much to have the work pushed forward*'.[30]

A further setback occurred in May when, as discussed previously, problems were discovered relating to the diagonal braces in the piers, Kennard having specified the wrong details and sizes to the foundry at Falkirk. Liddell suggested a compromise and wrote to Carr, adding '*The work on part of the contractor inspires me with no confidence in him*'.[31]

Some of the slow progress on the viaduct was not of Kennard's making – his father, on a visit to Crumlin, was '*exceedingly annoyed that castings from his Falkirk works had not arrived*'. He was sure that, apart from 20-30 tons, the whole of the order had been completed. According to Kennard's brother, Arthur, they had been laying awaiting shipment for two months but 100 tons had been loaded and were on their way, and he expected them to arrive at Newport within a week.[32]

A letter from Gordon to Carr in July sheds some light on the perceived relationship between the company and Kennard. Prior to the lifting of the first girder, Gordon forwarded to Carr documents and calculations for positioning loads on the girder, and how the test should be carried out. He also provided an interesting observation: '*I think Mr Kennard has no loophole by which to escape from making a workmanlike job save a confession of inability to meet his engagements which he is not likely to make without a struggle to avoid the necessity of doing so*'.[33]

Kennard, however, was in high spirits at this time and writing to Carr, he stated that '*Nothing is wanting, every tool is steadily at work and fully up to what is required to complete the viaduct in five months*', i.e. December 1854. The friction between Kennard and Liddell would appear to have still remained, as he was asking Carr to report his comments on to Liddell, '*as he knew he had not been pleased with the progress being made*'.[34]

It was at this time that Kennard was so short of money that he mortgaged his workshops and equipment to the company for £5,000. Under the terms of the deed, to be endorsed on the contract, Kennard agreed that the company were entitled to the possession and occupation of the workshops, sheds and other buildings, including engines, machinery, tools, utensils and implements. He was not allowed to let any part of the buildings or the use of machinery until the completion of the contract, when the workshops and machinery would revert to him.[35] What at first was seen as a simple contract between

Kennard and the company became more complicated when it was learned that he had occupied and made use of land belonging to a third party – he had not signed a lease for the land. When eventually signed, the lease was for twenty-one years, renewable then every twenty-one years up to a maximum of seventy-five years; for the first period, the rent was £70 paid quarterly, for what was described as *'all of the wharf land and premises called Blaencuffin Wharf ... land adjoining with manufacturing workshops, sheds, erections, and premises erected and built and all other premises if any'.* Under the terms of the mortgage agreement with the company, Kennard was to repay the £5,000 with interest at 5% by 18th May 1855. If he failed to comply with the deed, the company had the power to sell the land, workshops and buildings by public auction or private contract. The buildings and machinery were to be insured for £3,000, at least and if he failed to insure the property, the company could do so and charge the costs to him. The mortgage deed was agreed and dated 18th November 1854.

Switches, crossings, water tanks and other items were being ordered from the works throughout 1854 and 1855. In January 1855, Kennard agreed to make the girders for a boiler plate bridge, in accordance with outline drawings supplied by Carr, and to deliver the completed bridge to the nearest point to a site on the Crumlin to Pontypool road. Kennard's price was to be £20 per ton payable in cash on delivery at the site.[36] The purpose of the works, to be known as the Clarence Road Bridge, was to carry the Eastern Valleys line over the Taff Vale Extension near Pontypool Clarence Road station. The on site engineering works were to be undertaken by the company's main contractor, John Rennie.

The difficulty in obtaining horses to transport finished goods to site was a continual source of annoyance to Maynard and Kennard. In March, both were complaining that there was £500 worth of switches and crossings awaiting delivery and the Clarence Road Bridge was completed but they could not obtain horses to move it to the Western Valleys line for transshipment.[37] Kennard was still attempting to obtain the use of horses at the beginning of April.[38] Today, we are accustomed to the efficient transportation of goods by road vehicles covering large distances along surfaced highways, and it is sometimes easy to forget that the movement of many of the manufactured goods for the construction and early development of the railway network during the 19th century, depended entirely upon horse-drawn wagons or carts.

Towards the end of March, Kennard was quoting for the further supply of switches and crossings for the company. The prices were accepted by Carr, who ordered a supply of such, including rails and nuts. On completion of the Clarence Road Bridge, Kennard asked Carr if he needed any more of this style of bridge, because he found the works could *'make them very well and cheaply'*,[39] finding that they could be produced for less per ton than the viaduct. The weight of the bridge worked out to be 23 tons. His price for a similar bridge with 60 foot girders would be £10 per foot run.[40] Carr

PLATE 8.15: *Design for a warehouse crane, with a wooden post and jib, for internal use. Cranes such as this were installed inside railway goods sheds.*

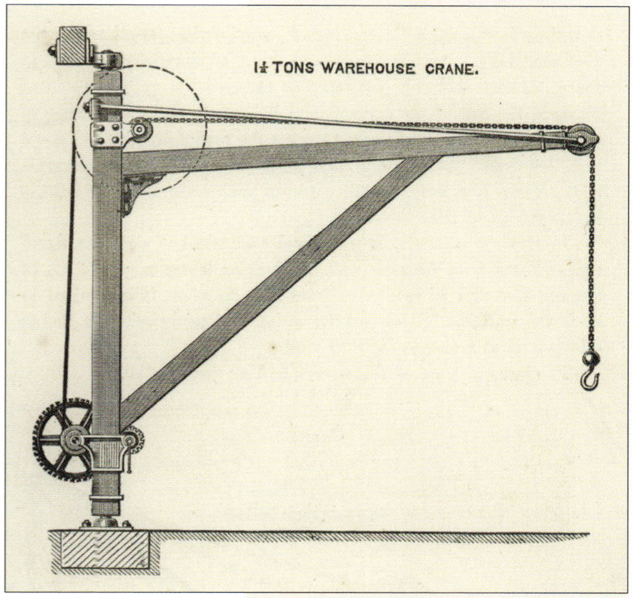

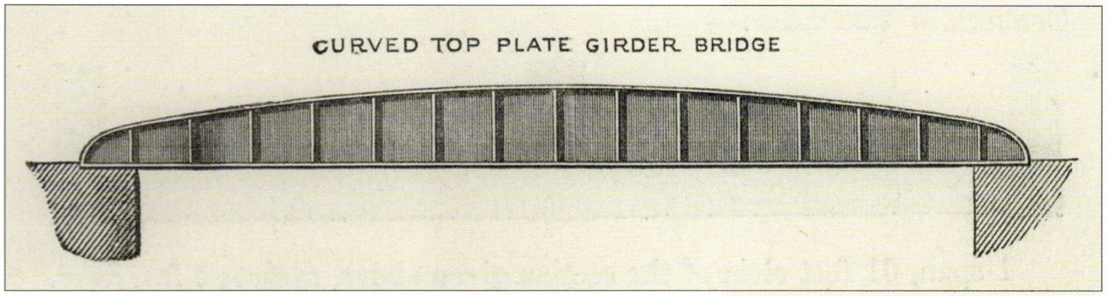

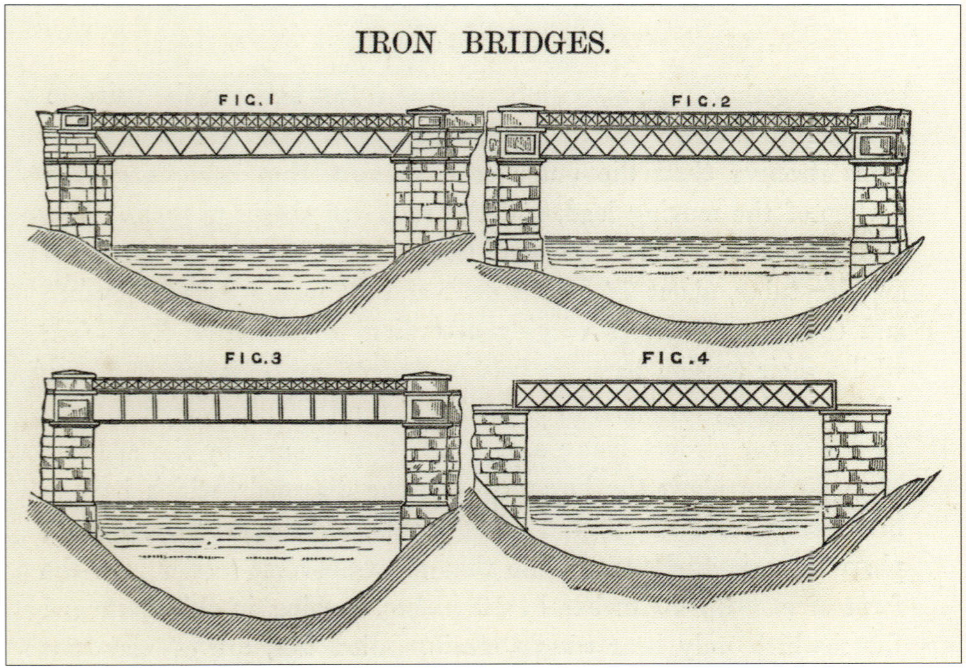

PLATES 8.16 & 8.17: *The Viaduct Works catalogue offered a large range of designs for wrought iron bridge spans.*

PLATE 8.18: A pre-First World War view of Pontypool Clarence Street station, on the NA&HR's Taff Vale Extension line. In the background is the bridge carrying the Eastern Valleys line over the TVE, supplied by the Viaduct Works and which was criticised by BoT inspector Captain Tyler for not being of sufficient strength. NEIL PARKHOUSE COLLECTION

asked Kennard to delay forwarding the bridge because he wanted some holes punched in the girders. Precise details in writing were not provided and Carr received a note in June that nothing had been done on boring the holes on the girders.[41] At the same time that Kennard had agreed to retain the bridge and bore the holes, he was expressing his delight about the capabilities of the new planing machine he had installed at the works. He anticipated that it would improve the production of switches and crossings, and he would welcome an order for a further 100 sets.

The Taff Vale Extension line from Pontypool to Crumlin Junction was inspected on behalf of the Board of Trade by Captain H.W. Tyler on 16th August 1855. He was not entirely happy with the strength of the Clarence Road Bridge, reporting that it was composed of three girders for carrying two lines of rails. He observed that it appeared to be a tolerably strong one but with the greatest load that was likely to travel over it, he thought the compression per square inch at the top in the centre girder and the tensile force at the bottom in all of the girders would be greater than desirable, as they would respectively exceed five and six tons.

A bridge across the River Shannon in Ireland was also causing Kennard problems. On his return from a visit to Ireland, in a note to Carr he wrote '*I hope now we shall make a finish of this infernal bridge*'. It had been designed and supplied from the Viaduct Works for the Limerick, Ennis & Killaloe Railway but the line failed early inspections because this long bridge over the River Shannon was found to be very unsafe and was reported to have been one of the worst bridges ever built. An inspector decided that it would be unsafe according to the drawings, whilst Kennard claimed that it had been built to another plan but when examined it complied with neither. The inspector considered it essential that the bridge be reconstructed but, in the end, more props were inserted and it was sanctioned for public use in November 1858. The railway company threatened to sue Kennard and the bridge was eventually replaced in 1909.

Water cranes installed at Abergavenny were a familiar

source of complaint, with Carr reminding Kennard at every opportunity that they had never been completed. A new one had been broken during its erection and never finished, and the valves on it were left *'leaking miserably'*. Carr threatened to employ his own men to complete the job and charge the expense to him. However, before doing so he suggested that Kennard's foreman meet the company's inspector and see for himself. In his response, he claimed that the fixing of water towers was not in his contract.[42]

Orders continued to be placed for railway associated apparatus with the works during the first months of 1855. Those switches and crossings ordered from March onwards were based on a sample set submitted by Carr. Other orders included the supply of 40 foot turntables, obtained by Kennard from Manchester. Although he was asking for tracings for the foundations, when questioned about late delivery to the various sites, he countered that it was not in his contract to fix the tables but *'he would take steps to send the necessary men to fix them'*. In one note to Kennard, Carr was reminding him of his comments when placing the last order – *'please to get the 14 underway as soon as possible'*.[43] By June, Carr was chasing Kennard and Maynard to provide the company with delivery dates for all of the items ordered and at one stage, Carr warned him that he would *'hold him bound not to go on disappointing the Company in such a needless manner and to get assistance from wherever you can to make up the deficiency'*. Kennard's excuse to the late delivery was *'a difficulty in the supply of iron due to the breakage of a roller at the iron works, a breakage to an arm on a lifting crane, that he was in Ireland at the time, and the shortage of horses'*.

Things could not get worse for the works when Carr discovered that some of the switches had been made curving to the right instead of turning to the left. This was followed by him accusing the works of turning out switches in a most *'extraordinary slovenly manner'*. Carr did not believe that Kennard's workmen appreciated the care required in producing switches, crossings and turntables and that better supervision was required. He asked Kennard to put the matter *'on a proper footing for me at once'*. Irrespective of these failings, Carr continued to place orders with the works and Kennard was asking for even more, as he wanted to keep the men together.[44] During the next few months, over seventy-five orders were placed at the works.

Carr wrote to Kennard at the end of December to inform him that, at the end of the year, he would hand over control for all of the stock in the points and crossings account to the company's storekeeper, Mr Gardiner, along with all outstanding orders. He asked Kennard to stop all deliveries and to let him have a list of orders outstanding. He would then withdraw those orders and reissue them in Gardiner's name and to whom all future orders were to be delivered.[45]

When making enquiries into the delivery of axle boxes and moulding boxes for the brass foundry, Carr was being told repeatedly that *'they had not come from Kennard yet'*. One can imagine his frame of mind when he wrote to Kennard *'Oh what weary gulf that will obtrude itself between the promise and the performance of even the best of men. How much longer will it take to cross it on this occasion?'*.[46]

Two years after signing the mortgage deeds, Kennard wrote to the company requesting their return. He claimed that he had made frequent applications for their return through the company's solicitors but they replied that they had received no instructions.[47] At their next meeting, the board resolved that *'the release be given of the mortgage of Mr Kennard to this Company'*.[48] A draft indenture was prepared by the company's solicitors and dated 31st December 1856. It stated that the £5,000 loan plus interest had been repaid to the company, and that

PLATE 8.19: *Directors of the Crumlin Viaduct Works pose with the directors of the London Stereoscopic Company at Crumlin. They are thought to be, from left to right, Howard John Kennard, George Swan Nottage, Thomas William Kennard and his father Robert William Kennard. A coloured version of this stereo slide was also issued, which is reproduced in the chapter on the LSC.*
STEPHEN ROWSON COLLECTION

in surrendering and yielding the document the company had not undertaken any works that would hinder the return of the premises to Kennard.

Kennard's brother HMK along with an unidentified gentleman called at the company offices in early 1857 and left a message that they would like the return of the deeds, because they had acquired the Viaduct Works but absolute ownership could not be signed until such time as the deeds were returned to them.[49] Under their ownership, the works were extended with the construction of an iron foundry on adjoining land, to which direct rail access was available from the Taff Vale Extension's Llanhilleth Branch. From this time on, all orders and correspondence was directed to the Kennard Brothers.

From late 1858, Kennard spent most of his time in America. In November 1858, *The Illustrated London News* reported that T.W. Kennard and George Francis Train had arrived in New York on the Cunard Line paddle steamship *Persia*, and had gone prospecting for railways in the west. Train was mostly concerned with street tramways but Kennard's interest would have been the Atlantic & Great Western Railroad Company of Pennsylvania (A&GWRR), formed earlier that year with the objective of constructing lines to Ohio and Pennsylvania.

However, difficulty was experienced in raising the required capitol and to overcome the problem, a deputation visited Europe to sell bonds and purchase iron. Don Jose de Salamanca, a Spanish nobleman and financier, came to the financial aid of the A&GWRR, and Birkenhead businessman James McHenry also agreed to invest in the company provided Kennard surveyed the route.

Kennard returned to England in 1859 to give evidence in the action he had brought against the NA&HR over the construction of the viaduct at Crumlin. He then went back to America in 1860, to take up the post of chief engineer of what became known as the Atlantic & Great Western Railroad of New York (A&GWRRNY), following the company's acquisition of the Erie & New York City Railroad, which was to run for 369 miles from Great Valley, New York to Dayton, Ohio. Construction began in May 1860. Great Valley was renamed Salamanca and a small settlement called Tyler Town was renamed Kennard to honour the financier and engineer. The first train from New York reached Jamestown, 33 miles away, on 25th August 1860 and a dinner was arranged for a few invited guests, including Kennard.

In January 1861, Kennard had returned to England to give evidence at the arbitration hearing, in support of

Plate 8.20: *As well as extolling the range of products that the Viaduct Works could manufacture, Maynard's book also included numerous examples of impressive bridges that they had supplied the ironwork for. This is the Velletri Viaduct in Italy, near Rome, which carried a double line of railway 185ft above the deep valley of the Rio Piscari. The wrought iron girders were supported on two decorative cast iron piers and the total length of the bridge, including the masonry abutments and arches, was 600ft. It was replaced by a five-arch masonry viaduct in 1892.*

A NEW AMERICAN YACHT.

New York, says a letter from that city, is undergoing a great revival on the subject of yachting. Clubs are to be formed and club-houses erected; challenges are to be issued to the world, and prizes accorded to the champions. Several of the leading people here have lately built fine yachts, which accounts for this new excitement. The following is a description of one of them:—

The new and beautiful steam yacht Octavia—named after the owner's lady—has been fitting at Allison's Yard, Jersey City, for ocean as well as coast and sound service. Mr. Allison is finishing her cabins with curled maple, rosewood, holly, satinwood, and other hard woods capable of taking a polish. The mirrors and upholstery work generally will be in the highest possible taste and excellence. The Octavia was built at Cleveland, Ohio, for Mr. Kennard, Superintendent of the Atlantic and Great Western Railroad Company, by Messrs. Peck and Masters. She is schooner-rigged, and is constructed in the most substantial manner, entirely of American wood, principally white oak, with combings and finishings of hard pine, cherry, curled maple, black walnut, &c., all of which were transported over the Atlantic and Great Western road. She is of 430 tons burden, 146 feet length, 25 feet breadth, 14 feet depth, with 250 nominal and 700 actual horse power. She is calculated to consume at the rate of one and a quarter pounds of coal per horse power per hour, and with two hundred tons of coal on board can make the circuit of the globe. Her propeller is nine feet six inches in diameter, with four feet six inches pitch. Her engines are constructed upon an improved plan—the invention of Mr. Kennard. They are a combination of both the low and high pressure styles—a union of the locomotive and marine descriptions—making the vessel, with her estimated rate of speed of fourteen to eighteen knots, a sort of locomotive on water. The engines have a surface condenser, calculated to use steam at the rate of seventy-five pounds to the inch. Dimensions of cylinders, high pressure, eighteen by eighteen inches; low pressure, thirty-six by eighteen inches. The cylinders are connected, and move on a beam. The steam first goes into the small cylinder, and, after having performed its functions there, goes into the larger one, and thence into the surface condenser, where it is returned to the boiler at a temperature of about one hundred and twenty-five degrees. The boilers are of the ordinary marine tubular kind, with about two thousand feet heating surface. All the machinery was manufactured at the works of the Atlantic and Great Western Railroad Company, Jersey City. The Octavia has two cabins—the state cabin forward, officers' cabin aft. The state rooms and saloons are forward, with pantries, closets, store-room, &c., together with a children's nursery, which is supplied with all family conveniences. She can handsomely accommodate about twenty guests, without interfering with the quarters of the officers. Her complement of crew will be fifteen men. Although a purely American notion, being constructed entirely of American material, and her seams sealed as if with some purely American hermetic solution, she will sail under British colours. Mr. Kennard, however, before going to Europe, intends her to pass the coming summer in American waters, where she will doubtless prove an attractive and agreeable feature in our forthcoming regattas and yachting cruises. The Octavia is estimated to be worth $150,000.

his action to recover money he claimed was due to him from the NA&HR regarding the costs involved in the construction of Crumlin Viaduct.

He was back in America by the summer of 1861, to discover that work on the A&GWRRNY had been held up due to a lack of capital, remaining in abeyance until the autumn of 1862. On 25th October 1862, Kennard organised a special excursion train that ran from Meadville, Pennsylvania to Jamestown and back, and consisted of an engine and two new passenger cars. Refreshments were provided, as required, and it was reported that the day's activities ended with three hearty cheers for Thomas Kennard, *'for whose superior business qualifications and unflagging industry they were mainly indebted for the active prosecution and prospective completion of the line'*. However, the railway company went into receivership on 1st April 1867 and Kennard lost his job, returning to England.

Whilst in America, Kennard spent money lavishly; in 1865, he fitted out a steam craft, rigged as a top sail schooner, valued at 150,000 dollars, naming it *Octavia* after his wife. The steam engines powering the craft were reported to have been invented by Kennard.

Plate 8.21: *The Cunard Line paddle steamer* Persia, *on which Kennard sailed in America in November 1858.*

Fig. 8.1: *Detailed decription of Kennard's yacht* Octavia, *from* The Globe, *14th April 1865.*

Plate 8.22: *This engraving is thought to be the only known illustration of Kennard's white-hulled, lavishly appointed steam yacht* Octavia. *It is shown on the James River in March 1865, exchanging gun salutes with Fort Powhatan. This was during the time of the American Civil war and Kennard had ventured into what was a war zone with his vessel and party of guests, in the rather optimistic belief that the Union flag they were flying protected them from artillery fire from the banks, whilst sailing up a river which was strewn with mines! He was rebuked by the Federal authorities but they continued onwards, reaching the ruined city of Richmond, Virginia, before making it back out again safely. After reportedly living beyond his means for some years, his US estate and the* Octavia *were sold around 1869 to pay off debts.*

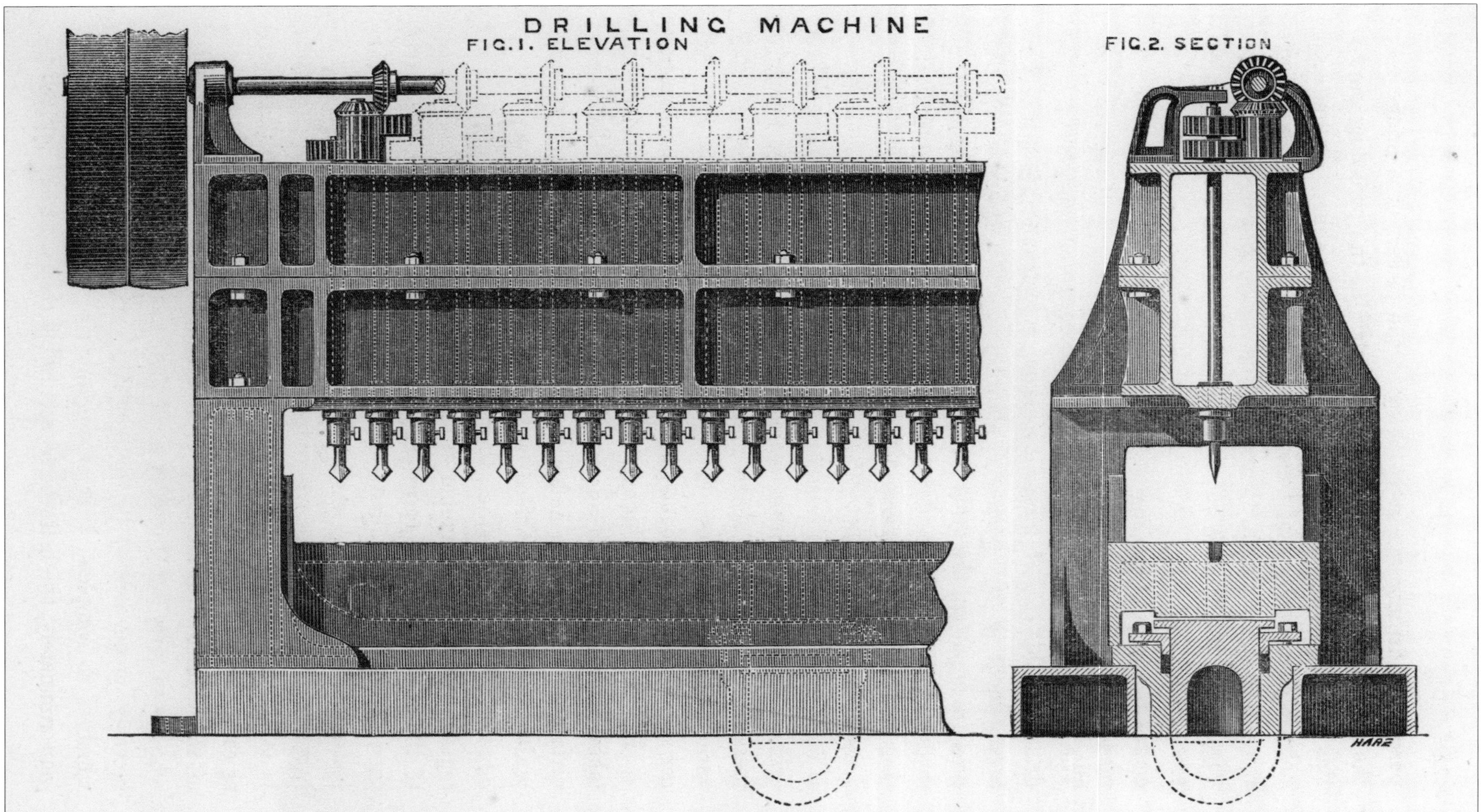

Plates 8.23 & 8.24: Kennard's own design of drilling machine, Above, was used in the works during manufacture for the viaduct. This ability to design and fabricate their own machines, required in the various manufacturing processes, led to the production of numerous other examples, such as the rivetting machine, Right. Unfortunately, little is known in regards to how many of these types of machines were made and sold, or indeed whether any have survived anywhere.

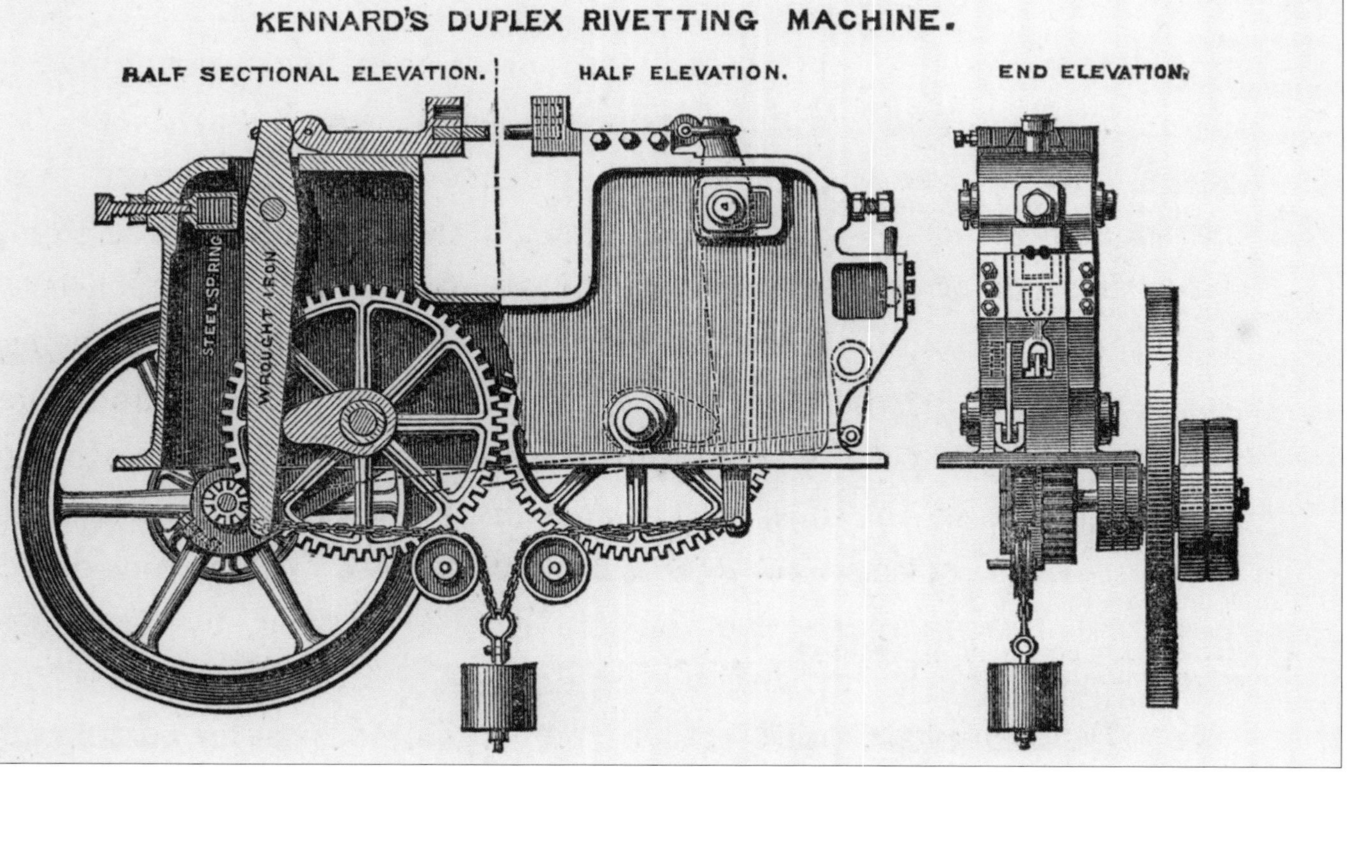

During the management of the works by the Kennard Brothers, their younger brother Howard John moved there after gaining experience at the family businesses at Falkirk and Blaenavon, and the Viaduct Works continued to export bridges all over the world. These included the Barrakur Bridge crossing the Barrakur River in India. Made on the Kennard and Warren principle, it was a bridge of ten spans of 150 feet each, with a total length of 1,650 feet, and was designed in such a manner that it could be assembled entirely with nuts and bolts,

PLATE 8.25, ABOVE: One of five spans fabricated for the Murray River Bridge in Australia.

PLATE 8.26, RIGHT: The Murray River Bridge in 2006. Built in 1873-79, the river piers go down to depths of up to 110ft, which made construction very difficult, whilst the height above water had to be raised from 20ft to 30ft to provide clearance for river steamers. In 1886 a railway was also laid across it, with the bridge being joint road/rail up until 1925, when the new railway bridge was built alongside. In 1981, it was added to the South Australia Heritage Register as a State Heritage Place.

PLATE 8.27, BELOW: The Viaduct Works supplied the ironwork, including the cast iron support columns, for the LC&DR's bridge spanning the River Thames at Blackfriars, shown in this engraving in Maynard's book.

PLATE 8.28: *Blackfriars Bridge from rail level, looking south circa 1880. It was designed by Joseph Cubitt and Frederick Turner, built by Kennards and opened in 1864, carrying two pairs of lines across the Thames from Blackfriars Bridge station to Ludgate Hill. Blackfriars Bridge station closed in September 1885 and an additional bridge was built to the east, leading to a new terminus named St. Pauls, opened in May 1886 (renamed Blackfriars in 1937). To the left, with the rounded top, is one of the cartouches, iron castings dating from 1864, embellished on the outer face with a relief of the LC&DR crest. There were originally four of these cartouches, two at each end of the bridge. When the bridge was demolished in 1985, by McAlpine's, one of them was rescued and put on display at Lord McAlpine's estate. The two at the southern end were restored and remained in position until moved to the new south entrance to Blackfriars station in 2012.* SOUTH EASTERN & CHATHAM RAILWAY SOCIETY COLLECTION

PLATE 8.29: *The river piers were left when the bridge was demolished and today form rare surviving examples in the UK of the Viaduct Works output.* THE WUB - OWN WORK, CREATIVE COMMONS LICENSE *CC BY-SA 4.0*

obviating the need to resort to riveting. A road and footpath bridge crossing the River Murray in Australia was designed by W. Dempsey, civil engineer of London, and consisted of five spans at 121 feet centres, carrying a road 22 feet wide and a footpath 3 feet wide. In Spain there was the Tagus Bridge, erected at Villa Nova da Constancia, which comprised 16 spans of 101 feet 10 inches centre to centre, with each girder having the top and bottom beams connected by equilateral triangles forming a double Warren truss. A similar design was used for crossing the Ebro River at Tudela, at Aragon over the River Aragon and at Assecca. In Portugal, the Mondego Bridge crossed the River Mondego along with the Seisse Bridge, on the Oporto line. A bridge comprising two 150 foot spans with a central lifting span was erected over the River

PLATE 8.30: A short series of photographs were taken by the Midland Railway official photographer of the reconstruction of the River Wye bridge at Whitney on Wye in 1887-88, after it had been badly damaged by raging flood water. Watched by a local boatman presumably employed to rescue anyone who fell in, removal of the original Viaduct Works girders is underway, supported either end on a pair of small 4-wheeled bogies, with MR 1868-built, Kirtley '480' Class 0-6-0 No. 639 about to gently haul it off the viaduct.
ALASTAIR WARRINGTON COLLECTION

Tiber in Rome and at nearby Valletri, a bridge of three 152 feet spans was said to have been erected in three months.[50]

In this country, the works supplied bridges to the Llanelly Railway & Dock Company, along with that over the River Thames at Blackfriars for the London, Chatham & Dover Railway, designed by Joseph Cubitt. By 1864, this was one of the largest bridges supplied from the Viaduct Works and parts of it still survive today. Three double Warren truss spans were supplied for the Hereford, Hay & Brecon Railway's viaduct spanning the River Wye at Whitney, constructed in 1863. Badly damaged by a flood in 1878, it was rebuilt in 1887, reducing it from double track width to single; it had only ever carried one track in any case. Plate girder bridges were also manufactured at the works, both parallel and arched styles, alongside other railway equipment and there were also jetties, landing stages, iron roof girders, iron-framed buildings and iron roofing.[51]

However, when orders gradually began to fall away, in September 1871 the Kennard brothers withdrew from the works and put them up for sale. The reason for them disposing of the concern was revealed in an undated letter, in which they agreed to sell to Maynard as they '*wished to retire from business*'. They sold to Maynard, at the time manager at the works, due to his '*zealous attention to detail*', whilst they were '*satisfied with his integrity and competence*'. Wishing to help establish the business, they were prepared to sell the works as it stood on the books and did not require any payment for good will. The asking price was £26,500, which was to include all buildings, offices, engines, tools, machinery, plant, gas works, fittings of upper and lower works, a hotel and two cottages. The existing ninety-nine year lease for about 80 acres, with about eighty years to run, was £200 per annum. The rent being obtained from the hotel, cottages and the farm of about 200 acres, covered this annual cost, leaving the works rent free. The farm and the Soffrydd Quarry had been rented and taken by H.M. Kennard from 10th July 1867. All of the existing stock was to be taken at valuation, along with an agreed price for orders in hand, which Maynard was to take over.[52]

During 1870-71, the works were turning out about 200 tons of finished ironwork a week. Estimated profits over the previous nine years was £120,000, providing a net return of 20% to 25%. Over the previous twelve months

profits were estimated to be £19,913. On completion of the sale, a new company was to make a 50% down payment, with the remaining 50% paid within eighteen months. As part of any agreed sale, the Kennard's would grant Maynard a free licence and authority, '*to use and work all of their existing patents without any demands to pay royalties*'.[53]

Working within the terms of the Companies Acts of 1862 and 1867, a new company, limited by 50,000 shares, to be known as the Crumlin Works Company Ltd was incorporated on 22nd September 1871. There were three directors, including Henry Maynard as managing director, and Captain Hayworth, a local colliery owner, as chairman. Early in 1872, the new company took out a mortgage for the remaining £13,250, the full sum being repaid to the bank two years later. To clear this debt, the new company had borrowed capital from a Mr Price of Tredegar, a sum of £5,000 at 6% interest per annum. For security against the loan, they deposited the deeds of the works with Price.[54]

Within twelve months of taking over and continuing the business interests established by the Kennards, they had acquired the manufacturing rights of the Davis Patent Steam Striker, exporting these through an agent across Europe. This association ran into trouble when their agent, Henry Gaerth & Co, suppliers of rails, plates, sheets, pig iron, *etc*, went into liquidation owing a sum of £306. A writ was issued against Gaerth, civil engineer, to be tried in the County of Monmouth. It was then established where he was living and it was reported that it was '*a new house with new wooden furnishings*'.[55]

Another more fruitful association was an agreement

PLATE 8.31, ABOVE: The Viaduct Works design for an arched girder bridge. No location was given for this, so it may simply be an example of another type of bridge that could be supplied and the background fanciful.

PLATE 8.32, RIGHT: A more exotic far eastern location was used for this design for a suspension footbridge but again it is not known if one was ever fabricated, supplied and erected anywhere.

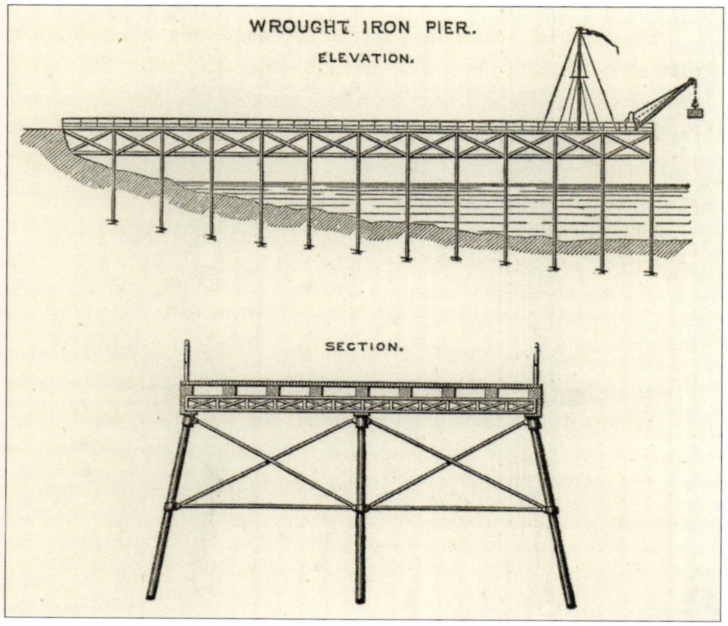

PLATE 8.33, RIGHT: A design for a wrought iron pier, complete with flagpole and crane. The latter indicates that this was a design for a working pier and not a seaside pleasure pier, although these were very much in vogue at the time of the Viaduct Works existence and no doubt they would have been able to supply the ironwork for one if requested.

entered into in 1873 with Easterbrook & Co., patentees for the manufacture of railway locking apparatus, signal boxes, points and connections. Under the terms of the agreement, the Crumlin Viaduct Works were to manufacture and supply goods contracted to be supplied to railway companies by Easterbrook.[56]

One of the best remembered viaducts was that built by the Severn & Wye Railway, across the lower end of the Lydbrook Valley. Completed in 1875, it was designed by G.W. Keeling, the S&WR engineer and was based on the Warren truss.[57] It comprised three spans, two 120 feet in length and the centre one 150 feet, supported on lofty stone piers. The Crumlin Viaduct Works supplied the ironwork, their tender of £7,396 being the cheapest of the three submitted but construction was carried out by the S&WR's contractor, J.E. Billups.

In their eleventh half-yearly report ending 26th April 1877, the secretary stated that '*the contract for a bridge in South Africa was most satisfactory and progress was such that it would be completed during the next few months*'. The *Cape Times* for May 1877 records that a bridge at Bethulie, put up twenty-one years ago by the Crumlin Company,

Plate 8.34: *Lydbrook Viaduct, which carried the Severn & Wye Railway's line over the lower end of the Lydbrook Valley, is seen here nearing completion in 1875. A small locomotive belonging to the contractor, Billups, can be seen with a rail mounted crane at the far end.* Ian Pope collection

Plate 8.35, Above: *Kennard patented this design for slip machinery, for hauling ships out of the water and up a slipway so that they could be worked on.*

Plate 8.36, Right: *A Kennard's Patent slip was installed at Evans Bay, Wellington, New Zealand, at a slip designed by the civil engineer James Abernethy. The equipment was supplied by the Viaduct Works in 1865-66, under a concession to build and operate the slip. However, because of contractual difficulties, it was not installed until 1871, after the Wellington Patent Slip Company had been formed and bought all of the equipment from the Viaduct Works. This 1920s photograph of the haulage machinery makes for an interesting comparison with the engraving.*
Collection Alexander Turnbull Library, Wellington, New Zealand

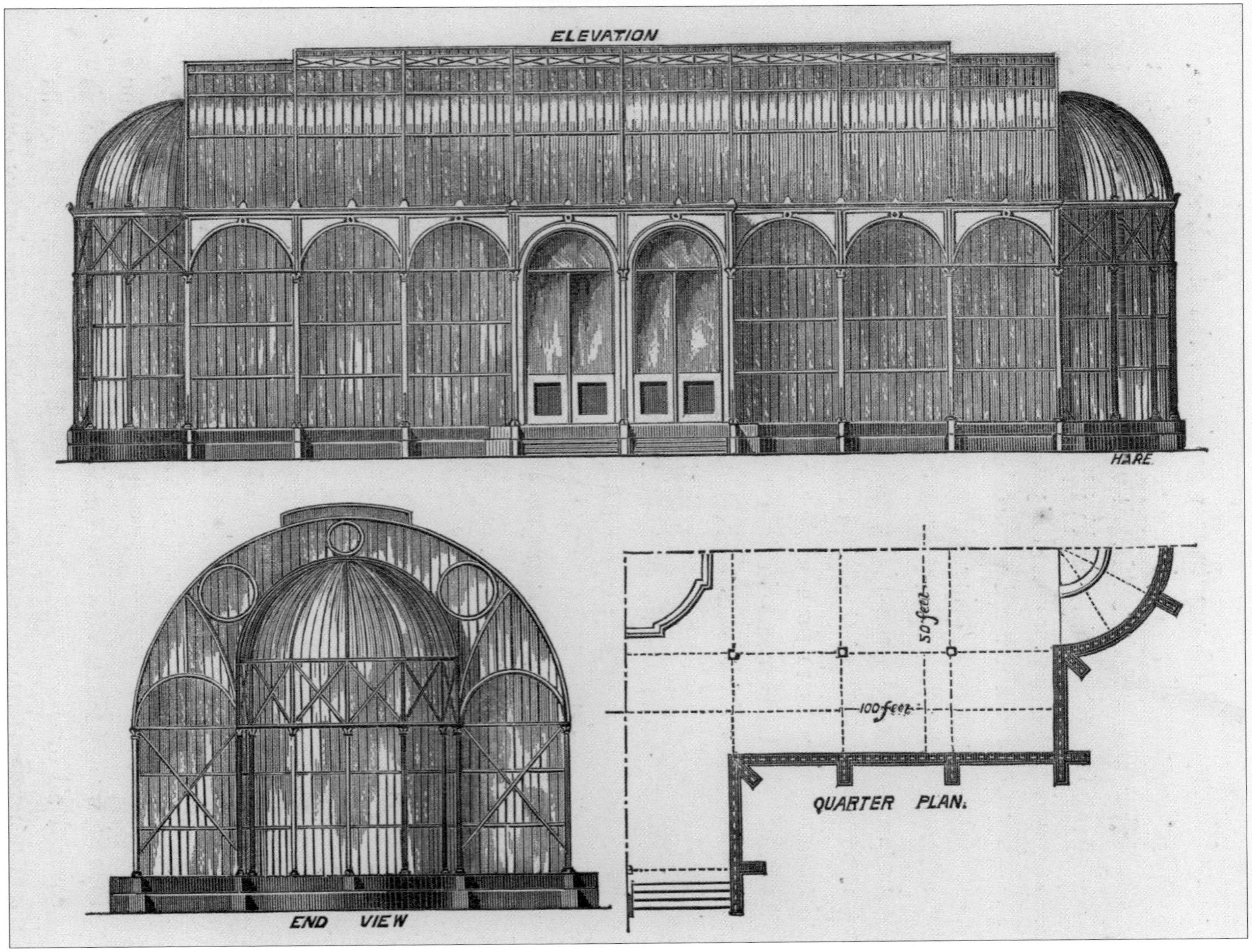

PLATE 8.37, ABOVE LEFT: *The schooner* Julius Vogel *and the steamship* Grafton *on the slip, circa 1880. It comprised a 200-ton, 180ft long cradle which moved on wheels along parallel rails. Twin chains hauled the cradle holding a vessel or vessels out of the water and lowered them back down again when work on them was complete. The power was supplied by two steam engines driving a cogwheel winch. The new facility was an immediate success and a second slipway was contructed alongside the first in 1922. Slipway No. 1 was taken out of use in 1969 and No. 2 in 1980 and sadly everything was demolished and much of the original machiery scrapped. A few items survive on display at what is now deemed a heritage site, named Cog Park.* NEW ZEALAND HISTORY ONLINE

PLATE 8.38, ABOVE RIGHT: *A punching and shearing machine.*

PLATE 8.39, LEFT: *One of the Viaduct Works more esoteric designs was this for a conservatory, which would have had cast iron framework and been some 250ft in length.*

PLATE 8.40: One of the most detailed views of the Viaduct Works is this photograph by Harvey Barton of Bristol showing it derelict following bankruptcy and closure in 1878. A workforce of 200 had been employed here and the order books were healthy but the company was operating at a loss and had run out of cash. A nuts and bolts manufacturer, John Paton & Co., bought the works in 1878 but went out of business in 1881 and the premises were eventually acquired by the Western Valleys Brewery in 1891, who continued to brew beer here into the 1950s. STEPHEN ROWSON COLLECTION

remained in excellent order and was as good as the day it was constructed. Maynard had left for South Africa to discuss the supply of a further bridge and attend the South African International Exhibition where they had products on display. The directors therefore thought it prudent not to charge any further profits on the '*current undertaking*'. Mention was also made of the supply of a bridge for Venezuela but the secretary warned that '*work was generally very slack*'. The balance sheet showed debts of £50,461 3s 10d.[58]

The closing years of the 1870s witnessed a period of economic recession, with an associated fall in the demand for coal and iron. The Viaduct Works Company was affected badly, suffering from serious cash flow problems and demand for the goods they supplied getting less and less. News of the problems the Viaduct Works Company was facing had reached H.M. Kennard, still a shareholder, who through the works' solicitors advanced, in late 1877, a sum of £1,000 to the directors. Weeks later, in January 1878, in the High Court of Justice, the Master of the Rolls, under the direction of the official liquidator, heard a petition from a number of creditors and ordered that the Crumlin Viaduct Works Company Ltd be wound up under the provisions of the Companies Acts of 1862 and 1867. This was followed by an action taken at the beginning of August 1878, when the Master of the Rolls, by an order of the High Court, declared that the Crumlin Viaduct Works be sold by public auction. The biggest creditor at that time was the West of England & South Wales District Bank, who were owed in excess of £13,000.[59]

PLATE 8.41: *This view of Crumlin Viaduct and the Viaduct Works is undated but was probably taken circa 1902. The Works now housed the Western Valleys Brewery, the extended buildings of which are not shown on the 1899 6 inch OS but which look quite new here. The Trinant Colliery tramroad incline is abandoned, the line having fallen out of use in 1897. However, sinking of Crumlin Colliery, which began production in 1908, had not yet started.*
NEIL PARKHOUSE COLLECTION

PLATE 8.42: As well as photographing the rising viaduct and various aspects of its construction, the LSC photographer also got some of the workers' children to pose, along with a few of the older lads at the rear, who were probably already part of the workforce. All male, apart from one little lady in the centre, many wear caps a size or two too large, with the little chap front left barely able to see past the peak!
DAVID DICKINSON COLLECTION

The first auction was to be held in London on Tuesday, 15th October 1878, with the sale of the leases for the '*Ironbridge and Girder Works, Plant and Machinery, Viaduct Hotel, Managers house, Stone Quarry and Farm, about 200 acres*'. The sale of the stores, tools and materials, consisting of 647 mixed lots, was to take place at the works over three days commencing 3rd December 1878.[59]

After twenty-six years, the Crumlin Viaduct Works was finished as a major manufacturer of bridges and railway apparatus. The buildings, however, remained in use into the 1950s but have now all gone.

References

1. Letter, Kennard to Carr, 18th Dec. 1852
2. Letter, Kennard to Carr, 21st Dec. 1852
3. Letter, Kennard to Kendall, 24th Feb. 1853
4. Letter, Kennard to Liddell, 24th Feb. 1853
5. Letter, Liddell to Kennard, 4th Apr. 1853
6. Letters, Kennard to Liddell and Gordon, 16th July 1853
7. Letter, Liddell to Kennard, 1st Aug. 1853
8. Letter, Liddell to Kennard, 6th Sept. 1853
9. Letter, Liddell to Kennard, 16th Sept. 1853
10. Letter, Kennard to Liddell, 19th Sept. 1853
11. Letter, Kennard to Liddell, 23rd Sept. 1853
12. Letter, Pritchard to Kennard, 3rd Oct. 1853
13. Letter, Pritchard to Kennard, 7th Nov. 1853
14. Letter, Pritchard to Kennard, 9th Nov. 1853
15. Letter, Liddell to Kennard, 9th Nov. 1853
16. Letter, Pritchard to Kennard, 11th Nov. 1853
17. Letter, Kennard to Pritchard, 12th Nov. 1853
18. Letter, Pritchard to Kennard, 19th Nov. 1853
19. Letter, Pritchard to Kennard, 21st Nov. 1853
20. Letter, Kennard to Pritchard, 21st Nov. 1853
21. Letter, Liddell to Kennard, 24th Nov. 1853
22. Letter, Kennard to Liddell, 13th Dec. 1853
23. Letter, Kennard to Liddell, 15th Dec. 1853
24. Letter, Carr to Kennard, 13th Dec. 1853
25. Letter, Kennard to Liddell, 4th Feb. 1854
26. *Monmouthshire Merlin* newspaper
27. Letter, Carr to Gordon, 24th Feb. 1854
28. Letter, Gordon to Carr, 26th Feb. 1854
29. Letter, Carr to Liddell, 10th Apr. 1854
30. Letter, Liddell to Kennard, 25th Apr. 1854
31. Letter, Liddell to Carr, 18th May 1854
32. Letter, R.W. Kennard to Kennard, 27th June 1854
33. Letter, Gordon to Carr, 13th July 1854
34. Letter, Kennard to Carr, 18th Sept. 1854
35. Indenture made and dated 18th July 1854 between Kennard §and the Newport, Abergavenny & Hereford Railway
36. Letter, Kennard to Carr, 26th Jan. 1855
37. Letter, Kennard to Carr, 25 Mar. 1855
38. Letter, Kennard to Carr, 2nd Apr. 1855
39. Letters, Kennard to Carr and Carr to Kennard, 27th Mar. 1855
40. Letter, Kennard to Carr, 16th Apr. 1855
41. Letter, Carr to Kennard, 8th June 1855
42. Letter, Carr to Kennard, 28th Mar. 1855
43. Letter, Carr to Kennard, 9th May 1855
44. Letters, Carr to Kennard, 4th June & 8th July 1855
45. Letter, Carr to Kennard, 21st Dec. 1855
46. Letter, Carr to Kennard, 1st Apr. 1856
47. Letter, Kennard to board of directors, 4th Nov. 1856
48. Board of directors meeting. 6th Nov. 1856
49. Note on the file
50. Maynard's publication *The Victoria Works*, 1868
51. *ibid*
52. Note dated 13th Sept. 1871 in Gwent Archives
53. From records held at Gwent Archives
54. From records held at Gwent Archives
55. From records held at Gwent Archives
56. From records held at Gwent Archives
57. *Severn & Wye Railway Volume 3*, Ian Pope & Paul Karau, Wild Swan, 1988, page 457
58. Half yearly report records held at Gwent Archives
59. From records held at Gwent Archives

MODIFICATIONS AND REPAIRS

CHAPTER 9

By December 1857, the horizontal columns bracing the girders together were starting to break, forcing Carr to place an order for a further six to be cast from the existing pattern. This would appear to have been a recurring problem. In 1858 it was reported that the '*distance pipes*' between the girders (horizontal columns) were breaking, owing to the awkward strain from bad fitting. Other reported failures included the heads of the pins of the diagonal braces in the piers breaking off. Professor Gordon considered that the provision for expansion and contraction was very defective, owing to '*Kennard's absurd junction plate put on top to join all the girders together*'. Gordon instructed Carr to examine these faults, remove the junction plates and investigate especially how the effect of expansion was damaging the piers and the abutments.[1]

In response, Carr was of the opinion that the pins in the viaduct turned around by vibration and so unscrewed themselves from the $1^1/_4$ inch bolts, and that this would require a simple remedy, '*but there was no hurry*'.[2] No further mention is made of how the problem was resolved but, a year later, structural works were being undertaken. Precise details are scant and the only identified reference to any remedial works appears in the minute books of the Newport, Abergavenny & Hereford Railway. The first mention occurs in April 1859, when it was reported that the viaduct had been repainted and that some alterations to the girders were necessary.[3]

At the September Board meeting, influential director Thomas Brown reported on the extent of correspondence he had been engaged in with H.M. Kennard, Edward Clarke, Gordon, the secretary and Charles Liddell.[4] This was accompanied by a report from McDonnell (Mark Carr's assistant), who explained that plans for suspending the girders had been put forward by Liddell. He was to be confronted with a similar problem at Worcester, when needing to strengthen the girders of a bridge across the River Severn on the Worcester and Hereford line. An alternative solution put forward by Gordon was subsequently adopted but no record has been found as to what the unspecified solution was. However, at the next meeting of the directors, it was reported that six of the girders had been successfully completed with Gordon's design but that the road as altered could not be opened for traffic until work on the remaining girders had been completed, and the road tested.[5] This was completed and it reopened in January 1860.[6]

Reporting on the success of the works, Liddell stated '*I have examined the alterations to the supports of the 'up line' of the girders on the abutments of Crumlin Viaduct and have to report that work well and solidly carried out and much stronger than original*'. Testing was completed by passing three engines over the same line with both '*up and down lines*' opened for traffic again by summer 1860.[7] An obscure entry in the company's ledger suggests that the cost of the works amounted to £2,000.

Whilst these works were in progress, the company were

PLATE 9.1: *No. 16 of Pumphrey's stereo views of the late 1850s, looking north-east across Crumlin village to the Viaduct Works and the viaduct towering behind.* STEPHEN ROWSON COLLECTION

involved in a further dispute with one of the Kennard brothers. Whether it was Thomas or Howard was not made clear but at the outset of the works a notice had been served stating that '*Kennard not to go upon the line of railway or any part of stations or works without the prior permission to do so from the Company secretary or the engineer*'. The board endorsed the notice and resolved to cancel all authority previously given (if any), and threatened to take proceedings for trespass if Kennard entered any of the stated sites or property.[8] At the request of director Mr Robinson, the notice was withdrawn in December and replaced by a special pass.[9] Under what terms the pass was issued was not disclosed but this was at a time when arrangements were being made to settle the differences between the company and Kennard by '*friendly arbitration*'. An article in the local press suggests that the public had become aware of how low their relationship had sunk when it was reported that '*Mr. Kennard chose to say things to the Company, and they could not shut his mouth*'.[10]

On the completion of the repair works the viaduct was painted but as soon as this had been completed, letters in the local press were accusing the directors of the company of '*causing the noble viaduct at Crumlin to be grossly disfigured by the cheap and nasty daubing of heavy looking paint in place of the lighter and appropriate colour previously employed*'. Instead of being painted in its original colour, which was described as white, the viaduct had been painted in a dark red-brown colour, and there were requests for '*those directors who were men of taste to return the colour to white*'.

At the beginning of 1865, the safety of the structure was being questioned by local inhabitants when it was observed that a larger than normal number of men were working on the viaduct. Letters expressing their anxieties frequently appeared in the local press, inducing others to write to the Board of Trade (BoT) with details of their concerns. One of the correspondents, who wrote to the secretary of the BoT and to the chairman of the Great Western Railway, was Lord Llanover, a man with considerable influence who owned estates in and around Crumlin.[11] In 1831, standing under the name of Benjamin Hall, he was elected the MP for Monmouthshire and during his term of office he was to serve as First Commissioner for Works. In that role he oversaw the construction of the clock tower attached to the Houses of Parliament, the name of its famous bell, 'Big Ben', being closely associated with him. He was created a baronet in 1838 and became the first Lord Llanover in 1859.

Reacting to Lord Llanover's letter, Frederick Saunders* had requested and received a report from his Divisional Engineer at Gloucester, W.G. Owen, the first of three individual reports he was to receive. Owen stated that Crumlin Viaduct received his constant attention and that his examination, only the previous day, indicated '*no grounds for alarm or safety*'. However, he did feel that the viaduct required repairs, as well as strengthening of the connections to the girders, brought about through the '*increase in the number of heavy goods trains passing over the viaduct and their associated increase in weight*'. Aware that further work was necessary, Owen had earlier imposed an 8mph speed restriction on traffic crossing the viaduct, with instructions to limit traffic to one train at a time, in order to reduce the effect of vibration.

Owen also noted that for some time he had been concerned with the state of the timber flooring, which was showing signs of rotting. To remedy this he mentioned that a contract was being prepared to have the timber replaced with sheets of wrought iron.[12] He also noted that the piers were in excellent condition. Saunders obviously wanted a further independent opinion other than that from the BoT and engaged a Mr Fowler, consulting engineer, and a Mr Brereton to examine and prepare a report on the condition of the viaduct. The latter is probably Robert Pearson Brereton (1818-1894), one of the seven resident engineers working under Isambard Kingdom Brunel on the construction of the Great Western Railway. His signature appears on the drawings for the bridge over the River Wye at Chepstow and he supervised work on the Royal Albert Bridge, spanning the River Tamar at Saltash. After Brunel's death in 1859, Brereton took over his role as chief engineer for a number of lines, working from Brunel's old office in London.

Lord Llanover's letter to the secretary of the BoT also brought an immediate reaction. He wrote to the chairman of the GWR and Llanover, informing them that Captain Tyler RE had been appointed to '*inspect and report on the condition of the viaduct*'.[13]

Prior to Captain Tyler's inspection, he had sent a letter to Joseph Armstrong, GWR divisional engineer at Hereford, requesting him to make available, for his use, a train made up of seven engines and their tenders, and a train of loaded coal and other trucks, sufficient to cover two spans on both lines, with a combined weight of 600 tons. The train of seven engines would be used to run back and forth over the viaduct, to allow an analysis of the action the weight had on the girders and piers.

Concerns were being expressed about Tyler's demands, with Armstrong being '*at his wits end*' in trying to obtain

** Frederick Saunders (1820-1901) was appointed Assistant Secretary to the South Wales Railway in 1844, becoming Chief Secretary in 1849. When his uncle, Charles Saunders, retired as Secretary to the Great Western in 1863, Frederick filled his place. On resigning his post in June 1886, he was made a Director of the company and then succeeded Daniel Gooch as Chairman of the GWR in 1889. He retired in June 1895 but remained a member of the Board until his death at Reading in 1901.*

PLATE 9.2: *Pumphrey's stereo image No. 1402 clearly shows the Trinant Incline in use. This now ran to a wharf and siding on the Up side of the MR&CC main line, whilst the narrow gauge waggons in the centre background are standing on the rails leading to the canal tip originally used for Trinant coal but which was now part of the Viaduct Works internal tramroad or trolley system. The standard gauge wagons are on the MR&CC siding into the Works, whilst the lads in the foreground, sitting around the saw pit, not only added some human animation but served to create a good stereo effect as well.* STEPHEN ROWSON COLLECTION

PLATE 9.3: Joesph W. Armstrong, GWR Divisional Engineer at Hereford, photographed at Grange Court Junction in May 1872 during the conversion of the South Wales Railway to standard gauge. His younger assistant standing alongside is William Lancaster Owen, son of William G. Owen, Divisional Engineer at Gloucester. He used the name Lancaster to distinguish himself from his father. In the year this picture was taken, he was appointed Chief Engineer of the Monmouthshire Railway & Canal Co.,which was taken over by the GWR in 1875. He was subsequently appointed as GWR Engineer for New Works, reporting to his father. The photograph was taken by R.H. Barrett, whose George Street studio faced the viaduct at the west end of Gloucester GWR station.
NEIL PARKHOUSE COLLECTION

seven engines, when he only had four at his disposal.[14] A further concern was the safety of the men working on the viaduct, as trains and engines would be travelling over a weaker section of the girders that were in the process of being strengthened. Irrespective of these concerns, however, Tyler continued with his plans. On the day of his inspection, he was accompanied by Lord Llanover, representatives of the GWR and the Kennard brothers.

On Thursday, 21st September 1865, Tyler had the seven engines, with an aggregate weight of nearly 300 tons, placed on one line stretching over two spans. The deflection of the girders was understood to be a little over one inch, whilst the measurement for lateral vibration was so slight that it hardly registered when viewed through a theodolite. For the second test, a train of loaded trucks was placed on the other line alongside the engines, the total weight on the two spans being about 600 tons, with the deflection and lateral movement no greater than that previously recorded. The engines were then driven backwards and forwards from end to end of the viaduct, and again it was understood that there was little change in the recorded measurements. The loading was considered to have been well in excess of what would have been expected during normal use. At the completion of the tests there was a general feeling amongst those present that the structure was perfectly secure.

Tyler's report contained a number of observations and specific recommendations. He noted that the piers had not been affected by traffic passing over the structure during the eight years since the viaduct had been opened to traffic but they had suffered in a number of places from the action of the atmosphere and from water. The ends of the vertical braces, particularly those that connected the columns together, had rusted in places to such an extent that it was considered '*exceedingly desirable*' that the whole of the piers be cleaned, carefully examined and painted without delay. Also included in Tyler's report was a recommendation that the holes or spaces left in the pockets into which the vertical braces rested should be filled in to prevent the ingress and pooling of water. There was no mention of any need to provide additional support to the distance girders at the junction they made with the columns.

It also contained a recommendation that the speed of trains should be restricted to between 6mph and 8mph because of the effects of centrifugal force that occurred when they travelled over the viaduct. It caused vibrations that, according to Tyler's working out, increased in proportion to the squares of the rate of speed. After a series of other calculations, Tyler noted that the girders had suffered as a result of the passing traffic causing the pins securing the braces to be worn away and work loose, as they were being forced up and down in the direction of the braces. He claimed that he was unable to accurately ascertain the extent of the damage without stopping the traffic altogether, to allow him to remove and examine the pins. If a situation arose where pins could be removed to examine any weakness, the opportunity should be taken to replace any defective ones as the safety of the viaduct depended upon them. He acknowledged that this fault had been recognised by the GWR and was being remedied by adding gusset plates at three angles of the upper and lower beams.[15]

An interesting feature that Captain Tyler mentioned in his report was that the motion created by passing trains and the reaction that this had on the pins, had been first detected by a workman specially employed to watch over the viaduct. His role was '*to keep the numerous screws, bolts and cotters located in the viaduct, screwed up in their position*'. The employment of a '*bridgeman*' was an important role in the continuing inspection and maintenance of the viaduct. In 1902, the GWR agreed to erect a cottage for his sole occupation, at a cost of £340.[16]

Tyler noted that arrangements were being made to remove and replace the rotting timber flooring with timber or iron. As part of these works, he recommended the addition of iron cross girders at 3-4 feet intervals to tie the two systems of girders together, and to add two extra girders under the platform for its total length, in order to add stability and to provide support for any new floor of sheets of wrought iron. He advised that the GWR should carry out and complete the works '*as soon as possible*' but to bear in mind that they would have an effect on the loading carried by the girders and the piers.

Forwarding a copy of Tyler's report to the chairman of the GWR, the secretary to the BoT commented: '*My Lords trust that the directors will see the importance of adopting, at once, the measures pointed out by Capt. Tyler as to be taken without delay for ensuring the safety of the public who may have to pass over the viaduct in question, and will give their attention to the recommendations for further strengthening the structure*'.

When Fowler and Brereton introduced their report, they stated that '*they were requested to prepare a report following comments made by Mr Owen that there was a considerable motion in the viaduct from passing trains that was exciting attention, and to inspect the bridge and consider what might be done to remedy the defects*'. Prior to its completion, they were provided with a copy of Tyler's analysis, allowing them to confirm many of the points he raised, along with his recommendations.

The first part of their inspection was concerned with the piers and commented that '*they appeared in good condition*'. In their opinion, they had stood up to the work well since the opening of the railway in 1857 but that it was desirable that they should, where necessary, be cleaned and painted.

When examining the girders, they observed that the trains passing over the viaduct resulted in movement of the struts and ties, which caused the pin holes to become an oval or oblong shape. A close examination of the pins indicated that there was no evidence of wear on them and they remained in a sound condition. They commented that some measures were in progress that had been previously suggested to remedy this, by riveting gusset plates in the angles formed by the diagonal braces at the top and bottom webs of the girders. As a safety measure, they suggested the suspension of traffic using the line immediately above where the men were working.

They considered that the timber floor was in such a poor condition that it should be removed but prior to it being replaced, they advocated the installation of wrought iron floor beams, which would add considerably to the stability of the structure. They also recommended that the viaduct should be strengthened, in order to reduce the strains to a figure that did not exceed 5 tons per sq. inch. According to Fowler and Brereton, the most economical way of achieving this would be to insert additional plates and angle irons to the existing girders, which could be done without difficulty. The estimated cost for strengthening was as follows:

Gusset pieces to diagonal braces	£2,800
Strengthening main girders	£8,400
New floor iron beams	£10,000
Painting	£1,300
Sub Total	**£23,500**
New timber floor	£4,500
Wrought iron floor	£11,000
TOTAL	**£34,000**

In Fowler's and Brereton's opinion, a wrought iron floor would offer a great increase in stiffness and durability to the structure. On receipt of the reports, the directors resolved to carry out the works as recommended at the estimated cost of £34,000.[17]

At the end of November, Owen reported to Saunders that he had met Kennard at Crumlin and had agreed to continue with work on the remaining gusseting and strengthening of the girders. He pointed out that the supplying and laying of the new flooring had not yet been let, although it had been authorised at the directors' August meeting and would follow the completion of the strengthening. Whilst the work was in progress, single line operation would continue.[18]

H.M. Kennard submitted a tender for supplying and fixing the wrought iron floor for £10,530, a sum that was sanctioned by the board at their January meeting[19]. It was felt that as he was already doing work on the viaduct, it could not be expected for another contractor to be engaged on the same site at the same time, especially as there would be a need to erect additional scaffolding that would render most other work inconvenient. On these grounds, the directors considered that they had no other option than to award the contract to HMK at the price he quoted.

PLATE 9.4: *These two men, Tom Kennard and another of the management (who is also shown in the picture on page 26), posed on the bank of the Ebbw River, add to the stereo effect of this unusual view looking north towards the viaduct in summer 1856. Note the well-cultivated vegetable plots just the other side of where the men are sitting.*
STEPHEN ROWSON COLLECTION

PLATE 9.5: This is the second of Francis Bedford's panoramic views from his visit in 1861, in which his photographic wagon can be seen parked outside the post office, just to the left of the canal bridge. Early photography involved a deal of bulky heavy equipment, plus a supply of glass plates to use as negatives, so a horse-drawn van was not just a useful means of travel, it was a necessity for transporting everything. By the time of this visit, the built-up land that connected the two portions of the viaduct was already becoming covered with trees. This short section of line was quite exposed and must have raised some concerns amongst train crews, as a high fence was to be erected as protection a few years later. The Trinant Colliery wharf at the base of Mark Philips' Tramroad incline appears to be out of use at this date and note too the gantry and overhead crane which had been erected in the Viaduct Works yard, by the head of the canal; this looks well maintained albeit appears quite low in water. There are two signals in the picture, one beyond the overhead crane and the other on the TVE line between the viaduct sections, both of which appear to be twin-armed, slotted post examples. Finally, the building on the far right of the picture, with the bell on the roof, was the village schoolhouse. This photograph was discovered in an album with the date '18th Oct$^{r.}$ 1871' inked beneath, indicating that copies of Bedford's picture were still being sold ten years after he had taken it. DAVID WESTCOTT COLLECTION

PLATE 9.6: A rare and unusual view of damage to the viaduct, the print of which carried no details. However, it almost certainly shows the aftermath of a derailment in December 1898, when a wheel on the wagon of an Up coal train shattered into pieces and smashed a section of railings at the eastern end of the Ebbw viaduct – fortunately it seems without injury to anyone. Where it occurred, close to the abutment, was clear of any housing or works below. A report into the incident noted that several yards of track had been ripped up, which must have been behind where the photographer was standing. A breakdown crew were sent out to effect repairs, with single line working on the Down side put into place until these were completed.
NEIL PARKHOUSE COLLECTION

Crumlin. However, between 1891 and the early years of the 20th century, a number of events associated with the viaduct led to parliamentary proceedings, new works, and further repairs and modifications.

It had become common knowledge amongst engineers that a section of a wrought iron beam supporting a bridge had failed and fallen onto a public highway.[25] Although they were not directly involved, the GWR reacted to this failure by forwarding a circular to each of their divisional engineers, calling on them to inspect all of the iron bridges on their system. A return was required that distinguished between bridges with flat girders, wrought iron, steel and timber. A report was then to be prepared advising on those that should be strengthened or renewed.[26]

Whether the next reported maintenance at Crumlin was identified as a result of the requested information was not mentioned but, in 1898 and according to a schedule that had been submitted to the directors, unspecified repairs to the viaduct were completed at a cost of £5,337 18s 9d and it was repainted at a cost of £778 17s 4d. These works were followed in 1899 by the repointing of the abutments stonework, whilst the telegraph wires were removed and replaced inside ducting.[27]

Erecting a structure the size of Crumlin Viaduct within an area containing an abundance of coal seams was to have its risks. In early 1854, the company commissioned a report from a Mr Llewellyn, a mining engineer, whose brief was '*to report back on the working of coal mines under the viaduct*'. At a subsequent meeting, the board resolved '*to purchase land from the Cwm Tillery seam at a cost not exceeding £300, and to make an offer to the owner of the Elled vein at no more than £200*'.[28]

The next reference to the issue of nearby coal seams occurs in 1902, when the GWR promoted a Bill seeking powers to restrict mining activities within a specified area from the viaduct and the right to purchase, by compulsory acquisition, any located within a specified area delineated by them. The main seams of interest to the company were those of the Llanhilleth mine to the north, at a depth of 312 yards, and the Newport Abercarn mine to the south, at a depth of 330 yards. Following the evidence put forward by one objector, who owned 9 acres of the 63 acres affected, and with the remaining landowners having agreed to treat with the company, the Bill was amended in the House of Lords. The subsequent Act of Parliament, entitled *The Crumlin Viaduct Act 1902*,[29] conferred '*further powers upon the Company with respect to the viaduct against injury by the working of mines or minerals under or in the neighbourhood*'. However, instead of absolute powers to restrict mining in the prescribed area and the ability to purchase coal seams by compulsory acquisition, these powers were limited to a predetermined timescale and where these conditions were not met, then mining activities were permitted but works directly beneath the viaduct were restricted to '*the making of airways, roadways, etc. no more than 13 feet wide and 8 feet high*'.

Between 1903 and 1911, the viaduct was subjected to further repairs, modifications and maintenance works. During April 1903, it was reported that temporary arrangements were being made to permit '*the working of traffic over the viaduct during the laying of the permanent way*'. Two months later, further arrangements were being made to reduce the double line to a single line whilst unspecified repairs were being undertaken.[30] Other than the reference to the permanent way, the only other mention of works being completed was of the electric staff system that was put into operation between the signal boxes at Crumlin Junction and Crumlin High Level. At a meeting of the board of directors in October 1903, the general manager reported that '*the time had arrived when the reconstruction of the bridge carrying the railway should be taken in hand*'. He produced a plan illustrating how it was proposed to lay a double line that '*associated with alterations to the goods and refuge sidings as well as alterations to the signalling could be completed at an estimated cost of £7,804*'. This was followed by a minute from the GWR's Traffic Committee, which mentions '*the reconstruction of bridge carrying the railway over the River Ebbw, estimated cost £7,804*'. No further details were provided but twelve months later it was reported that the single line workings were *'purely a temporary arrangement for the purposes of enabling the flooring of the Crumlin Viaduct to be repaired'*.

An article in the GWR's 'house' magazine in October 1907 describes the reconstruction works of 1904 as the laying of a new floor, consisting of steel plates 2 feet 6 inches wide and 1/4 of an inch thick, on top of the existing steel plate floor laid in 1865-66. The holes for rivets, etc., were prepared with the use of a pneumatic drill, obtained from the Consolidated Pneumatic Tool Co.of London. The work required the use of 24,000 rivets, with 18,000 existing holes and 24,000 in the new plate work, resulting in 42,000 holes in total. The rivetting plant was powered by a compressor working at a pressure of 80lbs per sq. inch located in a specially converted van. It had sufficient power capacity to run, simultaneously, two drills, a reamer, a hammer, a holder on and a forge. Work started on the reconstruction on 21st May 1904 on the Down line, which was completed on 7th August. Next day, work then commenced on the Up line, with normal working of trains across the viaduct being restored on 16th October.[31]

Other than the reports of 1865 and 1875, the next time that any structural work on the piers can be positively attributed to being undertaken occurred in 1905, the minute books of the board including the entry *'repairs to the piers Crumlin Viaduct £3,000'*, whilst the minutes of the Traffic Committee noted *'repairs to Crumlin Viaduct £3,000'*.[32] Also recorded in the Engineering Committee minutes is a reference to the supply of stone and that repairs had been completed to the stonework (of the abutments) at a cost of £750.

Plate 9.7, Below: *The GWR, worried about the effects of possible mining subsidence on the viaduct, attempted to compulsorily purchase coal seams belonging to two of the important nearby collieries. The Newport Abercarn Black Vein Steam Coal Company's Celynen Colliery was just over a mile to the south of the viaduct. Later renamed Celynen South – following the opening of Celynen North colliery in 1914 – it had three shafts, No. 1 Pit working the Nine-Feet (Black Vein) seam and No's 2 and 3 Pits the Five-Feet/Gellideg (Old Coal) seam. Coal was raised by steam power until 1971 and the colliery closed in 1985.*

Plate 9.8, Left: *The GWR also wanted to purchase the Black Vein seam worked by Llanhilleth Colliery, about a mile to the north, at the bottom of the Llanhilleth Branch, coming down from Crumlin Junction in the immediate foreground. Sunk in the 1850s, Llanhilleth Colliery closed in 1969.*

Both Neil Parkhouse collection

Plates 9.9, 9.10 & 9.11: *The juxtaposition of these pictures is the result of a fortuitous coincidence. The main view,* **Right,** *is a GWR official photograph showing work underway strengthening the bridge decking in 1904. As noted in the text, the work was described in a short article about the viaduct which appeared in the October 1907 issue of the* Great Western Railway Magazine. *The additional steel floor took a total of twenty-one weeks to lay, with the opportunity being taken to renew the timber baulks supporting the track as well. The photograph on the right shows timber baulks being used to apply a constant force whilst drilling down into the steel plate – note the neat line of holes leading to the nearer worker's foot. Another workman poses holding a rivetting machine behind to the left. The tools they are using were all powered from Engineering Department compressor van No. 14938, behind. This vehicle was converted from an iron covered goods van originally built in 1856 and condemned in 1903 but it was then rebuilt in the December of that year. This involved extending the chassis to incorporate a vertical steam boiler, which powered the air compressor. Water for the boiler was taken via hosepipe from the nearest supply, which here would have been the water tower seen in the background at Crumlin Junction. What was probably a works train headed by an 0-6-0 saddle tank can be seen alongside the water tower. The compressor van remained in service until 1937. Now to the fortuitous bit. During the period this work was in progress, one of the local photographers also took a picture and published it as a commercial postcard,* **Above.** *The enlargement,* **Below,** *shows the form of the compressor van rather well, silhouetted against the sky. Workmen are spread out over two of the spans and some sheeting had been draped in one area to protect the valley below against debris falling from the bridge.* Right: John Mann collection; Above: Neil Parkhouse collection

PLATE 9.12, ABOVE: *A view looking west along the walkway beneath the main deck. The photograph, which is dated 12th December 1916, was a GWR official, used as evidence to show James Dally saved his colleague in 1914 (see page 250). The timber platform used by the painters can be seen on the left.* JOHN MANN COLLECTION

PLATE 9.13: *In 1907, engineers from the Great Western Railway attempted to locate drawings or written material pertaining to the amendments to the original design, as discussed by Lord Llanover. The engineers failed but agreed that the additional strengthening work at the junction of the piers, then clearly visible, was the work referred to. This photograph of the only remaining section of a pier, on display outside San Diegio University in California, confirms to today's engineers the full extent and significance of the strengthening alterations then performed.* A. TUFNELL

Further reference is contained in a report dated 20th November 1905, in which the repairs mentioned include work on the diagonal braces, and to the iron straps attached to the columns, distance girders and diagonal braces. The examiners mention that, due to a lack of scaffolding, only one pier was inspected in detail but other examinations taken over the previous two years had identified problems where the diagonal braces were inserted into the distance girders and where they crossed each other. In nearly all of those cases examined, it was recorded that they were '*very badly rusted and must be repaired immediately*'. The method then adopted was to take out one brace at a time, remove the rusted section and weld on new sections. This work was completed on-site '*with materials taken from store*'.

Of concern to the examiners was the discovery of a weakness at the junction the distance girders made with the columns of the pier. The report indicates that, when the viaduct was quite new, the method for fixing the distance girder to the column was found to be unsatisfactory. In order to provide additional support, strength and rigidity, braces of cast iron of sufficient depth and width had been fitted between the flanges of each adjoining distance girder. Angled straps were attached to these braces and to the original diagonal braces above and below the distance girders. The original fixings for the vertical braces, packing pieces where they entered the pockets of the distance girder and their gib and cotter fixings, were retained. The upper section of the strap was attached above the gib and cotter. The latest examination revealed that, in some cases, the straps were severely rusted and broken, and were being renewed with the same design of metal castings. The broken straps were removed one by one and sent to Swindon for casting replacements. A drawing accompanying the report provided details of the design of the straps and the areas affected by rust. The estimated cost of £3,000 corresponds to the £3,000 figures in the board's and Traffic Committee's minute books.

Evidence as to the method used to strengthen the junction made between the vertical braces and the distance girders can be analysed further by examining the only remaining section of the piers of the viaduct, which stands in the grounds of San Diego University, California.[33]

After an extensive research of records held in national and local archives, local and national newspapers, and magazines, these were the only records found that could relate directly to the date when the modifications and additions were carried out but even then they only mention that no one knows when they were completed, just that it was soon after the viaduct had been finished.

That strengthening work had been completed on the piers by 1909 is indicated in a report that they were being repainted. However,

PLATE 9.14, RIGHT: A paint crew pose on one of the piers in 1914. At this period the viaduct was repainted every seven years and it was estimated that it took some 15 tons of paint to give it the required two coats.
ANON

the weather had apparently been so unfavourable that the contractors had been unable to complete the work, so a large portion of it had been carried over until the following spring and again in 1914.

A detailed report on the condition of the viaduct, prepared in 1919, records that over the previous two and half years, very careful records had been taken every six months of the deflection of the main girders, '*under Test Loads and actual working conditions*', along with measurements of stress in the cross girders and rail bearers. The records did not show any excessive deflection but, over the period of the study, measurements were increasing, albeit only by a very small amount. The stress records indicated that the cross and rail girders installed in 1865 to replace the timber floor were very lightly stressed. Measurements had been taken of all four girders simultaneously, when two girders under one road were loaded. It was found that the continuous cross girder transmitted some of the load to the inner girders under the unloaded road. In 1919, this was considered to be caused by deflections of the four girders comprising the two spans.

During May and June 1919, two stretchers between the bottom booms (tension beam) broke and as in previous cases, they were replaced by spares taken from stock. The stretchers and bracings between the top booms (compression beam) were considered to be '*not necessary*' and if any of these broke it was suggested that '*they need not be replaced*'; on the bottom booms, however, it was considered that the cast iron stretchers be replaced by steel ones at an estimated cost of £6,000. Other recommended works included the renewal of the remainder of the plate floor at an estimated cost of £8,900.

It was at this time that the Traffic Department was pressing for the unrestricted use across the viaduct for 'red route' engines (the heaviest). It was mentioned that the floor had been strengthened in 1904 but the engineers considered that if this requirement was to be achieved, then '*the Viaducts must be either strengthened or reconstructed ... strengthening would be expensive, very expensive and altogether unsatisfactory considering the age of the structures*'. As an alternative, it was suggested that '*red engines could be allowed over both viaducts by moving the roads to the centre over two strengthened inner girders and re-arranging the rail bearers and operating as a single line*'.[34] It would appear that no further action was taken on the renewal of the floor plating, because a letter from the Chief Engineer's Office in 1922 stated that '*if the viaduct has to be kept going for a further number of years then the repairs should be carried out*'.[35]

Between 1927 and 1930, further modifications and major repairs were completed. The tension beams of the two inside main girders were stiffened by replacing the existing angled gussets with ones of a larger and stronger section. Similar to the work carried out in 1904, the steel floor decking was replaced, owing to it having '*worn thin with age*', and, as on previous occasions when major work was being undertaken, one line of the permanent way was closed at a time, allowing three gangs of thirty men to be employed. Two gangs worked towards the centre from each end on the larger viaduct and another gang worked on the smaller one. As well as removing the steel decking, the lattice fascia and the supporting wooden flooring was replaced with rolled steel joists, to which the existing ornamental parapet was attached. Pneumatic drills were used throughout, with air supplied by steam and petrol driven compressors. A total of 1,140 new plates of different sizes and shapes were laid, all cut to fit on site, around 110,000 rivets being used to attach them to the girders. At the completion of the repair works and as a result of the gussets to the girders being strengthened, the permanent way was reinstated as a single line running down the centre of the viaduct. This was a logical outcome in any case, as the double line had been restricted to one train crossing the viaduct at a time for some years. The works when finally completed

PLATE 9.15: This February 1926 photograph, taken close to the eastern abutment, shows blocks of wood wound with rope and secured to the handrails, indicating that work was likely being carried out on the girders, outside of the walkway.
JOHN MANN COLLECTION

PLATE 9.16: An undated photograph from between the wars showing buckling of some of the ironwork on one of the inner girders. JOHN MANN COLLECTION

PLATE 9.17: Bridge Inspectors for some of the GWR's Divisions in 1926, including Mr J. Thomas of the Newport Division who had responsibility for Crumlin. The illustration appeared in the GWR's 'house' magazine.

had cost a total of £19,000, with £2,000 being spent in 1927, £5,300 in 1928, £5,500 in 1929 and £5,400 in 1930.[36]

For the intervening years, from 1930 to the end of the Second World War, no records have been found regarding any repair works to the viaducts. However, from the late 1940s on, the letter books contain regular items of correspondence in regards to repairs required to them. Most refer to the need to replace or strengthen parts due to rust and breakages but these were always considered to be a temporary measure lasting between eight and and ten years before consideration needed to be addressed to replacing the superstructure. On Monday, 11th June 1949, it was reported that an intensive appraisal of the viaducts had been completed using a Southern Region bridge testing van. Two ex-GWR '43xx' Class 2-6-0 locomotives were used to haul the testing van, under loaded conditions, across both the small and large viaducts, where it was found that the diagonal web members were overstressed. In the same year, the timber flooring to the walkway was replaced. An unspecified expenditure of £10,000 was recorded in the minute books of the Western Region of British Railways.[37]

Letters of February and November 1950 make passing comment to the prohibition of only the heaviest 'red' locomotives. During 1951, extensive repairs were carried out, which involved replacing the bearings on the short viaduct, along with repairs to the top booms, repairs to the floor and other works to the main girders. An attached warning mentioned that there was a gradual

worsening, which would require extensive works over the next five to six years.

Between January 1954 and October 1955, further defects were being reported, including corrosion to the top chords of the trusses, the gusset plates, and some of the cross girders and decking. It was later pointed out that the enclosed form of the top chords (*i.e.* the compression beam) would make it extremely difficult to repair them. The decking was suffering overstrain from floor interaction and required costly modifications. There was an opinion at that time that the general condition of the viaducts was beyond the '*normal margin of safety*'.

From the contents of a letter dated 28th November 1956, it is obvious that the corrosion of the metalwork in both viaducts was causing major concerns to the engineers. Although the reconstruction of two of the spans had been scheduled for 1958, it was mentioned that with the difficulties encountered in repairing the main girders, whether in fact it would be more prudent to consider the reconstruction of all of the spans of both viaducts between 1958 and 1960.[38]

The worsening condition of both viaducts was adding strength to proposals to reconstruct their superstructure. It had been pointed out that the line had been singled over them in 1929, whilst the 8mph speed restriction had been in force almost since opening, along with a prohibition on the use of heavier locomotives. A correspondent stated that '*Reconstruction has got to be faced in 1959 or 1960*'. If it was designed as a double line structure, then

PLATE 9.18: *It has proved quite a surprise to discover that several of the picture postcards of the viaduct published over the decades managed to capture unusual occurrences and this view is another example of that, showing the two GWR '43xx' Class 2-6-0 locomotives engaged in weight tests of the structure in summer 1949.* NEIL PARKHOUSE COLLECTION

PLATE 9.19: *One of a series of photographs taken on 14th July 1949, showing calculations being recorded during the strain gauge tests.* JOHN MANN COLLECTION

Plate 9.20: *A British Railways Western Region official photograph of the two 'Moguls' on the bridge during the strain gauge tests. Sadly, no picture seems to have been taken when the Southern Region Bridge Testing van was present. The significance of these tests is that they were being carried out eighteen months after the formation of British Railways, who were keen therefore to evaluate the condition of the viaduct, as although it was an important part of the Western Region network, it was also potentially a major liability.*
John Mann collection

strengthening and repairs would be required on the piers but if it was to be a single line, then no repairs would be required.[39] Four months later, it had been confirmed, following calculations and a site visit, that *'the existing piers and foundations were of ample strength and are in excellent condition to carry a new steel girder superstructure for 'red' loading on a single track at speeds up to 20 mph. The re-girdering of the ten spans for a single track then scheduled for 1959/ 1960 could be completed quite easily during thirty, 24-hour weekends occupation at a cost of about £325,000 or £450,000 for re-girdering for a double line on the existing piers, but any re-girdering was becoming urgent and should not be delayed beyond 1960'*.[40]

After a very thorough inspection of the piers on 13th June 1957, the bridge examiner, who had observed the viaducts for over thirty years, concluded that *'the condition of the cast iron parts of the piers was as good as it was a hundred years ago'*. He observed that there were odd places where blow holes showed up, some footings and a few horizontal bracing beams had cracked and been patched (probably at the time of erection) but there was nothing indicating movement either of the parts of the piers themselves or of the footing on the foundations.[41]

Following a further inspection in April and July, it was concluded that cracking within the structure was due to corrosion and not to overstress or settlement. This

PLATE 9.21: *Bridge testers on their work platform on 14th July 1949, during the strain gauge tests. Raised up above the walkway so they were positioned right underneath the deck, the two men on the left keep a close eye on their instruments as the locomotives pass over, whilst the third man had more measuring gauges mounted on the girder he is leaning on.*
JOHN MANN COLLECTION

PLATES 9.22, 9.23, 9.24 & 9.25: Although at first glance one could be mistaken for thinking that these photographs of 14th July 1949, show the bridge wired with plastic explosives, what they actually record is the wiring involved with the strain gauge testing. This led from various sensors which were cemented to girders and beams thought most likely to be affected by stress. Interestingly, this was a relatively new science at this date, the strain gauge having been independently invented by Edward E. Simmons (working in Cailfornia) and Professor Arthur C. Ruge (in Massachusetts) in the late 1930s, which was a by-product result of other researches they were involved in. The view on the right shows that safety netting had been strung around and below the men's work platform, as they were working at a much higher point of the viaduct than in the previous picture; the netting guarded against both falls and items being dropped.
ALL JOHN MANN COLLECTION

CLOCKWISE FROM TOP LEFT: All taken on the same day as the strain gauge pictures, this selection of photographs shows some of the issues with the metalwork:

PLATE 9.26: *A close-up of one the links at the east end of the Ebbw viaduct. Note the packing between the cast iron base and the stone.*

PLATE 9.27: *The links at the east end of the Kendon viaduct.*

PLATE 9.28: *Three of the links at the east end of the Ebbw viaduct.*

PLATE 9.29: *A close-up showing uneven packing between an 'A' frame and the deck beam on the Ebbw viaduct.*

PLATE 9.30: *Corrosion to a diagonal member on the Ebbw viaduct.*

ALL JOHN MANN COLLECTION

had not reduced the effectiveness of the lateral bracing connections but any further corrosion or cracking required attention and prevention. Water running down the diagonal bracing that found its way into the pockets in the distance girders, causing further corrosion, continued to be a problem, along with rusting where the diagonals crossed. As with previous recommendations, the pockets needed to be cleaned thoroughly and filled with a waterproofing compound. The report continued to find cracking and rusting at the ends where the iron straps and bracing were attached to the distance girder and to the column; this appeared to be the only serious defect and it was illustrated on an accompanying drawing (**Fig. 9.2**).[42]

A high powered meeting was held at Paddington on 12th March 1959, attended by seven officials from the Operating Department, five from the Commercial Department, one from Signalling, two from Running & Maintenance and one from Engineering. After completing a special review of all of the factors discussed, the officials present agreed to recommend via a memorandum that the viaduct should be reconstructed. In addition, the chairman mentioned the need to prepare necessary arrangements to deal with

PLATE 9.31: A close-up of the links at the west end of the Ebbw viaduct. JOHN MANN COLLECTION

PLATE 9.32: A detail study showing the underneath side of the decking on the Ebbw viaduct. JOHN MANN COLLECTION

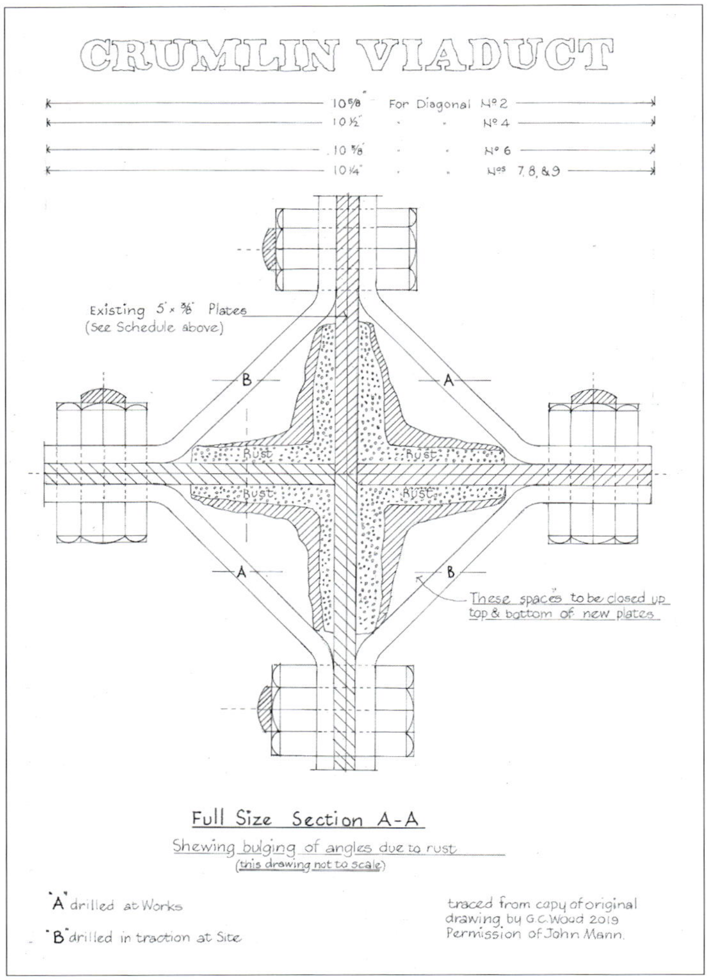

FIG. 9.2: Drawing illustrating the bulging of the angles caused by the ongoing problem of rust.

the working of traffic over them during the occupation of the viaducts by the engineering department.[43]

A letter in the chief engineers letterbook, dated 16th March 1959, endorsed the conclusion contained in the memorandum and the reconstruction of the viaducts was to proceed. This was followed by an agreement to prepare plans and tenders to strengthen them for a further life of ten years at an estimated cost of £50.000. In August 1960, the contract covering the cost of the repairs was awarded to the Fairfield Shipbuilding & Engineering Company of Chepstow, with an anticipated completion date of 31st January 1961. Later reports confirm that the repairs were nearing completion in February 1961 and that the work had been completed during June 1961. Further repairs had been identified, with these being completed by British Railways staff. A firm decision on the reconstruction of the viaducts was not forthcoming during 1961 and it was being pointed out by the engineers that one was required by 1964.[44]

Inspections of the viaducts during November 1961 reported that the earlier repair '*had not addressed the overstressing of the main girders*'. Special arrangements were made for further testing at 9.30am on Sunday, 7th January 1962, the work being completed by staff from the Civil Engineering Laboratory. To facilitate load testing, arrangements had been made for a BR 'Standard' Class '9' 2-10-0 locomotive, with a 5,625 gallon tender fully loaded and watered, to haul a train of five fully loaded 20-ton hopper ballast wagons (code name 'Herring'). These were to be available between 9.30am and 5.00pm and the train was to be marshalled with the wagons coupled to the smokebox end of the locomotive, which was to be facing Crumlin High Level station *i.e.* west.[45] Results of the testing showed that under existing engine working conditions, there was some overstress in the web member in tension but there was no need to further curtail running or alter the speed restrictions. Concern was raised regarding the safety of trains crossing the viaducts during gales and, with recorded wind speeds exceeding 50mph, it was felt that restrictions on traffic ought to be applied '*whenever gales of Force 8 and above were imminent*'.[46] Further consideration was given to the wind situation when it was pointed out that existing stresses on the tension web members of the inner girders exceeded the then enhanced British Transport Commission allowances for wrought iron bridges whenever wind speed exceeded about 70mph, equivalent to a Force 11 gale on the Beaufort scale. The reason for preparing these figures for Crumlin was the fact that the main viaduct was very exposed, the wrought iron was of low ductile quality, and that secondary stresses and deformation stresses were high.[47]

PLATE 9.33: *Looking west along the Ebbw viaduct walkway on 14th July 1949.*
JOHN MANN COLLECTION

A memorandum prepared in April 1962 clarifies a number of points previously discussed and completed. Referring to the proposed repairs and other works on the structure, these could continue, under existing working conditions, for a maximum period of ten years. The works recently completed at a cost of £9,120 were to ensure the continuity of the strength of the structure but made no provision for strengthening. In addition to this, work was in hand for the replacement of defective bracing and redecking the walkway, bringing the total cost of the works to £15,000. It was considered that the repairs that had been carried out to the structure enabled it to be kept in use without imposing any additional restrictions until 1969. However, concerns had been expressed all along about this limited life extension, as any decision on its reconstruction needed to be made by 1965 to allow for a period to design and obtain tenders for renewing the structure in 1969. The effect of the wind on the structure was dispensed with but it was recommended that the viaduct should be inspected every six months.[48]

The final letters relating to the future of the viaducts provide a strong indication on further actions to be considered on the future of the Taff Vale Extension line. The first was the result of a revised cost of £490,000

*PLATE **9.34:** Like several generations of picture takers before him, the BR official photographer took his own spectacular panorama on 14th July 1949, managing to encapsulate the full length of the entire viaduct. Dropping down the valley side at the west end of the Ebbw section, the Trinant Colliery tramroad incline still formed a clear scar on the landscape fifty years after it fell out of use. Smoke and steam rise from Navigation Colliery in the centre right background.*
JOHN MANN COLLECTION

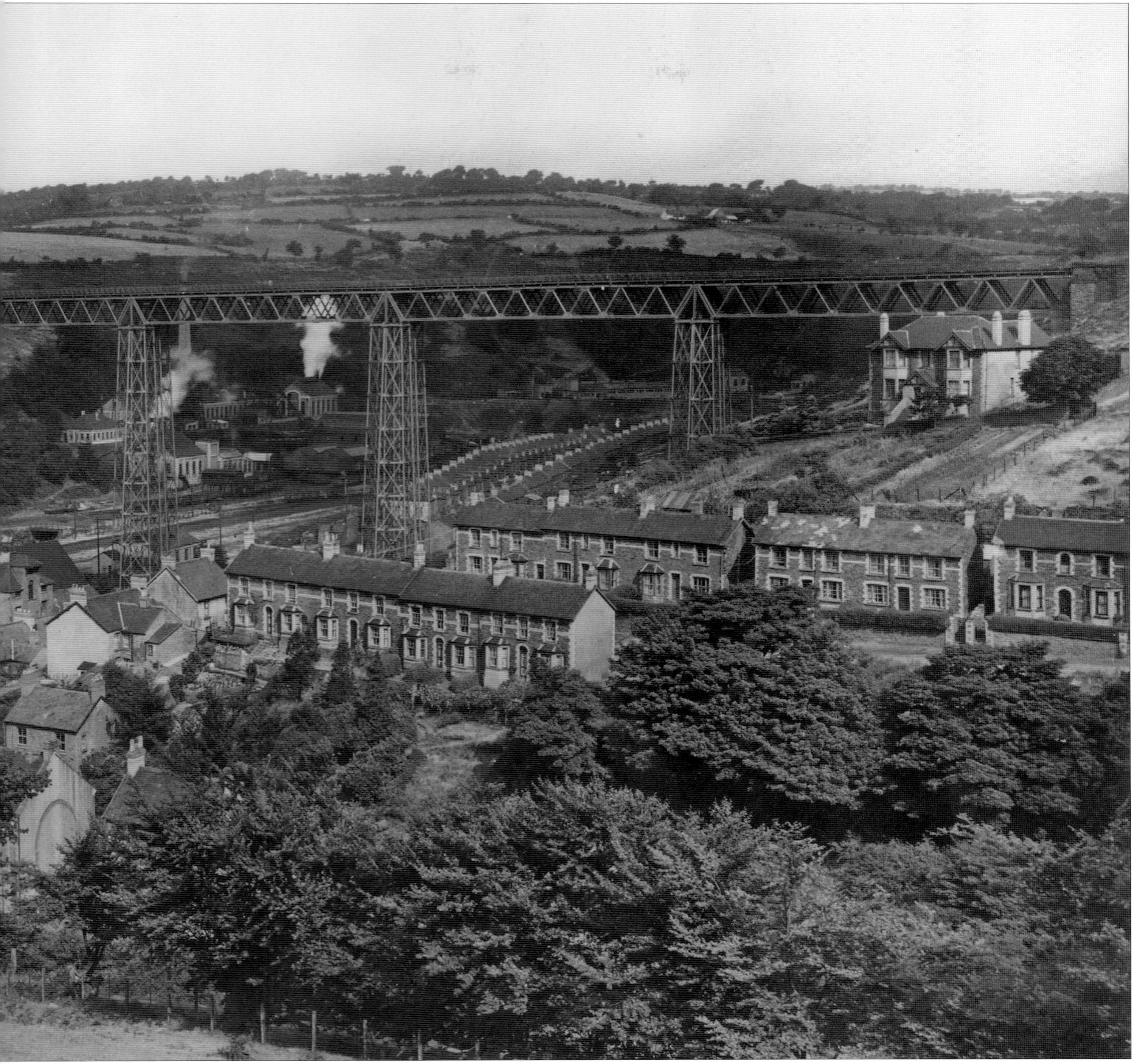

PLATE 9.35, PAGE OPPOSITE: The Ebbw section from the western abutment. This is one of a series of photographs taken on 19th August 1964, prior to any demolition work starting, which were commissioned as a record of the viaduct by the National Monuments Record of Wales.

PLATE 9.36, LEFT: Part of the same survey, this view is looking westwards along the south elevation of the Kendon section from the eastern abutment. Although a very wet day, the quality of the images was not affected.
BOTH RCAHMW/COFLEIN

for the reconstruction of the viaducts, followed by a letter asking about the future of the line. Whatever the outcome of that was to be, an assurance that a definite decision would be reached by 1965 was requested.[49]

References

1. Letter, Gordon to Carr, 21st July 1858
2. Letter, Carr to Gordon, 6th Aug. 1858
3. Minute, 9th April 1859, The National Archives (TNA)
4. Minute, 23rd Sept. 1859, TNA
5. Minute, 21st Oct. 1859, TNA
6. Minute, 17th Feb. 1860, TNA
7. Minute, 17th Feb. 1860, TNA
8. Board meeting, 21st Oct. 1860, TNA
9. Board meeting, 10th Dec. 1860, TNA
10. *Monmouthshire Merlin*, Oct. 1860
11. Letters. 4th Sept. 1865, Gwent Archives. Letters in *Hereford Times* and *Monmouthshire Merlin*, Sept. 1865.
12. Letter, 6th Sept. 1865, Gwent Archives
13. Letter, 5th Sept. 1865, Gwent Archives
14. Letter, 16th Sept. 1865, Gwent Archives
15. Report of Capt. Tyler to Board of Trade, 22nd Sept. 1865, forwarded to Saunders, 26th Sept. 1865, MT29/26, TNA
16. MT6/129, 19th Oct. 1904, TNA

PLATE 9.37: This final view from 14th July 1949 again emulates others taken decades before and shows a very tidy looking bridge deck. Crumlin High Level County Primary School and High Level station can be seen in the far left distance and on the hillside up above, the terraces of Treowen had all been added in the 1930s; steps leading straight down to the Up platform were provided when the estate was built.
JOHN MANN COLLECTION

17. Report, Fowler & Brereton, 13th Nov. 1865. Minute Locomotive & Carriage Committee. 15th Dec. 1865, RAIL 1057/2962, TNA
18. Letter to Saunders, 14th Nov. 1865, reported to Locomotive Carriage & Permanent Way Committee, 16th Dec. 1865, TNA
19. MT6/129/10, TNA
20. Letter, Owen to Saunders, 28th Nov. 1866
21. Letter, Owen to Saunders, 27th Nov. 1866
22. Letter, 27th Nov. 1866
23. *Monmouthshire Merlin*, 10th Nov. 1866
24. *Monmouthshire Merlin*, 1st Dec. 1866
25. Report, 5th August 1891, Rail 250, TNA
26. Circular letter, 6th Nov. 1891, Rail 250, TNA
27. Minute, 8th June 1898 & Aug. 1899, Rail 250, TNA
28. Board of directors minute No. 1310, 16th Feb. 1854, TNA
29. Great Western Railway (Crumlin Viaduct) Act, 1902, 8th Aug. 1902
30. Rail 250, 27th Apr. 1903 & MT/6/129, 30th June 1903, TNA
31. *Great Western Railway Magazine*, Oct. 1907
32. Rail 250/175, minute No. 2202, 30th Nov. 1905, Rail 250/48 TNA
33. https://www.waymarking.com/waymarks/WMJH4X_Remnant_of_the_Crumlin_Viaduct__San_Diego_CA
34. Report prepared by A.C. Cookson, 4th July 1919
35. Letter A.C. Cookson to W.W. Grierson, 17th May 1922
36. Reports contained in railway magazines
37. Report, 11th June 1949
38. Letter P.S.A. Berridge to F.R.L. Barnwell, 28th Nov. 1956
39. Letter P.S.A. Berridge to M.G.R. Smith, 13th Feb. 1957
40. Copy letter, F.R.L. Barnwell from P.S.A. Berridge, 17 June 1957
41. Letter, P.S.A. Berridge to M.G.R. Smith, 17th June 1957
42. Report, 7th July 1958
43. Memorandum of meeting held at Paddington, 12th Mar. 1959
44. Papers contained in chief engineer's letter books
45. Letter, P.S.A. Berridge to J.F. Bickerton, 18th Dec. 1961
46. Letter, P.S.A. Berridge to M.G.R. Smith, copy to J.F. Bickerton, 16th Feb. 1962
47. Letter, P.S.A. Berridge to J.F. Bickerton, 5th Mar. 1962
48. Memorandum, 5th Mar. 1962
49. Letter, May & 26th June 1962

A WORKING LIFE
LOCOMOTIVES AND TRAIN SERVICES

CHAPTER 10

When it opened in 1857, the Taff Vale Extension of the Newport, Abergavenny & Hereford Railway completed the vital link between the NA&HR main line at Pontypool Road and the Vale of Neath Railway at Aberdare Junction. Coal could now be transported eastwards across the South Wales valleys, from the collieries of the Aberdare coalfield to the Midlands. However, whilst the line ostensibly connected Pontypool Road to Neath, the Vale of Neath line was built to the broad gauge, so from the outset through traffic was not the priority. A third rail was laid along the line of the VoNR in 1864 and it was subsequently converted to standard gauge in 1872 but by this stage the pattern had been set and whilst some passenger services operated over the whole of the line, only a few general goods trains worked right through.

NEWPORT, ABERGAVENNY, & HEREFORD RAILWAY.

OPENING OF THE TAFF-VALE EXTENSION LINE TO TREDEGAR JUNCTION,
OVER THE CRUMLIN VIADUCT.

WHITSUNTIDE HOLIDAYS.

ON MONDAY and TUESDAY, the 1st and 2nd of JUNE, EXCURSION TRAINS will run to CRUMLIN VIADUCT and Back, as under :—

From HEREFORD, at 11.30 A.M. ; returning from CRUMLIN at 8.0 P.M.
FARES : Closed Carriages, 3*s.* 6*d.* ; Open ditto, 2*s.* 6*d.*

From ABERGAVENNY, at 8.0 30 A.M. ; returning from CRUMLIN at 6.30 P.M.
FARES : Closed Carriages, 1*s.* 6*d.* ; Open ditto, 1*s.*

From USK, by Special Train, at 10.0 A.M. ; returning from CRUMLIN at 7.30 P.M.
At Single Fares for the Double Journey.

Tickets will be issued to CRUMLIN from Hereford and Intermediate Stations as far as NANTYDERRY by all the Ordinary Trains, at Single Fares for the Double Journey.

In addition to the Ordinary Trains between Pontypool and Crumlin a Train will leave Pontypool at 3.0 P.M., for Crumlin ; returning from Crumlin to Pontypool at 9.0 P.M.

Tickets can be obtained at Hereford and Abergavenny, for the Trains from those Stations, any day during the current week.

General Manager's Office, May 25th, 1857. BY ORDER.

NEWPORT, ABERGAVENNY, & HEREFORD RAILWAY.

NOTICE.—ALTERATION OF TRAINS FOR JUNE, 1857

ON AND AFTER MONDAY, the FIRST DAY OF JUNE, the FOLLOWING ALTERATIONS will be made :—

The 11.10 A.M. Up Train will leave Newport at 11.0 A.M., and be proportionately earlier at all intermediate Stations, and Hereford.

N.B. This will be a Through Train to Shrewsbury, Birmingham, Liverpool, Manchester, &c.

The Taff Vale Extension Line is now open, over the Crumlin Viaduct, to Tredegar Junction (Blackwood), and slight alterations have been made in the times of the Usk, Crumlin and Tredegar Trains, for particulars of which see Time Bills of the Company. BY ORDER.

General Manager's Office, Hereford, May 25, 1857.

SHREWSBURY AND HEREFORD RAILWAY.

WHITSUNTIDE HOLIDAYS.

EXCURSION TO NEWPORT, PONTYPOOL, & THE CRUMLIN VIADUCT.

ON MONDAY, JUNE 1st, a SPECIAL EXCURSION TRAIN will leave SHREWSBURY at 7-15 A.M., calling at the principal Stations, and arriving at Pontypool and Crumlin, about 11-0 A.M.

FARES FOR THE DOUBLE JOURNEY:

	FIRST CLASS.	COVERED CARRIAGES.
SHREWSBURY ... ... CHURCH STRETTON	7*s.* 6*d.*	5*s.* 0*d.*
CRAVEN ARMS ... ... LUDLOW	6*s.* 6*d.*	4*s.* 6*d.*
WOOFFERTON... ... ... LEOMINSTER	6*s.* 0*d.*	4*s.* 0*d.*

The Return Train to leave Newport at 5-30, Crumlin at 6-0 P.M., and arrive in Shrewsbury about 10-0 P.M.

Traffic Manager's Office, Shrewsbury, May 20th, 1857. BY ORDER.

Fig. 10.1: NA&HR and Shrewsbury & Hereford Railway advertisements for excursion trains over the TVE and Crumlin Viaduct on 1st and 2nd June 1857, from the Hereford Journal *of 27th May. The NA&HR also gave notice of train service alterations as a result of the line's opening.*

Testing, First Trains, First Time Tables

As already noted, the first locomotives on the viaduct were West Midland engines supplied for weight testing purposes in May 1857. A single engine arrived first, in early May, and the success of that test led to six being sent down a week later, to allow for far more rigorous testing. The NA&HR fleet was quite small, comprising just twenty engines at this date, so it is not difficult to work out the likely candidates. The heaviest were the seven 0-6-0 tender engines built by E.B. Wilson & Co. in 1854-55 and numbered 1-6 and 10 by the NA&HR – No. 3 is illustrated on page 79. It is also likely that they worked regularly across the viaduct after it had opened to traffic and all seven were taken into West Midland Railway stock when that company was formed on 1st July 1860 (WMR No's 71-76 and 80) and subsequently into GWR stock on 1st August 1863, when they absorbed the WMR (GWR No's 253-258 and 268).

Sadly, none of the highly detailed accounts of the opening of the viaduct give any clue as to the locomotive which hauled the special excursion from Hereford, conveying the NA&HR directors and guests, on Whit Monday, 1st June 1857. However, as the 0-6-0s used for

Plate 10.1: This poor quality engraving appeared in the Hereford Times *for 6th June 1857, just five days after the official opening and thus almost certainly shows the special train, the only illustration thought to do so; it has not been found in any other newspaper of the time. Unfortunately, it is insufficiently detailed to identify anything about the train.*

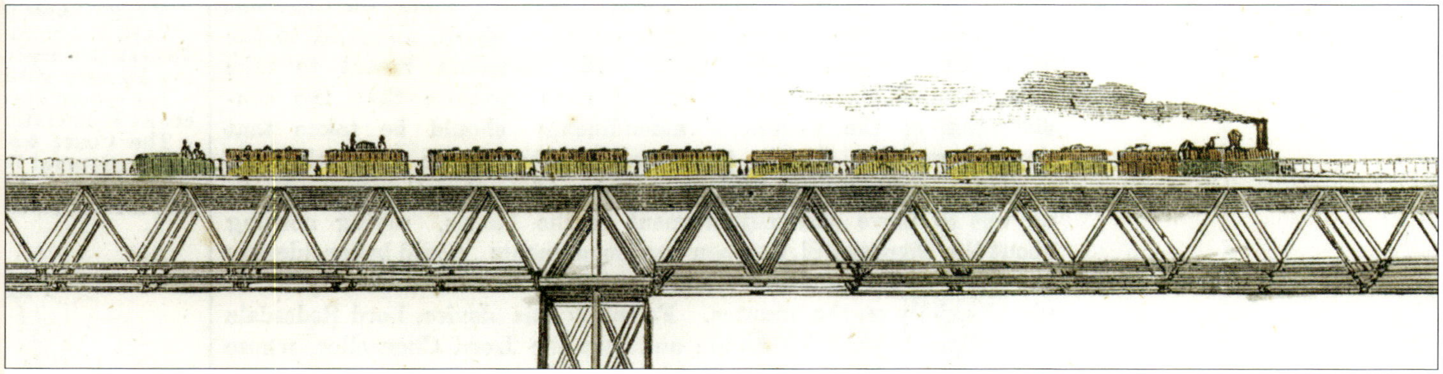

Plate 10.2: This enlargement from the Illustrated London News *engraving of 29th August 1857 was that paper's first picture of the completed viaduct. Published three months after opening, it almost certainly shows an ordinary passenger service, hauled by one of the NA&HR's passenger 2-4-0 engines, heading west.*

Plate 10.3: GWR No. 191 had started out as NA&HR No. 28 Reindeer. *The engine was rebuilt twice by the GWR, the first time in November 1873 when the wheelbase was altered from 7ft 9ins x 7ft 4ins to 7ft 9ins x 7ft 9ins. This photograph appears to date from before that was carried out, so shows the engine still in original condition.*
Neil Parkhouse collection

testing were officially designated as goods engines, it would seem likely that one of the E.B. Wilson & Co. 2-4-0 passenger tender engines was used, No's 27-30, the first three delivered in 1855, with No. 30 arriving in August 1856. As the newest of the four, was No. 30 perhaps the engine selected? We shall never know. Contemporary accounts note that the train first called at a temporary platform erected at the eastern end of the viaduct and then stopped on it, with the directors' carriage positioned above the central pier.

Whilst the completion of the viaduct allowed the Taff Vale Extension to be opened as far as Tredegar Junction (Pontllanfraith) in 1857, it was not until the following year that operations were extended on to Quaker's Yard. The opening of the Middle Duffryn line at Aberdare by the GWR in 1865 also finally allowed through passenger trains over the whole of the TVE/VoN route, which saw the commencement of a service of three trains a day each way between Hereford and Swansea in addition to the various local workings en route. An early circa 1857 sketch of Hengoed Viaduct with a train passing over shows a mixed goods and passenger consist, the carriages marshalled at the rear.

As noted above, the NA&HR's period of operation over the viaduct was short, just three years and one month, whilst the ensuing WMR era lasted for an identical time. Many of the former's fleet of engines would undoubtedly have continued to regularly work over it through the 1860s and into the 1870s. The number of 0-6-0 goods tender engines had grown to seventeen, with the construction of ten slightly smaller versions of the original seven, built between 1856 and 1858. E.L. Ahrons, in his series on the early standard gauge engines of the GWR published in *The Locomotive Magazine* in 1915, notes that these were split between Newport, Pontypool Road and Hereford.

There were also the four 2-4-0 passenger locomotives, No. 27 *Antelope*, No. 28 *Reindeer*, No. 29 *Elk* and No. 30 *Gazelle*. Of a standard E.B. Wilson & Co. design and therefore identical to engines supplied to the North Eastern Railway, they were rebuilt twice after coming into GWR ownership and enjoyed long careers of well over forty years each. The NA&HR stud also included two 0-6-0 tank engines, built by Wilson's in 1856 to work the Llanhilleth Branch (from Crumlin Junction), NA&HR No's 7 and 8. They were later used for many years banking heavy coal trains from Pontypool Road. Lastly, there were the three locomotives bought from the contractor Joseph Brassey, all 0-4-2 tender engines built

Plate 10.4: GWR No. 274, ex-NA&HR No. 16, seen here at Grange Court Junction in May 1872, was built in 1858 and thus was not one of the engines used in the weight tests but it is quite likely that one or more of its earlier classmates was – No's 9 and 11 of 1856 or No's 12 and 13 delivered in January 1857. These engines were slightly smaller than the earlier goods engine class illustrated by No. 255 on page 79, and two tons lighter. E.L. Ahrons notes that none of the NA&HR's goods locomotives were ever rebuilt by the GWR – so again the engine is seen here in as built condition – and that all were broken up between 1879 and 1883, No. 274 being withdrawn in October 1879.
Neil Parkhouse collection

by Dodds & Co. of Rotherham, which became NA&HR No's 20-22. No. 22 was rebuilt as an 0-4-2 side tank engine and used for passenger work.

What is not clear is where these engines would have been shedded. The NA&HR's main shed and workshops were at Hereford Barton, the domain of the company's Resident Engineer & Locomotive Superintendent Mark Carr. However, it would seem highly improbable that engines were sent out from Hereford every day, so where exactly were they stabled for working the TVE line? The only known sheds locally at this early period were those of the Monmouthshire Railway & Canal Company – one at Coed-y-Gric Junction, close to Panteg station, which opened in July 1852 and was arranged in roundhouse fashion around a turntable, although only two of the seven roads were covered; and another at Pontypool station (Crane Street from 1881), a single road shed with a spur to a turntable, which opened in October 1854. Use of the latter would seem most unlikely, as the MR&CC used it for the engine working their three trains each way per day passenger service between Pontypool and Newport Mill Street station. It was closed in November 1878 when a new shed was opened at Blaenavon.

Which leaves the shed at Coed-y-Gric Junction. After the NA&HR became part of the WMR in 1860, the latter made an attempt to lease the MR&CC but although the Bill was passed by Parliament, it was rejected by the Monmouthshire Company's shareholders. It does perhaps suggest a degree of cooperation between the two concerns though, so it may well be that the WMR were permitted the use of the shed at Coed-y-Gric. By the time that the MR&CC did agree a deal to lease their undertaking, to the GWR from 1st August 1875, a new shed had been established, built on a new site to the north in 1869. This was straight shed with eight covered roads and may have been a joint MR&CC/L&NWR construction, as the two companies had developed a close working arrangement. The design of the building

Plate 10.5: This ex-Thomas Brassey 0-4-2 tender engine was rebuilt as a side tank, probably by the NA&HR at their Hereford Barton workshops, and used for passenger work. As such, it quite probably worked local services from Pontypool Road to Crumlin and then beyond. NA&HR No. 22, it became WMR No. 92 and then GWR No. 227 but was then quickly deemed surplus to requirements and was sold to the Bishop's Castle Railway in 1870.

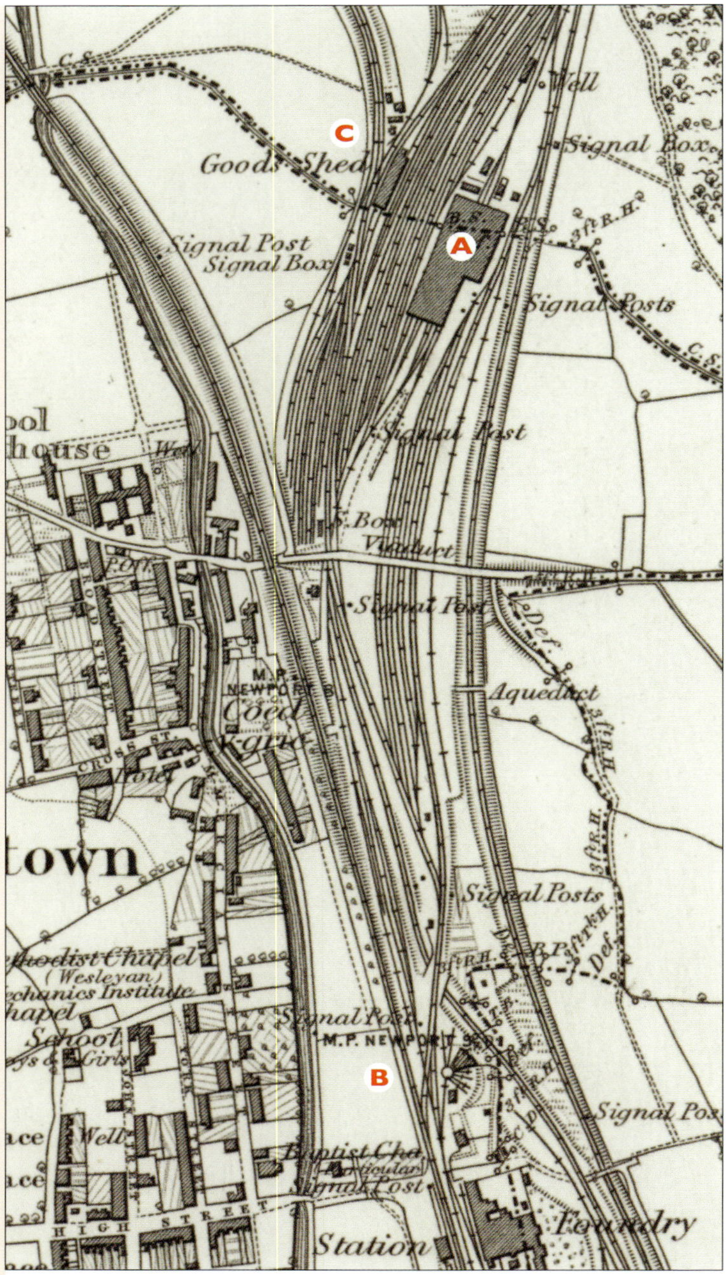

FIG. 10.2: *This extract from the 6 inch OS map surveyed in 1881 is interesting and contradicts what has previously been published in regards to the MR&CC's engine shed. The map clearly shows the GWR's roundhouse extension (the wider portion (A) at the north end of their Pontypool Road shed) but also includes the tiny MR&CC roundhouse style facility (B), just to the north of Panteg station, which was opened on 1st August 1880 and replaced the original station, situated on the NA&HR main line on the east side of the foundry but off the map portion here. The new station became Panteg & Griffithstown in 1898 and was closed in 1962. It will be noted that the TVE line, which starts its turn away to the west by the goods shed (C), had virtually a direct route through the yard to the MR&CC shed. That this is still shown as intact here also begs the question as to when in fact it did close?*

PLATE 10.6: *GWR No. 192, ex-NA&HR No. 29* Elk*, seen here posed at an unknown shed location after its second rebuilding in September 1890, makes for an interesting comparison with the unrebuilt No. 191 on page 162. It was withdrawn in June 1902 after a service life of forty-seven years.* JOHN ALSOP COLLECTION

had distinct echoes of L&NWR sheds built elsewhere on their system. It was enlarged in 1879, by which time the GWR were firmly in charge, with the addition of a Swindon-style roundhouse at the northern end of the building; this had one line running right through (and into the earlier shed, with twenty stabling spurs – ten on each side – all coming off the centre turntable. A large brick-built, Dean-type coaling stage was provided at the same time. Situated in the triangle formed by the GWR line from Abergavenny on the east side, the MR&CC line from Panteg to Pontypool on the west and the TVE line to the north, it was to provide much of the motive power for the trains using these routes for the next eight-six years. However, the 1881 OS map extract on the left severely calls into question the previously published circa 1865 closure date for the earlier MR&CC shed.

The first NA&HR passenger time table for the TVE, issued in September 1855, showed a service of four Down and three Up trains a day between Pontypool Road and Crumlin, which would been to the temporary platform erected at the site of what later became Crumlin Junction. Down trains departed Pontypool Road at 7.30am, 9.40am, 11.50am and 4.25pm, with returns departing Crumlin at 9.50am, 3.10pm and 7.50pm. The Sunday service comprised three trains a day each way, Down at 7.30am, 10.20am and 8.10pm, and Up at 8.20am, 4.20pm and 9.05pm. Journeys took either 20 or 25 minutes. The fares quoted, from Hereford, were 7 shillings (1st), 5s 1d (Second) and 3s 2d (Third Class), but whether this was single or return is not clear.

With the opening of the line on to Tredegar Junction in 1857, the service increased to five Down trains, departing Pontypool Road at 7.30am, 12.00 midday and then 1.42, 4.38 and 7.00pm. Up trains called at Crumlin at 10.00am and then at 1.30, 3.20 and 5.30pm. The Sunday service was three trains each way. The First Class fare from Hereford remained the same at 7s but Second and Third Class fares had dropped slightly to 4s 9d and 3s 1½d. By March 1868, with the line finally opened throughout to Quaker's Yard, the service remained at five Down and four Up trains (and three each way on Sundays) but tickets could be bought through to Merthyr Tydfil on all trains. Merthyr at that time was a great industrial centre and an enticing destination for any nascent railway company, so running powers were obtained over the Taff Vale Railway in order for NA&HR trains to reach it. Through tickets to all NA&HR stations for Third Class passengers from Liverpool and Chester were also advertised.

With such a small NA&HR fleet to work with, change

PLATE 10.7: GWR 'Standard Goods' No. 610 pictured here circa 1875, was new in 1871. It is seen here in almost original condition apart from the brass dome, which were fitted to the class from around 1875 in place of painted ones. Cast numberplates were fitted in place of painted numbers from 1876 and the class were fitted with cabs from 1879. Note the young lad on the footplate and the fine example of a disc & crossbar signal behind.
BRIAN ARMAN COLLECTION

under the WMR was probably driven by traffic levels, with WMR engines taking up the slack. However, the GWR had begun absorbing the 131-strong WMR stud of locomotives during the period June-December 1861 and only three remained to be taken under the GWR's wing on 1st August 1863. As a result, it may well be the case that GWR engines had also started to appear on the Taff Vale Extension prior to this date. However, early locomotive records are sparse in the extreme, so much of this must remain as speculation.

No time table has been seen for the short period of West Midland Railway operation but it is presumed that little changed until after the GWR had absorbed that company in August 1863. Initially, the GWR issued time tables for what had now become their West Midland Section. Little changed with the passenger time table through the decades during the later 19th century, what was essentially largely a local service proving sufficient, whilst goods and coal traffic were much more in evidence. A GWR West Midland Section Working Time Table for 1865 shows sixteen Down trains crossing the viaduct between 10.00pm and 11.00am, with the 10.00am service off Pontypool Road being the only passenger working – there were numerous trains of empty wagons, plus minerals workings, the Swansea goods and a pick-up goods.

Meanwhile, the concurrent GWR passenger time table listed the Pontypool Road-Swansea trains under the title '*GREAT WESTERN AND VALE OF NEATH RAILWAYS*'. Services were shown from Hereford to Pontypool Road,

PLATES 10.8 & 10.9, BELOW: Two further examples of 'GWR 'Standard Goods' 0-6-0s, showing their later development: No. 435 was built in 1868 and withdrawn in 1907 whilst No. 701 was in service from 1872 to 1919. No. 435 had been fitted with vacuum brakes and a Swindon cab, which went over the rear splasher. No. 701, seen here at Stafford Road shed, has a Wolverhampton pattern cab, which incorporated the rear splasher.
BOTH BRIAN ARMAN COLLECTION

GREAT WESTERN AND VALE OF NEATH RAILWAYS.

TIME TABLE OF TRAINS BETWEEN SWANSEA, ABERDARE, MERTHYR, AND PONTYPOOL ROAD,

And through communication to and from Shrewsbury, Chester, Liverpool, and Manchester, &c., &c.

DOWN TRAINS.

STATIONS.				WEEK DAYS.	3d Class between Swansea & Pontypool Road.				SUNDAYS.			
				Class 1, 2, P	Class 1 & 2	Class 1 & 2	Class 1, 2, 3	Class 1, 2, 3	Class 1, 2, 3	Class 1, 2, 3	Class 1, 2, 3	
				A.M.	A.M.	P.M.	P.M.	P.M.	A.M.	P.M.	P.M.	
Swansea (Wind Street)	dep.	.	.	8 0	10 50	3 0	5 15	7 50	8 30	.	6 45	.
Briton Ferry Road ..	”	..	..	8 10	11 0	3 10	5 25	8 0	8 40	..	6 55	..
Neath Abbey	”	...	...	8 16	11 5	3 16	5 31	8 6	8 46	...	7 1	...
Neath . .	”	.	.	8 21	11 10	3 25	5 36	8 11	8 51	.	7 6	.
Aberdylais	”	..	..	8 25	11 14	3 30	5 41	8 16	8 56	..	7 11	..
Resolven	”	...	.	8 35	11 24	3 40	5 52	8 27	9 7	...	7 22	...
Glyn Neath . .	”	.	.	8 43	11 32	3 48	6 0	8 36	9 16	.	7 31	.
Hirwain (for Aberdare)	”	..	..	9 10	11 50	4 11	6 20	9 0	9 43	..	7 58	..
Hirwain (for Merthyr)	dep.	..	.	9 10	11 51	4 11	6 25	8 58	9 45	.	7 58	.
Llwydcoed	”	..	..	9 16	11 56	4 16	6 30	9 4	9 51	..	8 1	..
Abernant	”	...	...	9 21	12 1	4 21	6 35	9 9	9 56	...	8 6	...
Merthyr . .	arr.	.	.	9 31	12 11	4 32	6 45	9 20	10 5	.	8 15	.
Aberdare . .	dep.	.	.	9 20	12 0	4 20	6 33	9 10	9 53	.	8 10	.
Mountain Ash	”	..	..	9 25	12 10	4 30			9 58	..	8 15	..
Quaker's Yard ...	arr.	...	...	9 40	12 20	4 40	...	...	10 13	...	8 30	...
	dep.	.	.	9 45	12 30	4 45	.	.	10 16	.	8 33	.
Llancaich	”	..	..	9 53	12 38	4 55	..	..	10 26	..	8 43	..
Rhymney Junction ...	”	...	...	10 3	12 45	5 5	...	...	10 36	...	8 53	...
Tredegar Junction .	”	.	.	10 8	12 50	5 12	.	.	10 41	.	8 58	.
Crumlin	”	..	..	10 18	1 0	5 22	..	..	10 51	..	9 [illegible]	..
Pontypool Town ...	”	...	...	10 30	1 13	5 37	...	...	11 3	...	9 20	...
Pontypool Road .	arr.	.	.	10 35	1 18	5 45	.	.	11 8	.	9 25	.
Monmouth . .	arr.	.	.	11 55	3 0	7 0	.	.	12 15	.	10 30	.
Pontypool Road .	dep.	.	.	10 53	1 51	5 57	.	.	.	4 7	.	.
Hereford (Barton) ..	arr.	..	..	12 28	3 5	7 31	..	..	..	5 40	..	..
Worcester . .	arr.	.	.	1 50	5 25	8 55	.	.	.	7 10	.	.
Dudley	”	..	..	3 22	7 5	10 30	..	..	..	9 25	..	..
Birmingham	”	...	...	4 0	7 45	...	...	...	...	10 25	...	...
Wolverhampton .	”	.	.	3 50	7 40	10 50	.	.	.	10 5	.	.
Leominster . .	arr.	.	.	1 5	3 45	8 33	.	.	.	8 33	.	.
Ludlow	”	..	..	1 25	4 10	8 55	..	..	..	8 55	..	..
Shrewsbury	”	...	...	2 25	5 5	10 0	...	...	...	10 0	...	...
Oswestry . .	”	.	.	3 20	6 13	11 35	.	.	.		.	.
Wrexham	”	..	..	3 46	6 35	11 50	..	..	..	..	..	..
Chester	”	...	...	4 10	7 0	12 15	...	...	...	...	...	...
Manchester (Vic. Station)	”	.	.	6 5	9 10	3 55	.	.	.	.	.	.
Birkenhead	”	..	..	5 0	7 45	3 5	..	..	..	..	..	..
Liverpool (Landing Stage)	”	...	...	5 20	8 5	...	...	...	...	...	...	...

UP TRAINS.

STATIONS.		WEEK DAYS.							SUNDAYS.			
		Class 1, 2, 3		Class 1, 2, P	Class 1, 2, 3	Class 1, 2, 3	Class 1 & 2		Class 1, 2, 3	Class 1, 2, 3	Class 1, 2, 3	
		A.M.		A.M.	P.M.	A.M.	A.M.		A.M.	A.M.	P.M.	
Liverpool (Landing Stage)	dep.	.	.	.	.	7 35	10 50	.	.	.	.	.
Birkenhead	”	..	..	..	..	7 50	11 10	..	..	..	..	..
Manchester (Vic.Station)	”	...	...	...	...	6 30	9 50	...	...	...	...	...
Chester . .	”	.	.	.	.	8 45	12 15	.	.	.	.	.
Wrexham	”	..	...	..	..	9 17	12 40	..	..	..	..	..
Oswestry	”	...	..	...	...	9 35	12 55	...	...	...	...	...
Shrewsbury . .	”	.	.	.	.	10 30	1 40	.	.	.	.	.
Ludlow	”	..	..	..	..	11 30	2 38	..	..	..	..	..
Leominster	”	...	...	...	...	11 56	2 58	...	...	...	...	...
Wolverhampton (L. Lev.)	dep.	.	.	.	.	7 55	10 30	.	.	.	.	.
Birmingham (New Street)	”	..	..	..	..	7 45	12 5	..	..	..	..	..
Dudley	”	...	...	...	...	8 25	11 0	...	...	...	...	...
Worcester . .	”	.	.	6 30	.	11 5	1 10	.	.	.	.	.
Hereford (Barton) . .	”	.	.	8 5	.	12 30	3 35	.	.	11 40	.	.
Pontypool Road ..	arr.	..	..	9 46	..	1 47	4 55	..	..	1 18	..	..
Monmouth . .	dep.	.	.	8 40	.	12 30	4 45	.	6 30	.	5 15	.
Pontypool Road .	dep.	.	.	10 0	.	2 0	6 0	1, 2, 3 Class.	7 35	.	6 25	.
Pontypool Town ..	”	..	..	10 5	..	2 5	6 5		7 40	..	6 30	..
Crumlin	”	...	...	10 18	...	2 20	6 17		7 53	...	6 43	...
Tredegar Junction .	”	.	.	10 28	.	2 30	6 27		8 0	.	6 53	.
Rhymney Junction ..	”	..	..	10 33	..	2 35	6 32		8 8	..	6 58	..
Llancaich	”	...	...	10 41	...	2 43	6 40		8 16	...	7 6	...
Quaker's Yard .	arr.	.	.	10 49	.	2 53	6 50		8 24	.	7 14	.
	dep.	..	..	10 55	..	2 58	6 55		8 30	..	7 20	..
Mountain Ash ...	”	...	...	11 5	...	3 7	7 5		8 35	...	7 25	...
Aberdare . .	arr.	8 20	.	11 15	.	3 17	7 15		8 45	.	7 35	.
Merthyr . .	dep.	8 40	.	—	1 30	3 0	7 0		8 30	.	7 30	.
Abernant	”	8 52	..	—	1 42	3 11	7 12		8 42	..	7 42	..
Llwydcoed	”	8 57	...	—	1 47	3 17	7 17		8 47	...	7 47	...
Hirwain . .	arr.	9 3	.	—	1 53	3 22	7 23		8 53	.	7 53	.
Hirwain . .	dep.	9 5	.	11 25	1 55	3 27	7 26		8 55	.	7 55	..
Glyn Neath	”	9 25	..	11 45	2 15	3 47	7 46		9 15	..	8 15	..
Resolven	”	9 34	...	11 54	2 23	.	7 54		9 23	...	8 23	...
Aberdylais . .	”	9 46	.	12 5	2 35	4 5	8 5		9 35	.	8 35	.
Neath	”	9 51	..	12 10	2 40	4 10	8 10		9 40	..	8 40	..
Neath Abbey	”	9 56	...	12 15	2 45	...	8 15		9 45	...	8 45	...
Briton Ferry Road .	”	10 1	.	12 21	2 51	4 18	8 21		9 51	.	8 51	.
Swansea (Wind Street)	arr.	10 15	..	12 35	3 5	4 30	8 35		10 5	..	9 5	..

June, 1865.

Return Tickets between Birmingham, Wolverhampton, Wellington, Manchester, Liverpool, Birkenhead, Chester, Shrewsbury, and intermediate Stations, and Stations on the South Wales and Vale of Neath Lines will be available for two days.
Passengers for Swansea may alight from Down Trains at the Ticket Platform, Eastern Depot, if they so desire.
Passengers from or for South Wales Stations, West of Swansea, will change at Swansea or Neath, at their option; & for Stations East of Neath, at Neath. Omnibuses meet the Trains at the South Wales & Vale of Neath Stations both at Swansea & Neath

I.

FIG. 10.3: Confusingly, the 1865 time table showed Swansea to Pontypool Road as Down and vice versa as Up in the table which covered the connections to and from Liverpool.

where passengers changed trains, but also showed the times of connecting services from Liverpool, travelling first by ferry across the River Mersey from Liverpool Landing Stage to Birkenhead and then via Chester and Shrewsbury. So for instance a 7.35am departure from Liverpool saw Swansea reached at 4.30pm – not unreasonable considering that 1865 was only thirty-five years out from the Rainhill Trials. The Liverpool end also provided a connection with transatlantic and Irish Sea shipping serving the docks.

PLATE 10.10: GWR No. 244 began life as WMR 'Goods' 0-6-0 No. 13, a replacement built at Worcester probably in 1860-61, the original WMR No. 13, an Oxford, Worcester & Wolverhampton Railway engine taken over in 1856, being in poor condition and scrapped. Some of these engines were shedded at Pontypool Road and thus would have worked over the TVE line. Note the polishing with oily rags.
BRIAN ARMAN COLLECTION

The first ex-NA&HR engine to disappear from the fleet was No. 22, which as GWR No. 227 was sold to the Bishop's Castle Railway in 1870. The rest of the fleet were withdrawn between 1876 and 1881, with the exception of the four 2-4-0s, No's 27-30, which as GWR No's 190-193 remained in service until 1899 (No. 190) and 1902 (No's 191-193). Shedded usually at Worcester, although they worked to Newport from time to time it seems unlikely they ever ventured across the viaduct again.

	Hereford (Barton)	dep.	8 5			12 30			2 50	3 35	7 5	8 0					11 40		7 50				
34½	Tram Inn		8 17						3 2			8 12					11 53		8 2				
37	St. Devereux		8 25						3 8			8 20					12 2		8 10				
40¼	Pontrilas		8 35			12 55			3 16	4 2	7 32	8 30					12 12		8 20				
45¼	Pandy		8 49						3 30			8 42					12 25		8 33				
48	Llanvihangel		8 57						3 38			8 50					12 32		8 40				
	Abergavenny Junction		9 7			1 21			3 45														
52	**Abergavenny**		9 12			1 26			3 50	4 25	7 55	9 4					12 45		8 53				
54½	Penpergwm		9 22							4 33	8 5	9 13					12 53		9 1				
57	Nantyderry		9 32	Class					4 5			9 23					1 0		9 10				
	Little Mill Junction			1, 2, 3												a.m.							
61¾	Pontypool Road	arr.	9 45	a.m.		1 49			4 20	4 55	8 27	9 35				1, 2, 3	1 8		9 25				
	Pontypool Road	dep.	9 50	11 0		1 56				6 0						11 15			9 35				
	Little Mill Junction																						
64	Usk		10 10	11 15		2 14				6 15						11 30			9 50				
67¼	Llandenny		10 20	11 25		2 24				6 25						11 40			10 0				
68¼	Raglan Road		10 25	11 30		2 29				6 30						11 45			10 5				
72¼	Dingestow		10 40	11 45		2 47				6 48						12 0		1, 2, 3	10 20				
76	**Monmouth**	arr.	10 50	11 55		3 0				7 0						12 15		p.m.	10 30				
	Pontypool Road	dep.	10 0			2 0				6 0						7 35		6 25					
62¾	Pontypool Town		10 5			2 5				6 5						7 40		6 30					
67½	Crumlin (for Western Valley)		10 18		1, 2, 3 Class.	2 20				6 17	1, 2, 3 Class.					7 53		6 43					
71	Tredegar Junction		10 28			2 30				6 27						8 0		6 53					
72¼	Rhymney Junction		10 33			2 35				6 32						8 8		6 58					
	Cardiff	arr.				3 30																	
	Rhymney	arr.	9 15			12 50																	
75	Llancaich and Nelson		10 41			2 43				6 40						8 16		7 6					
77½	Quaker's Yard		10 55			2 58				6 55						8 30		7 30					
	Aberdare		11 15			3 17				7 15						8 45		7 35					
	Hirwain		11 25			3 27				7 26						8 55		7 55					
	Neath		12 10			4 10				8 10						9 40		8 40					
	Swansea		12 35			4 30		class		8 35						10 5		9 5					
	Troedyrhiew		11 0			3 10		1, 2, 3		7 5						10 31		7 36					
	Merthyr	arr.	11 8			3 20		p.m.		7 15						10 38		7 43					
	Pontypool Road	dep.	9 48			1 51		5 50	4 22	4 55	8 28	9 36					1 18		9 25				
64	Pontnewydd		9 57					5 57	4 32			9 42					1 26		9 33				
69½	**Newport,** Mill Street	arr.	10 10			2 8		6 10	4 45	5 12	8 45	9 55		a.m.			1 38		9 45	a.m.			

All Trains are 1, 2, & 3 class between Monmouth and Merthyr. *Branch.*

Dist. from Newp					1, 2, Parl. a.m.	1, 2, a.m.	1, 2, 3 a.m.	1, 2, a.m.		1, 2, p.m.		1, 2, 3 p.m.		1, 2, p.m.			1, 2, Parl. a.m.		1, 2, 3 p.m.				
	Newport, Mill Street	dep.			6 10	7 35	9 15	10 30		1 30		2 0		5 30			9 20	Class	3 45			class	
5¼	Pontnewydd				6 24	7 49	9 29	10 44		1 44		2 14		5 44			9 32	1, 2, 3	3 57			1, 2, 3	
7¾	Pontypool Road	arr.			6 28	7 56	9 45	10 48		1 47		2 17		5 50			9 40	a.m.	4 5			p.m.	
	Merthyr	dep.						9 20		12 5				4 20				9 50				6 55	
	Troedyrhiew							9 29		12 14				4 29				9 57				7 2	
	Swansea (Wind Street)							8 0		10 50				3 0				8 30				6 45	
	Neath							8 21		11 10				3 25				8 51				7 6	
	Hirwain							9 10		11 50				4 11				9 43				8 0	
	Aberdare							9 20		12 0				4 20				9 53				8 10	
23¾	Quaker's Yard							9 45		12 30				4 45				10 16				8 33	
21¼	Llancaich and Nelson							9 53		12 38				4 55				10 26				8 43	
18½	Rhymney Junction	arr.						10 3	1, 2, 3 Class.	12 45				5 5				10 36				8 53	
	Rhymney	dep.						9 0															
	Cardiff	dep.						8 50															
17	Tredegar Junction	arr.						10 8		12 50				5 12				10 41				8 58	
14	Crumlin (for Western Valleys)							10 18		1 0	1, 2, 3 Class.			5 22	1, 2, 3 Class.			10 51			class	9 8	
8¾	Pontypool Town						1, 2, 3	10 30		1 13				5 37		1, 2, 3		11 3			1, 2, 3	9 20	
7¾	Pontypool Road	arr.					a.m.	10 35		1 18				5 45		a.m.		11 8			p.m.	9 25	
25¾	**Monmouth**						8 40			12 30				4 45		6 30					5 15		
22¼	Dingestow						8 50			12 41				4 55		6 41					5 26		
18	Raglan Road						9 5			12 57				5 10		6 57					5 42		
17	Llandenney						9 8			1 3				5 15		7 2					5 47		
13¾	Usk						9 20			1 15				5 25		7 14					5 59		
	Little Mill Junction																						
	Pontypool Road	arr.					9 40			1 35				5 45		7 35					6 20		
	Pontypool Road	dep.			6 30	7 57		10 53		1 51		2 20		5 57			9 45		4 7				
	Little Mill Junction																						
12¼	Nantyderry				6 45			11 5				2 30		6 8			10 2		4 19				
14¾	Penpergwm				6 54			11 15				2 40		6 15			10 10		4 29				
17½	**Abergavenny**				7 4	8 21		11 25		2 16		2 50		6 25			10 20		4 37				
	Abergavenny Junction					8 26								6 28									
21½	Llanvihangel				7 15			E				3 0		6 38			10 30		4 48				
23¾	Pandy				7 23			11 44				3 8		6 46			10 37		4 56				
28¾	Pontrilas				7 36	8 46		11 57		2 40		3 21		6 59			10 50		5 10				
32¼	St. Devereux				7 47			12 8				3 32		7 10			10 58		5 18				
34¾	Tram Inn				7 57			12 18				3 43		7 21			11 5		5 26				
39¾	**Hereford** (Barton)	arr.			8 10	9 11		12 28		3 5		3 55		7 31			11 15		5 40				

Branch.

Figs 10.4 & 10.5: From the same 1865 time table, these are extracts from the pages showing the West Midland Section services; those westwards from Pontypool Road are now correctly listed as Down trains and those heading east Up. Note the railway's spelling of Hirwaun as 'Hirwain'. All services between Pontypool Road and Swansea offered either Third Class or Parliamentary (P) tickets, as indicated by the VoN time table opposite. Parliamentary trains were a requirement of the Railway Regulation Act 1844 to provide inexpensive, basic rail transport for the less affluent – at least one service per day had to be run on every railway route in the UK.

Returning to the subject of engine sheds, although one was never provided anywhere on the TVE line between Pontypool Road and Quaker's Yard, the GWR did have another shed that would have supplied motive power for the route, namely the one at Aberdare. Opened as a four road shed in 1867, on the north side of the GWR's station (High Level added in 1924) on the Vale of Neath line, increasing traffic levels saw it doubled in size in 1874. During its lifetime, engines from its allocation would undoubtedly have worked freight turns over Crumlin Viaduct. It was closed on 11th November 1907 but was replaced by a larger roundhouse shed on a new site a little further north, which required a bridge over the River Cynon to reach it. From here and up until the shed closed on 1st March 1965, Aberdare-based, heavy freight type engines roamed much of the GWR and later British Railways Western Region system, delivering South Wales coal across the country.

Although Crumlin Viaduct was well photographed during construction and soon after, pictures showing trains crossing do not surface until the early years of the 20th century, when it became of interest to local and national postcard publishers. Consequently, the type of motive power crossing over during the last decades of the 19th century can again only be speculated at but GWR types would probably have started to predominate from the mid-1860s. The early 20th century views mostly show passenger trains in the hands of various types of tank engines and it would seem likely that this was much the same throughout the last two decades of the 19th

A SECTION OF CAMPION'S MAP OF THE COLLIERIES AND INDUSTRIES OF SOUTH WALES 1877

century. Chunky '1016' and 'Buffalo' Class 0-6-0 saddle tanks – of inside or outside framed variation – and the smaller '517' Class and 'Metro' 2-4-0 tanks, both built in large numbers from the late 1860s, would have been a common sight on passenger trains, as most services were local in nature. Most goods services meanwhile would have been in the hands of 'Standard Goods' 0-6-0 tender engines, another large class numbering over 300 built from 1866 to 1876. One lone '360' Class 0-6-0, No. 362 built in 1866, withdrawn in 1919 and one of a small class of just twelve engines, seems to have spent almost its entire career in the Newport Division, so quite possibly would have worked over the viaduct at some stage. Then, from 1883, construction began of Dean's inside-framed 'Dean Goods' 0-6-0s, with 260 built up to 1899. Like their 'Standard Goods' predecessors, the class was spread across the GWR network and some allocated to the Newport Division would have been regulars across Crumlin Viaduct.

Meanwhile, from April 1873, trains no longer ran along the TVE direct from Hereford, passengers having to change instead at Pontypool Road. Services running through to Merthyr via the TVR line from Quaker's Yard ceased in the early 1870s, probably around the time the Vale of Neath was converted to standard gauge. Instead, the GWR began serving it from Hirwaun (west of Aberdare and often misspelt by the railway as Hirwain), along tracks which they owned. Trains ran eastwards from Hirwaun and, at Gelly Taw Junction, took the branch to Merthyr that ran via Abernant and the 2,495 yards long Merthyr Tunnel.

An edition of the GWR Service Time Tables No. 5 for July 1877 (covering Shrewsbury, Worcester, Hereford and

PLATE 10.11: A 'Buffalo' Class 0-6-0 saddle tank heads east over the viaduct circa 1900, at the head of a typical passenger train of the period, comprising a 4-wheeled luggage/parcels van at the front, a bogie clerestory carriage, three 6-wheeled coaches and a bogie luggage/parcels van at the rear.
STEPHEN ROWSON COLLECTION

PLATE 10.12: The first six engines of the 'Buffalo' Class, No's 1076-81 of 1870, were built as double-framed side tanks. They were all later rebuilt as saddle tanks, No. 1077 being the last in 1902. They had shorter bunkers than the rest of the 'Buffalos' and after rebuilding always differed from their later classmates in this respect. The engine had gained a half cab in place of the original spectacle plate by the time it was seen here circa 1900 and was withdrawn in 1931.
BRIAN ARMAN COLLECTION

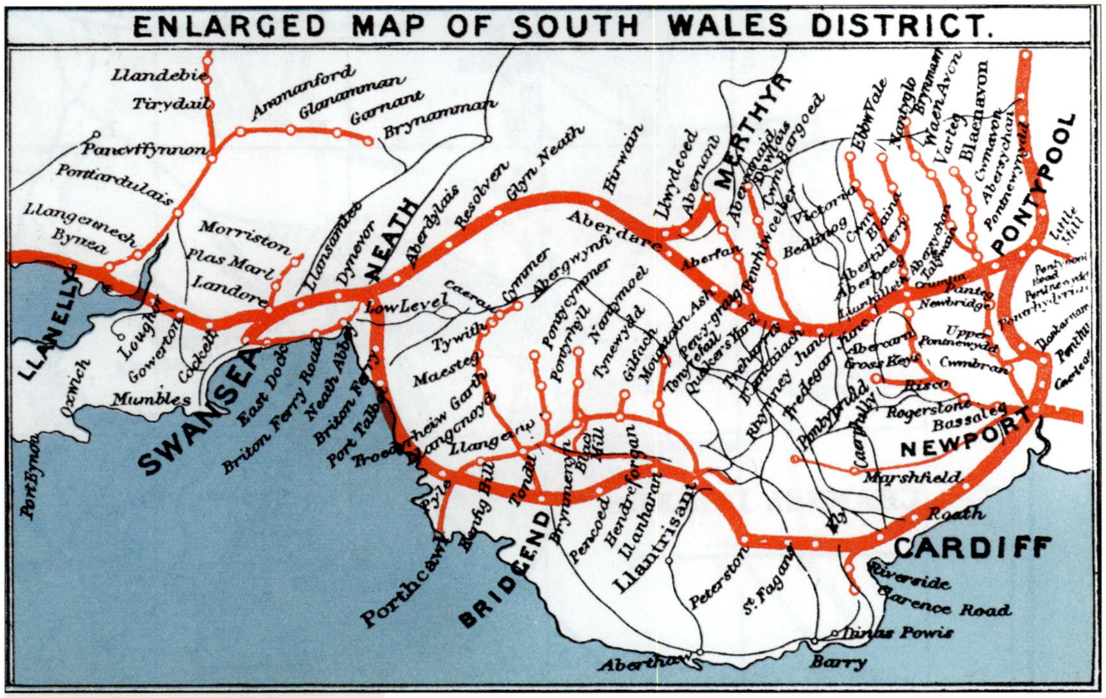

FIG. 10.6: Map showing the GWR's lines in South Wales. The more direct GWR&RR Joint line serving Merthyr is shown as of lesser importance than the line to the Vale of Neath; there were direct trains to and from Swansea.

PLATE 10.13: Outside-framed 'Buffalo' Class No. 755 was new in 1873 and is seen here circa 1880 with Dean chimney and lining on the cabsides and bunker. Note the slotted post signals behind and the Chepstow private owner wagon in the background. Rebuilt as a pannier tank in 1918, No. 755 was withdrawn in 1929.
BRIAN ARMAN COLLECTION

PLATE 10.14: Inside-framed '645' Class 0-6-0ST No. 770 takes water at Newport around 1905. Built at Wolverhampton in 1873, many of the class worked in South Wales and they went through various rebuilds over the years. Originally built with short saddle tanks, longer ones and a Swindon boiler with Dean chimney and brass dome cover were all part of a 1902 rebuild. Rebuilt as a pannier tank in 1925, it was superheated too, lasting in service then until 1936.
BRIAN ARMAN COLLECTION

borders, plus the TVE, Aberdare Extension and the VoN) provides a fuller picture. There were up to forty timetabled Down goods workings on a daily basis, including numerous trains of coal empties from places such as London, Basingstoke, Swindon, Gloucester, Birkenhead and Manchester, general goods and minerals workings (loadeds and empties), a single pick-up goods, station truck workings and the occasional light engine and van. There were only three passenger trains, which called at Crumlin at 9.16am, 2.21pm and 5.55pm.

The Up direction was not quite so busy, with twenty-seven goods workings, mainly coal heading out to the destinations mentioned above but some general goods and minerals trains, and again the odd light engine movement such as the Hirwaun pilot engine heading back to Pontypool Road. Up passenger services called at Crumlin at 10.05am and 1.37pm and 5.28pm. Sundays meanwhile were very quiet, with just two passenger workings each way and only one or two goods trains. This heavy imbalance of goods workings over passenger trains was to change little over the rest of the 19th century and there were to be only marginal improvements in the passenger service. The Special Notices at the rear of the time table included an instruction that '*The through Aberdare and London and Basingstoke and Aberdare and Birkenhead Coal Trains must in all cases have the precedence over the Local Trains*'; the signalmen had to keep track of the whereabouts of these trains, informing the boxes ahead of them and shunting local trains aside as necessary – their punctuality was paramount. Meanwhile, speed restrictions of 8mph across the viaduct and 10mph on the Llanhilleth Branch were also noted and these remained in place throughout their existence.

The situation as regards trains to Merthyr changed again in April 1886, when the Quakers Yard & Merthyr Railway was opened, a joint GWR and Rhymney Railway enterprise. It paralleled the TVR line to Merthyr but ran up the opposite side of Merthyr Vale. Cutting off the dog leg via Hirwaun, it halved the distance, with passengers to and from Merthyr changing trains at

Plate 10.15: *A plethora of colourful advertising signs add to this spectacular view of an eastbounds goods rumbling across behind a 'Dean Goods' 0-6-0 in 1911. Crumlin Low Level Middle Signal Box, left, closed in 1927 when the crossing was removed.* G.M. Perkins/Kidderminster Railway Museum

Plate 10.16: *One of the first batch of 'Dean Goods' 0-6-0s, No. 2309, built in 1883 with domeless boiler and flush smokebox. This engine lasted in service until January 1934. Used all over the GWR, members of the class would have been common on the viaduct.* Brian Arman collection

Plates 10.17 & 10.18: *These two circa 1912 postcard views of the viaduct were clearly taken moments apart. In the first picture, a 'Metro' tank heads across with a Down train that includes a 'Cordon' wagon at the rear, carrying tanks filled with gas for carriage lighting. In the middle of the bridge it crosses with an Up service hauled by a 'Standard Goods' 0-6-0 tender engine, now to the fore in the second view. Sinking of Crumlin Navigation Colliery, in the right background, had started in 1907 with the pit in full production by 1911.*
Both Neil Parkhouse collection

Quaker's Yard High Level station. However, the line from Merthyr to Hirwaun and the Vale of Neath retained its importance, as there was a regular service of direct trains between Merthyr and Swansea.

Thus, in the *Bradshaw's* railway time table for 1888, trains are shown leaving Pontypool Road for Quaker's Yard at 8.55am, 2.05pm, 6.07pm and 9.10pm, and at 8.50am and 5.05pm on Sundays. Up workings from Quaker's Yard were at 9.21am, 12.56pm, 4.56pm and 8.08pm on weekdays, and at 10.40am and 8.05pm Sundays. However, the 1895 Bradshaw shows a modest improvement on this, with the service increased to five Down and six Up trains a day: Pontypool Road departures were at 8.55am, 10.40am, 2.10pm, 6.10pm and 9.25pm, whilst times from Quaker's Yard were 8.07am, 9.18am, 12.58pm, 4.58pm, 6.56pm and 8.17pm. Two trains each way remained the norm on

Plate 10.19: *A 'Buffalo' 0-6-0ST rumbles eastwards to Pontypool Road with a four-coach train of clerestory bogie stock. The carriages all look to be in the all over brown livery that the GWR introduced in 1908, which was in vogue until 1912 when the company decided to change instead to an all over crimson lake for their coaching stock. This lasted until 1922, when the more familar chocolate & cream livery was brought back.*
Brian Arman collection

Plate 10.20 Left: *Passenger services crossing on the viaduct circa 1908. The eastbound train is headed by an 0-6-0 pannier tank, whilst that heading west has an 0-6-0 side tank in charge.* Neil Parkhouse collection

Sundays and journey times to Crumlin High Level on all trains were approximately 20 minutes from Pontypool Road and 30 minutes from Quaker's Yard.

The GWR passenger time table for 1902 showed a more frequent service, with Down trains leaving Pontypool Road at 7.45, 8.55 and 10.55am, and then at 2.10, 3.25, 6.20 and 7.20pm. There was an extra later service on Saturdays at 9.35pm but the Sunday service was now just two trains. In the Up direction, trains left Tredegar Junction at 8.40 and 9.43am, and then at 1.21, 4.16, 5.21 and 7.18, with an 8.40pm departure on Saturdays and again just the two Sunday trains. Journey times between Pontypool Road, Crumlin and Quaker's Yard remained as above. Five of these services, in both directions, ran through to and from Swansea as also did both of the Sunday trains. The map which accompanied this time table showed the Merthyr to Hirwaun line as of the same importance as the rest of the Vale of Neath route and the South Wales main line but the GWR & RR Joint line as a branch to Merthyr.

However, the Edwardian era was to see a better service introduced, with the 1908 *Bradshaw* showing nine Down and six Up trains on weekdays, although the Sunday time table was still just two each way. Pontypool Road departures were at 7.20 (terminating at Llancaiach), 7.50, 8.50 and 10.55 mornings, and at 2.14, 3.25, 6.20, 7.50 and 9.30 afternoons/evenings. Up trains calling at Crumlin High Level left Quaker's Yard at 8.38 and 9.16 in the morning, whilst after midday, the 12.42 to Pontypool Road

Plate 10.21 Below Left: *'Metro' tank 2-4-0 No. 3564 was new in 1894. It is seen here after fitting with a new boiler and larger side tanks in 1914. Built originally for working the Metropolitan lines in London, the class spread over the network as they grew in number, performing useful work across the GWR. Generally long-lived, No. 3564 was withdrawn in early 1944.* Brian Arman collection

Plate 10.22 Below: *No. 1635 is an example of a 'Buffalo' Class saddle tank after rebuilding with side tanks. Carried out in August 1911, the pristine condition of the engine, complete with lined out livery and Great Western crest, suggests this picture may have been taken shortly after that date. The location is thought to be Gloucester possibly after a running in turn from Swindon. By 1921, No. 1635 was allocated to Merthyr shed and it was withdrawn in 1932.* Brian Arman collection

Plate 10.23: *An Up mixed goods behind a 'Buffalo' tank straddles the hill between the two sections of the viaduct circa 1908.*
Stephen Rowson collection

Plate 10.24: *Looking north-east over the viaducts and back towards Crumlin Junction, as a pannier tank arrives at Crumlin High Level station with a Down passenger working circa 1910.*
Neil Parkhouse collection

did not stop but the 12.56, 3.56, 4.55 and 7.07 services did. The 8.24pm Up ran Saturdays only and there was also a Tuesdays only train which started from Pontllanfraith at 8.05am, calling at Crumlin High Level and Pontypool on its way to Pontypool Road.

Postcard views of the viaduct from the Edwardian period show a cetrain uniformity of motive power, with largely 0-6-0 saddle tanks, and 2-4-0, 0-4-2 and 0-6-0 side tanks featuring on passenger and goods workings, along with some 0-6-0 tender engines. The GWR had a plethora of different classes of 0-6-0 saddle tanks in the later years of the 19th century and early part of the 20th century, with designs emanating from the company's works at both Swindon and Wolverhampton. Many lasted in service for fifty years or more, in their later lives as pannier tanks, a conversion process which the GWR commenced in the early 1900s. In this guise, engines built in 1860s, '70s and '80s were still hard at work into the 1920s and beyond. Pontypool Road had three members of the 1864-65, Wolverhampton-built '302' Class on its allocation in 1921, all by then fitted with pannier tanks; No. 303 was finally withdrawn in July 1932, after a working life of sixty-eight years and one wonders how many times it had crossed over the viaduct during that time. Eight of the nine strong class chalked up totals of over a million miles in traffic.

Along with these three veterans, Pontypool Road also still had numerous other 0-6-0 tanks of various vintages, such as '645', '1076' ('Buffalo'), '1854' and '2021' class engines. The shed also still had two 2-4-0 'Metro' tanks on its allocation at this time but no longer any of

Plate 10.25: *A line up of tank engine power at Swindon, showing further types that would have worked on the TVE. Two '2021' Class saddle tanks bookend a '517' Class 0-4-2 tank, No. 544, built in 1869 and withdrawn in 1928. No's 2124 and 2135, meanwhile, were both built in 1903 and both were later fitted with pannier tanks, coincidentally in line with their numbers – No. 2124 in 1924 and No. 2135 in 1935; withdrawal took place in 1950 and 1953 respectively. The picture dates from the first decade of the 20th century and all three were possibly at Swindon for attention in the works.* Neil Parkhouse collection

the '517' Class 0-4-2Ts. The only member of this class which might still have been seen crossing the viaduct by then, No. 537, was based at Aberdare, which also had two of the GWR's steam railmotors, No's 50 and 51, which are seen in a couple of postcard views.

Plate 10.26: *Outside-framed 'Aberdare' Class 2-6-0 No. 2664 on the GWR main line near London, with a lengthy train of coal empties heading back to South Wales circa 1930. New in 1902, the engine was based at Severn Tunnel Junction shed when seen here and was withdrawn early in 1936.* John Alsop collection

As regards larger tender engines, from the early 1870s 'Standard Goods' would have become a common sight, being widespread across the GWR system, and then the equally ubiquitous 'Dean Goods' Class from the 1880s. In the absence of any confirmatory photographic evidence, it can only be a matter of speculation as to whether any passenger tender engines were to be seen, from any of the 2-4-0 classes, a few examples from which spent time working from Hereford, or the later 4-4-0 classes which certainly when first built were used on main line expresses in any case.

The first truly 'heavy' engines to venture onto the viaduct were the outside-framed '2600' or 'Aberdare' class 2-6-0s, construction of which commenced in earnest in 1901 (the first of the class, No. 2600, was built as No. 33 in 1900). A goods version of the 'Bulldog' 4-4-0s, they were built essentially as coal engines, working between Neath/Aberdare and Swindon, hence the nickname. Numerous members of the class were stationed at Aberdare from the outset and soon at Pontypool Road too, such that both still had thirteen and eight of them respectively on their allocations in 1921. However, we need to step back in time a few years at this point, to examine the role that they and the viaduct played during the 1914-18 war.

PLATE 10.27: A glimpse of the conditions that stokers worked in on coal fired steam ships. This pre-First World War view, taken below decks on an unnamed Naval vessel, shows coal supplies being unloaded into the hold. NEIL PARKHOUSE COLLECTION

The First World War and the 'Jellicoe Trains'

Crumlin Viaduct was to play an important role during the First World War but to explain why and how, perhaps a little bit of background would be useful to begin with.

Britain's status as an island nation was brought into sharp replief following the declaration of war on 4th August 1914. The entire fleet of the Royal Navy suddenly became responsible for the defence of the British Isles against enemy attack by sea and of the major sea lanes against mines, submarines and maruading enemy ships. As the war progressed, the navy were forced into action in the Mediterranean, the Irish Sea, the Atlantic Ocean and Scandinavia, where the most famous sea battle of the conflict occurred; at Jutland in May-June 1916, the pride of the Royal Navy was severely dented, when twelve ships were sunk, and 6,102 British sailors were killed. The loss of two of the battlecruisers, HMS *Queen Mary* and HMS *Indefatigable*, both of which blew up and sank, provoked Admiral Beatty's now infamous outburst – "*There seems to be something wrong with our bloody ships today!*".

What is perhaps less appreciated nowadays, over a century later, is that at this time all of these ships were still coal fired. Huge teams of stokers, working in three shifts and in generally appallingly filthy conditions below decks, were required to keep the fires stoked and the boilers producing steam to power the engines. A large battleship, for instance, would have a compliment of a thousand men, of whom around 600 were employed in the engine room, mostly as stokers. And this roughly 60 per cent figure can be applied through the ranks of the smaller vessels in a battle fleet.

It can immediately be appreciated, therefore, that coal, in huge quantities, was neeed to keep the fleet operational and on the move – and the best steam coal was mined in South Wales. However, by the outbreak of war, the Navy had moved the bulk of its ships from the big South Coast bases at Portsmouth, Devonport and Plymouth, to Scotland, to Rosyth and Scapa Flow, where they were better positioned to prevent the German fleet from breaking out to attack the

FIG. 10.8: The first two pages of a GWR document giving details as regards the operation of the Admiralty coal specials. The fact that this seems to have been part of pre-war planning for a possible European war is shown by the date of issue – January 1912.

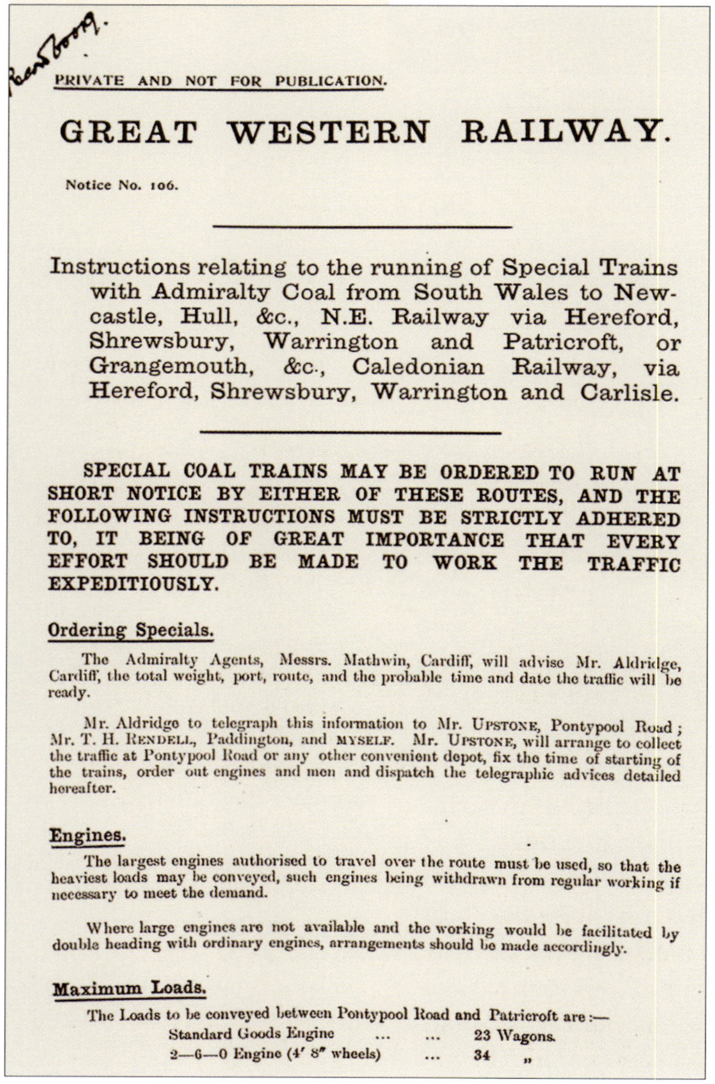

PRIVATE AND NOT FOR PUBLICATION.

GREAT WESTERN RAILWAY.

Notice No. 106.

Instructions relating to the running of Special Trains with Admiralty Coal from South Wales to New-castle, Hull, &c., N.E. Railway via Hereford, Shrewsbury, Warrington and Patricroft, or Grangemouth, &c., Caledonian Railway, via Hereford, Shrewsbury, Warrington and Carlisle.

SPECIAL COAL TRAINS MAY BE ORDERED TO RUN AT SHORT NOTICE BY EITHER OF THESE ROUTES, AND THE FOLLOWING INSTRUCTIONS MUST BE STRICTLY ADHERED TO, IT BEING OF GREAT IMPORTANCE THAT EVERY EFFORT SHOULD BE MADE TO WORK THE TRAFFIC EXPEDITIOUSLY.

Ordering Specials.

The Admiralty Agents, Messrs. Mathwin, Cardiff, will advise Mr. Aldridge, Cardiff, the total weight, port, route, and the probable time and date the traffic will be ready.

Mr. Aldridge to telegraph this information to Mr. UPSTONE, Pontypool Road; Mr. T. H. RENDELL, Paddington, and MYSELF. Mr. UPSTONE, will arrange to collect the traffic at Pontypool Road or any other convenient depot, fix the time of starting of the trains, order out engines and men and dispatch the telegraphic advices detailed hereafter.

Engines.

The largest engines authorised to travel over the route must be used, so that the heaviest loads may be conveyed, such engines being withdrawn from regular working if necessary to meet the demand.

Where large engines are not available and the working would be facilitated by double heading with ordinary engines, arrangements should be made accordingly.

Maximum Loads.

The Loads to be conveyed between Pontypool Road and Patricroft are:—
Standard Goods Engine ... ... 23 Wagons.
2—6—0 Engine (4′ 8″ wheels) ... 34 „

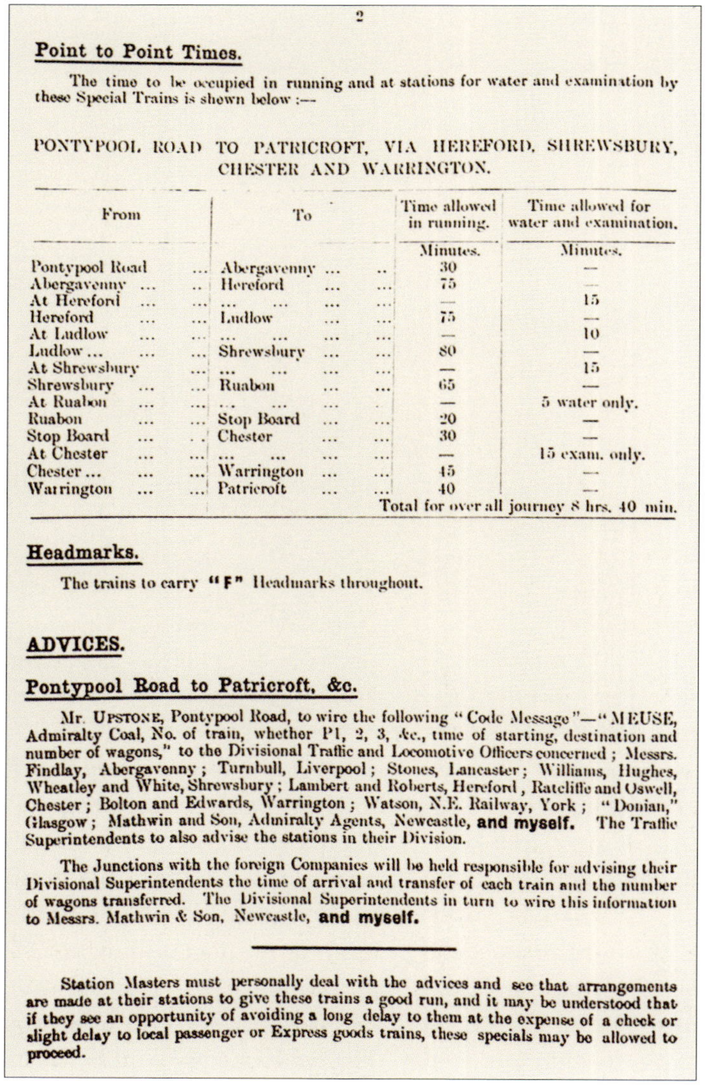

2

Point to Point Times.

The time to be occupied in running and at stations for water and examination by these Special Trains is shown below:—

PONTYPOOL ROAD TO PATRICROFT, VIA HEREFORD, SHREWSBURY, CHESTER AND WARRINGTON.

From	To	Time allowed in running.	Time allowed for water and examination.
		Minutes.	Minutes.
Pontypool Road	Abergavenny	30	—
Abergavenny	Hereford	75	—
At Hereford	...	—	15
Hereford	Ludlow	75	—
At Ludlow	...	—	10
Ludlow	Shrewsbury	80	—
At Shrewsbury	...	—	15
Shrewsbury	Ruabon	65	—
At Ruabon	...	—	5 water only.
Ruabon	Stop Board	20	—
Stop Board	Chester	30	—
At Chester	...	—	15 exam. only.
Chester	Warrington	45	—
Warrington	Patricroft	40	—

Total for over all journey 8 hrs. 40 min.

Headmarks.

The trains to carry "F" Headmarks throughout.

ADVICES.

Pontypool Road to Patricroft, &c.

Mr. UPSTONE, Pontypool Road, to wire the following "Code Message"—"MEUSE, Admiralty Coal, No. of train, whether P1, 2, 3, &c., time of starting, destination and number of wagons," to the Divisional Traffic and Locomotive Officers concerned; Messrs. Findlay, Abergavenny; Turnbull, Liverpool; Stones, Lancaster; Williams, Hughes, Wheatley and White, Shrewsbury; Lambert and Roberts, Hereford, Ratcliffe and Oswell, Chester; Bolton and Edwards, Warrington; Watson, N.E. Railway, York; "Donian," Glasgow; Mathwin and Son, Admiralty Agents, Newcastle, **and myself.** The Traffic Superintendents to also advise the stations in their Division.

The Junctions with the foreign Companies will be held responsible for advising their Divisional Superintendents the time of arrival and transfer of each train and the number of wagons transferred. The Divisional Superintendents in turn to wire this information to Messrs. Mathwin & Son, Newcastle, **and myself.**

Station Masters must personally deal with the advices and see that arrangements are made at their stations to give these trains a good run, and it may be understood that if they see an opportunity of avoiding a long delay to them at the expense of a check or slight delay to local passenger or Express goods trains, these specials may be allowed to proceed.

British mainland, and from where they operated then throughout much of the conflict.

The possibility of a major war breaking out in Europe had been foreseen for some time, to the extent that a certain amount of advance planning had taken place, of which the movement of the battle fleets was a part. Newspaper reports from 1911 mention the Admiralty's accumulation of supplies of Welsh Steam coal at Newcastle, Hull and other places easily accessible by the North Sea fleet. However, it was now reported that '*the Admiralty coal agent at Cardiff has given explicit instructions to hurry forward Rhondda Valley steam coal to the west coast of Scotland at any cost*'. Some 15-20,000 tons were despatched over a two day period, in wagons labelled 'Urgent' and 'OHMS', in what the Admiralty described was '*an experiment on a large scale*'. It was noted, however, that the experiment, if that was what it was, '*must prove a costly one*'. The fact that this was far from being an isolated occurrence would seem to be borne out by the GWR circular (***Fig. 10.8***), dated 1912.

And although at first glance it might have seemed the sensible option to send ships to the various South Wales ports for bunkering with coal, in practice it would have been dangerous to expose them to the long journey round the coast, either via the Channel or the Irish Sea, whilst also taking them 'off station' for much longer. Consequently, several million tons of coal were carried from South Wales to Scotland and to other points round the country during the war, keeping the Grand Fleet of the Royal Navy active at the battlefront and the fires of its steam powered fighting vessels ablaze. The pre-war planning was also clearly based on these factors.

It having been deemed equally dangerous to send unprotected collier ships coastwise to the various naval ports, it was thus incumbent upon the railways to deliver these huge quantities of coal to where they were required. They were officially known as 'Admiralty Special Coal Trains' and such was their frequency and importance that they were deemed worthy of a special bell code on the GWR and a special headcode on the London & North

Fig. 10.9: *Extract from the 1916-17 6 inch OS showing Pontypool Road station and the junctions just to the south, where the ex-MR&CC's Eastern Valleys line, the TVE and the ex-NA&HR main line all met. The specially laid in Admiralty sidings can be seen branching off just to the south of The Highway road bridge and ending against the embankment carrying the Monmouthshire Canal past the west end of Pontymoile tinplate works.*

PLATE 10.32: Having noted in the previous caption that GWR steam railmotors never worked services across the viaduct, to find a second sighting of one on another commercial picture postcard of the early 1920s is quite a coincidence. The houses just above the far end of the viaduct are on the uniquely named Load of Hay Road, a steep and narrow lane which is no longer a through route, being blocked off near the bottom.
STEPHEN ROWSON COLLECTION

and 8.05pm (5.40pm off Swansea High Street), continuing the slight imbalance between the number of Up and Down trains. There were no Sunday trains at this time.

The time table shows that a number of the local services on the Vale of Neath section of the line were covered by steam railmotors (SRMs), with No. 82 based at Neath shed and No's 50 and 51 at Aberdare in 1921. Both sheds had long associations with these machines, receiving their first examples in 1905. Aberdare subsequently had four in 1911, whilst Neath then had two. Aberdare was to give up its two SRMs in 1925 but Neath continued to use them on services right up until September 1935, when the last few were taken out of service. Coincidentally, there are two postcard views from the early 1920s showing SRMs crossing over Crumlin Viaduct but there were never any scheduled services that used this part of the route. It seems therefore that their recording was the result of fortuitous circumstance and that they were probably SRMs from Aberdare or Neath heading to or from Swindon Works for overhaul.

The first post-war visible sign of change on the railways was a momentous one, the 1923 Grouping, a result of the Railways Act of 1921. From 1st January, most of the main line companies in Britain were grouped into one of four new concerns, albeit the Great Western Railway was able to retain its name and identity (the only company to do so) when swallowing, amongst others, the larger South Wales concerns: the Alexandra (Newport & South Wales) Docks & Railway, the Barry Railway, the Cardiff Railway, the Rhymney Railway and the Taff Vale Railway. Also involved in running railways in South Wales, however, was another of the so called 'Big Four', namely the London, Midland & Scottish Railway, which had absorbed the Midland and London & North Western railways.

The new era also brought the first major change to Crumlin Viaduct, when the line over it was singled in the late 1920s, between Crumlin Junction and Crumlin High Level station. The *Great Western Railway Magazine* carried extensive reports from all of the various departments of the company, listing work that was being carried out, coupled with annual reports at the start of each year as to what had been done. Frustratingly, however, through this period there was very little mention of the viaduct. In the January 1927 edition, the Engineering Department's annual report stated that '*Crumlin Viaduct ... is being repaired*', the only mention it received in that year. The repairs were actually work to strengthen the bridge, as detailed in the previous chapter. The Engineering Department's annual report in the January 1929 edition noted under '*Works in Progress*' that '*the flooring of Crumlin Viaduct ... is being renewed*' but again no further mention follows for that year. Singling work clearly entailed alterations to the working arrangements at Crumlin Junction and High Level signal boxes but the Signalling Department made no mention of these in their report for that year either.

In the relevant section of Cooke's *Track Layout Diagrams*, dates are given for the start of permanent singling, which was carried out in conjunction with renewal of the flooring and states '*Line singled from 22.4.1928*'. The accompanying diagram shows the Up line removed, with short headshunts left in place on the Down side at both ends of the viaduct. Having renewed the flooring on the Down side, that line was then relaid and the Up side lifted, with the added note '*Down line used as single line from 21.7.1929*' and with a headshunt in place at the High Level station end only. However, signalling historian Garth Tilt has provided a slightly different date for the start of singling, noting that it commenced on 15th April 1928 over the existing Up line. The disc block & bell between Crumlin Junction and Crumlin (High Level) was taken out of use and replaced by Electric Key Token working. The single line was then slewed to the Down side of the viaduct on 21st July 1929 but when exactly it was subsequently realigned to the centre of the viaduct has not been ascertained, although it would have been soon after completion of the new floor in 1930.

Doubts regarding the strength of the viaduct had been held for many years but it is clear from some of the postcard views that Up and Down trains were still permitted to cross at the same time right up until the start of the First World War and almost certainly then through the years of conflict, given the amount of extra traffic generated by the war. The wish to single track the line therefore seems to have been driven as much by the Traffic Department's desire for it to be suitable for use by 'Red route engines,

Plate 10.33: *A '43XX' Class 'Mogul' 2-6-0 heads west over the Ebbw Valley in the mid 1920s, with a Down service made up of a motley selection of carriage stock.* NEIL PARKHOUSE COLLECTION

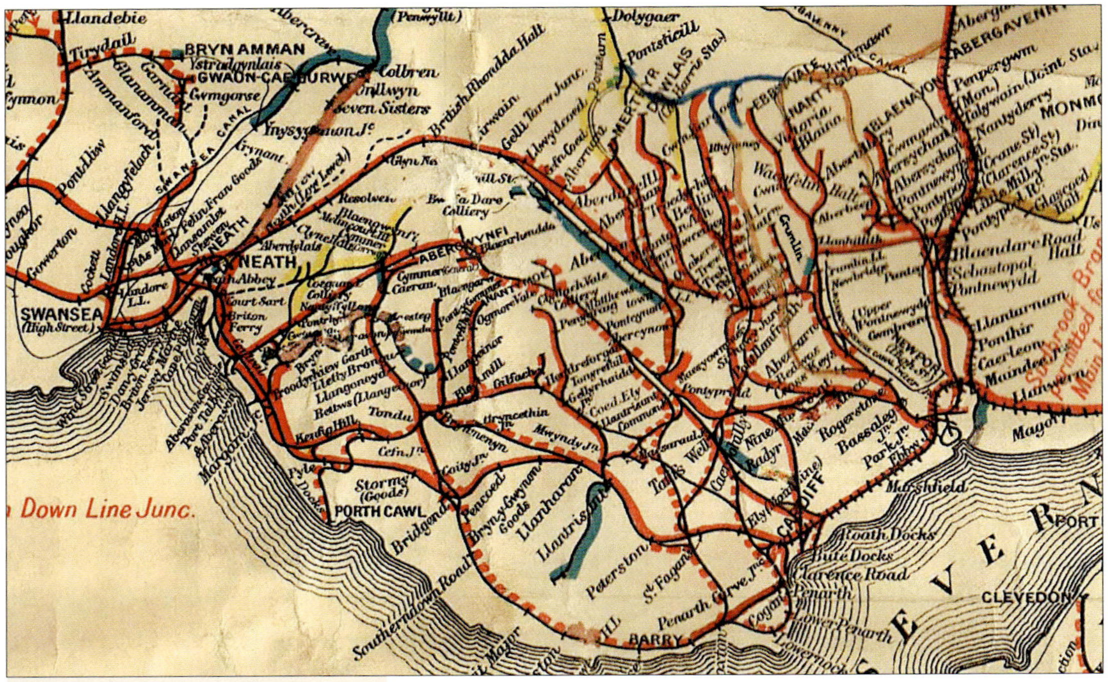

Fig. 10.12: Extract from a GWR Route Availability map, saved from Worcester shed. Note the VoN/TVE was entirely Red apart from the very short Blue section over the viaduct. HTTP://WWW.MICHAELCLEMENSRAILWAYS.CO.UK

PRIVATE, AND NOT FOR PUBLICATION.

No. 11.

GREAT WESTERN RAILWAY.

SERVICE TIME TABLES

PONTYPOOL ROAD

AND

NEATH JUNCTION

SEPTEMBER 14th, 1931,

AND UNTIL FURTHER NOTICE.

IMPORTANT NOTICE.

The Time Specified in the Time Tables is the Departure from the Station when the Times of Arrival and Departure are not stated; and in such cases the Trains should ARRIVE in sufficient time to enable the work to be done, in order to leave the Station at the time appointed.

25.

such as the new heavy goods '47XX' Class 2-8-0s built from 1919 (they were never permitted on the bridge), the '56XX' Class 0-6-2 tanks (which became synonymous with coal traffic in South Wales) built between 1924 and 1928 and the mixed traffic 'Hall' Class 4-6-0s, construction of which began in earnest in 1928. The colour coding system, introduced by the GWR from 1st July 1905, denoted the haulage capabilities and weight restrictions of their classes and maps were produced showing what colour code the respective routes were. The TVE/VoN line was restricted to an extent by the viaduct being colour coded blue, when the rest of the route was red (***Fig. 10.12***).

Reference to Section 11 of the *GWR Service Time Tables, Pontypool Road and Neath Junction*, dated 14th September 1931, gives a fuller picture of all train services over the viaduct as the country began to recover from the economic turmoil of the 1920s. In recognition of the new signalling arrangements, a note under the header on the first page stated '*SINGLE LINE – Crumlin Junction to Crumlin (High Level), worked by Electric Train Token*'. Thus all goods workings were marked 'CS' at Crumlin HL – '*Call at Single Line Stations for Train Staff, or Tablet, or Ticket only.*'. Opening times for the boxes controlling traffic over the viaduct were as follows: Crumlin High Level Station opened at 4.15am on a Monday morning and was then open continuously until 3.10am on the Sunday morning, or after the last goods train had passed; Crumlin Junction Signal Box was slightly different, opening at 4.00am on the Monday and closing at 3.30am on the Sunday; however it was then reopened from 8.15am to 11.10am and 6.45pm to 9.40pm for the passage of the Up and Down Sunday passenger services. Note that in what follows, capital letters have been used (in place of apostrophes) to indicate how each train was referred to in the time table, *i.e.* Coal, Goods, Passenger, etc.

The first Down train through was the 12.17am Coal from Crumlin Junction to Aberdare, later to be followed by the 4.00am Merthyr Goods, the 4.40am New Tredegar Goods and Empties, and the 5.00am Little Mill Junction to Swansea Goods (Mondays excepted – MX). Next came the 5.25am Pontypool Road to Quaker's Yard, Workmen and Passenger, which got to Crumlin HL at 5.44am and did not depart until 6.03am, arriving then at its destination at 6.40am. The 6.28am Little Mill Junction to Porth Goods was next, to be followed by the 6.40am auto train from Pontypool Road, which called at 6.59am. On arriving at Nelson & Llancaiach at 7.19am, it then formed the 7.26am departure from there to Swansea High Street.

Back at Crumlin HL, the auto was followed by the 6.45am Pontypool Road to Aberdare Goods and the 7.42am Pontypool Road to Swansea High Street Passenger. A Motor service for schoolchildren ran from Crumlin HL (8.37am) to Hengoed HL only, so did not cross the viaduct and did not run either during the school holidays. The next train was another Passenger, the 8.42am from Pontypool Road to Swansea High Street, which was marked 'CS' at Crumlin Junction, and there was then another freight, the 10.00am Oakdale Goods off Pontypool Road, before another Passenger, the 10.58am Pontypool Road to Swansea High Street. At 11.10am, another Merthyr Goods left Pontypool Road and completed the morning's Down workings.

On Saturdays Only there was what was termed the Cardiff Passenger, which left Pontypool Road at 12.25pm and ran to Hengoed HL, where a connection was made with a Cardiff train. Otherwise, on weekdays, the timings off Pontypool Road were, successively, an 11.45am Goods to Aberdare (arrive Crumlin Junction 12.15pm), the 1.11pm Passenger to Aberdare HL, the 1.40pm Motor which ran to Oakdale Halt, the 2.26pm Passenger to Swansea High Street, the 3.45pm Passenger to Aberdare HL, the Fridays

Only (FO) 4.00pm Motor to Oakdale Halt ('CS' at Crumlin Junction), the 4.50pm Passenger to Swansea High Street, a 6.00pm (FO) Motor service from Crumlin HL to Oakdale Halt, the 6.20pm Passenger to Aberdare HL, the 6.35pm (SX) Goods and Minerals to Hengoed HL, the 6.35pm (SO) Ferndale Goods to Ystrad North, the 6.55pm (SO) Goods to Maesycmmer Junction, the 7.40pm Passenger to Swansea High Street, the 7.15pm (SO) Llanhilleth Empties (which ran down the branch from Crumlin Junction so did not cross the viaduct), the 8.05pm (FO) Motor to Oakdale Halt, the 8.25pm Goods and Minerals to Aberdare HL, and the 9.00pm Aberbeeg Empties, whcih again ran down to Llanhilleth from Crumlin Junction.

Down workings were completed by the 9.35pm (SO) Passenger to Aberdare HL, the 9.35pm (SX) Workmen Passenger to Oakdale Halt, the 9.40pm Goods to Gadlys Junction (just beyond Aberdare HL), the 10.15pm (SX) Ferndale Goods, which ran to Ystrad North, the 10.20pm (SX) Workmen to Llanhilleth Colliery Sidings and the 11.30pm Coal to Gadlys Junction, which started at 9.40pm on Saturdays. Sundays, meanwhile, saw only two Down trains crossing the viaduct, both Passengers, the 8.20am and 6.50pm to Swansea High Street, with no freight trains time-tabled.

Up workings, times for which are given off Aberdare HL unless otherwise indicated, began with the 12.40am Coal (MX) and the 11.40pm Maerdy Goods (SX, when it started at 8.30pm), which left Hengoed HL at 3.22am. These were followed by the 3.30am (MX) Coal and then the 7.05am Oakdale Halt to Crumlin HL Auto, which terminated here but formed the 7.29am to Pontypool Road during the school holidays when the 8.37am was not running. The 5.10am Merthyr Goods formed the 6.10am off Quaker's Yard HL and this was followed by the 4.50am Goods and Minerals from Aberdare, which departed Hengoed HL at 9.10am.

The 7.56am Passenger was followed by an Empty Coaching Stock (ECS) working, which went on to form the 9.16am from Pontypool Clarence Street to Pontypool Road. At 9.10am, an Empty Motor working passed through Crumlin HL and over the viaduct, which again only ran during the school term, and this was followed by the 7.15am Passenger from Swansea High Street, which stopped at the station at 9.19am. There was a gap then until the 9.35am Passenger from Neath General, which called at 11.08am, and the 9.10am Porth Goods, which left Hengoed HLat 11.27am. Climbing the hillside from Llanhilleth Junction and therefore missing the viaduct was the 9.00am Abertillery Goods, which arrived

PLATE 10.34: *Another unidentified 'Mogul' rumbles across with a westbound mixed freight in the mid 1920s. Both this and* **Plate 33** *were clearly taken before the line across had been singled.*
NEIL PARKHOUSE COLLECTION

Crumlin Junction at 11.30am and left ten minutes later. The 11.50am ex-Aberdare Passenger and the 11.05am ex-Swansea High Street Passenger were the next Up trains over the viaduct, the latter passing through Crumlin HL at 1.40pm. Similarly, it was 3.50pm before the 11.00am Coal crossed over, having been preceded by the 1.10pm Passenger from Swansea High Street, which called at Crumlin HL at 3.30pm. An hour and a quarter later, the 3.48pm Passenger also then called at the station.

The rest of the day's Up workings, in the order in which the time table lists them, were made up by the 4.55pm (FO) Motor from Oakdale Halt to Crumlin HL, the 3.10pm Passenger from Swansea High Street, the 5.30pm Goods from Penar Junction, the 11.05pm (9.00pm SO) Hengoed HL to Pontypool Road Goods, the 6.22pm (FO) Oakdale Halt to Pontypool Road Motor, the 1.45pm Pembroke Dock Passenger (5.35pm off Neath General), the 8.45pm (FO) Oakdale Halt to Pontypool Road Motor, the 8.55pm (SO) ex-Hengoed HL Coal and the 9.49pm (SO) ex-Hengoed HL Coal, the latter noted as '*Commences June 11th, 1932*'. Meanwhile, the 9.50pm Cardiff Passenger, which left Hengoed HL at 10.27pm, was listed '*Will not run after June 11th, 1932*'. On Saturdays Only, the last passenger train of the day was the 8.45pm from Swansea High Street, which called at Crumlin HL at 11.11pm, whilst on weekdays there was an 11.05pm Motor off Oakdale Halt which called at 11.21pm. This was followed by the 11.20pm ex-Hengoed HL Coal, which started at 8.55pm on Saturdays Only, the 9.05pm Goods and finally the 12.05am Coal from Maesycwmmer Junction. As well as these, there were three further workings up the Llanhilleth Branch, at 4.46pm off Penar Junction and at 8.05pm and 1.00am (SX) from Llanhilleth Junction, the latter being at 11.40pm on Saturdays.

Sunday workings comprised a 12.15am Coal train from Aberdare HL and two passenger trains – the 8.46am off Swansea High Street and the 5.30pm Carmarthen Passenger, which left Swansea at 6.55pm, the two calling at Crumlin HL at 10.47am and 9.17pm respectively.

The Motor services in the time table, which in places are also referred to as Auto Trains, would have been 'Push/Pull' trains, comprising auto-fitted tank engines usually with one or two auto trailers. These trains could be operated from a driving compartment at one end of the trailer and therefore did not need to run round. When working in Push mode, the fireman remained on the footplate, communicating with the driver in the front of the trailer by means of a bell. In 1934, for instance, Aberdare had 0-6-0PT No. 6400 on its roster, built in 1932 and the first of the '64XX' Class, which were constructed specifically for auto work. Some of the earlier 'Buffalo' Class 0-6-0PTs were also auto fitted in their later days, following withdrawal of the steam rail motors.

Other motive power to be seen working over the viaduct during the post-Grouping GWR era would have included examples of the 'Large Prairie' 2-6-2 tanks, represented by the '41XX', '51XX' and '5101' classes, '56XX' Class 0-6-2 tanks and the 'Aberdare' Class 2-6-0 tender engines. The longer distance passenger services, running the whole length of the TVE/VoN to and from Swansea High Street would have been handled by 4-4-0 tender engines for much of this period. In 1921, for instance, Hereford shed had eleven 'Bulldogs' on its roster, any of which may have worked through to Swansea, whilst Neath also had one, No. 3338 *Swift*, that may have worked to Carmarthen and back (which shed had half a dozen of its own) but equally could have worked through passenger trains to Pontypool Road.

Interestingly, in 1921 Neath also had an allocation of six of the ex-Railway Operating Department (ROD) 2-8-0s, built to a design by John G. Robinson originally for the Great Central Railway, of which a further 521 were built in 1917-18 to assist in the war effort. Most of the initial batch – some 311 engines in total – were sent straight to France and when they were brought back after the war, they were purchased or loaned to various of the railway companies to cover shortages caused by many of their locomotives requiring overhaul and repair. The GWR bought twenty initially in 1919, numbering them 3000-3019, and then hired a further eighty-four in 1921, which became No's 3020-3099, but these were returned in autumn 1922. However, in 1925 they purchased another

PLATE 10.35: *'Bulldog' No. 3338* Swift, *photographed here at Old Oak Common probably in May 1913 by J.B. Sherlock, was allocated to Neath shed in 1921.* JOHN ALSOP COLLECTION

Plate 10.36: Looking north-east from the towpath of the Tennant Canal, an unidentified 'Bulldog' 4-4-0 makes its way across the new River Neath viaduct as it heads a Down express away from Neath General station in 1906. The original wooden viaduct it replaced can be seen immediately to this side of the new structure. The viaduct visible in the right background carried the Vale of Neath line into Neath General. Through services off the TVE/VoN heading to Swansea branched off at Neath Junction to join the Neath & Brecon line and head through Neath Riverside station. This was situated just off to the left of this view, on the other side of the canal, with the train about to cross that line too. John Alsop collection

eighty, which became No's 3020-3099 again. The six members of the class on Neath's allocation were from the hired batch of eighty-four that were returned in 1922, all being in the 3020-3099 number series. Whilst they would all have been employed working along the South Wales main line, it may well be that locomotive shortages at this time could have seen one haul the occasional freight or coal train via the Vale of Neath line to Pontypool Road.

The eighty further members of the class that the GWR subsequently purchased in 1925 had something of a chequered history, with many of them being in poor condition. The worst fifty were given only minimal maintenance and all of them had been withdrawn by 1931. The other thirty, however, along with the original twenty bought in 1919, were overhauled, given copper fireboxes and painted GWR green, and were spread around the system where needed. Thus, in 1934, three were at Neath (No's 3000, 3006 and 3010), one was at Aberdare (No. 3036) and four more were at Pontypool Road (No's 3018, 3023, 3037 and 3038), with fifteen of the rest at other South and West Wales sheds. However, much of the heavy freight was worked at night, so whilst members of the class worked over the viaduct on the longer distance goods, no photograph has been found to date. In 1934, Aberdare also had thirteen of the '28XX' 2-8-0s on its allocation, whilst Neath had two and Pontypool Road six.

In part because of night time working, photographic evidence is sadly lacking for us to be able to expand the range of classes that we know for certain worked over the viaduct. However, what we do know about railway operation is that needs must at times and with only the very heaviest engines prohibited, undoubtedly there would have been occasions when a shed foreman sent out what he had to hand. The classes detailed here were all represented at Pontypool Road, Aberdare and/or Neath sheds, so it is highly likely that larger engines crossing over was a not unusual occurrence. The fact that the various 2-8-0 tender engine classes, for instance, are specifically mentioned as being permitted in the service time tables

Plate 10.37: GWR No. 3040, ex-ROD No. 2154, was built by North British at their Atlas Works in Springburn in 1919. When first leased in July that year it became GWR No. 3042 but was returned in October 1922. Purchased subsequently in 1925, it was added to GWR stock after a full overhaul as No. 3040 in January 1927 and is seen here on Neath shed on 26th July 1936, fitted with a Class '47XX' chimney. It lasted in service until June 1956. John Alsop collection

USE OF TROLLIES ON CRUMLIN VIADUCT.

When it is necessary for a trolley to work on or pass over the Single Line between Crumlin High Level and Crumlin Junction or vice versa, the ganger or loading man in charge must, before placing the trolley on the Line, be in possession of the Token, which must be obtained from the Signalman at Crumlin High Level or Crumlin Junction.

The trolley must be signalled in accordance with Electric Train Staff Regulation 9 appearing on page 39 of the General Appendix, and this Regulation must be strictly adhered to by all concerned.

The Signalman must, when delivering the Token, have a proper understanding with the Engineering Department Staff as to the time they may be allowed to occupy the Single Line Section when loading or discharging materials on the Viaduct, in order that no delay may occur in clearing the Single Line for the passage of trains.

CRUMLIN VIADUCT.

The list of engines on page 53 of No. 11 Appendix should be deleted and substituted by the following :—
All engines in the Red Classification are prohibited from passing over the Viaduct.
Under no circumstances may more than two engines coupled together work over the Viaduct.
Other engines may work over the Viaduct as under :—

Classes.	Engine Numbers.	Are allowed to work over
2-8-0 "G" & "K" (R.O.D.) ... 2-8-0 "T"	3000 to 3099 ... ... 2846, 2856 to 2883	Unassisted only.
2-8-0 "C" ... ... 2-8-0 "D"	2800 to 2830 ... ... 2831 to 2845, 2847 to 2855	Unassisted, coupled, assisted by any 0-6-0, 0-6-0T, 0-4-0T, 0-4-2T or 2-4-0T not in the Red classification, or to those of the 0-6-2T in Yellow or uncoloured classifications only.
2-6-0 "L" ... ... 2-6-0 "M" ... ... 2-6-0 "F" ... ... 2-6-0 "I" ... ... 4-4-0 ... ... 2-6-2T 0-6-2T	4301 to 4320 ... ... 4300, 4321 to 4399, 5300 to 5399, 6300 to 6399, 7300 to 7321. All engines of 26xx classification ... All except those in Red classification	Unassisted, coupled or assisted by any 0-6-0, 0-6-0T, 0-4-0T, 0-4-2T or 2-4-0T not in the Red classification.
0-6-0, 0-6-0T, 0-4-0T, 0-4-2T, 2-4-0T. Any other engine in Yellow and uncoloured classification.	All except those in Red classification	Unassisted, coupled or assisting any engine not scheduled as "Unassisted only."

FIG'S 10.13 & 10.14: Extracts from the 1931 STT in regards to Crumlin Viaduct.

is perhaps the clearest indication that they did in fact cross the viaduct regularly. Pictures are moments in time and the number taken is actually quite small in comparison. 'Grange' Class 4-6-0s appeared in the final few years, including (as we shall find out later in this chapter) No. 6836 *Estevarney Grange* on the last day but a photograph showing one of the class on the viaduct has yet to surface.

In contrast to the conflict of 1914-18, it is unlikely that the Second World War had any significant effect on traffic on the Pontypool Road to Neath route and therefore over the viaduct. By 1939, the British Navy was no longer powered by steam, so there was no repeat of the 'Jellicoe Specials'. The line was not of particular strategic importance and did not directly serve any military establishment of note (apart from, indirectly, ROF Glascoed, of which more shortly) but was kept clear on Sundays to allow for extra traffic, with the passenger service now restricted to weekdays and Saturdays only. Neath General was now the western destination, services no longer running through to Swansea High Street. Other noticeable wartime effects would have been the general dimming or extinguishing of lights and the painting of white lines on platform edges to prevent anyone falling off in the dark – a practice which was then continued after the war.

The passenger service in 1942 did not differ greatly from pre-war levels in number, with departures off Pontypool Road at 6.40am (to Nelson & Llancaiach,

PLATE 10.38: An undated view from the hillside below Crumlin High Level station, showing both sections of the viaduct.
STEPHEN ROWSON COLLECTION

PLATE 10.39: Quite a number of picture postcards included what was deemed the important facts as regards the viaduct's construction in their captions. This view includes open wagons in the foreground lettered LMS and SR, so the picture is clearly post the 1923 Grouping. However, the GWR 'Small Prairie' tank heading across with an Up train looks close to the railing, which would indicate it is prior to the line being singled in 1929. NEIL PARKHOUSE COLLECTION

Third Class only), 7.45am (to Aberdare HL), 8.16am (to Hengoed HL, Saturdays & School Holidays Excepted, Third Class only), 8.40am and 11.00am (both to Neath General), 1.15pm (to Neath General, Third Class only), 2.28pm (to Neath General), 4.04pm (to Aberdare HL, SX, Third Class only), 6.20pm (to Neath General) and 7.50pm (to Aberdare HL).

Up trains calling at Crumlin General were the 7.45am off Nelson & Llancaiach (Third Class only), 7.50am off Aberdare HL, 7.45am off Neath General, 11.43am off Aberdare HL (Third Class only), 1.35pm off Neath General, 3.57pm off Aberdare HL, and the 3.39pm and 6.01pm, both off Neath General. Totalling nine Down trains and seven Up, this did not represent a significant increase on 19th century levels.

Unfortunately, little has been ascertained about wartime freight traffic levels over the TVE/VoN line. However, a February 1943 *Appendix to Section 12 of the Service Time Tables, Worcester, Hereford and Newport*, which covers Pontypool Road, makes no mention of any wartime conditions or restrictions, or has any special working instructions. The only one relating to the TVE line is headed '***Freight Trains from Taff Vale Extension Line terminating at Pontypool Road***' and reads: '*Guards must inform the Signalman at Cwm Glyn how many wagons they have on. The latter must telephone the information to Pontypool Road West Junction Signalman, who will transmit to the Middle Yard Shunter and Yard Inspector so that arrangements can be made for trains to be drawn in clear of the Main line at West Junction when necessary, to avoid delay*

Plate 10.40: *A typical 1930s Motor Train working, with '57XX' Class 0-6-0PT No. 5728 hauling a pristine two coach 'B Set' forming an Up local to Pontypool Road on 9th July 1936. The GWR used the term 'Motor Train' in its time tables for many of its shuttle operated, short distance services, whether or not they were auto trains. None of the '57XX' Class were ever auto fitted, so this is a standard two-coach local working but indicated as a Motor Train in the time table. New into service in February 1929, No. 5728 spent much of its life based at Pontypool Road shed, in its early years working from the sub-shed at Branches Fork, near Abersychan, which closed in January 1952. It transferred to Merthyr in 1957 and was withdrawn off Duffryn Yard shed on 7th May 1962. As an incidental aside, it is quite noticeable how, through the years of its existence, the roof of the old Viaduct Works building seemed to be in a continual state of disrepair*
FOX PHOTOS LTD/
NEIL PARKHOUSE COLLECTION

to Down Freight and Passenger trains from Station South Box.' (Cwm Glyn Signal Box was situated about mid way between Blaendare Sidings and Pontypool Clarence Street station). This would suggest that most wartime traffic was being routed via the main line and that the TVE/VoN was of secondary importance.

However, it may be that any services that could have been deemed a security risk, such as to and from a secret munitions base (the existence of which was never acknowledged on OS maps), simply did not feature in the time table and a clue to this is gleaned from a 1949 STT, which details Up and Down Workers Trains to the Royal Ordnance Factory at Glascoed (officially ROF54), situated a short way up the Monmouth Branch from Little Mill Junction and served by an extensive rail network. It was opened in 1940 and had its own station, as well as being served by three halts on the branch, whereby three daily trains brought up to 13,000 workers in and out of the site from various towns and villages in the Valleys. Raw materials and components were also all brought in by rail and finished munitions were despatched the same way. It would seem therefore that the trains bringing in workers via the TVE – from Brynmawr and Ystrad Mynach via the Llanhilleth Branch and from Rhymney across the viaduct in the 1949 STT – were not mentioned in the time tables, as traffic to and from Glascoed would have been deemed secret.

PLATE 10.41, ABOVE: *Glascoed Halt on 8th August 1961. Opened on 16th May 1927, it was replaced by the platform seen here, opened on 22nd April 1938 and built on the opposite side of the line to allow for the new railway into ROF Glascoed. It closed officially with the branch passenger service on 30th May 1955 but was used by Glascoed workers up until 13th October 1957. At the date of the picture, the line remained open to Usk for goods, so the signal box was still in use to control the junction into the factory.* MICHAEL HALE

PLATE 10.42, LEFT: *Glascoed Factory West Access Halt on 11th April 1955. Opened on 12th June 1941, it closed probably with the branch passenger service.* H.C. CASSERLEY

PLATE 10.43, FAR LEFT: *Glascoed Factory East Access Halt from the front of a GWR railcar on 11th April 1955. Opened on 3rd January 1943, it had closed by June 1954.* R.M. CASSERLEY

UP	Ruling Gradient 1 in	B 5.15 a.m. Brynmawr Workers	B 5.42 a.m. Ystrad Mynach Workers	B 5.50 a.m. Newp't and 5.50 a.m. Blaenavon Workers	B 5.35 a.m. Rhymney Workers	G 2.30 p.m. Aberbeeg LE	G 2.0 p.m. Ebbw Jn. LE	C ECS
		SX am	SX am	SX am	SX am	SX PM	SX PM	Q SX PM
PONTYPOOL ROAD dep	—	6 20	[illegible] 27	6 30	6 37	2 53	3 0	3 †0
Little Mill Junction	103F	6 24	[illegible] 31	6 35	6 41	2 57	3 4	3 4
Glascoed Halt	—	......	......	......	......	......	......	......
Glascoed Loop	—	6 28	5 35	6 39	6 45	3 3	3 9	3 9
Glascoed R.O.F.	—	6 30	5 36	6 40	6 46	3‖ 5	3‖10	3†10

DOWN	Ruling Gradient 1 in		G To Newport LE	G LE	C ECS	B To Brynmawr	B To Rhymney	B To Newport and Blaenavon
Glascoed R.O.F.	—	...	5‖50	7‖10	7†20	4 32	4 37	4 42
Glascoed Loop	—		5 51	7 11	7 21	4 33	4 38	4 43
Glascoed Halt	—	...	......	......	......	......	......	......
Little Mill Junction	100R		5 55	7 15	7 25	4 37	4 42	4 48
PONTYPOOL ROAD arr	104R	...	7 0	7‖20	7†30	4 41	4 46	4 52

FIG. 10.15: *The summer 1957 Pontypool Road to ROF Glascoed time table.*

Plate 10.46: *High Level station in all its Victorian splendour, looking east on 26th May 1956. Built of stone, the steeply pitched roofs and awnings were an attractive feature. Note that the doors and windows are at a slightly lower level, suggesting that the platform had been raised at some stage.*
Stephen Rowson collection

Plate 10.47: *Crumlin High Level Signal Box photographed shortly before closure of the line in 1964.*
Desmond Coakham/
Welsh Railway Research Circle

Penar Junction), 6.50pm (6.40pm Little Mill Junction to Margam Sidings Freight – SX and SO trains but they ran to exactly the same timings), 7.30pm (Coke Ovens Freight, SO, to Ystrad Mynach North), 8.25pm (Freight to Aberdare HL), 10.15pm (Coke Ovens Freight, SX, to Ystrad Mynach North) and 10.40pm (10.30pm Little Mill Junction to Margam Sidings Freight – '*Terminates Hirwaun Pond Saturday nights.*').

The change in origination points and destinations over the pre-war years is immediately apparent, as well as the increase in both the number and frequency of trains. This was mirrored by the time table of Up freights: 3.17am off Ystrad Mynach North (2.05am Coke Ovens Freight, MX), 3.00am off Aberdare HL (Freight, MX), 4.50am off Aberdare HL (Freight), 5.00am off Aberdyalis (Saltney Freight, OW – stop for water at Hirwaun, BE from Mountain Ash (Cardiff Road), BE from Crumlin Junction, note – '*Carries "H" Headlamps when conveying grease axlebox tanks.*'), 9.30am off Quaker's Yard East Junction (8.30am Merthyr Freight), 11.25am off Ystrad Mynach North (9.50am Porth Freight), 11.00am of Aberdare HL (Freight – '*Shunter at Bird-in-Hand to advise Quaker's Yard particulars of the traffic to be picked up so that the load of train may be kept down to clear. Quaker's Yard to pass the information on to the Guard of train.'*), 2.20pm off Penar Junction (Oakdale Coal, SO), 1.55pm off Aberdare HL (Freight – note '*SUSPENDED*'), 2.10pm off Neath Junction (11.15am Llandilo Junction to Stourbridge Junction Freight, note – '*Carries "H" Headlamps when conveying grease axlebox tanks'.*, BE from Glyn Neath, CT – Change Trainmen at Pontypool Road), 2.55pm ex Oakdale Coal (SX, N (*or later as required*) at Bush Colliery 3.55-4.05pm, 5.50pm off Ystrad Mynach North (Engine Ystrad Mynach to Glascoed, SX, '*Runs empty Coaches FO Ystrad Mynach depart 5.46pm.*'), 7.50pm off Penar Junction (Loco Coal – '*To Saltney WO. To Wolverhampton ThFO*', BE from Crumlin Junction, CT at Pontypool Road), 7.40pm off Fleur-de-Lis (Return of 4.55pm Pontypool Road Freight, BE from Crumlin Junction), 9.10pm off Penar Junction (Freight, SO, BE from Crumlin Junction), 5.28pm off Neath Riverside (2.30pm Llandilo Junction to Saltney Freight, '*Carries "H" Headlamps when conveying grease axlebox tanks.*' BE from Glyn Neath, EW – Examination and Water at Aberdare HL, BE from Mountain Ash (Cardiff Road), OW – stop for water only at Penar Junction, BE from Crumlin Junction, CT at Pontypool Road), 9.30pm off Hengoed HL (Freight, SX, '*Return of 5.40am Pontypool Road.*'), OW at Penar Junction, BE from Crumlin Junction), 9.45pm off Aberdare HL (Freight, SX), 10.30pm off Aberdare HL (Freight, SO), 9.32pm off Neath General (7.55pm Landore Freight, '*Runs 5 minutes later on Saturdays*', BE from Glyn Neath, OW Aberdare HL, BE from Mountain Ash (Cardiff Road), BE from Crumlin Junction, arrive Pontypool Road 2.41am) and the 12.10am off Ystrad Mynach North (11.00pm Coke Ovens Freight (Sats.), '*Return of 7.30pm (Sats.) Pontypool Road*', BE from Crumlin Junction).

As well, once again, of the variety of places mentioned, the difficulties of working heavy Up freights in the days of steam over the length of the VoN/TVE line are graphically indicated here by the extra notes, with three stops being made by some workings for a bank engine to come on to the rear and assist, along with two stops for water. So the 7.55pm freight from Landore (Swansea), took over five hours to make the journey from Neath to Pontypool Road. It also seems clear, however, that much more use was being made by British Railways of the single line over Crumlin Viaduct than had their predecessor, the GWR.

The *Working Time Table of Passenger Trains* for the summer 1957 period showed services (Ordinary unless otherwise noted) leaving Pontypool Road at 4.30am (as ECS on Mondays and as a Light Engine (LE) working MSX), 6.40am (Rail Motor to Nelson & Llancaiach), 7.40am (to Aberdare HL), 8.40am and 11.00am (to Neath General), 12.10pm (SO, to Ystrad Mynach North for connection to Cardiff and Barry Island), 1.05pm (to Neath General), 2.25pm (to Swansea High Street and Carmarthen), 3.50pm (to Swansea High Street), 4.46pm (SX, 4.37pm Glascoed Workers to Ystrad Mynach North), 5.00pm (to Aberdare HL), 6.20pm (to Neath General), and 8.31pm (to Aberdare HL).

Up departures were at 5.42am (off Ystrad Mynach North, Glascoed Workers), 5.35pm (off Rhymney, Glascoed Workers), 7.45am (Rail Motor, off Nelson &

PLATE 10.48: *The fireman of a westbound train has his arm out ready to slot through the hoop of the single line token permitting entry onto the single line over the viaduct at Crumlin Junction.* ROD BLENCOWE

PLATE 10.49: *Class '57XX' No. 9797 brings a four-coach Down train in uniform crimson and cream livery off the viaduct and into High Level in August 1958.* TREVOR OWEN/COLOUR-RAIL

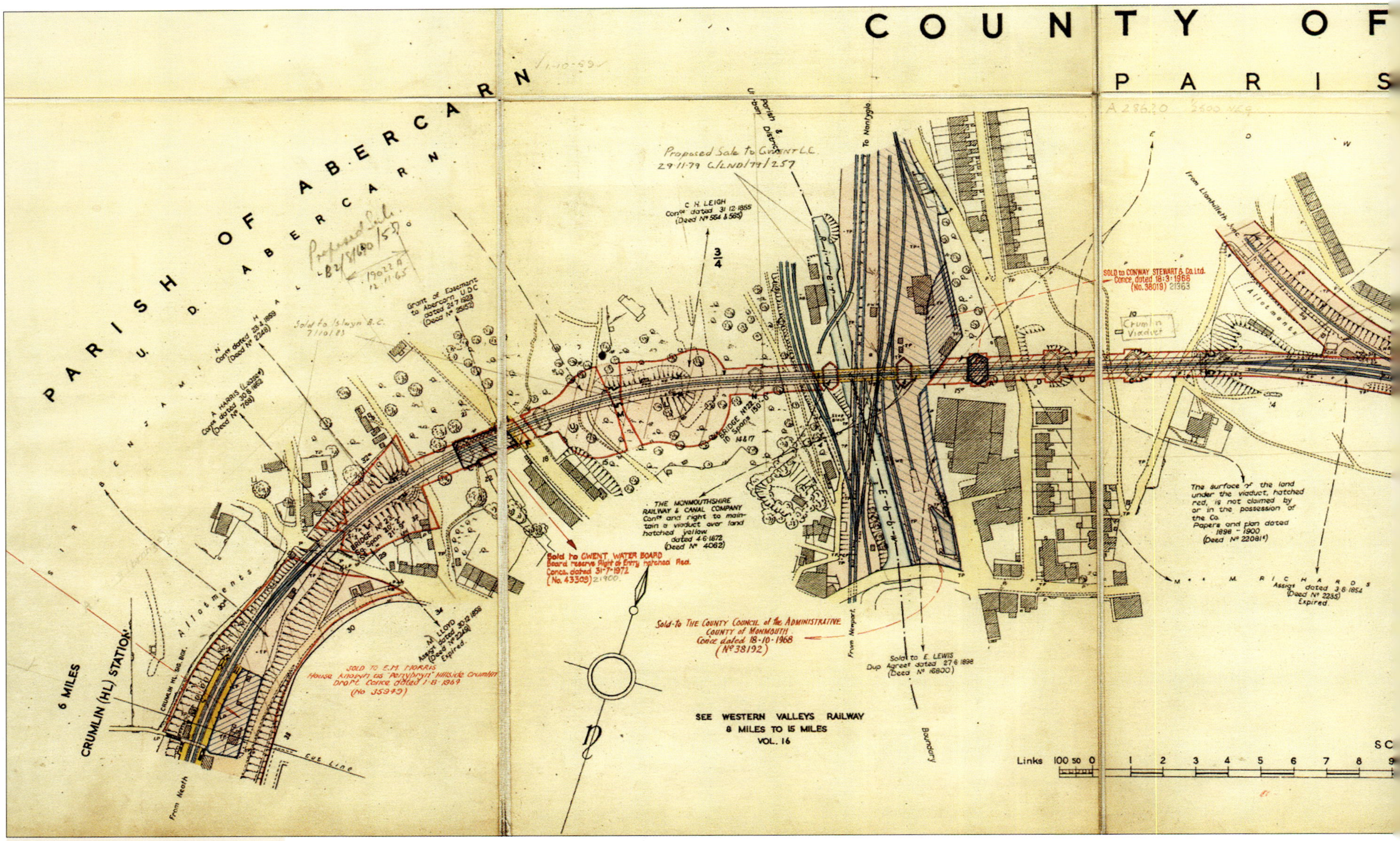

FIG 10.16: The British Railways Western Region 2-chain survey of 1954, which had been updated with land and property sales to 1979. The survey covers from Hafodrynys Halt in the west, through Crumlin Junction and over the viaduct to High Level station, along with the goods yard at Crumlin Low Level.
ALASTAIR WARRINGTON COLLECTION

Llancaiach), 8.06am (off Nelson & Llancaiach, 7.38am from Dowlais), 7.45am (off Aberdare HL), 7.40am (off Neath General), 11.15am (off Aberdare HL), 11.19am and 1.55pm (off Neath General), 3.00pm (off Swansea High Street), 5.50pm (off Ystrad Mynach North, Workers Train), 5.37pm (off Swansea High Street), 8.54pm (off Ystrad Mynach North, 7.45pm from Barry Island '*Will run on Saturdays only 29th June to 31st August inclusive only.*') and the 10.06pm (off Aberdare HL). There were no Sunday trains in either direction.

Freight workings around this period are gleaned from the September 1960 to June 1961 *Working Time Table*, with times off Pontypool Road unless otherwise indicated: 11.34pm (7.25pm, Coleham to Margam, SX), 1.47am (MX, 8.05pm Saltney to Margam Hump Yard), 4.18am ('MX, AE' – change engine, 9.50pm (SX) Bordesley Junction to Llanelly), 4.35pm (off Pontypool Road Goods (PRG) to Merthyr) 5.16am (MX, off Crumlin Junction, 3.50am from Ebbw Vale to Penar Junction, 'Q' – runs when required), 5.45am (off PRG to New Tredgar), 6.10am (off PRG to Ebbw Vale LL), 6.40am (MX, to Llanelly), 6.55am (MO) and 7.05am (MX, off PRG to Stormstown Junction), 9.15am (off PRG to Aberdare HL), 9.25am (SX, off PRG to Oakdale), 9.45am (off PRG to Aberdare HL), 1.10pm (off PRG, to Quaker's Yard), 3.00pm (off Hafodrynys East, to Aber Junction), 3.05pm (SX, off Crumlin Junction, return of 10.20am SX, Aberdare to Crumlin Junction), 2.35pm (off PRG, to Stormstown Junction), 5.05pm (SX, off PRG, to Aberbargoed Junction), 5.35pm (SO, off PRG, to Aberdare HL), 6.20pm (SO, off PRG, to Hirwaun Pond. 6.20pm SO, off Pontypool Road), 7.55pm (SO, off Crumlin Junction, to Aberdare HL, arrives 9.51pm), 7.55pm (SX, off Crumlin Junction, to Aberdare HL, arrives 10.56pm), and the 9.15pm (SX, off PRG to Aberdare). Most noticeable

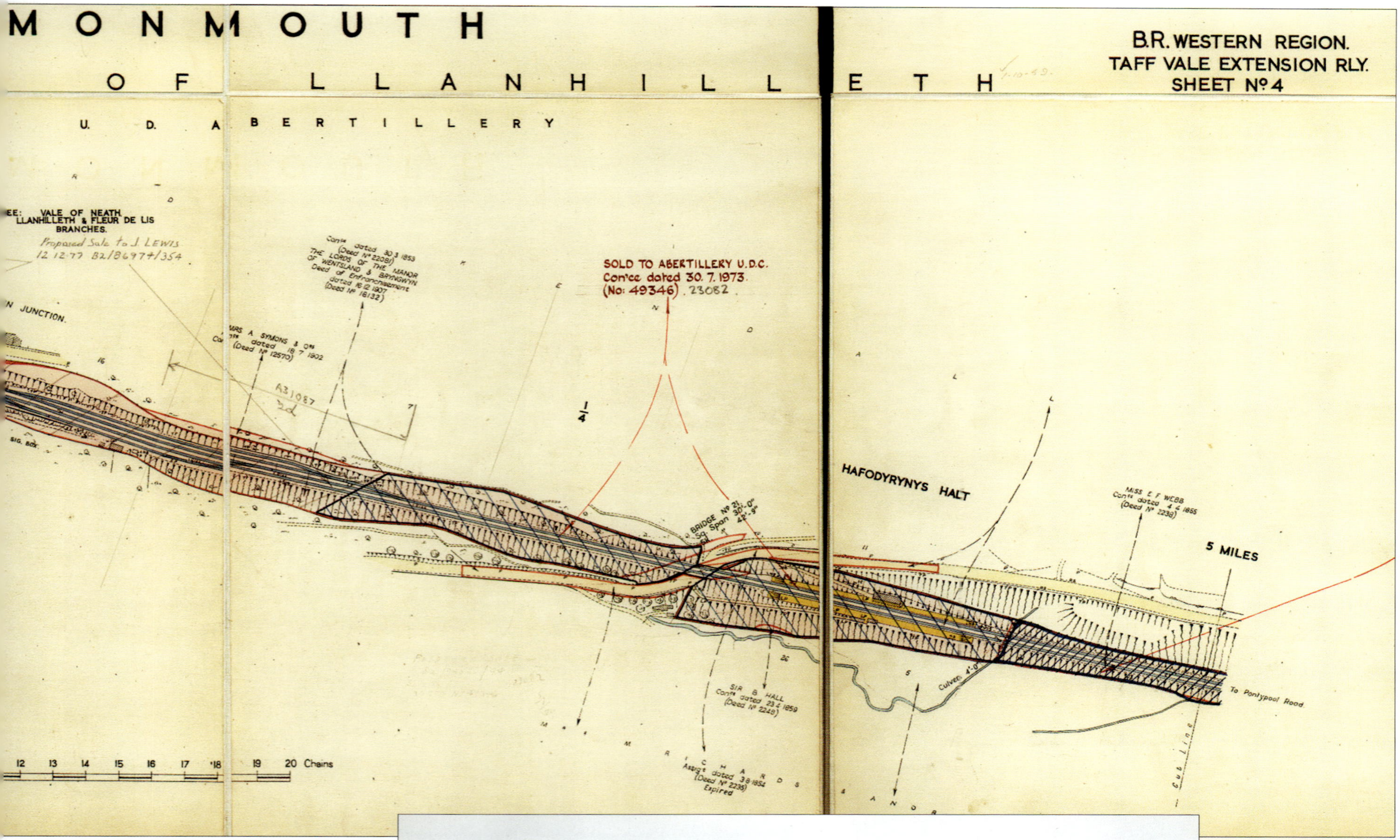

here is the diminishing number of longer distance freights, with only three scheduled, running in the early hours.

Up goods workings began with a Mondays excepted (MX) Pilot engine that had departed from Aberdare HL at 10.10pm, and then from Hengoed HL at 12.15am, which passed through Crumlin HL at 12.26am. Services then were as follows: 12.14am (MX, off Hirwaun Pond, 9.15pm (SX, Llandilo Junction to Stourbridge Junction), 12.06am (off Aberdare HL, 7.55pm SX, off Landore), 2.05am (MX, off Ystard Mynach North Junction),

PLATE 10.50: Looking north-east towards Swffryd school and the surrounding terraces, as 0-6-2T No. 6661 makes a spirited getaway from High Level station with an Aberdare to Pontypool Road service in August 1958. The locomotive was based at Aberdare shed from September 1953 to April 1964. TREVOR OWEN/ COLOUR-RAIL

Plate 10.51: *Looking west from the hillside below the Llanhilleth Branch on 26th June 1958. The six-coach loading of the Down train, hauled by a 'Large Paririe' tank, suggests this may be one of the 'through' workings, bound for the western end of the line, to Neath or Swansea.*
Neil Parkhouse collection

2.30am (off Aberdare HL), 6.45am (MX, off Penar Junction – '*Or as ordered by Control*'), 7.50am (MSX, off Aberdare HL, to Pontypool Road), 9.25am (off Quaker's Yard East Junction, 7.55am from Merthyr), 7.40am (off Swansea Eastern Depot, to Shrewsbury Cotton Hill), 10.35am (SX, off Nelson & Llancaiach, 9.30am from Aberdare), 12.32pm (off Penar Junction, 6.55am Aberdare to Pontypool Road), 11.55pm (off Ystrad Mynach North Junction, 10.10am from Stormstown Junction), 1.19pm (SO, off Nelson & Llancaiach, 10.40am (SO) from Aberdare), 1.40pm (off Hengoed HL, 10.40am (SX) from Aberdare), 3.10pm (SX, off Penar Junction), 5.50pm (SO, off Penar Junction, return of 3.40pm Hafodrynys East to Aber Junction), 2.55pm (off Aberdare HL, to Crumlin Junction), 4.50pm (off Quaker's Yard East Junction, return of 1.10pm Pontypool Road to Quaker's Yard), 8.10pm (SO, off Penar Junction), 8.30pm (SX, off Fleur-de-Lis), 8.51pm (SO, off Penar Junction, return of 2.35pm (SO) Pontypool Road to Stormstown Junction), 10.50pm (SX, off Hengoed HL, return of 5.45am Pontypool Road), 8.21pm (SX, off Neath General, 7.55pm Margam Abbey Yard to Salisbury) and 10.10pm (off Aberdare HL to Pontypool Road.

There were now no freight workings on Sundays either, so signal box opening hours were rationalised to suit. Crumlin Junction and Crumlin High Level Station boxes both now opened on a Monday morning at 4.30am, with the former closing after the last train had passed on in the early hours of Sunday morning, usually the 11.55pm up from Llanhilleth, which then left for Pontypool Road at 12.15am. The last train through High Level on a Saturday evening was the 6.50pm SO from Stormstown Junction, which was scheduled to pass at 9.01pm, after which the box could shut. Neither signal box had the facility to be switched out.

PLATE 10.52: An undated view but probably early 1960s, with an ex-GWR 'Hall' Class 4-6-0 silhouetted against the sky as it trundles across with a westbound mixed freight. Intriguingly here, note the panels of narrow gauge track laid along the old canal towpath in the right foreground. Petering out part way along, no explanation has been found as to why they were here or what they were being used for.
STEPHEN ROWSON COLLECTION

PLATE 10.53: In evening sunshine and watched by a local standing at the rear gate of his property, No. 6682, one of the GWR's '56XX' Class 0-6-2 tanks, makes it way gingerly westwards with a train of 'W ↑ D' lettered suphuric acid tanks on 31st October 1962. Two open wagons have been marshalled at the front as barrier wagons, whilst the tanks are presumably empties on their way back from ROF Glascoed to one of the chemical plants in the Swansea/Neath/Port Talbot area.
BILL POTTER/
KIDDERMINSTER RAILWAY MUSEUM

PLATE 10.54, BELOW: *Looking up from Hafodrynys Road Bridge as a '57XX Class 0-6-0PT heads east on 27th July 1963.*
ALAN JARVIS/SLS ARCHIVE

PLATE 10.55, BELOW RIGHT: *No. 6144 of Aberdare shed had only a month left in service when it was photographed on its way eastwards to Pontypool Road on 23rd May 1964.*
ALAN JARVIS/SLS ARCHIVE

Closure

The early 1960s were to see the crystalisation of plans for the entire British railway network to undergo a serious rationalisation, a process begun in the 1950s and which was ultimately to lead to Dr Beeching's now infamous report, *The Reshaping of British Railways*. In the 1950s, in a rapidly changing post-war world, the 1955 Railway Strike by members of the Associated Society of Locomotive Engineers & Firemen (ASLEF), for seventeen days from 28th May to 14th June, was to prove something of a watershed. Emergency arrangements had to be put into operation, vast amounts of freight turned to road transport and never returned, and Government lost patience with an industry that was haemorraging money.

Whilst the passenger service between Pontypool Road, Aberdare HL, Neath General and Swansea High Street was mentioned in the Beeching report, it was under a sub-heading of '*Passenger Services under Consideration for withdrawal before the Formulation of the Report*'. Many of them had already been implemented by the time the report was published, which suggests that these closures had already been decided. Pontypool Clarence Street, Crumlin HL and Aberdare HL were on the list of stations to close along, with all the others on the route.

There seems little doubt now, looking back, that the condition of Crumlin Viaduct was a major factor in the decision to close the TVE/VoN line but this also rather flies in the face of the 1959 Paddington Memorandum (see **Appendix 6**), which had recommended its retention. At that time, the line was still generating some 700,000 passenger journeys per annum, whilst due to the nature of the route – crossing from valley to valley rather than travelling along them – replacement of the passenger service by buses was impossible. However, whilst much work had already been carried out on the viaduct, another £415,000 needed to be spent urgently (£12.1 million in 2024), to bring it up to 'Red' route standard and allow the speed limit to be raised to 20mph but also to keep it going beyond 1961. In the light of this, the Chief Civil Engineer refused to recommend that any costly short term repair work be carried out. The conclusion of the memorandum was never acted upon, however, and with freight traffic declining and in a world where the motor car was fast becoming king, within five years the decision to close the line had been taken.

The impending closure seemed to attract very little attention from the contemporary railway press, however. In the March 1964 issue of *The Railway Magazine* there was first a very brief indication under the subheading '***Branch Closures Approved***': '*Agreement to withdrawal has been given ... Vale of Neath line ...*' – no mention of the fact that this would mean the loss of train services over the viaduct. This was followed up by a more detailed description under a similar subheading in the August 1964 issue '***Last train on South Wales branches***, by which time of course the line had shut:

'*From June 15 six branch lines in South Wales were closed to passenger traffic ... The last train over the Neath to Pontypool Road (Vale of Neath) line was hauled by a pannier-tank No. 4639. On the front was a headboard with the words "Vale of*

PLATE 10.56: *Photographer Bill Potter made the most of the fine sunshine available during his visit to Crumlin on 31st October 1962, during which he took a couple of pictures of the viaduct from Low Level station – one with a pannier tank and brake van standing at the Up platform and this one of an Aberdare-Pontypool Road service making its way over behind a '56XX' 0-6-2T. Low Level station had closed to passengers six months earlier on 30th April and nothing remains of it today.*
BILL POTTER/ KIDDERMINSTER RAILWAY MUSEUM

Plate 10.57: A child's tent in the garden of the station master's house, a lone car parked in the High Level station forecourt and the signalman chatting to the driver of '5101' Class 'Large Prairie' No. 4121, which was part way through a six month allocation to Aberdare shed – a timeless and delightful scene but one that was about to come to an end. The date is Wednesday, 10th June 1964 and there was only three days to go before the end of services. High Level was purely a passenger station, having no goods yard or sidings.
Colour-Rail

Neath 1851-1964", and on the bufferbeam was a badge with the Welsh dragon emblem. The four-coach train was packed with both local passengers and enthusiasts, and for many it was "standing room only". At each station crowds had gathered to bid farewell to the line and photograph the train. At Glyn Neath the train was 18 min. late and by the time Aberdare was reached more than 20 min. had been lost. Aberdare, which once had two stations, is now without rail communication. The train was cheered on its way by local residents, whose houses bordered the line, waving, cheering and throwing streamers. The locomotive whistle gave a continuous blast and at the stations detonators had been placed on both rails. Detonators had been placed every few yards across the famous Crumlin Viaduct and, together with the whistle, echoed across Ebbw Vale. At Pontypool Clarence Street it seemed that the trip was too much for the engine and a delay of 20 min. resulted. Many passengers from Newport, Cardiff and farther afield missed the last train at 11.43p.m.: however, the authorities saw fit to run a special train at midnight to get everyone home.'

The journal of the Railway Correspondence & Travel Society, *The Railway Observer*, also carried a report of the closure in their August 1964 issue: '*NEATH–PONTYPOOL LINE. The 42-mile cross-country line from Neath to Pontypool Road saw its last passenger train on Saturday, 13th June. This line remained all steam to the last, and on the final day the following were on passenger duty: 3713, 4110/21, 4639 and 6836. The appearance of a Grange was most unusual. Much of the line east of Aberdare has lost its freight traffic as well, and no trains are now running over that imposing structure, Crumlin Viaduct. It seems likely that this will be dismantled shortly.*' The engines noted comprised two '57XX' Class pannier tanks, two '5101' Class 'Large Prairie' tanks and

Plate 10.58: *Bill Potter made one last trip down to the line before it closed, on Friday, 12th June, taking a number of shots at High Level station as a record of its working existence. Here, hands in pockets and passing comment with another of the station staff on the Down platform, the signalman waits to collect the single line staff from the driver of 'Large Prairie' No. 4110, which was working its way back to its home shed at Neath, although this service would only have been going as far as Aberdare. Note the Crumlin High Level totem on the lamppost – at least one of these has survived, selling for £6,100 at auction in 2020!*

Plate 10.59: *Later that day, Bill travelled across the viaduct for the last time behind an unidentified pannier tank. The west portal of Glyn Tunnel can just be seen in the centre right distance, whilst Hafodrynys Halt lay inbetween Crumlin Junction Signal Box and the tunnel.*
Both Bill Potter/ Kidderminster Railway Museum

No. 6836 *Estevarney Grange* of Pontypool Road shed, which transferred to Worcester immediately after the closure.

The last Down passenger train over the viaduct was the 8.55pm from Pontypool Road to Aberdare HL, which stopped at Crumlin HL at 9.20pm. The very last Up train over the Vale of Neath line was the 8.45pm from Neath General to Aberdare HL, which on Saturdays was extended to Pontypool Road, arriving there at 11.18pm after calling at Crumlin HL at 10.54pm. However, the *Railway Magazine* report shows that with No. 4639 in charge, it was running very late on this last day. Photographs of the final train are few and not one has been seen of it on the viaduct – even on a day close to the summer solstice, the very late running meant that it was probably crossed in the dark.

Perhaps the strangest aspect of all, however, was the complete absence of any rail tours running over the viaduct as the end drew near. Given the propensity of rail enthusiasts to ride lines slated for

Plate 10.60: Sporting a 'Vale of NeatH 1851-1964' headboard, No. 4639 makes the very last stop by a passenger train at Glynneath station on its way to Pontypool Road on 13th June 1964. Note that the pannier tank's smokebox door hinges and handle, and the buffers and front coupling had all been painted white for the occasion. The photograph was sourced from the https:gwrachtimeline.co.uk website, where it is missidentified as Cwmgrach station.

closure for the last time, it seems odd to say the least that, having scoured the Six Bells Junction website, the last rail tour to run over Crumlin Viaduct was the Railway & Canal Historical Society's 'South Monmouthshire Rail Tour' of 7th May 1960, the proposed running of which was reported in the April 1960 edition of *The Railway Magazine* and which was open to anyone: '*... a 70-mile tour ... of lines in Monmouthshire and Glamorganshire ... three sections of the route have never had passenger services and other sections have been closed to passengers for many years. The special train will leave High Street Station, Newport, at 12.50pm, and will run via Machen, Waterloo Halt, Caerphilly (reverse), Fountain Bridge Halt, Bassaleg (reverse), Nine Mile Point and Sirhowy Junction (reverse) to Crumlin Viaduct. From Crumlin, the journey will be continued via Penar Junction (reverse), Hall's Road, and Park Junction to Dock Street and Mill Street Stations in Newport. The train will return to Newport High Street (where the tour will end) via Cwmbran Junction (reverse), Caerleon, and Uskmouth (reverse). The fare for the tour, including a copy of the itinerary, is 12s 6d ...*'.

Precise timings are not known and neither is the identity of the locomotive which worked the tour. To those who do not know the lines, the eastwards journey from Sirhowy Junction along the TVE took the train across the viaduct to Crumlin Junction, where it would have then reversed direction, travelling back over the bridge as it returned to Penar Junction. From there, the train reversed again, to head south on Hall's Road, passing through the short Penar Tunnel and making its way down the valley to Hall's Road Junction and Risca.

And that was it as far as tours were concerned. Whether the closure came too suddenly in 1964 for anything last minute to be arranged or whether there was an embargo

Plate 10.61: The SLS's 'Last Brynmawr and Last Blaenavon LL Passenger Train' rail tour of 6th May 1962, seen here coming off the Llanhilleth Branch at Crumlin Junction, behind 0-6-2T No. 6656. The line across the viaduct stretches temptingly off in the background but tour participants were denied the opportunity to travel over it – although they had passed beneath – as the train was bound for Panteg & Griffithstown, south of Pontypool Road, where it reversed direction to take the branch up the valley to Blaenavon Low Level. Based at Ebbw Junction shed when it hauled the tour, No. 6656 transferred to Barry a few days later.
E.T. Gill/SLS Archive

on tours over the viaduct in its last years is unknown but also unlikely. Perhaps, despite having started life as a 'wonder of the world' in the mid 1850s, by the end it only mattered to locals that outside their doors stood the tallest railway viaduct in the UK and the third tallest in the world. Having been fêted and photographed when first built, it seems that this marvel of the Victorian age, this triumph of British ingenuity and engineering, albeit one whose crown had become a little tarnished, simply slipped quietly off the railway map as the line over it closed for good.

And as predicted in the closure report in the *The Railway Observer*, demolition was not to be long in coming.

Anecdotes and Observations

There are numerous tales concerning railwaymen and members of the public who worked on and travelled over the Crumlin Viaduct. Engine drivers and firemen have many a story to tell and one that has become part of local folklore concerns the first driver to take an engine across the viaduct. Referred to locally as 'Hellfire Jack', for this, his debut run, he apparently spent time in the local inns gaining sufficient 'dutch courage' before he could carry out his duties. Railway company regulations were very strict at this time and anyone suspected of drinking alcohol would not have been allowed onto the footplate of a locomotive. However, 'Hellfire Jack' would appear to have been a common nickname for enginemen and it was also bestowed on the driver of *Gypsy Lass*, an engine belonging to the contractors working on the Worcester to Hereford line. Other more substantiated reports state that it was Mark Carr who was the first to take an engine over the viaduct as, on a number of occasions, he had driven locomotives across whilst completing tests prior to inspections by Board of Trade officials.

A feature of early locomotives (the GWR were no exception) was the lack of protection their open cabs gave to drivers and firemen during periods of inclement weather. Working on the footplate of an open-cab 0-6-0 engine 200 feet above ground level during high winds, driving rain, hail and snow was not a pleasant experience. In the early years, during winter months it was not unknown for a driver or fireman to acquire a covering sheet from any available open wagon and drape it over the cab in order to provide some protection. Such sheets later came to be fitted to locomotives, although their effectiveness was always limited.

One of the sources referred to in compiling this chapter has been Arthur J. Pritchard's slim volume *Historical Notes on The Railways of S.E. Monmouthshire*, published posthumously in 1962. Pritchard had died earlier that year, at the age of 84, so was born in 1878 and could claim a close connection with Crumlin Viaduct, writing in the relevant section of his chapter on the NA&HR: '*The completed viaduct was the sight of the times and excursions were run from the neighbouring districts to view it. The writer's parents and some relatives travelled from Abergavenny by one of these trains. Passenger carriages were scarce and recourse had to be had to cattle trucks into which the people packed. Many ladies "crinolines" were damaged in the crush that day!*'.

The railway industry, officially and unofficially, was very quick in naming engines and trains. One of the open cab engines which regularly travelled over the viaduct was known as 'Pneumonia Castle' to many of the railwaymen who had to take it across. One engine driver, fearful of heights, who was rostered regularly to work over the viaduct, would cover his head with his jacket and instruct his fireman to inform him when they were safely across. Another driver used to joke that if they were to fall off, he hoped it would be above the Navigation Inn, and that they would finish up in the bar, whilst one other was heard to comment that '*it's a long way up there*'. Enginemen not affected by the height would comment that, at night, the traffic lights and pedestrian beacons in the centre of the town below looked like flashing marbles.

Many passengers also had concerns over the height. For those who did it was not unknown for them to move to the centre of a carriage when travelling across the viaduct, so that they could not see over the edge and ground level way below them. There is a story of a grandmother petrified of heights and travelling over the viaduct who refused to let her grandson stand against a window, in case it unbalanced the train and toppled over. Author Gordon Wood's wife has a friend who used to live in Aberdare and from an early age travelled across the viaduct at regular intervals but when with her grandmother, was made to sit in the centre of the carriage in order to 'balance' it.

Only engines below a certain weight were permitted to work over the viaduct. Another friend, who's father was a signalman at High Level, had an overweight 'Castle' Class 4-6-0 arrive one day, sent over 'Light Engine' apparently by the Crumlin Junction signalman; however, his father refused to accept it and promptly sent it back!

One regular long distance train that had to cross it was the Stourbridge Junction to Swansea via Hereford goods train. One of two 'Grange' Class 4-6-0s were rostered regularly for this turn, No. 6853 *Moorhampton Grange* or

PLATE 10.62: Detested by Western men on this route were the ex-LM&SR '8F' 2-8-0s, mostly because of their heavy water consumption on the steep grades, requiring regular watering stops, but also because they caused the viaduct deck to oscillate more than normal. Here, on 8th June 1962, an unidentified member of the class drifts slowly over with a mixed goods train. Crumlin Low Level footbridge and the Hafodrynys Road bridge beyond replaced the level crossing seen in the view on page 169.
COLOUR-RAIL

No. 6866 *Morfa Grange*. Changing crews at Hereford, the local drivers and firemen used to hope that one of these 'Granges' was on the front of the train, as they dreaded the sight of a '43xx' or '53xx' Class 2-6-0, because the force of each thrust on the cylinders, even at slow speed, made the viaduct oscillate more than normal. However, the worst, as far as they were all concerned, were the ex-LM&SR '8F' 2-8-0s, which were also very heavy users of water over the route. Those on the early morning return journey meanwhile, hoped to arrive at Tredegar Junction early or on time, where, having to wait, they could listen to the miners singing as they travelled on trains taking them to the coal mines further up the valley.

Ignoring all concerns for their personal safety, the viaduct's open ironwork construction provided a special attraction for local youths to climb amongst the piers and gain access to the walkway – feats that kept the bridgeman and local police fully occupied. And talk to many residents of Crumlin and they will recall experiences of climbing the piers in search of jackdaws nests and eggs.

A final observation; as far as is known, the viaduct was only ever crossed by steam locomotion. Neither Pontypool Road or Aberdare sheds ever had allocations of main line diesel engines and there is no recorded instance of a diesel locomotive or a multiple unit working over Kennard's steel spans, although an unobserved nighttime working remains a possibility.

Sources

A full list of sources for this chapter is given on page 295.

CLOSURE AND DEMOLITION

CHAPTER 11

During the decades through the middle of the 20th century, the nation's dependency on the railways for travel and the distribution of freight was gradually overtaken by a more convenient and efficient means of transport for passengers and goods. In 1955, in an effort to arrest and reverse the downward trend, the British Transport Commission promoted a modernisation plan. However, although it was an in depth study, the plan failed to reverse the trend, with losses increasing from £23 million in 1954 to £177 million in 1962[1] (various sources quote different figures but they all fall within a similar range). Cutting these losses was to overrule other considerations.

The decision as to whether to repair or reconstruct the viaduct, or deviate the Taff Vale Extension Line, first raised at the turn of the century, was still being discussed almost sixty years later. However, it was now about to be overtaken by national policies and the social attitudes of the 1960s. Economics and efficiency became a fundamental influence on major and local decisions.

The earliest substantiated indication that serious consideration was being given to the future of the viaduct appears in a handwritten note of 1917, headed '*Memo as to the Reconstruction of Crumlin Viaduct*'. It was pointed out that reconstructing the viaduct at the location suggested, about a mile and a quarter to the east, would involve crossing a valley with an extreme difference of 300 feet when measured from the floor to the summit. Deviating the existing line would require a new one about three miles in length, involve boring a new tunnel a mile and a half long and the construction of a new viaduct about 1,003 feet in length. It was considered that the extent of the works suggested would render the construction of such a deviation line at moderate cost impracticable (this information was overwritten in pencil '*Scheme B*'). The estimated cost was £210,000 (a figure deleted in pencil) but with a note suggesting that to this figure would be added the cost of the purchase of mineral rights from the surrounding area. As an example it was pointed out that the purchase of the mineral rights at Crumlin had cost £26,122. As an alternative, it was suggested that without further investigation, it would '*probably be found advisable to replace the existing viaduct by constructing another alongside*'. Although crossed out in pencil, there was a suggestion that '*it may even be possible to substitute ferro-concrete piers for the existing cast iron ones*'.[2]

Added to the memo, in pencil, were details of the suggested Scheme B:

'Viaduct, 470 yards long 120 feet high	*£150.000*
Tunnel 400 yards long	*£ 50.000*
Tunnel 200 yards long	*£ 22.000*
Railway 3¼ miles long	*£100.000*
Gradient 1 in 60 in each direction	
Tunnel and Viaduct on curve of 20 chains radius	
Mineral support required at Celynen Colliery	*£ 26.000*
Additional mileage traffic = ½ mile, on inferior gradients in each direction	
Total	*£348.000'*

In 1919, when considering a request from the Traffic Department to use '*red engines*' across the viaduct, it was explained that due to its condition, it would require strengthening or reconstruction, concluding: '*It is therefore a question whether the viaducts should be reconstructed entirely or the line deviated round the end of the valley: This scheme has already been considered*'.[3] No further action appears to have been taken until 1922, when information was being sought on '*whether any decision has been arrived at relating to a proposed deviation of the line, with a view to avoiding further maintenance on the Viaduct*'.[4]

In 1926, one of the company directors was seeking information on a scheme that he understood had been under consideration, '*for deviating the Pontypool Road and Neath line in order to avoid Crumlin Viaduct*'.[5] Exhaustive searches through the offices of the Chief Engineer have proved unsuccessful and the only information available was an Ordnance Survey-based map defining various deviation schemes but the only substantive information related to Scheme B, presented in 1919. In conclusion, the Chief Engineer suggested that, with the limited information available, he did not think that the General Manager would wish him to proceed with preparing details for a deviation scheme.[6]

Plate 11.8, Right: Work apparently came to something of a standstill after the removal of the side girders whilst options were considered for the best way forward. Evidently, lowering the inner girders to the ground using crane lorries was contemplated and the two machines here are different from those in the earlier pictures, obtained from Sparrows Crane Hire Ltd and presumably of heavier duty. The thought of working in the operating cabs of these on a narrow platform 200ft up does not bear thinking about but, fortunately, wiser heads were to prevail.

Plate 11.9, Below: A view of the work site from over the roofs of the houses in the appropriately named Kennard Terrace.

Both Neil Parkhouse collection

fencing, possession of running lines beneath the viaduct, access to private property and that any articles of value or antiquity discovered on the site would remain the property of the Railway Board. Copies of drawings were provided showing the general layout of the viaduct, along with a note that details were inaccurate and the contractor would be responsible for obtaining accurate ones from a site visit. The work would be supervised by the Chief Civil Engineer and the tendered price would be paid on completion of the work to his satisfaction.[28] As previously, the Chief Civil Engineer insisted that any demolition work was undertaken by a competent firm approved by him, pointing out that it was not a viaduct that could be demolished by such people as those who had been involved at Boughrood.[29]

Of the nineteen contractors who had been invited to submit an interest in dismantling and removing the viaduct, only five attended a special on site meeting during March 1965: G. Robinson & Co. Ltd, Birds (Swansea) Ltd, Carter-Horseley (Engineers) Ltd, The Fairfield Shipbuilding & Engineering Co. Ltd and John Cashmore Ltd. The offer of £41,750 submitted by Birds

PLATE 11.10: *In an echo of a famous staged photograph taken during the building of the RCA Building in 1932 – which showed a group of workers having their lunch on a girder hung from a crane hundreds of feet above the streets of New York – four of the demolition men sit with their feet dangling over the 200ft drop below. The removal of the side girders has exposed the walkway across the viaduct.*
NEIL PARKHOUSE COLLECTION

This Page: Plate 11.11 Right: Looking up from near the base of the Isabella pier on 31st July 1965, showing dismantling of the viaduct in its early stages.
Michael Gates/SLS Archive

Plate 11.12, Below: Another view looking up from the village, taken on 31st July 1965, as Crumlin's defining monument slowly begins to disappear. It would appear that the mobile cranes had already been dispensed with.
Michael Gates/SLS Archive

Page Opposite: Plate 11.13, Top: Looking skywards at the part dismantled span No. 2, from the Viaduct Works site on 4th July 1965. Stark against the skyline, the Crumlin Junction Up Home bracket signal stands forlorn and out of use, awaiting its fate. The silver paintwork of the piers looks remarkably fresh.
Trevor Owen/Colour-Rail

Plate 11.14, Bottom Left: The first task in the dismantling was to lift the track (done under a separate contract) across the viaduct and this view looking west across the Ebbw Valley section on 7th August 1965 shows that work was complete, with track panels stacked on the left.

Plate 11.15, Bottom Right: Walking across the viaduct, the photographer next took this view looking across the raised ground which linked the two sections, with the Kendon Valley spans beyond, curving away towards High Level station.
Both Brian Mills/Trackbed.com

(Swansea) Ltd was accepted by the board in April 1965.[30]

At a meeting held in September, members discussed progress made and the method the contractor was going to adopt for lowering the main girders. Since their last meeting held in June, the two outside girders of trial span No. 2 had been lifted up onto the deck of the bridge by crane lorries positioned on the piers on either side of the span. However, it was found that the use of cranes at such a high level had proved unsatisfactory.[31] At a meeting held in August, the contractors proposed to launch a single tier, reinforced, twin-beamed Bailey bridge above the existing girders, with bearings centrally placed on each of the piers (**Fig. 10.2**). The existing girders would then be hung from and supported by the Bailey beams and with the use of winches fixed to the ends, the centre 50 foot section of two girders could be cut and lowered to ground level. The end sections would then be lowered in a similar way. After the two centre girders of span No. 2 had been dismantled, a start would be made on removing the floor plate of span No. 3. After the removal of the floor plate, in sections, the Bailey bridge would be

PLATE 11.21: *Span No. 1 looking up from in front of the Viaduct Hotel on 12th December 1965, To the left is the Western Valleys Brewery, housed in the now demolished old Viaduct Works buildings.*

PLATE 11.22: *The contractors used the High Level station site as a temporary storage yard for recovered materials, with pieces of the railings stacked on the Down platform in the foregound. The contractor's car, which was also driven out onto the Kendon section of the viaduct at least once, is a swish 1960 6-cylinder, 2,912cc Wolseley with Farina styling. Stephen Rowson also recalls that the contractor had a pet jackdaw that used to perch on his shoulder and fly off around the site.*
BOTH A.N.H. GLOVER/ KIDDERMINSTER RAILWAY MUSEUM

suggested that work should proceed in arranging the occupation of the main line and colliery siding on the weekend of 16th-17th April, *'for winching the pier over and for clearance of the steelwork'*.[37]

A briefing note prepared by the engineers for a meeting with the UDC, scheduled for the beginning of April, contained a number of facts that the Council should be made aware of, including that:

a) the structure had already been sold for demolition therefore they would have to negotiate a price for the pier with Messrs. Bird

b) the pier stands on land owned by the British Railways Board and they would have to purchase the freehold of the land

c) a legal document would have to be drawn up, absolving the British Railways Board from all liabilities under the Constructing of Railways Act, in respect of the remaining pier

d) any additional cost involved in demolition brought about by possible abortive negotiations, and any claim brought by Messrs. Bird would have to be met by the Council, and this must be accepted in writing at once

e) advise the Council that whereas support for this bridge had been retained by purchase from the Coal Board, our rights in this have now been withdrawn and the Coal Board are at liberty now to extract coal from underneath, and I understand are beginning to do so: therefore the pier may become liable to subsidence and collapse

f) the cast iron in the columns has a number of cracks, and is not in a stable condition as it was when it had a load upon it

g) the Council will have to be responsible for its maintenance and painting, which is a fairly expensive item

h) try to influence them that they are being unwise in suggesting the retention of the pier, since they may thereby be incurring possible heavy liabilities.[38]

Within days, the Council had decided against taking any further action and instead they proposed to investigate the possibility of erecting a small memorial.[39]

The final act in the demolition process was a note from Monmouthshire County Council mentioning that the demolition was complete apart from the abutments[40] and that British Railways had no intention of removing them.[41] The final reference to the demolition was an enquiry, requesting information on the possibility of finding the items placed in the column of the Isabella pier at the ceremony to mark the start of works in 1852. A curt reply stated *'nothing'*.[42]

Today, only the abutments stand as a visual reminder of the scale and size of Crumlin Viaduct – *'This singularly graceful and beautiful bridge'*.[43]

Plate 11.23: *A view of the lofty Ebbw section piers standing proud and erect after removal of all the spans. . A mid-December progress report noted that all of the spans were now down but pier No. 6 was being referred to as still standing; however, here it can be seen that the ironwork of pier No. 6 is now lying on the hillside, so it would seem likely that we are looking at a date around Christmas 1965.*
Neil Parkhouse collection

References

1. *The Railways: Nation, Network and People*, Simon Bradley, Profile Books, 2015, page 413
2. Memorandum prepared by A.C. Cookson, 21st Jan. 1917
3. Report of Traffic Department, 4th July 1919
4. Letter from A.C. Cookson, 17th May 1922
5. Letter from J.C. Lloyd, 12th Aug. 1926
6. Letter from J.C. Lloyd, 12th Aug. 1926
7. Letter, P.S.A. Berridge to M.G.R. Smith, 17th June 1957

Plate 11.24, Right: *Pier No. 5, the last standing directly on railway property, seen amidst snowy conditions in January 1966. This was the pier that Abertillery UDC expressed an interest in saving but the BR Board were not keen and it was winched over in April 1966.* Stephen Rowson collection

Plate 11.25, Far Right: *Pier No. 1 in the process of being winched over on 27th March 1966.* Stephen Rowson collection

Plates 11.26 and 11.27: *Snapshots from above and below of the bridge spanning Hillside being demolished. The Bridgend Inn's painted sign only vaguely resembled the viaduct. Sold in 2020, the inn was no longer in business at the time of writing.* Stephen Rowson

8. Memorandum, 12th Mar. 1959
9. Letter, P.S.A. Berridge to J.F. Bickerton, 18th Dec. 1961
10. Memorandum, 29th June 1962
11. Letter, R.E. Hatton to F.R.L. Barnwell, 16th Nov. 1964
12. Papers held at Gwent Archives
13. *The Reshaping of British Railways*, Mar. 1963
14. Hansard, HoC debate, 20th Dec. 1963, vol. 686, cc1634-63
15. Letter, F.R.L. Barnwell to C.F. Fiennes, 24th June 1964
16. Request to Stores Controller Swindon, 18th Aug. 1964
17. Recommendation of Bridge Assistant, Paddington
18. Note from Bridge Assistant Paddington: '*Boughrood Bridge: On Sunday, 5th July 1964, the steel girders of Boughrood Bridge, which had carried the Brecon to Moat Lane line across the River Wye, collapsed into the water during demolition. Three workmen, along with two 13-year old boys who were playing on the bridge, were plunged into the river and one of the men, 27-year old Granville Evans of Pentre, Rhondda, was drowned. A manslaughter verdict was returned against the demolition contractors, the Northern Strip Mining Co. of Sheffield, at the subsequent inquest.*'
19. Letter, F.R.L. Barnwell to R.B. Hoff, 28th Feb. 1965

Plate 11.28, Left: *The gap! An undated view looking east from Load of Hay Road, before tree growth obscured the few remains of the viaduct's existence. The stone abutment still stands today but is largely hidden in the undergrowth but note here also the very visible scar left by pier No. 1.* Neil Parkhouse collection

Plate 11.29, Below: *The gap from the other side, looking west towards the site of High Level station on 3rd August 1967. The station master's house can be clearly seen and also the western abutment of the viaduct. The metal footbridge in the foreground spanned the Llanhilleth Branch but with the rails having been lifted, it has since been taken down and the footpath lowered to cross the trackbed on the level. Down below, an English Electric Type '3' (later Class '37') heads down the valley with a train of empty coal hoppers.*
Bill Potter/Kidderminster Railway Museum

Plate 11.30: Earlier in the day on 3rd August 1967, Bill Potter took this lovely shot of green liveried English Electric Type 3 No. D6907 (later Class '37' No. 37207) passing through the site of the viaduct with an Up freight. Signs of decay abound, however – in the left foreground are the concrete piers which held the columns of the water tower, Navigation Colliery had closed three months earlier and the goods yard sidings had been lifted, with scrap merchants lorries being loaded with the cast iron chairs
Bill Potter/ Kidderminster Railway Museum

20. Papers held at Gwent Archives
21. Meeting held on 16th July 1964
22. Papers held at Gwent Archives
23. Report in *South Wales Echo*, 21st July 1964
24. Papers held at Gwent Archives
25. Papers held at Gwent Archives
26. Letter, RCA&HMW, 23rd Oct. 1964
27. Letter, Ministry of Housing & Local Government, Cardiff, 23rd Oct. 1964
28. Tender letter, 19th Mar. 1965
29. Memo from Chief Engineer, Feb. 1965
30. Minutes of meeting, 8th Sept. 1965
31. Minutes of meeting, 8th Sept. 1965
32. Letter, F.R.L. Barnwell to R.B. Holt, 2nd Sept. 1965
33. Minutes of meeting, 26th Oct. 1965
34. Report of Resident Engineer, 26th Oct. 1965
35. Report of Resident Engineer, 19th Dec. 1965
36. Letter to Messrs Birds. 25th Mar. 1966
37. Report of Resident Engineer, 31st Mar. 1966
38. Briefing note, 31st Mar. 1966
39. Minutes of Abercarn Council, 7th Apr. 1966
40. Letter from County Planning Officer, Monmouthshire CC, to British Railways 17th May 1966
41. Letter from British Railways to County Planning Officer, 24th May 1966
42. Papers held at Gwent Archives
43. *Usk Observer*, 6th June 1857

ASSOCIATED WORKS AND EVENTS

CHAPTER 12

Whilst the main theme of this book is obviously the viaduct, it would be perverse to ignore some of the other façets of the industrial and railway landscape in the immediate vicinity upon which it had an effect, along with other works that were a part of the local scene. Some of these associated works, such as the colliery tramroads, were already in existence, whilst others, such as Crumlin Siding and Crumlin Hall, came about as a direct result of the viaduct's construction. Others still, such as the Llanhilleth Branch and Crumlin Navigation Colliery, were simply an integral part of the local scene and thus are mentioned in the text as well as featuring in many of the photographs.

This chapter, therefore, looks at the history behind some of these other enterprises and aspects that were once a part of the local scene.

Soffrenydd/Swffryd Quarry

Thomas Kennard's activities in and around Crumlin were not concentrated solely on establishing a base for his bridge building and the manufacture of railway apparatus. Whenever Kennard was presented with an opportunity to acquire – by leasehold or purchase – additional land or property close to the works, he was quick to react. Amongst his early acquisitions were a farm, an inn and a quarry. The construction of the branch line from Crumlin Junction to Llanhilleth cut across the direct access from farmland and also what was referred to as Soffrenydd Quarry to the Old Quarry Road below. Stone from the quarry was being used in the construction of the eastern abutment of the viaduct and for Crumlin Hall, built for and occupied by members of the Kennard family. Soffrenydd, incidentally, is the Welsh word for 'Sovereign'.

In 1856, following the opening of the Llanhilleth Branch for goods traffic the previous year, H.M. Kennard, along with his brothers, had purchased the Viaduct Works and the leasehold of the surrounding land, which included the quarry. He wrote to Liddell, seeking permission to construct a bridge across the line, at a location that the two of them had identified at a previous meeting.[1] Liddell referred the letter to Mark Carr, considering it to be more a question for a resident engineer to resolve but added that any design for a bridge should make provision for protecting the line from stones, or any other matter being dropped on to it.[2]

Maynard then becomes involved, sending to Carr a rough sketch of a '*stage or bridge that the Kennard Bros. wished to construct over the branch line*'. The reason given for wanting the bridge was to take paving stones over the branch line by truck, then to let them slip to the base of the existing wall and out on to the Old Quarry Road. The bridge was to be made with a timber frame on the Down side and a stone abutment on the quarry side of the line. It was to be 6 feet wide, with a clear headway of 15 feet when taken from the level of the rails.[3] Carr's reaction was to treat the request with caution, suggesting that '*they should, before starting any works memorialise the board*'. Carr also pointed out that '*any plans prepared would require my approval ... will not approve anything that fails to make provision for clearing two lines of railway, and did not have substantial fencing between any tramway and the line, in order to protect the line from falling stones and derailing any tram*'. Referring to a rough sketch prepared by Maynard, Carr added that his comments were '*intended to be no more than useful hints*'.[4]

Maynard's next communication with Carr raised an interesting point; he wanted to know '*if any other line of rails was required on the branch, and if so, how would they be positioned, on the inside or on the outside of the existing branch line*'. If there was any possibility of doubling the line, Carr's response was not at all helpful, suggesting that neither of the routes suggested would be adopted but it would probably be somewhere between the two. Carr promised to discuss the subject next time they met but this is the last occasion that any reference is made to doubling the line in any of the correspondence.[5]

Nothing further appears in the records until the beginning of October 1856, when Mr Kidd, the Viaduct Works manager, writes to Carr informing him that he was '*getting a few stones from 'Sovereign Quarry' for building Mr Kennard's house*' but he was also complaining that Mr

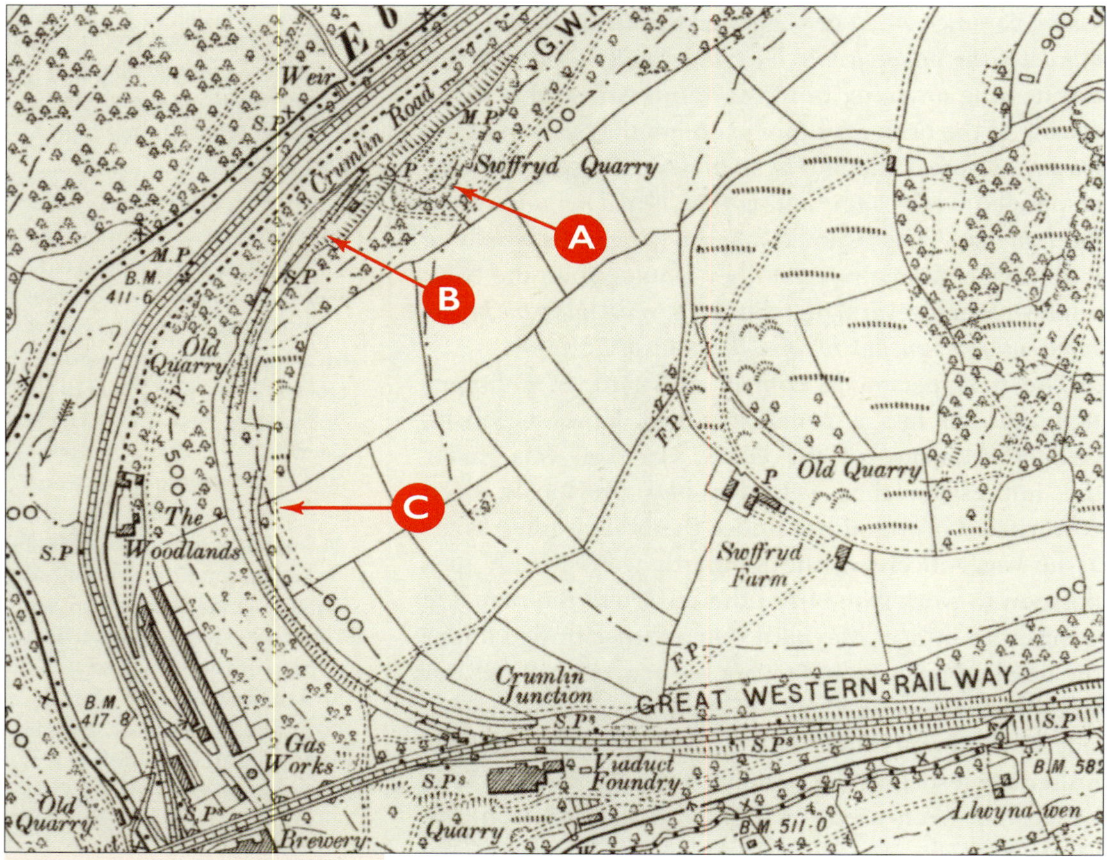

FIG. 12.3: A section of the 2nd edition 6 inch OS for Crumlin, as revised in 1899 and published in 1902:
A – the same quarry, now clearly named Swffryd after its location. A short length of tramroad runs to the loading wharf.
B – the loading wharf and loop siding provided by the GWR in 1886. There were ground frames at each end and the map also shows signal posts.
C – the upper private siding.

quarry, was in fact still in place at this date. However, by the time of the OS survey on page 228, it would appear that by 1878-79 the temporary bridge had gone and an underbridge had been built.

Everything then went quiet for over twelve months, before a John Monks wrote to Maynard asking whether he had heard anything from the GWR. Monks was keen on renting the quarry, with a proviso that he could send stone over the branch line by making use of an existing landing stage by the quarry from which he could load trucks.[24] The approach from Monks to rent the quarry prompted Maynard into action and, months later, he received, from the GWR, a copy of a plan of the branch with a proposed line marked on it. Their engineer wanted to know if he had interpreted correctly a large scale plan signed by Maynard on 6th May 1875, and if it was still what he wanted.[25]

The next record of any communication from Monks occurs over twelve months later, when he asked Maynard how much he would put up a bridge across the railway for and let the '*old quarry for as it was, but, supposing that the Great Western will put in a siding*'.[26] Having failed in his initial approach to rent and operate the quarry, Monks made a further offer to Maynard in July to rent it at a reasonable price, adding that if so he would pay any rent in advance.[27] From this time on, Maynard's attention was directed towards the GWR's engineers and the operational problems he was experiencing – problems that he never appears to have resolved.

Before making any arrangement with Monks, Maynard wrote to the GWR's Engineering Department with a request to be informed the reason for the delay in carrying out the arrangement to lay a siding into the quarry.[28] It transpired that the proposals then being put forward differed from those originally agreed by the landowner, Kendall. On the death of Kendall, there was no one who could release the company from the works originally agreed upon and a situation could arise that the GWR would remain obliged to construct it as originally agree upon. As far as they were concerned, they would require an indemnity against any claim being made against them from Kendall's representatives but the only way that the situation could have been resolved was to secure the indemnity and submit it to the GWR's board of directors.[29] A reminder was sent to Maynard four weeks later but to no avail.[30] The following year the leasehold of the quarry, the adjoining farmland and properties, and the freehold of the Viaduct Works were sold at public auction.[31] A siding was eventually installed by the GWR and an agreement arranged between Monks and the railway in 1886, some thirty years after the initial approach by the Kennards.

The Llanhilleth Branch

The Llanhilleth Branch opened at the same time as the TVE and although little traffic coming off it at the top travelled over the viaduct – the connection at Crumlin Junction was towards Pontypool Road and the vast majority of wagons were bound to and from there – it was very much a part of the local scene so its history is included here. With a ruling gradient of 1 in 43 and turning from south to east during its climb, banking assistance was generally required for Up trains. The Board of Trade inspector had tested and passed it for passenger working too in 1857 but it never had a timetabled public service, although from 1939 to 1957, the branch was used by ROF Glascoed workmen's trains originating from further up the Ebbw Valley. After these ceased to run, the branch was only ever to see one more passenger working, this being the SLS's 'Last Brynmawr and Last Blaenavon LL Passenger Train' rail tour of 6th May 1962, which climbed up from Llanhilleth before heading off east at Crumlin Junction. Information about this tour is sparse and the only known photograph of

PLATE 12.2: A detail enlargement from the circa 1880 picture on page 4, showing the steep course of the branch as it heads down and around the mountainside. The siding can be seen above the Kendon section of the viaduct. It looks to have been gated – which certainly would not have been the case if it was a safety siding leading to a sand drag – but otherwise there is no obvious clue as to what it was being used for. NEIL PARKHOUSE COLLECTION

PLATE 12.3: The same section of the branch and the course of the siding around seventy-five years later, photographed from the closed and under demolition viaduct on 12th December 1965. The branch had also been lifted by this date. Note the aerial ropeway on the horizon, carrying waste from Navigation Colliery to a succession of tips. A.N.H. GLOVER/ KIDDERMINSTER RAILWAY MUSEUM

it on the branch shows it arriving at Crumlin Junction (page 204). It surely must have been banked up from Llanhilleth, which was a requirement of how the branch was worked, but no reference has been found to confirm this nor to identify the banking locomotive. The views available from the line as it climbed and curved round Swffryd mountain, particularly of the viaduct, would seem to have been tailor made for rail tours but perhaps the banking requirement proved restrictive.

The 1 mile, 27 chains long branch was single except for short sections at both ends where it became double to join with the double track route of the Taff Vale Extension at Crumlin Junction at the top and the Western Valleys line at Llanhilleth Branch Junction at the bottom. It also served two private sidings en route, both on the sharp curve round from Crumlin Junction, although little is known about what the first of them was used for. Situated approximately 18 chains from Crumlin Junction, it was a single siding coming directly off the running line and was in existence by 1875, at which time there was a Private Siding Agreement (PSA) in place for the use of it between the GWR and an E. Lewis.[32] The siding also climbed sharply as the branch dropped down, so the two were quickly on different levels.

However, what Mr Lewis used the siding for is not at all clear. The 1st edition 25 inch OS extract on page 228 appears to show it ending in a sand drag, which would have provided protection against runaways from Crumlin Junction but if that were the case, any other use of it would have been prohibited. Successive OS surveys fail to indicate exactly what it served, with no evidence of any industrial enterprise in the immediate vicinity, a fact emphasised by the two pictures on this page. However, on 16th February 1907, a new PSA was signed by Vipond & Lewis[33] and there are further complications.

From 1916, the OS appears to show a catch point and run off siding slightly higher up the bank but a 1949 diagram for Crumlin Junction Signal Box[34] shows this as being below the point for the siding, with the notation '*sprung points, slotted by 34*'. The same diagram also shows '*Lewis's Siding GF*' (ground frame), which indicates it

PLATE 12.4, RIGHT: English Electric Type '3' No. D6866 gently rounds the steep curve at the start of the branch with a mixed freight on 27th September 1963. The track bed of the old Lewis siding can be seen on the right, just ahead of the locomotive. The photograph was taken from the footbridge carrying a footpath from Swffryd down to Crumlin village. This does not appear on maps until the 1948 revision, so would appear to have been a wartime provision, probably due to blackout restrictions making stepping across the tracks more dangerous. No. D6866 was very new when seen here, having gone into traffic at Cardiff Canton depot eighteen days earlier on 9th September.

PLATE 12.5, BELOW: Photographed from the same vantage point on the same day, Class '57XX' pannier tank No. 3708 nears the top of the climb with a train made up of several sheeted opens and some loaded coal wagons, which was being banked by 0-6-2T No. 6634. Both engines spent most of their BR era careers based at Pontypool Road shed.
BOTH BILL POTTER/ KIDDERMINSTER RAILWAY MUSEUM

was worked by the train crew but they had to get a key to unlock it first from the Crumlin Junction signalman. The 1938 revision of the 6 inch OS shows the siding now extended to the full extent of the boundary and it was still in situ on the 1948 revision. By this date, Swffryd Road, the school and the terraces of houses in Lewis Street had all been built on the hillside looking down upon the branch. It is thought that the siding fell out of use soon after Nationalisation and it does not feature in any of the accompanying photographs but a date for its removal has not been found. Cooke's *Track Plans* volume also indicates that the siding was gated.

The second private siding, a little further down, was that serving Swffryd Quarry. It is shown on the 6 inch OS extract on page 22), for which a PSA was signed by J. Monks & Co. on 26th October 1886.[35] This took the form of a loop siding alongside a loading dock, onto which ran a short narrow gauge line from the quarry, that may have been horse-worked as the gradient would have been against loaded tubs. Oddly, having been shown on the 1899 6 inch OS revision, this siding does not appear again, despite much evidence that it remained in place and in use, although when it ceased to be used by Monks has not been ascertained but it certainly seems to have fallen out of use for some time.

The siding was then taken over by new owners the Crumlin (Mynyddislwyn) Collieries Company – '*The old*

Crumlin Quarry siding, of J.H. Monks, assigned to T. Evans and J.H. Jones by agreement dated 12.9.1919'.[36] Working here commenced in 1920 and, for such a small level, it was to have quite an involved history.

The Great Western signed a new PSA with Crumlin (Mynyddislwyn) Collieries Ltd on 25th February 1924,[37] who were presumably going to work the tiny Swffryd Colliery, up on the top of the mountain, to the north-east of the quarry. This is shown as 'Coal Level' on the circa 1875 6 inch OS, with a tramway running straight down the hillside to what was presumably a wharf on the branch itself, near the Royal Oak public house at Llanhilleth. The mine was disused by the date of the 1899 OS revision and the tramway is also not marked but its route is shown on the 1916 revision as is a new coal level, a few yards to the south which also had a short length of tramway internally. The GWR's new agreement included the provision of new Upper and Lower ground frames at each end of the loop siding, which suggests it had been out of use for some time.

The PSA was then transferred to new owners the Erskine Colliery Co. Ltd on 30th December 1927.[38] The coal level with its short length of tramway continues to appear on the OS up until the 1948 revision but the PSA was subsequently terminated in 1949, with the siding and ground frames being taken out on 10th July 1949,[39] which makes it odd indeed that it was not shown on any OS map after 1899. A *Working Time Table* for the period that the siding was in operation has not been seen but with it being situated part way down an incline, it would have to have been worked with the engine at the lower end at all times to guard against any wagon runaways, whilst wagons in the siding would have to have been 'locked in' for the same reason, *i.e.* the point leading to the runaway

Plate 12.6: *Looking from Lewis Street, Swffryd back towards the viaduct, as an unidentified '56XX' 0-6-2T heads an Up four-coach Aberdare to Pontypool Road service across at the required 8mph. The trackbed of the siding is clearly seen in the foreground.* Trevor Owen/Colour Rail

Branch, trains were restricted to 22 loaded and 40 empty wagons in length, provided the guard and driver were satisfied that the wagon brakes were in good working order. The brakes on every wagon and the brake van had to be carefully examined, and those on the wagons had to be pinned down before starting. When two engines were working up the incline, one engine had to be at the rear.

The impending closure of the Taff Vale Extension/ Vale of Neath line to through traffic, coupled with the loss of much of the freight traffic at the eastern end, meant that the Llanhilleth Branch would become redundant. As a result of this, closure of it preceded the line over the viaduct and it was taken out of use on 17th May 1964. Today, much of the trackbed is now a foot and cyclepath, leading down from Lewis Street at Swffryd to Crumlin Road, south of Llanhilleth.

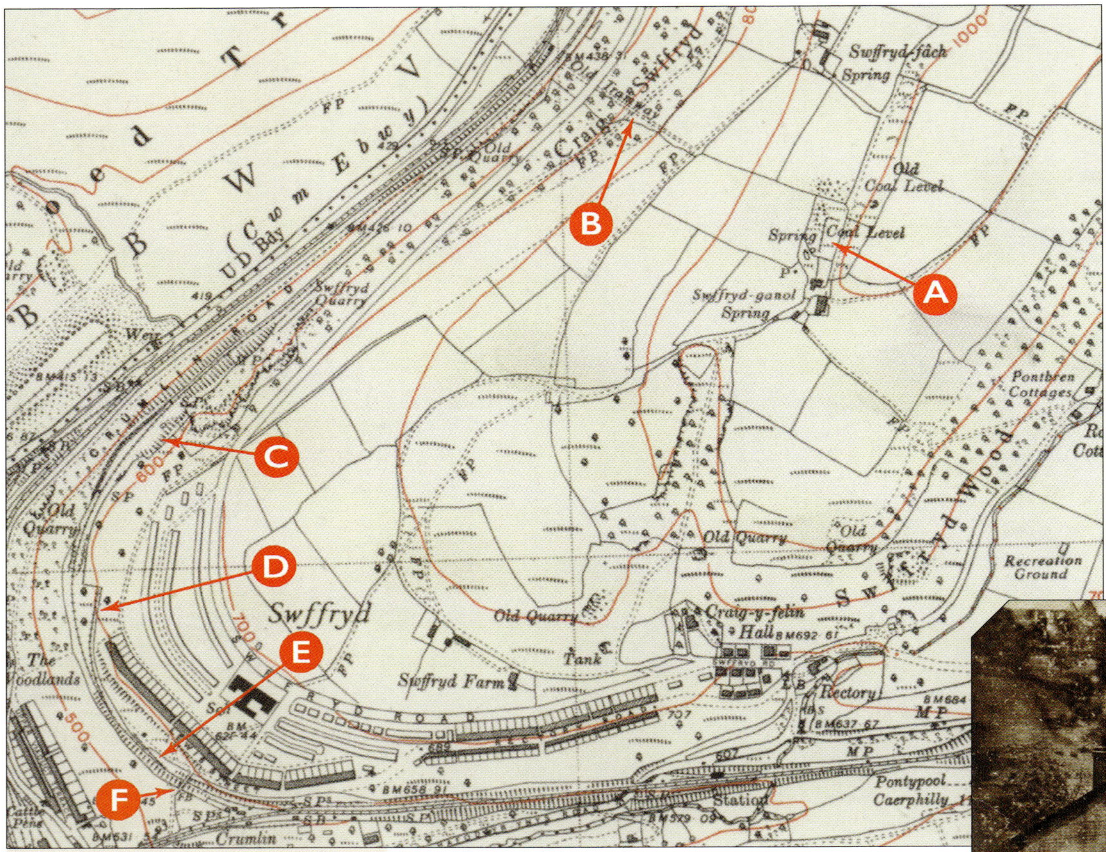

Fig. 12.4: An extract from the 1948 revision of the 6 inch OS, published in 1953:
A – the Swffryd coal level latterly worked by the Erskine Colliery Co. Ltd.
B – route from the earlier Swffryd coal level – which is shown as working on the mid-1870s revision – of an old tramway down to a loading bay on the Llanhilleth Branch.
C – site of Swffryd Quarry sidings. Despite remaining in use until circa 1948 and not being lifted until 1949, they were not shown on any revision after 1899.
D – Lewis's Siding, now extended to the edge of the land boundary
E – apparent catch point and run off track
F – footbridge

stub and the point connecting to the running line would have been set away from each other and clipped in position as an extra precaution. With ground frames at either end, the siding would have been worked by the train crew.

Plate 12.7, Above: A postcard view of the Royal Oak pub – the taller building near the far end – at Llanhilleth circa 1910. In the foreground, the branch can be seen climbing the hillside to Crumlin Junction. The terrace, facing onto Crumlin Road, remains today but the Royal Oak is now a private residence.
Neil Parkhouse collection

Plate 12.8, Left: An '87XX' 0-6-0PT on its way up near the bottom of the branch on 31st July 1963. The train is about to pass in front of the terrace containing the Royal Oak pub.
Alan Jarvis/SLS Archive

Plate 12.9, Left: *A circa 1905 postcard view of Llanhilleth Colliery No's 1 and 2 pits. The first workings here dated from circa 1865, with the colliery being acquired by Partridge, Jones & Co. in 1889 after it had been out of use for a year. As well as restarting work on the House coal seam, they sank a new shaft to reach the Steam coal seam, after which it became a very profitable operation that, at its height in 1909, employed over 1,800 men underground and around another 250 on the surface. The colliery closed in March 1969 and its site is now covered by a sports complex and the ground of Llanhilleth Rugby Club.* Neil Parkhouse collection

Plate 12.10, Below: *Taken on the same day as* **Plate 12.7**, *this impressive panorama shows the branch curving round in the right foreground to join the main line at Llanhilleth Branch Junction and makes for an interesting comparison with the postcard view from nearly sixty years earlier. The site of Llanhilleth Branch Signal Box is in the immediate right foreground but it was closed in 1933 and operation of the junction was then passed to Llanhilleth Middle Signal Box, in the centre left distance. Llanhilleth Colliery straddled the Western Valleys main line, along the Down line of which another pannier tank makes its way south.* Alan Jarvis/SLS Archive

Fig. 12.5: The route of Mark Philips' Tramroad as shown on the 1st edition 6 inch OS surveyed between 1873 and 1879. The site of Trinant Colliery – here marked as Trinant Level – has been picked out in blue for clarity. The tramroad (picked out in red) was single track except for the incline, which was double and worked on the gravity principle, with loaded trams pulling empties back up the slope. Also shown here is the route of the branch to the level at Llanerch Isaf (picked out in blue). Philips' Tramroad had run to the head of the Crumlin Arm of the Monmouthshire Canal, where the trams were tipped straight into waiting boats. After the extension of the MR&CC tramroad to Risca, coal was loaded instead into wagons at a wharf and siding provided on the west side of the line and this arrangement continued after the conversion of this line to an edge railway in the early 1850s.

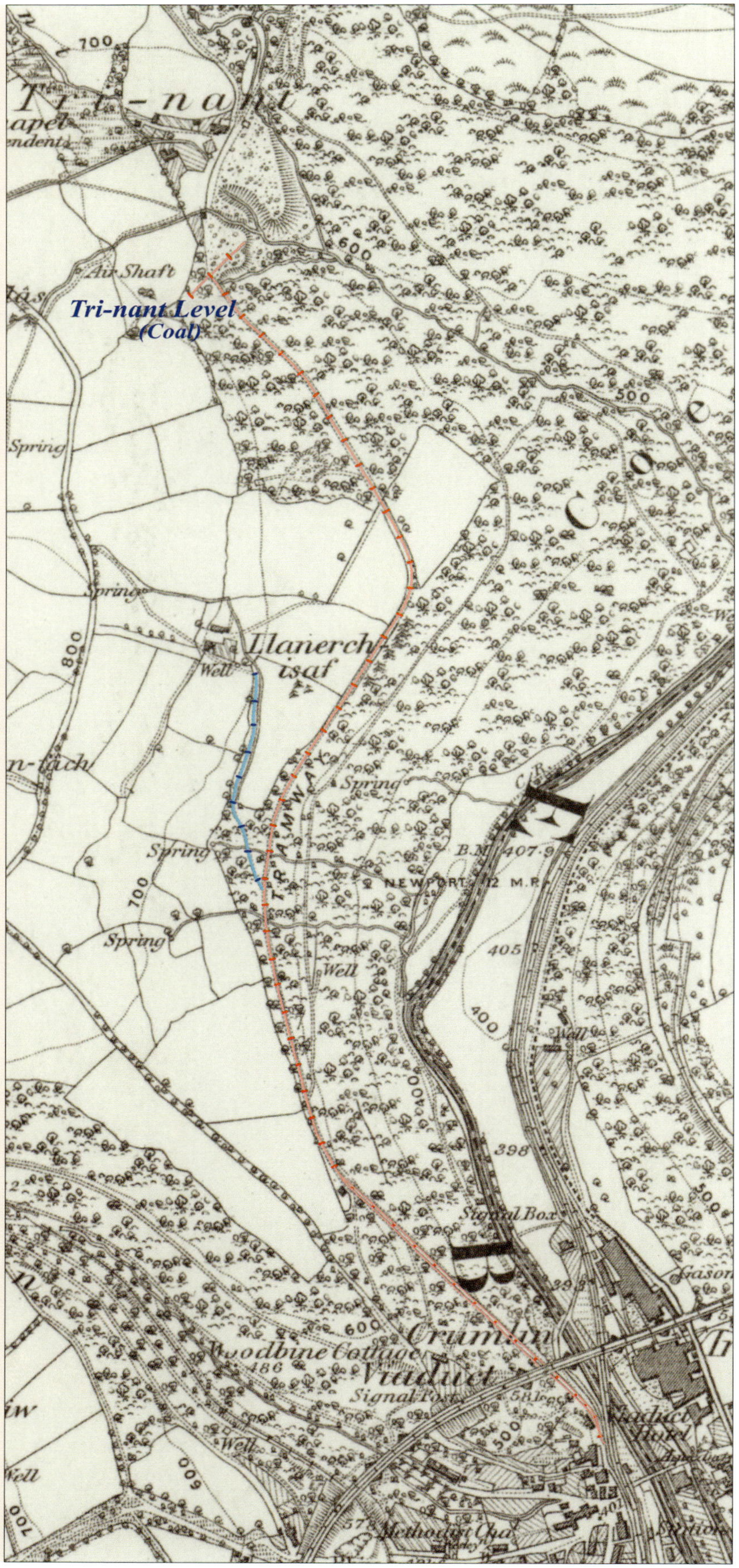

Early Tramroads at Crumlin 1 – Benjamin Hall and Mark Philips

The new viaduct at Crumlin spanned both the River Ebbw and the head of the Monmouthshire Canal's western arm, north from which the connection to Beaufort continued as a tramroad. Crumlin therefore established itself as a lively interchange spot where Newport-bound iron and coal was transshipped from tram waggon to canal boat. The wharves at Crumlin also became a focus for feeder tramroads from coal levels in the vicinity. Although these businesses were not connected to the viaduct or the Taff Vale Extension line, evidence of them appears in the background of photographs and so they are worthy of note.

In the late 1820s, well before the viaduct's time, the Monmouthshire Railway & Canal Company's tramroad had been extended south towards Risca and this section of the canal then became moribund. T.W. Kennard leased the original wharf at canal head and established his Viaduct Works there, whilst the tramroad south was made to cross to the river's right bank; it is the various generations of this bridge that appear in the photographs. In the early 1850s, the main tramroad was converted to a standard gauge edge railway, which came to be referred to as the Western Valleys line. The wharf at Crumlin was also the terminus of tramroads from collieries to the east of the river, around Blaencuffin and Llanhilleth, and was thus named Blaencuffin Wharf. From the late 1790s, coal masters and landowners of collieries high up on that land had had to decide whether to send their coal to Newport on the canal's Pontypool Arm or its Crumlin Arm and therefore to build tramroad inclines accordingly, to the east or to the west. Those which built to the west concern us and it was collieries such as Sir Robert Salusbury's that brought their coal to the Bleancuffin Tramroad and then to the canal at Crumlin.

Across the canal to the west on the river's right bank sat Mynydd Islwyn where, from early days, coal levels were driven into the mountain to the north of Crumlin and several collieries manifested themselves with the coming of the canal. From Penyfan, near Aberbeeg, a steep tramroad incline led down across the Ebbw

PLATES 12.11, RIGHT, & 12.12, BELOW: Both of these views are enlargements off previously seen plates, presented here to show the detail of the Trinant Incline and the railway loading wharf at its base. To the left of the head of the man holding the saw, a loaded tram waggon on its way down is about to pass an empty waggon being hauled back up by gravity. Meanwhile, a short rake of railway wagons stands alongside the loading wharf. The building on the wharf has a sign on the end wall – sadly not readable – and possibly another above the front door and is likely to have been offices for the old tramroad. The wooden bridge spans carry the main line of the MR&CC over the Ebbw River, whilst the siding curved away to head beneath span No. 6 of the viaduct. It then curved back, crossing the river on its own span to connect to the MR&CC line by the Viaduct Works. In the lower picture, on the incline the rope or wire and the rollers over which it ran can be clearly seen. To the right of the picture, behind the group of boys, the rudimentary canal tip and line of dram waggons are part of the Viaduct Works internal tramroad system.
BOTH STEPHEN ROWSON COLLECTION

and directly to the MR&CC's tramroad. Just south of Penyfan was Trinant Colliery, whilst to its west (still on the mountain) was Kendon Colliery and others such as Cefn Coch. Some of these had permission to run tramroads down the Kendon Road to canal head but early in the 19th century, the new Lord Llanover, Benjamin Hall, entered the scene and built a long tramroad on his own manorial land to a basin further down the canal. By offering inducements, he hoped to swallow up all of the colliery traffic and collect the equivalent canal tonnages. Hall's new Kendon Tramroad swept past Crumlin and ran down to the canal at Newbridge. When the TVE was built the tramroad was rerouted to run under the viaduct's Kendon Valley portion.

Mark Philips was an outsider whose father had invested in colliery land on Mynydd Islwyn following, it is believed, encouragement by fellow unitarians John Hodder Moggridge and Richard Perkins, who had land and collieries in nearby Blackwood. Philips was bemused that Hall should claim galeage as Lord of the Manor on top of his own galeage as landowner. He stood up to him and Hall therefore would not allow Philips' tenants to send their coal over his land. So, in 1824, Philips built his own tramroad on a ridge of Hanbury land to the canal at Crumlin, dropping down at its end via the incline that can be seen in many of the viaduct photographs. The tramroad is shown on contemporary maps (*e.g.* Edward Davies of 1834 and T. Morris of 1839) described as '*Mark Phillips' Tramroad*', albeit the family name was spelt Philips with one 'l' not two.

From the foot of the tramroad incline, the coal waggons passed across a river bridge to a wharf on the canal. With the extension of the MR&CC's tramroad to Risca (and its having crossed the river at Crumlin), Trinant Colliery

Plate 12.13: The first of two further enlargements, both taken off the photograph that features as the front endpaper, looking closely at the coal wharf at the bottom of the incline. The arrangements have clearly changed from the earlier photographs and it is thought that the picture dates from circa 1894-95, during the brief few years when Trinant Colliery had been reopened by the Waterloo Colliery Co. The incline bottom was now at a slightly higher level, the tramway no longer running onto the wharf in front of the offices, and three loading screens had been built to make tipping into railway wagons less labourious, with a fourth by the office building for land sale coal, tipped into carts. There also appears to be only one set of rails on the lower part of the incline.

Plate 12.14: A glimpse of incline top, which appears to show two sets of rails still in situ. The house, provided originally for the incline operator, is no longer there. Oxford House Industrial History Society collection

had no need to use the canal any more. A main line siding was built to the foot of Philips' incline and coal was then tipped from tram waggons directly into main line trucks. By 1855, from which time we have the first of the viaduct construction photographs, the main line had been converted to a railway and it is this siding and waiting coal wagons that are shown in the pictures. However, Philips's river bridge from the foot of the incline to the canal wharf was retained, perhaps simply as a footbridge (also shown in the early photographs) for access and with the tramplates removed. The waggon tip on the canal wharf was probably used by the viaduct works' internal tramway, described in the 1878 sale catalogue as '*trolley roads*', which totalled 1,456 yards and ran through both the lower and upper works, plus the incline connecting them. There were also seven turntables 6ft 6ins in diameter but none is apparent in any of the views. Some of the stereo photographs do show the narrow gauge trolley roads and trolleys/waggons, and the incline between the works is also depicted.

Trinant Colliery

Trinant Colliery is shown on the 1839 map of Monmouthshire, along with the tramroad that ran from it down to the canal basin at Crumlin. One online source quotes the tramroad as having opened circa 1795 *'from Trinant colliery and the other levels'* but without noting what these other levels were. A circa 1829 6 inch OS map shows that the two other nearby collieries, Cefn Coch and Kendon, were both served by the Kendon Tramroad, which ran down to Newbridge.

Cooke's *Gazetteer of the South Wales Coalfield* notes that Trynant Colliery [*sic*] was working by 1829 and was for sale by auction in August 1838, when it included *'the use of levels in lands called Llanarch Colliery'*. Ownership changed hands again prior to 1854 – a Mr Morrison was mentioned in 1842, whilst Martin Morrison and William Evans were trading as the Trynant & Pen y Coed Cae Coal Co. in 1844 and also as coal merchants under the title Martin Morrison & Co. However, by 1851, Trynant was being worked by Carr & Co., the sole representative being John Carr, with the MR&CC recording tonnages received in January, February and May 1855 of 547, 487 and 829 respectively. By August 1857, however, the colliery was in financial trouble and a meeting was held in respect of creditors of Messrs Carr Bros.[40]

Martin Morrison had acquired it again by 1861, working it up to 1863 as Morrison & Co. but then as Morrison & Martin up until the venture was again beset by financial problems in 1865 and it passed to John Godfrey of Crumlin, who was possibly the major creditor. No production figures are available for the period of Morrison's ownership and after this working ceased.[41]

In 1890, working at Trinant was resumed by the Waterloo Colliery Co. who renamed the pit Manger. However, production did not begin until late spring/early summer 1892, when it was noted that they had *'struck the Mynyddyslwyn seam after two years' effort'*; they also reverted back to the name Trinant for the pit at this time. In 1894, there were fifty-four men working underground and nine on the surface, which had increased to fifty-eight and ten respectively the following year. Returns, though, must have been disappointing, as in 1896 only eight men were underground with just seven the following year, and two on the surface, and the colliery was then abandoned for the final time on 9th October 1897.[42]

At the time they reopened Trinant, the Waterloo Colliery Co. were also working the Waterloo Levels, sending their output via the GWR's Penar Branch – the old Hall's Tramroad. However, they were clearly intent on sending out coal produced at Trinant via the abandoned incline, as the following report indicates: *'Construction, for the proper working of the Trinant Incline Siding and to connect it with the Waterloo Coal Co.'s colliery, of junction, spur and dead end for weighbridge. The Coal Co. to pay the cost estimated at £367.5.0, a rent of £15 p.a. for the existing siding and £5 p.a. for the additions about to be made. They will also carry out the necessary earthwork and provide weighbridge and house. Authorised 29.11.1893 [but deferred]'*. In June 1896 it was reported that the siding had not been used since November 1893, whilst in July 1896 it was expected to be *'used shortly'* but in the following month the PSA expired and was not renewed.[43]

The reference to the *'Trinant Incline Siding'* must equate to the wharf at the base of the incline, so the inference that it was out of use between 1893 and expiration of the PSA in August 1896 is odd. Connecting it to *'the Waterloo Colliery Co.'s colliery'* meanwhile, must refer to Trinant and the resurrection of Philips' Tramroad, out of use since circa 1865. The picture on the page opposite clearly shows both the wharf and the incline in use circa 1895 and it can be assumed that for the two years when over fifty men were working underground, a reasonable amount volume of coal was won, although no figures exist to confirm this.

The photographs taken during the viaduct's construction in 1856 are rare views of the incline fully at work. As many of the pictures show, its course down the valley side remained visible for decades after it was finally abandoned and the tramroad rails lifted around the turn of the century; it is hidden by trees today but still walkable.

Early Tramroads at Crumlin 2 – The Kendon Branch

Whilst the Kendon Tramroad passed through Crumlin it had no interaction with the village at all but on the way it did run beneath the Kendon section of the viaduct so it merits inclusion here, particularly as the construction of the Taff Vale Extension involved rerouting it to a slightly lower level, below the site of Crumlin High Level station.

Completed in 1814, the Kendon Tramroad was a branch of Hall's Tramroad, which it left at Penrhiwbicar, just to the south of

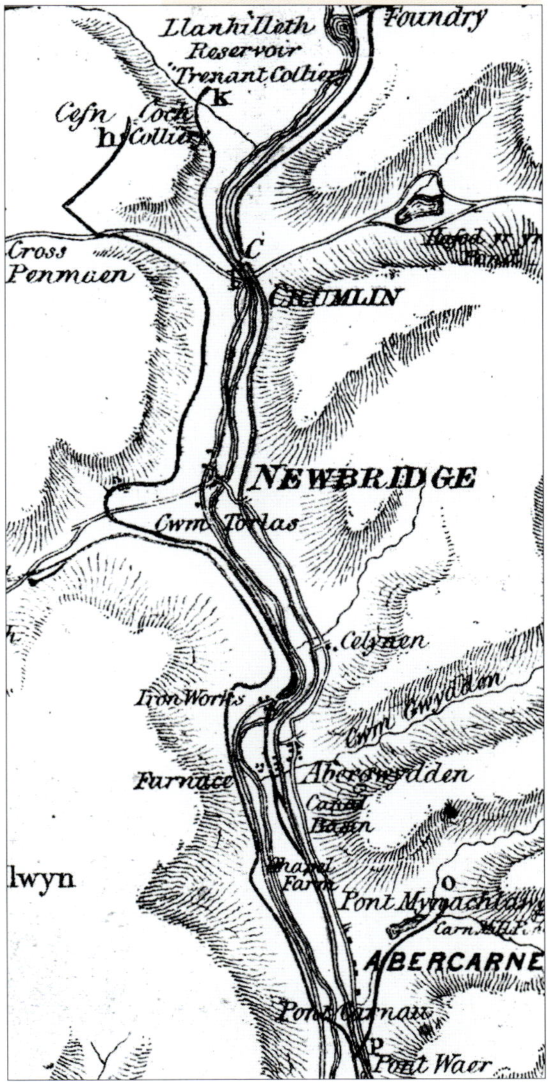

Fig. 12.8: An extract from Thomas Morris's Plan of the Canals and Railroads communicating with the town of Newport Monmouthshire 1839, *showing both the route of Philips' Tramroad from Trinant Colliery and the Kendon Branch south from Cefn Coch Colliery. The latter joined the main line of Hall's Tramroad after executing a 180° turn west of Newbridge. Loaded trams then travelled to the canal basin at Abercarn.*

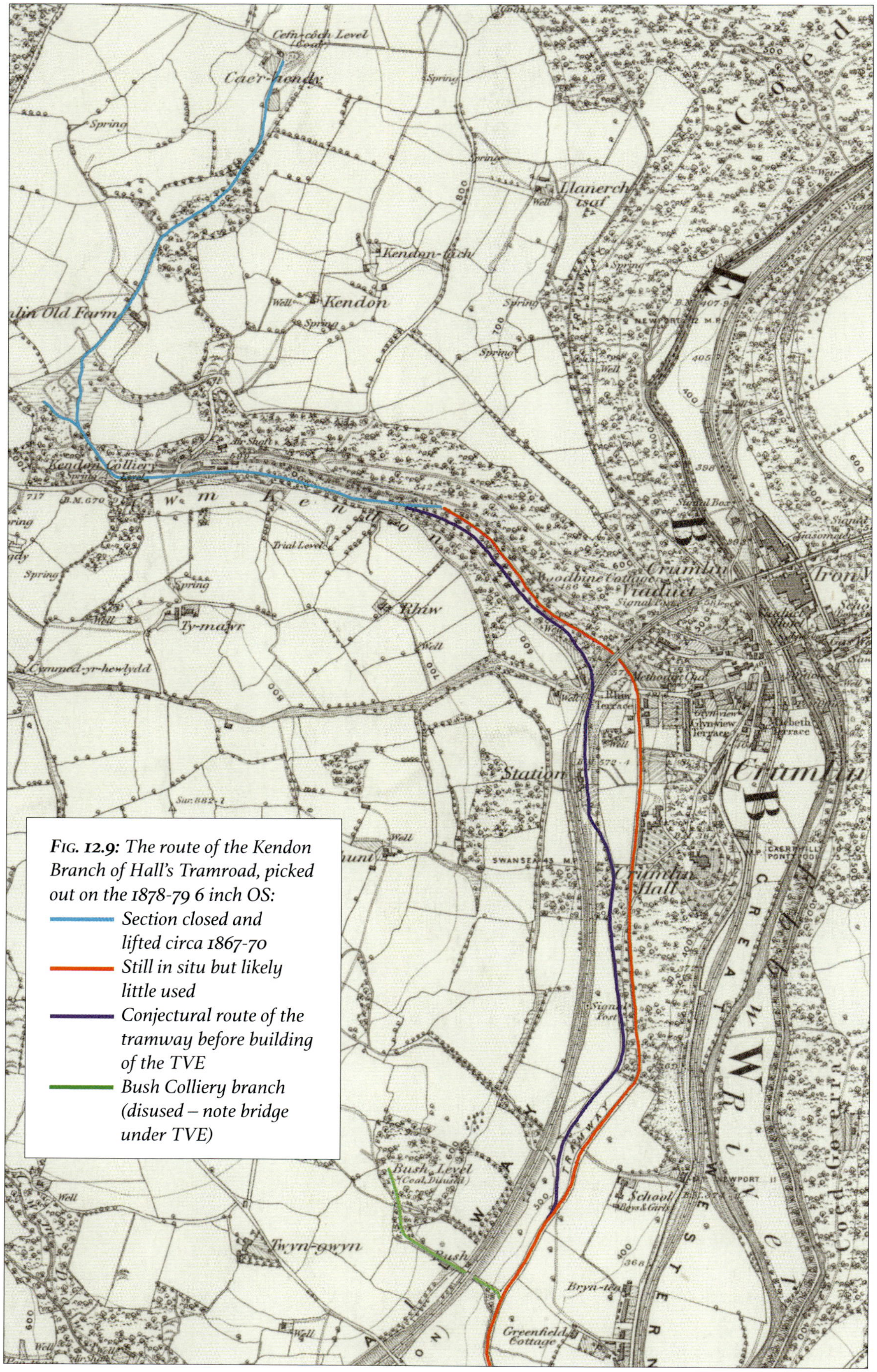

Fig. 12.9: The route of the Kendon Branch of Hall's Tramroad, picked out on the 1878-79 6 inch OS:
- *Section closed and lifted circa 1867-70* (blue)
- *Still in situ but likely little used* (orange)
- *Conjectural route of the tramway before building of the TVE* (purple)
- *Bush Colliery branch (disused – note bridge under TVE)* (green)

Newbridge.[44] After executing a sharp 180 degree turn from west to east around Cwm-dows, it then turned north at Newbridge running along the western side of the valley. It served three small collieries – Cwm-Dow, Twyngwyn and Bush – all reached by short branches off the main line. It then ran to two further pits to the north-west of Crumlin – Kendon, from which the tramroad took its name, and Cefn-Coch, where it terminated.

Between Newbridge and Crumlin, the tramroad was moved from its original route during the construction of the Taff Vale Extension – its original course was at a higher level and passed through the site of what became High Level station. At Crumlin, the later course ran roughly along the line of Manor Park and then between Oakland Terrace and Commercial Road, passing on the upper side of Crumlin High Level primary school. The deviation, which began near the junction for the short branch to Bush Colliery, at Newbridge, was nearly a mile long, so was clearly engineered to minimise the change in gradient.

After Crumlin, the tramroad curved round to the west to pass under the viaduct and enter the Kendon Valley. Here it reached Kendon Colliery, which had Old and New levels that were worked independently of each other, after which the line turned sharply north again, running for another half a mile to Cefn Coch Colliery. At its southern end, meanwhile, after joining Hall's Tramroad, loaded waggons were then taken down to the Monmouthshire Canal basin at Abercarn.

Little seems to be known about the early period of working at Cefn Coch Colliery, with Cooke's *Gazetteer* not having any details of it prior to 1886. However, the colliery is shown on Morris's *'Canals and Railroads'* map of 1839, so one presumes that it must have been in operation prior to that for the tramroad to have been built and opened in 1814. The OS mapping of the 1870s shows Cefn Coch Level still in operation but no longer served by the tramroad, which had been truncated short of Kendon Colliery. It is possible that coal was now being sent out via Mark Philips Tramroad, as Cefn Coch and Trinant Colliery were only around 250 yards away from each other and the journey down to the MR&CC wharf at Crumlin Low Level was considerably shorter than that to Abercarn. As Cefn Coch was no longer sending coal out via Kendon, its later history need not detain us here, except to say that working there was only finally abandoned in 1949.

Kendon Colliery is not shown on the 1839 map

Plate 12.15: *This rare and historic view, which provides us with the only known glimpse of the Kendon Tramroad in use, was taken around the time the viaduct was completed in 1856. The construction of the TVE had necessitated the rerouting of the tramroad a little lower down the side of the Kendon Valley but this view shows tram rails that would appear to have been in place for some time. Are we perhaps in the quarries, shown as 'Old Quarries' on the 1878-79 OS extract (***Fig. 12.10, Bottom Left***) and which may have been established to provide stone for the viaduct abutment and embankment infill. The tram waggon in which the man and two boys are sitting stands on the junction between two lines or sidings and there is another spur behind with a loaded waggon. This faces towards a counterbalance on the left, possibly for a chute leading down to the new line of the tramroad at a lower level. Note too the scattering of tram wheels in the foreground, probably a mixture of broken ones and replacements – made of cast iron, they were prone to breaking.*
Stephen Rowson collection

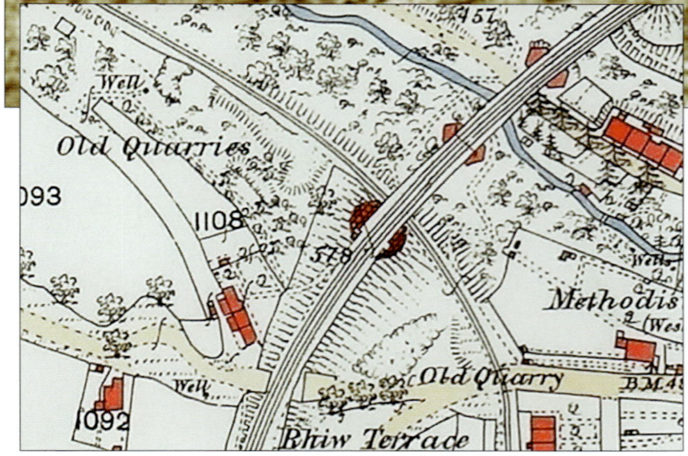

but Cooke's *Gazetteer* has '*New Kendon leased by Thomas Protheroe from Mr Barnes – MM 12.8.1831*' (MM was the *Monmouthshire Merlin* newspaper). From the same source, another report states '*Kendon Colliery, about 60 acres, capable at present of working 40 tons per day – MM 16.6.1849*' and then '*To be let with immediate possession, Kendon Colliery. This colliery is now opened and in a fit state for immediate working. Mr William Davis, proprietor. MM 2.5.1851*'. However, it seems its availability was due to the

Plate 12.16: *A glimpse of the Monmouthshire Canal at Abercarn, with a loaded horse-drawn barge on its way up circa 1910. This could be the general cargo boat, which operated a twice a week service from Newport to Crumlin until 1915. It is seen here between locks by Prince of Wales Colliery – lock No's 23 to 29 took the canal up and through Abercarn and this view shows No. 23 in the right foreground and No. 24, with a badly leaking lower gate, beyond. North from Pontywaun, most of the Crumlin Arm has been buried beneath the A467.*
Neil Parkhouse collection

previous lessors having gone bankrupt, a situation not untypical of these small scale workings.

By late 1853, the colliery was working again: '*Tonnage of coal conveyed on the Monmouthshire Rly from Edmund Jones's Kendon Colliery Dec 1853 nil by rail but 101 tons by canal to Newport* [presumably loaded at Abercarn basin], *Jan 1854 32 tons, Feb., Apl, and May 1854 nil, Jan. 1855 113 tons, Feb. 1855 nil and May 1855 193 tons. Also from T.P. & D. Price's Old Kendon Colliery Feb. 1854 23 tons, May 1854 32 tons and Jan. 1855 36 tons. MM*'.[45] Note the tonnages involved are pitifully small and production very intermittent.

Edmund Jones continued to be involved with the pit until September 1857, when it was reported that '*Kendon colliery of Edmund Jones was let to two persons who continued to work it until 19.6.1858, when they abandoned it.*'. Subsequently, the *Monmouthshire Merlin* reported that it was '*For sale by auction on 10.7.1862, all the remaining stock and colliery plant of Estate of Thomas Thomas, mainly at Pennar Colliery, but also at Kendon Colliery a weighing machine, spring tip, seven yards of parting, plates & sleepers.*'.[46] The pit was not listed in 1865 but two years later, on 22nd June 1867, the *Merlin* carried another report: '*For sale by*

Plate 12.17: *Another enlargement from the circa mid-1890s view of Crumlin, showing the route of the tramroad beneath the westernmost span of the Kendon section of the viaduct. It then crossed the road on the level, before heading off down the valley towards Newbridge. By the date of this picture, the tramroad had been further truncated and now terminated just off picture on the left, on the far side of the houses. There is a faint suggestion here that its original course may have run past the bottom of the Hillside Road overbridge wing wall. The viaduct abutment was built on its trackbed, which on the other side of the span looks to be about 20ft above the later course.*
Oxford House Industrial History Society collection

auction on 1.7.1867 at Kendon Colliery, the following, taken in execution by the Sheriff; 10 tons of old tram plates, about one mile of old tram plates laid down in and out of the level, two weighing machines, 35 small trams, two carriages on incline and various tools.'.[47]

This seems to be the end of the story. Clearly, the sale of a mile of laid down tramplates referred to the section of the tramroad from below Kendon Colliery north to the terminus at Cefn Coch, which is why that part of the line disappears from the OS map. An attempt was made to sell the colliery again in 1888, whilst working did resume at Kendon in 1894 but it was on a new site and none of the coal was sent via the tramroad. By this date the tramroad had been shortened further, now terminating alongside the Crumlin High Level primary school, just below the station and shown as such on the 1899 revision of the 6 inch OS published in 1902.

However, the whole of the Kendon Branch must have been out of use by this date, although it was not officially closed until 1912. The 1901 25 inch OS shows a section of the line removed near Newbridge and another section apparently blocked with quarry waste. In 1879, the GWR had taken possession of Hall's Tramroad and converted it to a standard gauge railway, although this was seemingly done fairly cheaply and the company upgraded it again in 1912. Later workings of Cwm-dows, Twyngwyn and Bush collieries all loaded their coal at railway sidings provided on what was always referred to as Hall's Tramroad, right up until it finally closed in 1990.

Plate 12.18: *The course of the tramroad heading northwards beneath the viaduct, as depicted on a circa 1905 postcard. Although looking in the opposite direction and from the other side of the span, the view equates well with the lie of the land as shown in the earlier stereo photograph on page 241.*
Stephen Rowson collection

Siding at Crumlin Junction

Immediately the Kennard brothers had acquired the Viaduct Works from Thomas Kennard in 1857, they began to seek ways of improving and expanding their business opportunities. One of their first ideas was to make an approach to Mark Carr, with a suggestion that the NA&HR install, for their particular use, a siding at Crumlin Junction. If the siding could be located close to their existing incline, it would provide the necessary facilities. Carr promised that he would make arrangements for their request to be '*duly laid before the directors at their next meeting*'.[48]

On receipt of a notification agreeing to the proposed works, which included an estimate for carrying them out, H.M. Kennard was alarmed at the prices being quoted for the supply of goods. He considered that the charge for the supply of rails at £8 were excessive when he could supply them for £5 10s, and that he could make and supply switches and crossings at a much lower price. Accepting the company's offer, Kennard added that he considered the facility would be as much to the benefit of the NA&HR as it would be to the Kennard brothers and believed therefore that it should be completed at cost price.[49] Carr responded by pointing out that he had tried to keep the estimate for the works as high as possible but that the final account would be a reasonable one. He added that the cost for the rails would be charged to Kennard at the market price at the time that they were being laid. However, the switches and crossings were a different matter, Carr was proposing to lay better ones than those supplied from his works but to charge Kennard what he would normally pay him for the work.[50] HMK agreed to the work being commenced straight away but in doing so, he added that '*if the price you name in the estimates is our own price it is not the cash price, and besides the rails are at a much less price*'.[51]

The year 1858 opened with HMK and Maynard chasing Carr to complete laying the siding as they were '*anxious to make use of our incline in course of the next 10 to 14 days*'.[52] The final communication was a letter from the Kennard brothers, explaining that they were expecting a quantity of iron over the company's lines within weeks and were pressing Carr to make all of the necessary arrangements to begin the work for finally connecting '*your line with our siding and incline*'.[53]

The OS extract (***Fig. 12.11***) shows the siding as a single line of rails running from a trailing connection with the Down line. It is thought that no PSA was ever signed for the siding, either by Kennard or by the Crumlin

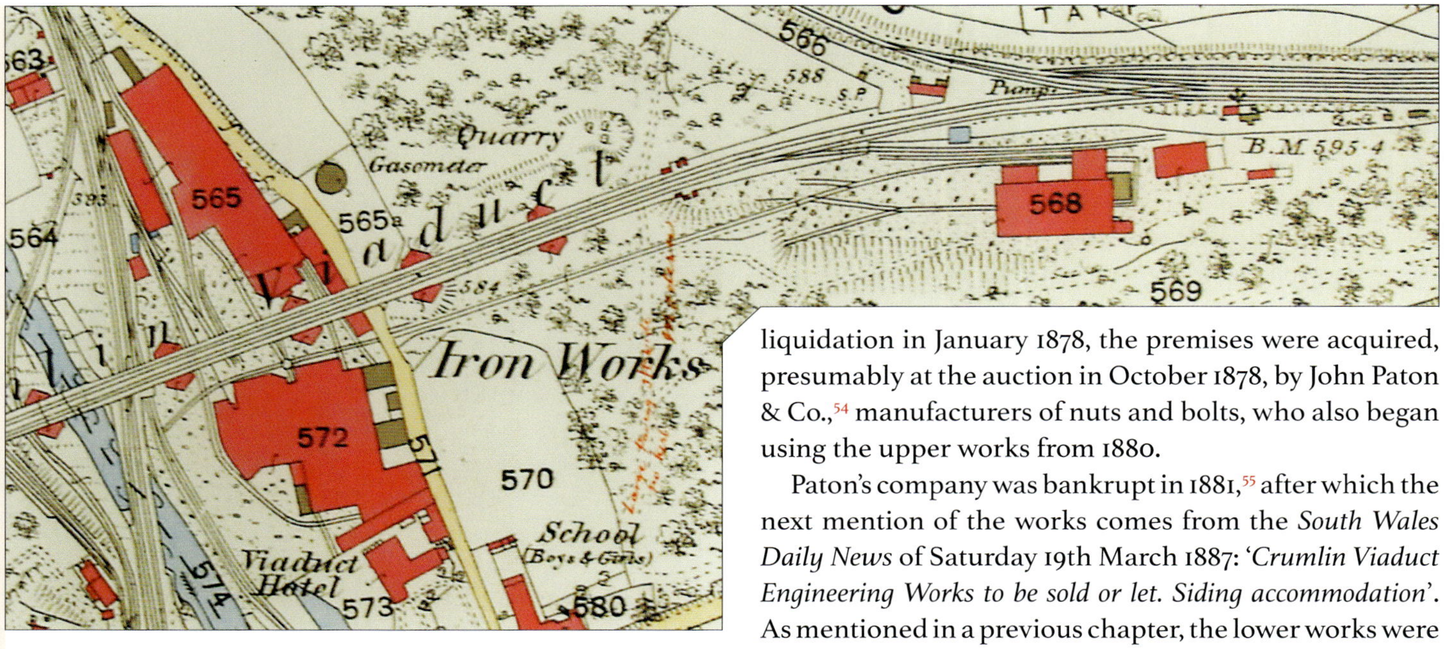

Fig. 12.11, Right: The Viaduct Works incline and siding as shown on the 1st Edition 25 inch OS of 1878-79. Although the incline is shown here as still extant, it was already derelict, and had probably not seen any use since the early 1860s.

Plate 12.19, Below: An enlargement from Plate 0.3, showing the course of the incline dropping down from Crumlin Junction. The dark coloured sheds, which are marked on later maps as Viaduct Foundry, were the upper works of the Viaduct Works Company.
Neil Parkhouse collection

Plate 12.20, Below Right: Taken from a Down train about to cross the viaduct on 11th April 1955, the catch point marks where the siding joined with the running line. H.C. Casserley

Bridge Works Ltd, the company established in 1871 to take the works over. Its early installation in 1858 perhaps preceeded such arrangements but the GWR seems not to have formalised things with subsequent owners either. After the Crumlin Bridge Works Ltd went into liquidation in January 1878, the premises were acquired, presumably at the auction in October 1878, by John Paton & Co.,[54] manufacturers of nuts and bolts, who also began using the upper works from 1880.

Paton's company was bankrupt in 1881,[55] after which the next mention of the works comes from the *South Wales Daily News* of Saturday 19th March 1887: '*Crumlin Viaduct Engineering Works to be sold or let. Siding accommodation*'. As mentioned in a previous chapter, the lower works were taken over by the Western Valleys Brewery Company in 1891 but uncertainty surrounds the upper works. The 1899 6 inch survey shows it as Viaduct Foundry, which Cooke's Track Plans, Section 47B, notes as '*Closed c.1904*'; by the time of the next map survey in 1916 the works had gone but the siding remained and was still in situ on the 1948 survey, although Cooke shows it as gone by 1930.

Crumlin Navigation Colliery

In the first decade of the 20th century, construction and sinking began of Crumlin Navigation Colliery, which was to become very much a part of the local industrial landscape, a backdrop to the viaduct and one of the few links with Crumlin's past which still remains today. Closing in 1967, it outlived the bridge's existence by a couple of years but much of the complex survives today due to a mixture of Grade II and Grade II* listings attached to the buildings, which are regarded as being

of national importance. Its construction also involved covering over a significant length of the Ebbw River, as the surface buildings, screens and sidings were all built on the west or river side of the valley

Partridge, Jones & Co. Ltd were formed in March 1874[56] and owned several collieries in the Western Valleys, including Nos' 1 and 2 Pits at Llanhilleth. They began surface building work at Crumlin late in 1906, with sinking of the first of the two shafts commencing on 1st January 1908.[57] Meanwhile, to facilitate construction, a PSA was signed with the GWR on 12th October 1907, which was reported as being for '*a temporary one, connected with the company's Trenant* [sic] *Incline siding*'.[58] After the Waterloo Colliery Co's interest in the incline siding had lapsed in 1897, a PSA for it had subsequently been signed on 4th August 1903 with one E. Bowen[59] but for what purpose is unclear and, in any case, the siding had been cut back to terminate beneath the viaduct by 1905.

The first permanent sidings at the colliery were authorised in October 1908 and laid in soon afterwards, with a PSA being signed on 20th October, which included '*diversions and covering in of River Ebbw, bridge for sidings over same and provision of a footbridge over railway*'. In February 1909, the *Western Mail* was reporting that '*The new North and South pits will be 400-500 yards deep and both have been sunk 100 yards. A number of men avail themselves of the new workmen's train from Newport*'. Two years later, in March 1911, the *Iron & Coal Trades Review* noted that '*South pit is now completed (to 515 yards). Expect that North pit will be completed in about three weeks*'. Finally, on 19th May 1911, the *Colliery Guardian* reported that '*Partridge, Jones & Co. have reached coal*'.[60]

After production started in 1911, the number of men employed over the years varied between around 350-550 underground and between 80 and 100 on the surface, with highs of 621 below (1928) and 126 above (1914), and lows of 119 below (1918) and 65 above (1961). Unsurprisngly, perhaps, given that the shafts were sunk beneath a river, flooding was a periodic issue, with the Meadow vein being abandoned in January 1914 as the company was unable to deal with the water, whilst in November 1917, '*an inrush of water ... has necessitated the suspension of operations*'. It seems that this stoppage may have been for some time, as in January 1918 it was being reported that the owners had '*refused to pay the War Wage for more than three weeks in the case of a temporary stoppage consequent of an inrush of water.*'[61]

On 8th Febraury 1926, by which time the company had amalgamated with others to become Partridge, Jones &

PLATE 12.21, ABOVE LEFT: Sinking underway at the new colliery in 1908. The stationary horizontal steam winder is nicely on view prior to being encased by brick.

PLATE 12.22, ABOVE RIGHT: The engine house and chimney were now completed but coal production had yet to commence in this circa autumn 1909 view.

PLATE 12.23, BELOW: This postcard probably dates from shortly after production had started in May 1911. Everything looks new, including the screens on the right and a rake of Partridge, Jones & Co. wagons occupy the foreground.
ALL NEIL PARKHOUSE COLLECTION

PLATE 12.24: Looking from the hillside known as The Woodlands, just below the Llanhilleth Branch, this locally produced postcard shows Navigation Colliery now in full production just before the First World War. At the bottom, facing across the Western Valleys line is Crumlin Low Level North Signal Box, which was opened in 1905. It was closed on the last day of 1952 and replaced by a ground frame.
NEIL PARKHOUSE COLLECTION

John Paton Ltd, a fire broke out in the engine house. It was reported as causing '*much damage to plant & buildings. Pits will be idle for repairs for some time*', which may have not been until November 1926, when it was noted that '*P.J. & J. P.'s Aberbeeg Pits opened on 15.11.1926*'.[62] There was a further problem with flooding in 1938, causing nearly two months of idleness before work could resume in two of the districts but the rest remained inundated. A 1939 proposal to drive a new roadway to provide a second way out from Crumlin and Celynen may in part have been a result of this.[63]

The colliery was Nationalised on 1st January 1947 along with the rest of the coal industry, coming under the control of the National Coal Board but Partridge, Jones & John Paton Ltd were not brought under public control until 1951, the delay no doubt due to the bureaucracy involved and the need to agree a compensation package for the company. Sample annual production figures under the NCB start with 97,000 tons raised in 1947, 142,664 tons in 1955, 87,329 tons in 1960 and 83,157 in 1965, whilst latterly the type of coal being produced was classed as 'Coking High Volatile'. In 1967, the three seams being worked were abandoned successively over the months, with final closure coming on 15th September.[64]

Surprisingly perhaps, the colliery buildings were not demolished and the site cleared immediately after closure, as happened with most other South Wales collieries, but whether this was by accident or design is not clear. The headgears were removed and the shafts subsequently filled with washery tailings in 1970. However, the horizontal, 4-cylinder, triple-expansion steam fan engine was saved and is preserved at the

PLATE 12.25: A GWR 2-6-2 tank, possibly one of the '31XX' series with a straight bunker, pauses alongside the colliery whilst heading down the valley with a train of loaded Ebbw Vale Company wagons in the early 1920s. A number of colliers can be seen around the engine, possibly crossing on their way into the mine, with some having a brief word with the footplate crew. In the decade or so since the colliery began production, a combination of weather, smoke and coal dust had coloured the pristine buildings seen in the earlier pictures.
NEIL PARKHOUSE COLLECTION

Amgueddfa Cymru – Museum Wales. The colliery is now regarded as a nationally important, nearly complete collection of both Grade II* and Grade II listed buildings, the best preserved colliery complex in South Wales. Their exhibition design was of unusual architectural quality, with the main walls in red brick, set off by yellow brick pilasters, marrying functionality with style. The complex includes two winding engine houses, a fan house, the chimney, a pumping house, stores and workshops, a heapstead, a powder store and the baths.

Disused since closure, they have since led a chequered and perilous existence, which only now appears to be reaching some sort of conclusion. A proposed housing development fell through in 2009 due to the financial crisis – fortuitously some might think for the site's relevance and credibility. Currently, a group called the Friends of The Navigation are working in partnership with the site owners, South Wales Building Preservation Trust, with the aim of restoring and regenerating the buildings and surrounds for the future benefit of the community. They have deteriorated significantly over the years, with many having lost their roofs but in 2023 the Friends group had cleared the site of fifty years of accumulated vegetation and although funding remains a significant issue, perhaps at last Navigation's future is being secured.

Plate 12.26: *Navigation Colliery and the Western Valleys line as seen from the deck of the viaduct on 7th August 1965 – in the period after trial dismantling had started but ten days before the filming of* Arabesque. *The single line of rails on the Up side (up the valley) is all that remains today.* Brian Mills/Trackbed.com

Plate 12.27: *All change at Crumlin Low Level. A circa 1980 view from the eastern side of the valley, showing the derelict colliery buildings, with the rerouted A467 cutting a swathe through Crumlin and completely obscuring the railway. The road actually crosses over it here, with the bridge just visible centre left bottom of the picture. The fan house in the left foreground is distinguishable by the square vent of its Walker fan. The tramroad incline in the left background was still very visible at this date too, as was the route then northwards, along the edge of the hill. Several of the colliery buildings have lost their roofs since this picture was taken.* Neil Parkhouse collection

From the LLANHILLETH BRANCH

Plate 13.16: *A view from alongside the Llanhilleth Branch on 5th June 1962.* Mark B. Warburton

Plate 13.17: *From a similar spot in May 1961, as a '72XX' 2-8-2T heads up the valley with a trainload of iron ore for the steelworks at Ebbw Vale. In the distance through the left-hand span, the line is four track between Crumlin South and Newbridge, with the outer two lines being loops – the Down Loop was installed in February 1897 and the Up Loop in March 1902. The footbridge serves the twin-sided single platform Celynen North Halt, opened on 10th August 1936, sited in between the main running lines and provided for miners working at Celynen North Colliery. The siding heading off to the pit, which was brought into use in August 1913, made a trailing connection with the Up line.* Colour-Rail

Plate 13.18: Class '72XX' 2-8-2T No. 7230 nears the top of the climb with a freight working of which only the lead tank wagon is in view on 9th August 1961. It may be that the 'Large Prairie' tank waiting 'light engine' on the viaduct was going to couple onto the other end of this train at Crumlin Junction and take it west, albeit working regulations for the Llanhilleth Branch meant that there would have been a banking engine on the other end of it anyway. However, perhaps the banker was required to return to Llanhilleth Junction. No. 7230 was new as '5202' Class 2-8-0T No. 5265 in March 1926 but the class were rebuilt as 2-8-2 tanks with extended bunkers between 1934 and 1936 to increase their working range and reclassified as '72XX'. As such they were the largest tank engines in the GWR fleet and the only 2-8-2Ts built by a British railway.

Plate 13.19: Same day, different train! The long rake of WD tanks suggests that this Up freight was bound for ROF Glascoed and was heavy enough for the '56XX' tank working bunker first at the front to require assistance from a 'Large Prairie' tank at the rear.
Both Trevor Owen/Colour-Rail

Views from the VALLEY SIDES

Plate 13.20: *The first of two views taken looking north-west from the lower slopes of Coed Cillonyd on 31st October 1962. Proving that coal moved in various directions around South Wales, a loaded train which had probably originated from Hafodrynys Colliery (on the east side of Glyn Tunnel), heads west behind a '28XX' 2-8-0.*

Plate 13.21: *Some time later, another load of coal is seen travelling east behind a '56XX' 0-6-2T. The realigned A472 Hafodyrynys Road now cuts down through here, on the near side of the Jerusalem Church in the foreground but almost all of the houses and buildings in view still remain today.* Both Bill Potter/Kidderminster Railway Museum

PLATE 13.22: In glorious summer sunshine on 5th June 1962 and with the hill between the two sections of the viaduct covered in verdant greenery, a two-coach Up service makes its way over behind a '94xx' pannier tank. Pontypool Road shed had two of these on its allocation in summer 1964, No's 8495 and 9488, so it is likely to be one of those. ALAN JARVIS /SLS ARCHIVE

PLATE 13.23: This viewpoint, from near the top of the Viaduct Works incline, is worth comparing with the early stereo photographs on pages 63 and 109. Photographed coming over at the head of a Neath to Pontypool Road working on 14th October 1963 was '56XX' No. 6690, which was based at Aberdare shed at this date. BILL POTTER/KIDDERMINSTER RAILWAY MUSEUM

From HIGH LEVEL

Plate 13.24: *Whilst Glascoed services from the north had ceased in 1957, those from the west continued for a while longer. On 27th April 1960, Aberdare shed's '57XX' 0-6-0PT No. 9712 draws into High Level station with a returning workmen's train heading to Ystrad Mynach.* E.T. Gill/SLS Archive

Plate 13.25: *On 18th April 1964, No. 4107 heads over the infill which raised the hilltop to join the two viaducts. The engine was based at Hereford shed, so it would appear that the Pontypool Road shedmaster had sent it on a quick out-and-back to Aberdare before despatching it back home.* E.T. Gill/SLS Archive

PLATE 13.26: *The Crumlin High Level signalman holds out the single line token for the fireman of No. 6641 to collect on 27th April 1960. The train would be stopping here but handing over the token by the box steps saved him a walk down the platform. New in September 1928, 0-6-2T No. 6641 had transferred from Llanelly shed to Neath Court Sart a week or so before the picture was taken, its final posting, withdrawal coming on 1st September 1962.* E.T. GILL, SLS ARCHIVE

PLATE 13.27: *Turning round, the photographer captured this second view a few minutes later as No. 6641 coasted over the viaduct towards Crumlin Junction at the regulation 8mph. In the foreground below is Crumlin High Level County Primary School, opened in 1912 and which still today has an image of the viaduct on its school badge.* E.T. GILL, SLS ARCHIVE

PLATE 13.28: Few today will probably know or indeed remember that one of the world's most famous steam locomotives made a trip over the viaduct but here we have the proof. The occasion was the running of an Ian Allan railtour, 'The Daffodil Express', on 18th May 1957, which started out from Paddington at 8.40am behind No. 4090 Dorchester Castle *and ran to Gloucester Central. From there it was taken on by No. 3440* City of Truro *piloting ex-GWR 'Mogul' No. 4338 and travelling via Ross-on-Wye, Hereford and Pontypool Road. The tour reached Crumlin Junction at 2.37pm, where* City of Truro *was detached and sent over the bridge first 'Light Engine' due to the restriction on two engines coupled together crossing over, with the rest of the train then following. Coupled up once more, the tour then headed off to Swansea, from where the direct route via the Severn Tunnel was taken back to Paddington. E.T. GILL/SLS ARCHIVE*

PLATE 13.29: The unknown photographer who took this shot had adopted a slightly higher position at the eastern end of the viaduct for this view of an unrecorded 'Large Prairie' tank heading across with a five-coach train from Neath circa 1960. The smoke and steam from the locomotive largely obscures High Level station but the school and the terraces that surround it can all be seen. The collection of sheds in the foreground are interesting, not least because GoogleEarth shows something very similar still here today in the same location. The elevated shed with the chap on the balcony looks to be a pigeon loft and it is perched on top of what are presumed to be old stone-built pig pens.
NEIL PARKHOUSE COLLECTION

Plate 13.30: *An impressive view looking up at the Kendon section from Kendon Road, as a '57XX' Class pannier tank ambles across with a loaded coal train on 31st July 1967.* Alan Jarvis /SLS Archive

Plate 13.31: *Looking east towards Crumlin Junction, Hafodyrynys Halt and Glyn Tunnel from above Kennard Terrace on 31st July 1963, as a pannier tank ventures onto the Ebbw spans with a three coach local from Aberdare. Coed Cillonyd mountain rises up in the right background and the realigned A472 Hafodrynys Road, mentioned a little earlier, climbs the valley below to the right of the houses, to meet up with the former course of the railway. It then climbs over the higher ground pierced by Glyn Tunnel. Recently, this well-used road climbing steeply out of Crumloin has been the most polluted in the UK.* Alan Jarvis /SLS Archive

PLATE 13.32: On Friday, 5th June 1964, warm sunshine quietly bakes the viaduct in the last few days of the line's operation. No. 4110, which also worked some of the last day services on 13th June, is seen here coming over the Kendon section with a two-coach Pontypool Road to Ystrad Mynach stopping train. The photographer, aware that the line was closing, made two visits to Crumlin to make a final record of the viaduct, of which this was the first, returning then a week later. BILL POTTER/ KIDDERMINSTER RAILWAY MUSEUM

PLATE 13.33: Another unidentified pannier tank crosses the shorter Kendon section on its way eastwards with a short train of steel mineral wagons loaded with coal circa 1960. In the foreground, the unnamed High Level station approach road curves down to meet High Level Road, which was climbing steeply to pass beneath the line near the end of the viaduct. This road is today named simply Hillside. Note the GWR lamp in the foreground. NEIL PARKHOUSE COLLECTION

From DOWN BELOW

PLATE 13.34: A Duple Roadmaster coach, which is possibly on a tour, outside the Railway Hotel on 11th May 1957, as up above a '28XX' 2-8-0 rumbles across with a Down train comprised mainly of steel mineral wagons. The Railway Hotel is still open today but the little tobacconist's has been demolished and the bridge is now closed to road traffic, replaced by a new structure a few yards to the north.
BEN BROOKSBANK/CREATIVE COMMONS LICENSE 2.0

PLATE 13.35: A nice juxtaposition of viaduct and Viaduct Works on 31st October 1962. Note that Waite & Son Ltd's sign on the end of the white painted building in the right foreground still referred to is as 'Viaduct Works'; in 1938, the company were listed as Candle & Lamp Manufacturers and based at Mitcham in Surrey. The buildings all look in a good state of repair here but none have survived sadly, just the Viaduct Hotel which creeps into the picture on the right. Up above on the Llanhilleth Branch, a very heavy freight requiring two bankers – a 'Large Prairie' and a pannier tank bunker to bunker – was nearing the top of its ascent to Crumlin Junction.
BILL POTTER/ KIDDERMINSTER RAILWAY MUSEUM

Plate 13.36, Above, and 13.37, Right: *As the 20th century progressed, the situation of the large steelworks at Ebbw Vale began to count against its continued viability. Despite modernisation and the introduction of new processes, it could not compete with other works in the UK and around the world which were sited near to deep water ports and, in some cases, close to the source of the raw materials required. Iron ore and coking coal had all to be hauled up the Western Valleys line to Ebbw Vale, up gradients as steep as 1 in 65, and the finished product brought back down again. One efficiency measure was to increase the length and thus the weight of the trains carrying the coke and ore and to this end, from their introduction in 1954, Newport Ebbw Junction shed had an allocation of BR 'Standard' Class '9F' 2-10-0s, supplementing their roster of ex-GWR and ex-WD 2-8-0s. Even then, often two were required as these views show. The main picture shows No. 92230 banking an unidentified classmate through Crumlin and beneath the viaduct with a trainload of coke on 27th July 1963, whilst the second view, right, shows the same two engines returning 'Light' apart from a brake van later that day. No. 92230 was based at Newport Ebbw Junction from January 1960 to October 1965, apart from a short stint at Old Oak Common (in October 1962) and a few months on Lickey Incline banker duties at Bromsgrove (January to August 1964).* Both Alan Jarvis /SLS Archive

Plate 13.38: *The viaduct as seen from Celynen North Colliery sidings on 12th April 1965. Sinking of this colliery began in 1913, after negotiations to lease the mineral rights were concluded between the Llanover Estate (of the late Benjamin Hall, of Hall's Tramroad fame) and the Newport Abercarn Black Vein Steam Coal Co. Ltd, who had already been operating Celynen South Colliery for forty years at this time. Opening of this pit allowed them to work the northern end of their mineral stake and in 1924 they also opened Marine Colliery at Graig Fawr to reach more of it. The latter closed in 1962 but Celynen North worked until December 1985. The wooden bodied wagon was unusual by this date and may have been internal user, and note the stacks of freshly cut pit props on the left.* Terence Dorrity

Plate 13.39: *A driver's eye view of the bridge, from the cab of a DMU approaching Low Level station on 23rd April 1962. The passenger service to Ebbw Vale was scheduled for withdrawal a week later, on 30th April, hence why the photographer made the trip. The DMU had just pulled away from Celynen North Halt which, being provided for use by miners at the colliery, did not appear in the public time tables. The trailing connection into the mine, off the Up line, can be seen just ahead of the train.* Paul Strong/ Neil Parkhouse collection

Plate 13.40: *A northwards view showing the bridges spanning the Ebbw River on 31st July 1965. Navigation Colliery in the background was still working but all looks quiet here and the mine sidings are empty. On the right, a pair of steel mineral opens have brought in house coal for the local merchant to distribute and the goods shed can just be made out behind the pier. The goods yard sidings were all lifted in late July 1967, which rendered the bridge span on the right redundant. Final closure of the Ebbw Vale steelworks in 2002 saw the last freight trains, removing scrap metal from the site, operate in 2003, after which proposals to reopen the branch to passengers began to be brought forward. The new service, starting from Cardiff, commenced on 6th February 2008 and further upgrades are planned, with more frequent trains also running to and from Newport. This will require more of the line to be double tracked again, to which end the river bridge here at Crumlin was rebuilt in 2020.* Michael Gates/Gerry Nichols collection

Plate 13.41: *A dizzying view straight down onto the Ebbw River bridges and the crossover, taken from the closed viaduct on 7th August 1965. The rust covered line top left was a short runaway siding whilst coming off the Up line opposite was the gated siding leading to the screens and colliery sidings. This had divided to four lines by the time it crossed the river a little further upstream from the other two bridges. Following closure of the colliery in 1967, the PSA for the sidings was terminated from 22nd January 1969.* Brian Mills/Trackbed.com

PLATE 13.42: *Nearly sixty years after the viaduct was demolished, this next selection of views will attempt to provide a flavour of what it was like to ride across. This is Crumlin village centre and the closed Low Level station from a train on the Ebbw section on 5th June 1964. Looking down the valley, Celynen North Colliery is in the centre right distance and the tower of Crumlin Hall can just be seen in the top right corner.* BILL POTTER/KIDDERMINSTER RAILWAY MUSEUM

VIEWS from a BRIDGE

PLATE 13.43: *Taken moments later, we are now looking back from the Kendon section. The gap caused by the loss of the passenger service on the lower line had clearly been filled by Western Welsh, with four of their vehicles – two single deckers and two double deckers – on view, along with the orange and cream coach of another operator on the road down from Hafodyrynys, by the Jerusalem Church. The new road now runs to the right of this.* BILL POTTER/KIDDERMINSTER RAILWAY MUSEUM

PLATE 13.44, OPPOSITE PAGE TOP: This view was taken on 12th December 1965, with the photographer having walked out onto the spans from High Level station during the demolition. Road improvements, including a new bridge over the line, have contributed to the change in this scene today. The B4251 Kendon Road was realigned to run from the new bridge and behind the Railway Hotel. Main Street was also then realigned and now runs behind the large red brick buildings, albeit only the one to the right of the Railway Hotel still survives. Over three years after closure, Celynen North Halt still remained in place, including its footbridge – which incidentally had come second-hand from Usk station – used by miners to reach the colliery. A.N.H. GLOVER/KIDDERMINSTER RAILWAY MUSEUM

PLATE 13.45, OPPOSITE PAGE BOTTOM LEFT: Looking across to High Level station from a Down train on 11th April 1964. Crossing must have been even more terrifying for those who did not like heights when the line across was double track and trains were therefore even closer to the edge! A.N.H. GLOVER/KIDDERMINSTER RAILWAY MUSEUM

PLATE 13.46, OPPOSITE PAGE BOTTOM RIGHT: A view from an Up train on 29th April 1964, looking towards Swffryd School and the surrounding terraces. Below the latter, the Llanhilleth Branch has begun its descent of the hillside, passing beneath the footbridge carrying the Swffryd to Crumlin footpath over the line. ALAN JARVIS/SLS ARCHIVE

PLATE 13.47, BELOW: After snapping the top picture opposite, the photographer moved to the other side of the carriage to capture Crumlin Navigation Colliery and the view northwards. A Western Welsh single decker is making its way along Crumlin Road and up the Ebbw Valley to Llanhilleth. Today, the A467 road cuts through Crumlin village immediately in front of the Viaduct Hotel and then over the site of the goods yard. It then crosses the railway where the footbridge is here, after which it curves round to the right, following the line of the colliery sidings, to run up the opposite side of the valley to Aberbeeg, bypassing Llanhilleth on the way. A.N.H. GLOVER/KIDDERMINSTER RAILWAY MUSEUM

PLATE 13.48: A Christmas card scene, photographed from a train calling at High Level station on 11th January 1963, with the viaduct casting its shadow on the hillside behind.

IN all WEATHERS

PLATE 13.49: A short while later, as the train made its way east over the viaduct, our hardy photographer took this second view looking down on some more of the bitter wintry conditions of early 1963, as a pannier tank headed up a snowbound valley with empties for loading at Llanhilleth Colliery. The snow had first arrived in a blizzard which swept across the country just after Christmas 1962 and temperatures throughout Janaury 1963 averaged -2.1°C, making it one of the coldest Janaury months ever recorded. There were further heavy snowfalls in the February, such that it was not until early March that temperatures finally rose and the snow melted away. Note the brick-built, ARP-style control cabin in between the screens sidings; loaded wagons coming out could be weighed either side. BOTH MARK B. WARBURTON

Plate 13.50, Above: Fog created its own atmosphere in the valleys and when heavy, crossing over the viaduct in a carriage must have been a surreal experience. Wearing BR lined green passenger livery, No. 5628 of Swansea East Dock shed adds to the mist with an impressive head of steam whilst on its way to Pontypool Road, on 23rd October 1962.

Plate 13.51, Below Left: With the valley clouded in mist, a loaded coal train heads west behind another '56XX' 0-6-2T.

Plate 13.52, Below Right: On the same day, another heavy coal train was seen making its way east, hauled by No. 5624 and assisted in the rear by 2-6-2T No. 5164. The train engine was based at Aberdare shed whilst the banker was on Pontypool Road's allocation. All Bill Potter/Kidderminster Railway Museum

Plate 13.53: *With the TVE/Vale of Neath line having closed on 13th June 1964, just over a fortnight later, on 29th June, the aerial photography specialists Terence Soames (Cardiff) Ltd made this stunning record of Crumlin Viaduct. Although not quite showing the full length of the Kendon section, it does show just about everything else. Crumlin Junction and the Llanhilleth Branch, curving away round the hillside, can be seen top right, along with Swffryd and the school. The line of Mark Philips' Trinant Tramroad can clearly be seen running along the ridge from the head of the incline, northwards to Llanerch Isaf and Trinant. On the valley floor, the bed of the Crumlin Arm of the Monmouthshire Canal curves round just below the tree line bottom right, with the Ebbw River flowing down the valley parallel on its left. The new A467 road was built on the bed of the canal and carries on then in front of the Viaduct Hotel, whilst the new bridge carrying the B4251 over the railway was constructed just the other side of the existing one, with the realigned road then running behind the Railway Hotel and up the hill towards Kendon. Modern day vegetation and tree growth is a little more lush than seen here but closely mirrors it in pattern.* Amgueddfa Cymru – Museum Wales

Crumlin Viaduct In The Stereoscope

CHAPTER 14

STEPHEN ROWSON

Thomas William Kennard (TWK), the man who won the contract for building Crumlin Viaduct, was a son of the London banker and industrialist Robert William Kennard (RWK), who in turn had inherited the wealth of his father the City banker John Kennard (1776-1838). In the 1830s, foreseeing the railway mania's demand for iron, Robert had invested in the Falkirk Ironworks in Scotland and developed it into the second most important of a number of ironworks in that area. In 1848, he bought the Falkirk Ironworks outright and placed his third son, Howard John (HJK), in charge. Three of his other sons also became involved over the years, although HJK and Arthur Challis Kennard (ACK) were the senior partners.

When the Blaenavon Ironworks in South Wales became a joint stock company in 1836, RWK also invested in that and he became its chairman, with his sons being involved there too. In all, our hero TWK had six brothers – Robert Bruce Kennard (1824-95), HJK (1829-96), ACK (1831-1903), Henry Martyn Kennard (HMK, 1833-1911), John Kennard (1836-1925) and Edward Kennard (1842-1910). The eldest brother entered the church but the others, all younger than Thomas, participated over the years in the management of Blaenavon and Falkirk, whilst also investing in and becoming directors of several railway companies (including the Northern & Eastern, Great Eastern and Eastern Counties railways).

The sales and administrative headquarters for the iron company was at 67 Upper Thames Street in London. Working there as accountant since 1836 was their cousin George Swan Nottage (1822-85). By 1854, Nottage and HJK were jointly operating another business in London, selling ornamental ironwork and bronzes cast at Falkirk. To add to this retail outlet, they began selling stereoscopic viewers, stereo daguerreotypes and paper images imported from France, where there was already

Plate 14.1, Far Left: George Swan Nottage, 1823-1885, founder of the London Stereoscopic Company. He was elected Lord Mayor of London in 1884 and is seen here wearing the mayoral regalia but sadly died in office the following year. As mayor, Nottage was entitled to a burial in the crypt in St. Paul's Cathedral.
Stephen Rowson collection

Plate 14.2, Left: This stereoscopic slide provides a dramatic view of the classical dome of St. Paul's Cathedral from across the Thames upstream of Southwick Bridge. To offer this slide for sale must have given Nottage and Kennard much satisfaction because for them the central subject is the London riverside premises of their father's company , lettered 'R.A. Kennard Iron Wharf' and which was their place of work (for sixteen years in the case of Nottage). River barges are clear evidence that the company relied on river and canal for transport of their products.
Stephen Rowson collection

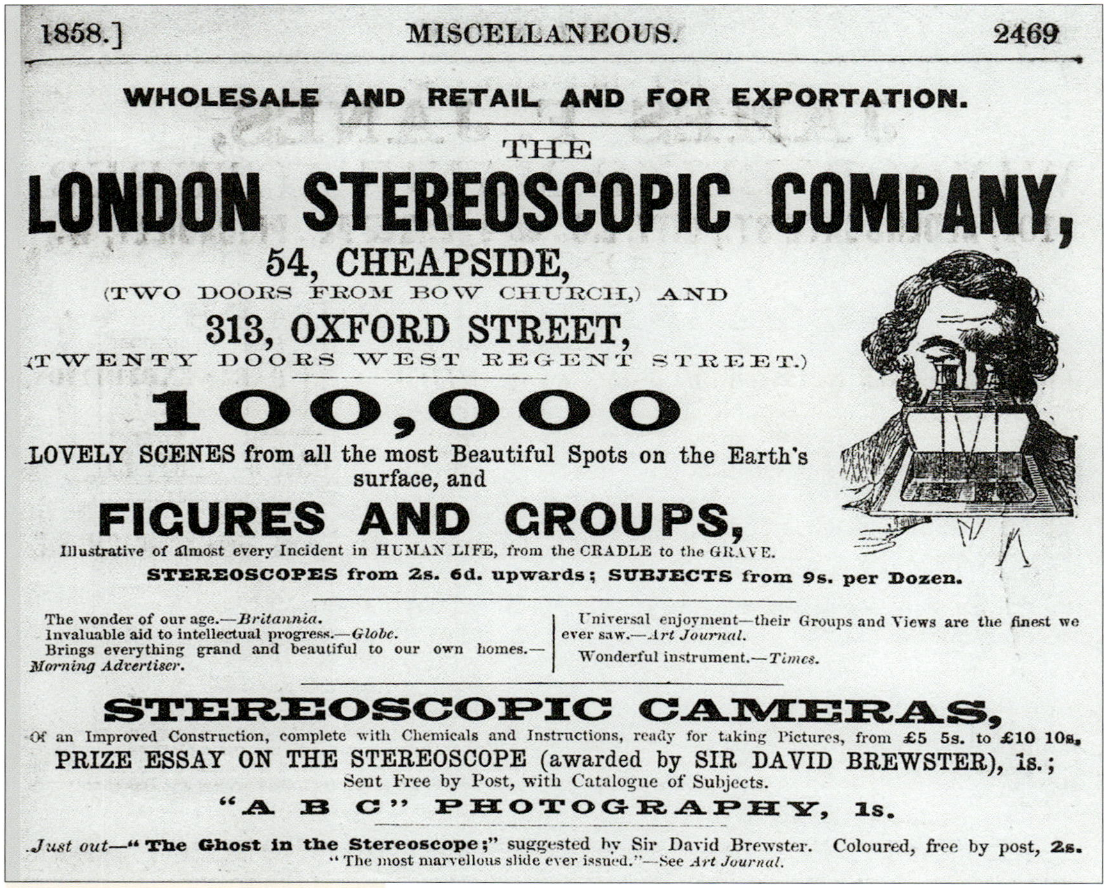
1858.] MISCELLANEOUS. 2469

WHOLESALE AND RETAIL AND FOR EXPORTATION.

THE
LONDON STEREOSCOPIC COMPANY,
54, CHEAPSIDE,
(TWO DOORS FROM BOW CHURCH,) AND
313, OXFORD STREET,
(TWENTY DOORS WEST REGENT STREET.)

100,000
LOVELY SCENES from all the most Beautiful Spots on the Earth's surface, and
FIGURES AND GROUPS,
Illustrative of almost every Incident in HUMAN LIFE, from the CRADLE to the GRAVE.
STEREOSCOPES from 2s. 6d. upwards; SUBJECTS from 9s. per Dozen.

The wonder of our age.—*Britannia.*
Invaluable aid to intellectual progress.—*Globe.*
Brings everything grand and beautiful to our own homes.—*Morning Advertiser.*
Universal enjoyment—their Groups and Views are the finest we ever saw.—*Art Journal.*
Wonderful instrument.—*Times.*

STEREOSCOPIC CAMERAS,
Of an Improved Construction, complete with Chemicals and Instructions, ready for taking Pictures, from £5 5s. to £10 10s.
PRIZE ESSAY ON THE STEREOSCOPE (awarded by SIR DAVID BREWSTER), 1s.;
Sent Free by Post, with Catalogue of Subjects.
"A B C" PHOTOGRAPHY, 1s.

Just out—"The Ghost in the Stereoscope;" suggested by Sir David Brewster. Coloured, free by post, 2s.
"The most marvellous slide ever issued."—See *Art Journal.*

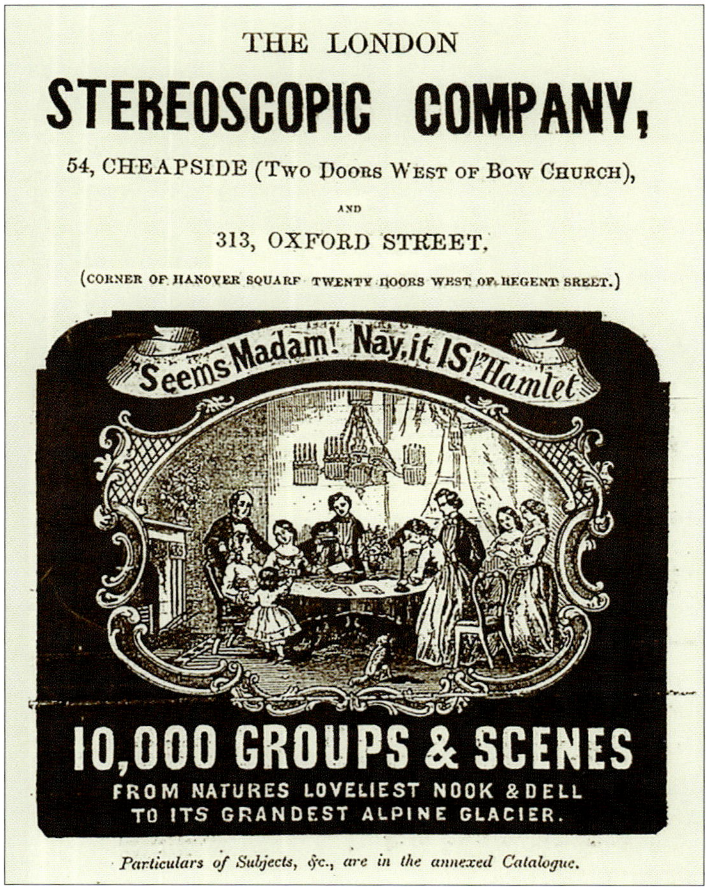
THE LONDON
STEREOSCOPIC COMPANY,
54, CHEAPSIDE (Two Doors West of Bow Church),
AND
313, OXFORD STREET,
(CORNER OF HANOVER SQUARE TWENTY DOORS WEST OF REGENT SREET.)

10,000 GROUPS & SCENES
FROM NATURES LOVELIEST NOOK & DELL
TO ITS GRANDEST ALPINE GLACIER.

Particulars of Subjects, &c., are in the annexed Catalogue.

Fig. 14.1, Above: An 1858 newspaper advertisement for the LSC.

Fig. 14.2, Above Right: The front page of the London Stereoscopic Company's catalogue for May 1856, which showed the stereoscope in use in a family living room. Clearly this leisure hobby was not aimed at the working classes of Crumlin!

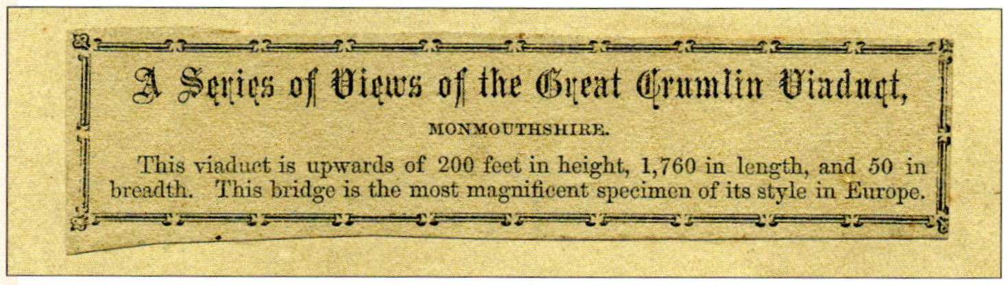

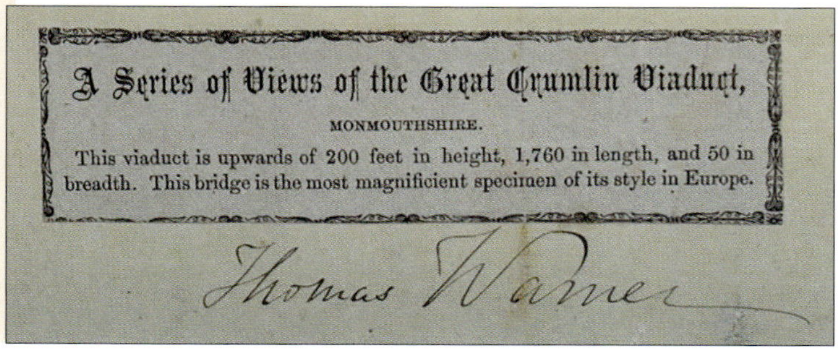

Fig. 14.3 -14.6, Right: Variations in design for the labels on the reverse of LSC stereo cards. Stephen Rowson collection

an active domestic market for collecting photographs. In Britain, Henry Fox Talbot's patent restrictions had imposed something of a stranglehold on commercial photography but his attempt to renew the patents was defeated in December 1854. This opened up the market and in that same month the setting up of the London Stereoscopic Company (LSC) was announced in *The Times*. As well as importing stereo slides for resale, Kennard and Nottage now used freelance photographers to provide the LSC with a growing stock of available images of Britain and Ireland. By May 1856, the LSC was advertising the availability of 10,000 slides, although the bulk of those on offer were still of French origin and were either genre subjects or romantic landscapes suitable for family viewings at the drawing room table (as suggested by the illustration on the front of their catalogue).

In early 1856, Nottage and HJK turned their thoughts towards testing a specific market, sending their photographer to Crumlin, where the Kennard family were involved in a major project to bridge the valley. Stereo slides would be produced to show architects and engineers the progress T.W. Kennard was making on the viaduct that was already being reported in the *Illustrated London News*. The next LSC catalogue, in September 1856,

PLATE 14.3: *This image is from a French stereo slide and depicts the interior of a workshop manufacturing such slides. Multiple positives would be printed from multiple negatives, pasted to card then dried and cut. The long time exposure required to take photographs at this period means that this picture would have had to have been posed but the photographer has still managed to achieve quite a natural feel of a busy manufacturing room, with various processes in the making of a stereo card on show.*
STEPHEN ROWSON COLLECTION

PLATE 14.5: *In 1866-67, the LSC moved from their Oxford Street premises to a new location at 108-110 Regent Street, on the corner of the junction with Glasshouse Street, as shown here on this circa 1912 picture postcard.*
NEIL PARKHOUSE COLLECTION

something the catalogue entry suggests with its appeal to civil engineers. Perhaps it was Lewis Gordon who had suggested the viaduct would be a good subject. Bridges became particularly popular for stereographs because of the depth they offered the photographer to provide a good three-dimensional effect.

Study of examples of the LSC slides that Stephen Rowson has collected or seen over many years has drawn him to conclude that there were at least two visits by the LSC photographer to Crumlin – in winter/spring 1856 and then again in summer 1856. Perhaps the first lot of twenty views were successful enough to prompt production of the next thirty. Examples from the second lot show evidence of leaves on trees and the extension to the Navigation Inn complete.

Many of the LSC images are taken of the workforce within the confines of the Viaduct Works site, although sadly there is no image of the interior of the erecting shops and forges, no doubt because of the poor sensitivity of the chemicals used on the glass plates in those early years.

keep a stock themselves or simply take orders blind?

These slides of the Crumlin Viaduct were ground breaking images. Stereo photography had missed out on recording the building of Stephenson's Britannia Bridge across the Menai Straits, completed in 1850. Moreover, these Crumlin stereo slides were published two years before Robert Howlett's celebrated stereographs of the launch of the *Leviathan* (the *Great Eastern*) and three years before the LSC published its own series *The Great Eastern in the Stereoscope*. The stages of erection of Brunel's bridge across the River Tamar at Saltash were documented in detail by both local and visiting photographers from 1857 but the Crumlin images were not like that and did not try to provide a record of construction; rather they paved the way to a wider interest in the industrial stereograph,

PLATE 14.6: *Cropped from Bedford's fine panorama of 1861, (pages 238-39) showing the Navigation Inn with its completed timber-sided extension.*
STEPHEN ROWSON COLLECTION

The placement of figures at differing distances from the camera adds to the three-dimensional effect but is crude in an obvious way. They show groups of workers, the engineer and contractors, whilst some also are more intimate portraits of the directors and management, and even their wives and children. One wonders why distant unconnected members of the public would want some of these anonymous images in their collections but such was the sensibility of the Victorian upper-middle class. We do not know who the LSC photographer was at Crumlin nor even whether the cousins practised the skill themselves. The Kennards were society people in London and selling their portraits would have added to their celebrity.

Helped by mentions in the *Illustrated London News*, Crumlin Viaduct, which was awarded the accolade of highest bridge in England and Wales, could be visited either in person or in the comfort of your own living room. And it was added as a detour from the well established grand tour of the Wye Valley and South Wales, in which Victorian tourists visited Chepstow (for the castle and River Wye bridge), Tintern Abbey, Monmouth, Ross-on-Wye and Raglan Castle.

Other stereo photographers also travelled to the viaduct, the foremost of whom was the Birmingham-based photographer Alfred Pumphrey. He offered four images from his first trip to Crumlin and three more probably from a later visit. Pumphrey really knew about three-dimensional composition and the stereo effect in his photography is generally superb. As well as showing how the viaduct sat sympathetically within the village of Crumlin, he, of all the stereo photographers, gives us some engineering aspects in context, such as his views of the saw pit and the inclined plane between the lower and upper works.

After Pumphrey came Francis Bedford, who was one of the first commercial photographers to cover a wide area of the country – particularly Wales (north and south) and the West of England. He built up an impressive catalogue of slides and maybe as early as 1861, when he is known to have travelled to

A. PUMPHREY'S STEREOGRAPHS OF ENGLISH SCENERY.

Chester.

356...Chester Cathedral
337... " " West Door
352...God's Providence House, Watergate
351A...Bishop Lloyd's House, ditto
355, 356...Row in Bridge Street
350, 351...Ditto in Eastgate Street
338...St John's Church
339...Ditto ditto, and Suspension Bridge
340, 342...Ruins of St. John's Abbey
344...Old Bridge from N.E.
245, 349...Victoria Bridge
347, 348...Suspension Bridge
360...City Walls from Watergate
357, 359...The Water Tower
358...King Charles's Tower
361, 362...Old Houses in Bridge Street
363...Old House in Foregate Street
364...Grosvenor Lodge
366...Eaton Hall, West Front
373, 374...Ditto, East Front
376, Ditto, South Window
367, 368, 369...Statuary at Eaton Hall

Chepstow.

732...Chepstow Castle from the Bridge
71...Interior of Chepstow Castle
69...Bridge over the Wye
64, 66...Iron Railway Bridge

Crumlin Viaduct.

14...General View from top of Embankment
13 & 16...Ditto, from the Valley
15...From halfway down the Embankment, shewing the Construction of the Piers.

Gloucestershire and Wiltshire.

276...Docks at Gloucester
290...Cirencester Town Hall
289...Ditto Abbey Church and Town Hall
286...Ditto Agricultural College
288...Ditto Abbey Gateway
299...Malmesbury Abbey, the Transept
302...Ditto ditto, from the South
304...Ditto ditto, from S.W.
305...Ditto ditto, the West End
306...Ditto ditto, the Transept from W.
307...Ditto ditto, from the North
300a, 303...Ditto ditto, South Door
301...Ditto Market Cross
35...Nailsworth
278...Ditto Institute
34...Village of Newmarket
37 & 38...Large Hollow Elm Tree, near Stroud
42, 44, 46...Gloucestershire Beech Woods
40...Weir at Horsley

Herefordshire.

696...East End of Hereford Cathedral
3...Booth's Porch ditto ditto
700, 701...Hereford Cathedral, Interior
698, 699...Ditto ditto and Bridge
1, 6...Ditto ditto, from N.E.
9 ....Ditto ditto and Palace
17 ....Ditto ditto Cloisters
4...Castle Green, Hereford
12...Railway Bridge over the Wye, Hereford
695...Old House, Hereford
01, 03, 686...White Cross, Hereford
697, 689, 504a...Black Friars' Cross, ditto
690...Ruins of Black Friars' Hospital, ditto
735, 733,...Old Town Hall, Leominster
736...The Church, ditto

Malvern.

468...Malvern from the foot of the North Hill
486...Worcestershire Beacon from ditto
467...Rocky Valley, ditto ditto
487...Ivy Rock, ditto
479...Malvern Hills fr. Herefordshire Beacon
193, 458, 460, 461...The Abbey Church
172, 490...St. Ann's Well
180...The Holy Well, Malvern Wells
188, 463...The Abbey Gateway
192...Belle Vue Terrace
218...The Tanks, North Malvern

Malvern continued.

464, 465...Pickersleigh, near Malvern
485...The Church at Maddersfield
483, 484, 481...Maddersfield Court (a moated Grange)
470...West Malvern Church
471...Newland Church
473...Little Malvern Church
475...The Wych Pass
476, 478, & 477...Eastnor Castle
451...The Priory, Malvern
200...Tudor House, ditto (Dr. Gully's)
454...Ditto ditto, ditto, from upper road
169...Dr. Wilson's, ditto, from the garden
449...Ditto ditto, from the road
450, 197...Malvern House
198...Porch of Malvern House
205...The Abbey Boarding House
213...Hardwicke House and Baths
212...Ditto ditto from garden
453...Ditto ditto from road
208, 209, 210...Townsend House (Dr. Grindrod's)
455...Dr. Johnson's Hydropathic Establishment
456...Dr. Ayerst's ditto ditto

Raglan Castle.

709...Raglan Castle, general view
712...The Water Gate
710, 711, 714...Raglan Castle from the Moat
705...Entrance to Raglan Castle
706, 707...Window in the Great Hall
715...Grand Staircase
716...The Picture Gallery
704...The Well at Raglan Castle
708...Gateway leading to Bowling Green

Shropshire.

737...Iron Bridge, Coalbrookdale
755...Waterfall, ditto
752...Large Waterwheel at Broseley
754...Buildwas Abbey
748...Madeley Court
749...Ditto ditto, Ancient Sun-Dial at
750...Ludlow Castle
761, 751...Stokesay Castle
753...Excavations and Roman Wall at Wroxeter
756...Littleshall Abbey
757...Ditto ditto, Norman Arch at

Tintern Abbey.

63...East Window, interior
718, 53...South Aisle
728, 729, 731...Interior Views across the transept
727...West Window from Interior
730, 57...Ditto, Exterior
722, 723, 58...South Window
724...The Cloister Gate
721...East Window, Exterior
725...West Door
55...Ditto from across the River

Warwickshire.

77...Kenilworth Castle, general view
78...Ditto ditto, ditto, more distant
87...Ditto ditto, Cæsar's Tower
88...Ditto ditto, Banqueting Hall
90...Ditto ditto, Windows of ditto looking to Cæsar's Tower
91...Kenilworth Castle, Windows of Banqueting Hall, opposite side
92...Kenilworth Castle, part of Leicester's Buildings
95 & 95a...Kenilworth Castle, Views in the Farm Yard
1102...Warwick Castle and Bridge
1103...The Old Bridge, Warwick
740, 741...The Town Hall, Birmingham
950, 951...Handsworth Church, ditto
952...Church of England Cemetery, ditto
954, 963...General Cemetery, ditto
955, 957, 958...Aston Hall, ditto
959, 960, 962...Exhibition, Aston Hall, ditto
964...Edgbaston Old Church, ditto

A Complete List of English and Welsh Scenery on application to any dealer.

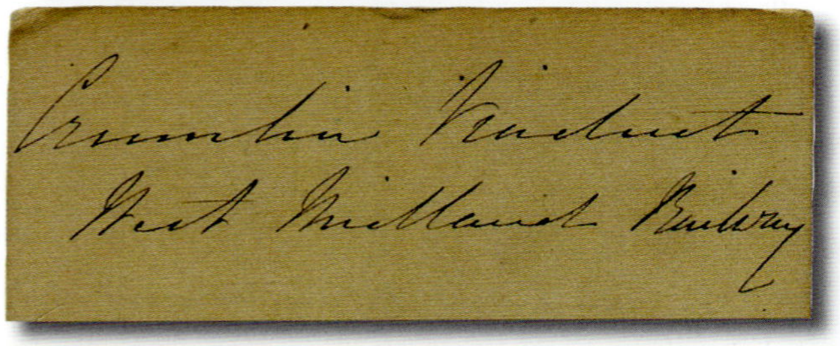

FIG. 14.11, ABOVE: Advertisement for stereos by Pumphrey. Note that Brunel's tubular bridge at Chepstow also featured, along with the Wye railway bridge at Hereford, the docks at Gloucester, the Iron Bridge at Coalbrookdale and the large waterwheel at Broseley.

FIG. 14.12 & 14.3, ABOVE LEFT: Pumphrey stereo front title and ink reverse, with West Midland Railway notation.

PLATE 14.7, LEFT: An unnumbered Pumphrey Crumlin stereo.
ALL STEPHEN ROWSON COLLECTION

PLATES 14.8 & 14.9: These two images are repeated from earlier chapters to emphasise the different photographic styles of these early photographers. In 1861, Francis Bedford had chosen more or less the same aspect as Alfred Pumphrey had for one of his slides but how different were the two outcomes – Pumphrey's study is full of vigour whilst Bedford's is almost a still life, albeit still with plenty of interest. BOTH STEPHEN ROWSON COLLECTION

I dedicate my contribution to this book to two sorely missed fellow collectors of Crumlin stereographs – Geoff Gilbert and Gwyn Nicholls. Without their insights and encouragement, this chapter could not have been written. Stephen Rowson

South Wales, he too joined the club and visited Crumlin. Bedford's soulless images of the Viaduct Works contrast with what the LSC and Pumphrey managed to produce with people included. Nevertheless, Francis Bedford's stereographs (and *cartes-de-visite*, which were printed directly from the negatives of one of the stereo pair) were a quality product and by the late 1860s they were available easily from newsagents and dealers. One wonders whether they were on sale at Crumlin Post Office, on the canal bridge and where he parked his carriage during his stay. Were any of these photographic products sold on site or did the visitor have to wait until he/she got home to the city? In North Wales the photograph collecting industry matured more quickly and, by 1860, the products of several Midlands-based photographers were on sale by bookshops and newsagents at or near well-known beauty spots, who again acted as photograph agents.

Stereo slide collecting took off very quickly and many provincial studios took the opportunity of publishing some local views of interest. Robert Waugh, for example, who had a books and fancy goods shop at 1-2 Church Street, Monmouth, published his own stereoscopic views of the Wye Valley which he offered to tourists and he also added Crumlin to the list.

There were other photographers too but the Victorians' craze for stereo photography had waned by the end of the 1870s, at around the same time that the Viaduct Works went into liquidation. The Kennards had already sold out to its manager, Henry Maynard, but the Kennard name remains in the memory.

164. Crumlin Viaduct—From the South-East.

PLATE 14.10: A Francis Bedford carte-de-visite of the viaduct, No. 164, which was a cropped down version of his Crumlin panorama. NEIL PARKHOUSE COLLECTION

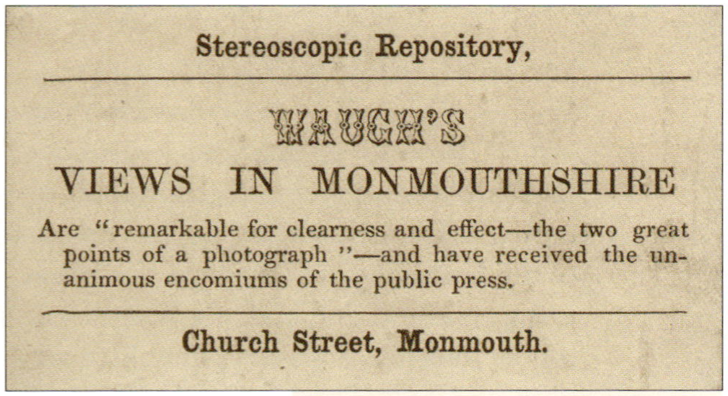
Stereoscopic Repository,

WAUGH'S

VIEWS IN MONMOUTHSHIRE

Are "remarkable for clearness and effect—the two great points of a photograph"—and have received the unanimous encomiums of the public press.

Church Street, Monmouth.

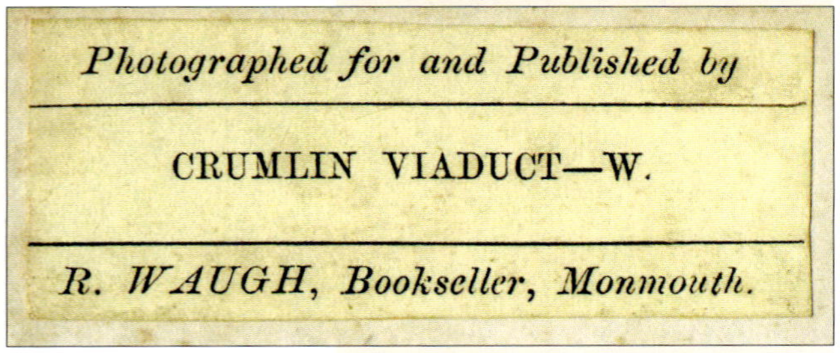
Photographed for and Published by

CRUMLIN VIADUCT—W.

R. WAUGH, Bookseller, Monmouth.

Maynard's books of the 1860s on the viaduct and on the Works' other world-wide products are well illustrated but not with photographs, this at a time when many books were being published with tipped-in real photographic prints. The conclusion must be that Nottage's innovative 1856 series of fifty stereographs of the viaduct was not really embraced by the rest of the family as a basis for future marketing and that the part photography played in the raising of the viaduct as a national monument may have been an accident.

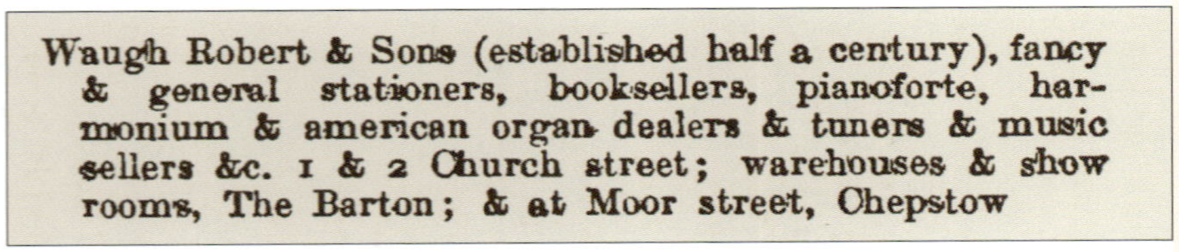
Waugh Robert & Sons (established half a century), fancy & general stationers, booksellers, pianoforte, harmonium & american organ dealers & tuners & music sellers &c. 1 & 2 Church street; warehouses & show rooms, The Barton; & at Moor street, Chepstow

The pictorial postcard first came to Britain in 1894 but at first the reverse was only for the address, so the front contained a small picture, with the rest of the space left for writing a message. Postcards only surged in popularity after 1902, when the backs were allowed to be divided, with one half now for the address and the other for a message, with the result that the collecting of them became the new craze for the decade or so leading up to the First World War.

It was during this period that the viaduct again became a common subject, as can be seen by the large selection reproduced in this book. Although the golden age of postcards is generally accepted to be the years prior to the First World War, during which era almost anything and everything in terms of subject matter was covered by picture postcard publishers, they continued to be popular into the 1960s and certainly images of the viaduct were still being used into the late 1950s. With diligence and a reasonably deep pocket, a dedicated collector could amass a collection of fifty or more different postcards of Crumlin Viaduct dating between 1900 and 1960.

PLATE 14.11, ABOVE LEFT: One of Waugh's Crumlin stereos. They lack the quality of those by the LSC, Bedford and Pumphrey but are also rare.
STEPHEN ROWSON COLLECTION

FIG. 14.11, TOP: An advertisement for Robert Waugh's Stereoscopic Repository in Church Street, Monmouth.

FIG. 14.12, ABOVE: The reverse of one of Waugh's Crumlin stereos.
STEPHEN ROWSON COLLECTION

PLATE 14.12, LEFT: A circa 1900 view of Church Street, Monmouth. Robert Waugh's premises, No's 1 & 2, are those on the right far corner of the alleyway by the cart. The two properties are both Grade II listed today whilst, coincidentally, the next two shops in the street on the same side are both bookshops
NEIL PARKHOUSE COLLECTION

FIG. 14.13, LEFT: The entry for Waugh, Robert & Sons in the 1895 edition of Kelly's directory.

Above, Right & Below:
Alfred Pumphrey

Above: *Alfred Pumphrey*

Below: *Probably London Stereoscopic Company*

Above & Below: London Stereoscopic Company.

CHAPTER 10: A WORKING LIFE – SOURCES

Books

Encyclopedia of British Railway Companies, Christopher Awdry, Patrick Stephens Ltd, 1990

Great Western Steam Rail Motors and Their Services, John Lewis, Wild Swan Publications, 2004

The Locomotives of the Great Western Railway, Part 3 Absorbed Engines, 1854-1921, The Railway Correspondence & Travel Society, 1956

The Railways of S.E. Monmouthshire, A. Pritchard, The Oakwood Press, 1962

The Vale of Neath Line, Gwyn Brwnant Joes & Denis Dunstone, Gomer Press, 1996

Track Layout Diagrams of the GWR and BR WR, Section 40 Western Valleys, R.A. Cooke, 1984

Track Layout Diagrams of the GWR and BR WR, Section 47B Vale of Neath Part 2: Aberdare to Pontypool Road, R.A. Cooke, 1981

Journals & Peridicals

Admiralty Coal Traffic During the First World War: The Jellicoe Trains Pts 1 & 2, Keith Turton, *Railway Archive* No's 19 & 20, Lightmoor Press, 2008

Great Western Railway Magazine – various issues

Hall's Tramroad: Abercarn, Pts 1, 2, 3 & 4, Foster Frowen, *Archive* No's 55, 56, 59, 60, Lightmoor Press, 2007-08

The Railway Observer – various issues

The Railway Magazine – various issues

Various contemporary newspapers

Various GWR & BR/WR *Working* and *Service Time Tables*, and *Bradshaw's Guides*

Websites

https://www.sixbellsjunction.co.uk – for rail tour info

https://www.brdatabase.info/index.php – loco allocations

https://maps.nls.uk – OS maps

ACKNOWLEDGMENTS

Completing the story of Crumlin Viaduct has been a complicated and intricate research project based on my interpretation of primary source material. It has also involved extensive discussions with staff, officials and members from national and local archives, libraries, museums, Government departments and professional institutions. Their advice and constructive comments have been invaluable, as well as that of enthusiasts and residents of Crumlin.

In particular I would like to express my thanks to a limited group who without their help and assistance, this story could not have been completed in such detail. Firstly, Richard Wood and Ian Coulson of the then Centre of British Rail Historical Records, who made special arrangements to relocate boxes of original documents and allowed me to examine and copy relevant material.

Jennifer Prothero Jones of Amgueddfa Cymru – Museum Wales, for making arrangements to view and then retrace each of the original contract drawings. The originals were in a very poor condition. Also ex-British Railways civil engineer John Mann, for providing access to his personal archive material detailing, in particular, the demolition of the viaduct

Stephen Rowson for his chapter on stereographic photographs, many of which are included in this publication, along with a selection of photographs and documents from his private collection.

Neil Parkhouse for his chapter on the viaduct's working life, for contributing numerous pictures from his personal archive and for sourcing many of the others contained herein. Overall they have served to wonderfully bring the viaduct back to life. In addition, his overall design and layout of this publication has brought my original manuscript to a state I could only have dreamed.

Gordon Wood, Hereford, 2024

We would also like to acknowledge the assistance received from other institutions and individuals in regards to images used: Coflein (National Monuments Record of Wales), Colour-Rail (Paul Chancellor), Kidderminster Railway Museum (David Postle), Oxford House Industrial History Society and the SLS (Gerry Nichols, archivist). Also John Alsop, Richard Casserley, David Dickinson, Terry Dorrity, Geoff Gilbert, Peter Klein, Brian Mills/Trackbed.com, Gwyn Nicholls, Russell Norton, Mike Thomas, Alastair Warrington and David Westcott, and to Ian Pope for redrawing the maps in Chapter 1.

Neil Parkhouse & Stephen Rowson, Lydney & Cardiff, 2024

APPENDIX 3 LIST OF DRAWINGS SUBMITTED TO THE ARBITRATION HEARING

Number on Contractor's Tracing	Number of Drawing	Number on Drawing	Date of Drawing When Made	Title *(Marked 'Illustrated' in red indicates a drawing included here)*
251	1	250	May 7th 1853	General Elevation both valleys
252	2	125	Jan. 6th 1853	Elevation & Plan of Girders
253	3	136	Jan. 20th 1853	Half Section Plan of Compression Bar
254	4	107	Dec. 1852	Section of Diagonals
255	5	173	Mar. 19th 1853	Sections Compression Bar
256	6	108	Dec. 1852	Joint No. 1C
257	7	109	Dec. 1852	Joint No. 1T
258	8	110	Dec. 1852	Joint No. 2C
259	9	111	Dec. 1852	Joint No. 2T

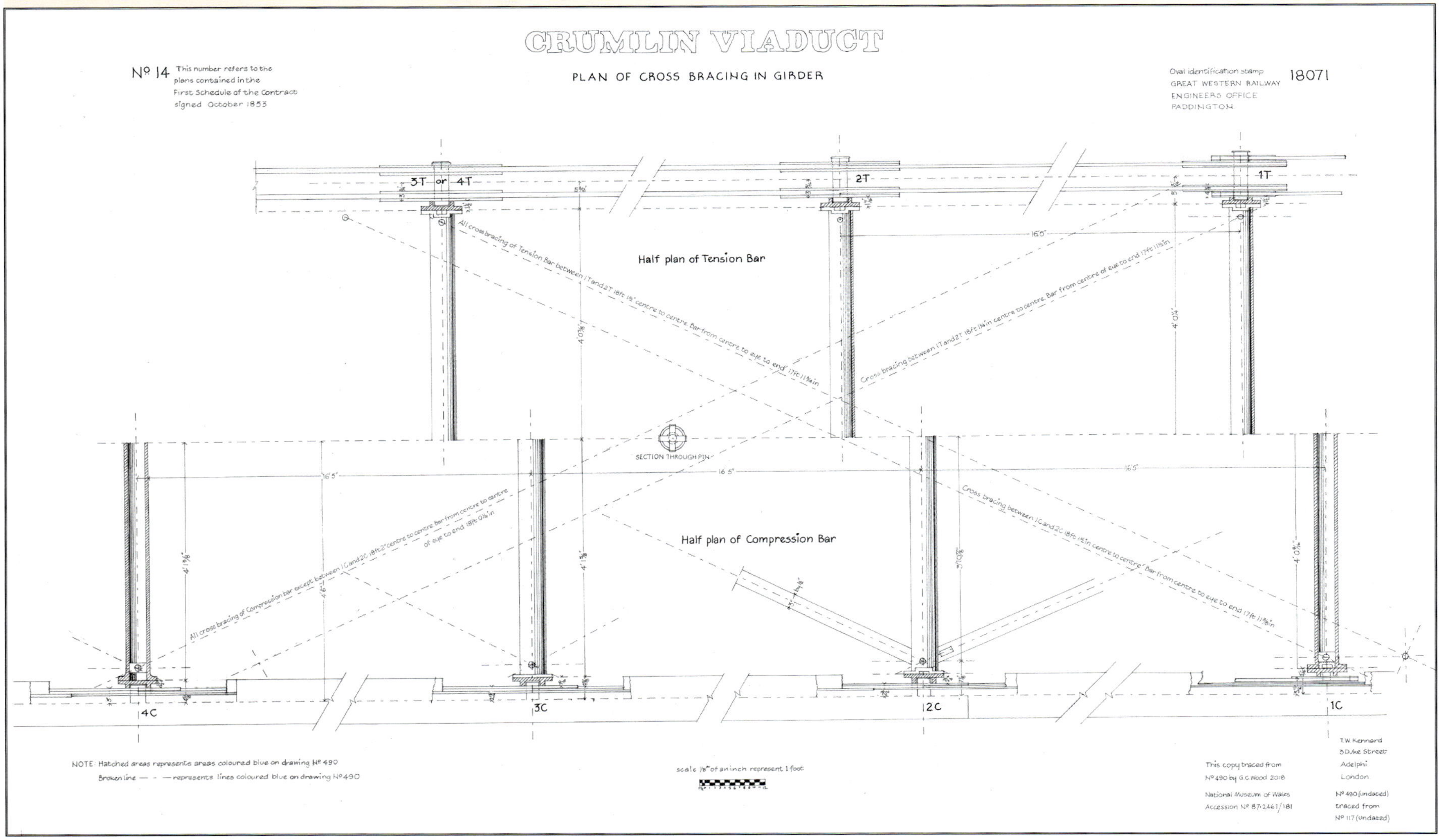

260	10	112	Dec. 1852	Joint No. 3C
261	11	113	Dec. 1852	Joint No. 3T
262	12	114	Dec. 1852	Joint No. 4C
263	13	115	Dec. 1852	Joint No. 4T
264	14	117	Dec. 19th 1852	Plan of Girder Bracing.................... Illustrated
265	15	118	Dec. 22nd 1852	Column for Ditto .... Illustrated
267	16	266	May 12th 1853	Handrail Panel................................. Illustrated
268	17	217	April 4th 1853	Elevation to Piers
269	18	104	Dec. 1852	Skeleton Dittto .... Illustrated
270	19	210	Mar. 24th 1853	Plan Foundation Tier No. 6
271	20	211	Mar. 24th 1853	Plan Foundation Pier No. 7........... Illustrated
272	21	212	Mar. 24th 1853	Plan Foundation Pier No. 10
273	22	213	Mar. 24th 1853	Plan Foundation Pier No. 11

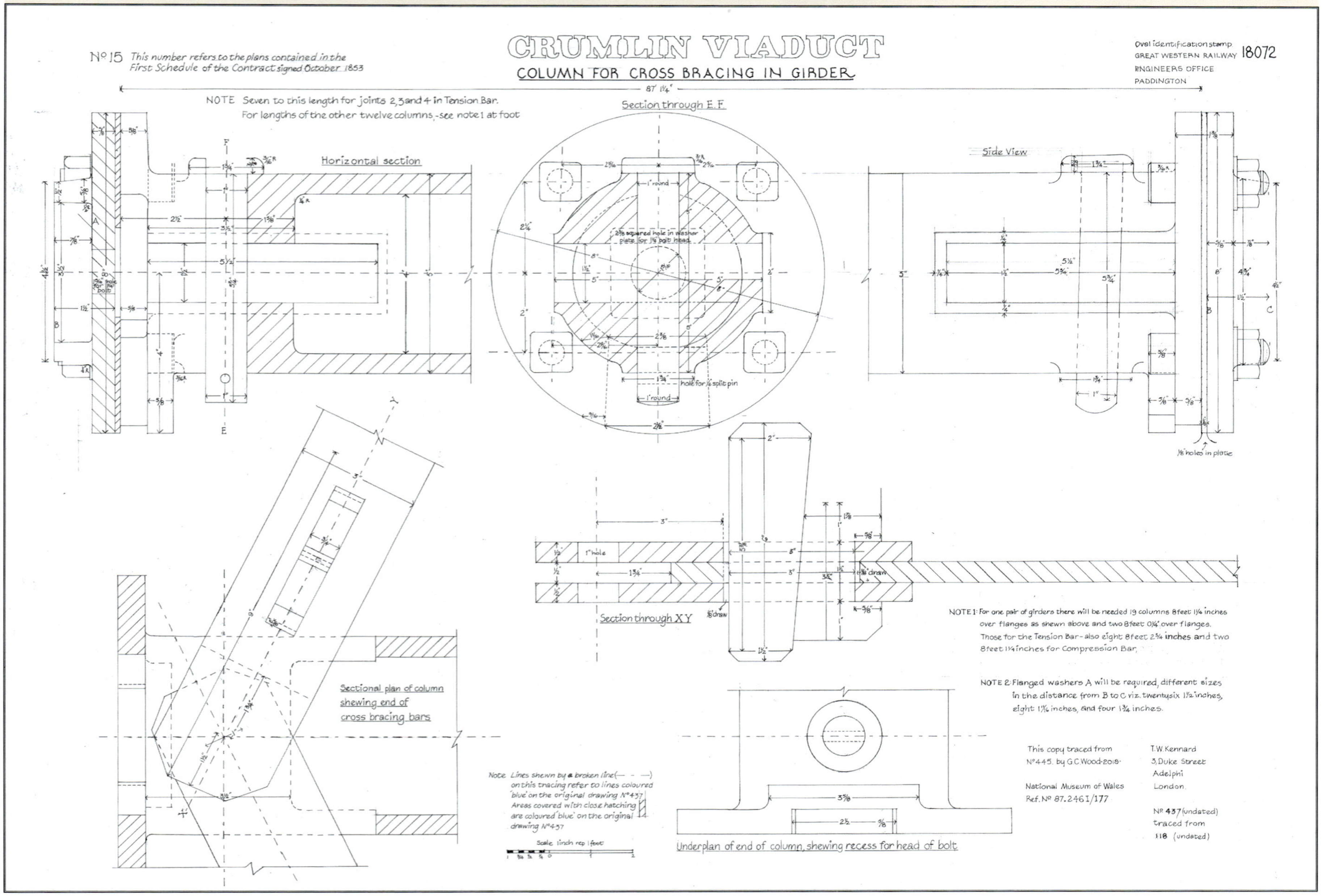

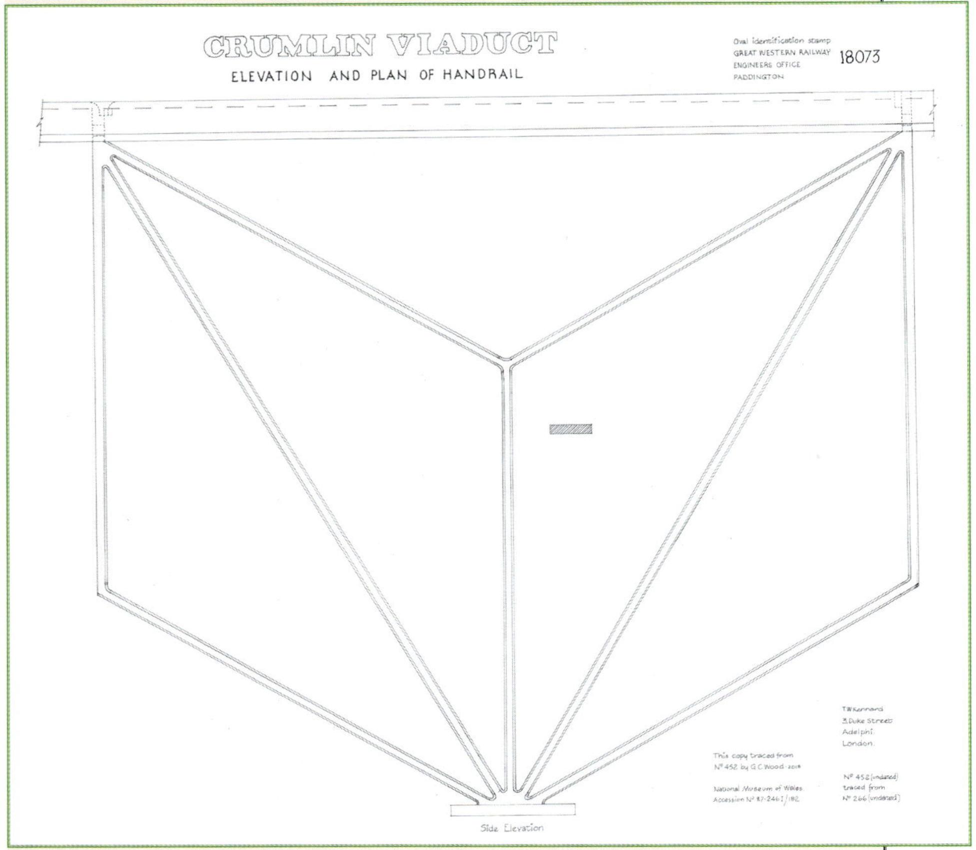

Plate A.1: *Taken on a very wet 19th August 1964, the neatness of this scene, looking east around the curve of the Kendon section and nicely showing the design of the handrails, rather belies the fact that the line had been closed for two months.* RCAHMW/Coflein

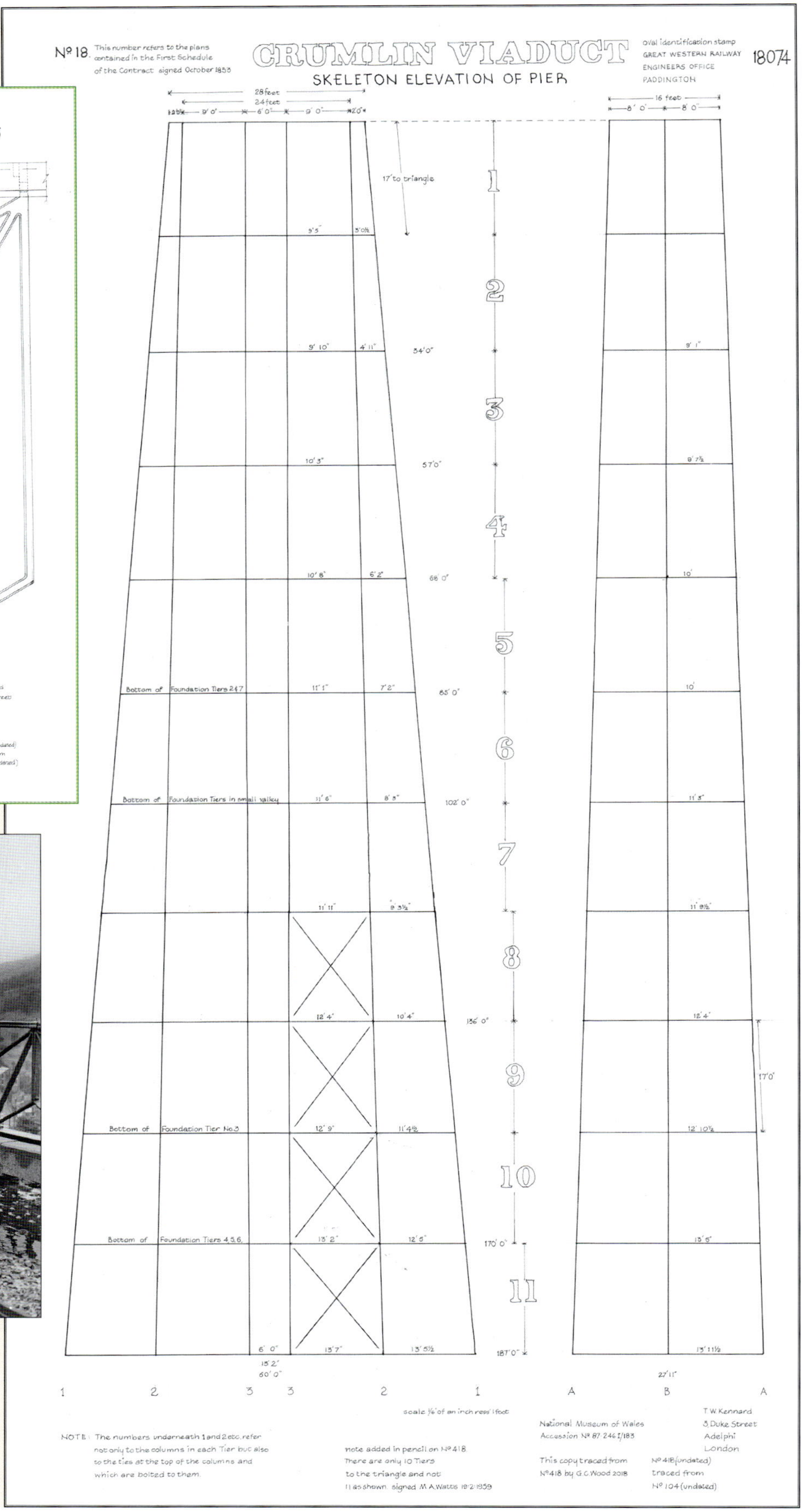

274	23	126	Jan. 8th 1853	Feet of Columns........ Illustrated
275	24	207	Mar. 24th 1853	Girders at feet of Column........ Illustrated
276	25	208	Mar. 28th 1853	Skew Girder for No. 6 Foundation Tier....... Illustrated
277	26	209	Mar. 24th 1853	Skew Girder for 10 & 11 Foundation Tier
278	27	100	Nov. 2nd 1852	Raking Column for Pier
142	28	120	Dec. 1852	Columns 2A, 3A, 2B, 3B
138	29	103	Dec. 1852	Girder between 1 & 2B Pier
279	30	122	Dec. 1852	Girder between A2 & B2
147	31	123	Dec. 1852	Girder between A3 & A2
152	32	124	Dec. 1852	Girder between A3 to A3
280	33	167	Dec. 1852	Girder between 1 & 2A........ Illustrated
281	34	121	Dec. 1852	Tier No. 6 to Skew Bracing
282	35	116	Dec. 17th 1852	Heads of Columns No. 1 Tier........ Illustrated
283	36	105	Dec. 1852	Triangle top of Pier........ Illustrated

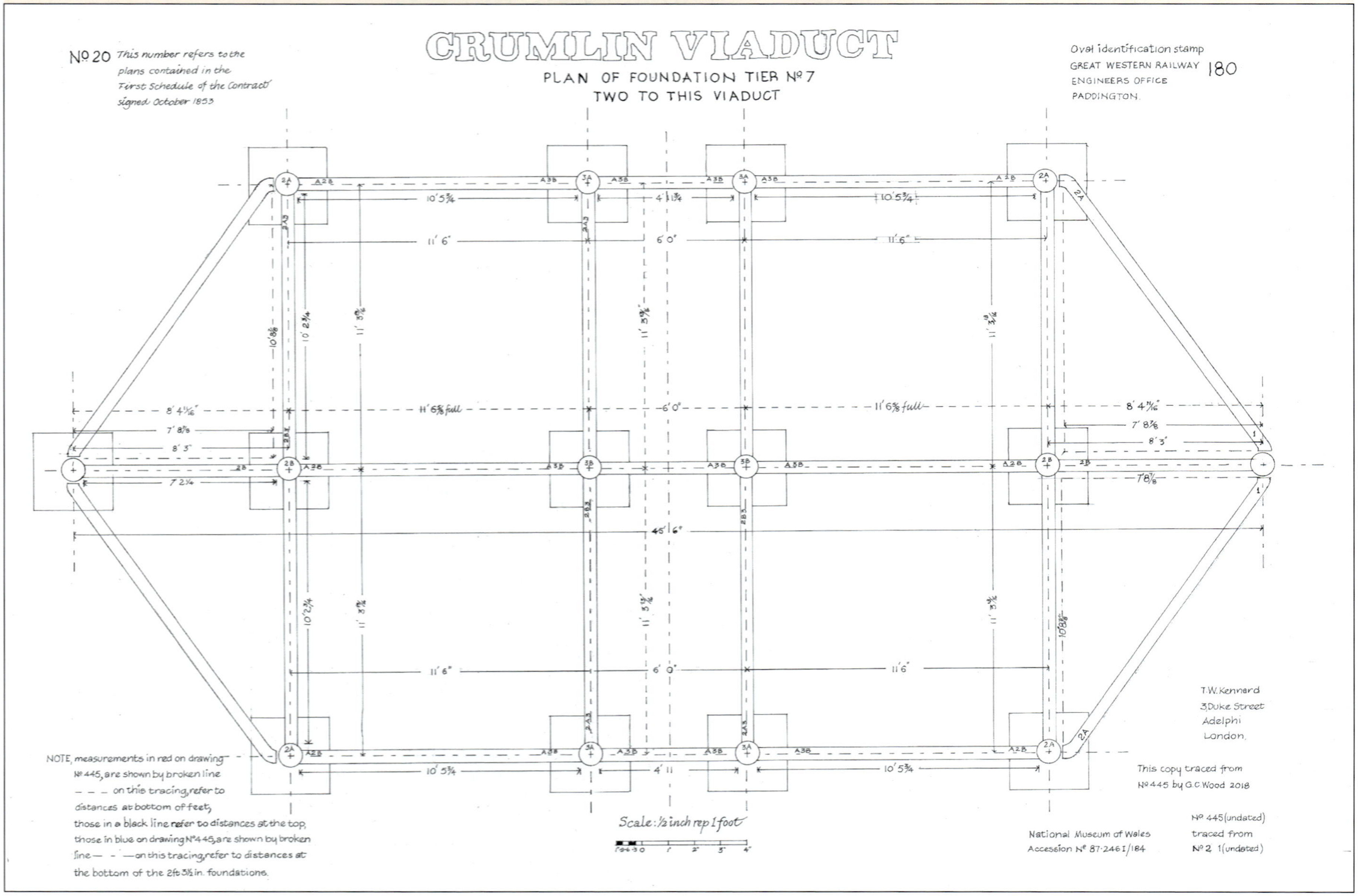

Liddell sent in his report to the directors on the same day, 10th July 1857, as follows:

'*The amount charged according to the Contract is correct.*

The charge for abutments in regard to quantities is not quite correct and Mr Kennard is now making further inquiries into the measurements.- The prices are greatly in excess of the same description of work done by the Company, and I cannot estimate the prices higher than those shewn in red figures in my account.

The charge for foundations of Piers is not admissible by the terms of the Contract. – The second schedule specifies that the foundations are 'where practicable to be laid on the solid rock,' *and 10 gives minute instructions as to the thickness of concrete, and as to the manner of building up the rubble and Ashlar work.*

The foundations of the Piers were very little different from what was anticipated when the Contract signed.

The charge for alterations of Abutments is correct as to quantities but the prices are too high.

The deduction of £1,100 should be from the amount of Abutments only – By the design on which the first tender was made the Abutments were to be made of Iron – On making the working drawings the Viaduct was lengthened one span and the Abutments being reduced in height were reduced from £2,600 to £1,100 – Masonry was finally substituted on account of the objection to the Iron Work being buried by embankment the wrought iron cross bracing being liable to rapid decay, and the difference of Cost between the two kinds of structure only has to be paid. – The Cost of the Iron Abutments was estimated as above stated at £1,100, and as this Cost, had been in Iron, would according to Mr Kennard's statement have been exceeded, the whole of it at least must be deducted from the cost Price of Abutments as executed.

By reference to my account the extra amount due on this change is shown.

The items of extra work all have been settled and agreed for the amounts marked in red ink excepting items 25, 26, 27, of these No. 25 is, if done without orders and without any knowledge on my part of its being done, or that it was intended to raise any claim for it.

No. 26 I of course know nothing

No. 27 I am entirely at a loss to understand upon what grounds it is put forward.

According to the terms of the Contract the amount due is in my opinion correctly stated by the red figures in the account and annexed – There is however I fear little doubt that the Contractor has lost considerably by this Contract.

Many circumstances in combination have produced this result into which it is needless now to enter, and it is for the directors alone to consider, whether for a work of such novelty and extent, an allowance in mitigation of this loss may be fairly made.

My own opinion is that on Mr Kennard's settling the account the directors might fairly make up the payment to £46,000.

Your Obedient Servant Charles Liddell.

The following is a summary of the whole account admitted by the Company

Balance of Contract price due to the Plaintiff	*£1,677 10 00*
Extras	*£3,328 19 01*
Balance due for Switches and Crossings	*£ 223 00 00*
Balance due for Road over Viaduct (£1812 16 00	*£ 312 16 00*
Balance of Goods Account	*£ 482 17 01*
Total	*£6,025 02 08*

Set off claimed by the Company		
Tonnage	*£ 4,171 12 07*	
Engineering account (admitted)	*£ 358 01 03*	
Old Rails (admitted)	*£ 126 17 00*	
Timber	*£ 200 00 00*	
Completing Viaduct	*£ 214 00 00*	
		£ 5,081 03 10
		£ 943 18 10

The other claims made by the Plaintiff are for hindrances caused by the Company in the completion of the Works and for loss arising upon the negotiation of the Debentures – as regards the former we are unable in Mr Liddell's absence to ascertain whether there is any foundation for it, and as regards the latter there is no trace in the correspondence or Minutes of any such Agreement as that alleged in the Declaration and moreover no account has ever been furnished by the Plaintiff shewing in what manner and in respect of which of the debentures he has sustained the alleged loss of £1,500.

INDENTURE

APPENDIX 5

Thos. Wm. Kennard
and
The Newport, Abergavenny and Hereford Railway Company
Deed endorsed on Contract
Dated 18th July 1854

This Indenture made the 18th day of July 1854 Between the above named Thomas William Kennard of the one part and the above named Newport, Abergavenny and Hereford Railway Company of the other part. Whereas the said Thomas William Kennard has recently erected and built on ground adjoining the Line of Railway of the said Company certain Workshops, Sheds, Warehouses and other Buildings and Erections and has fitted up and furnished the same with Engines, Machinery, Tools, Utensils and implements sufficient and requisite to enable him to complete the above written Contract and for the purposes of his other business. Now this Indenture witnesseth that for the considerations expressed in the said Contract and in furtherance of the objects thereof He the said Thomas William Kennard for himself his heirs, executors and administrators doth hereby covenant with the said Newport, Abergavenny and Hereford railway Company their successors and assigns that the said Company shall have and be entitled to the possession and occupation of the said Workshops, Sheds and other Buildings so erected by him the said Thomas William Kennard as aforesaid and that the said Engines, Machinery, Tools, Utensils and Implements thereon shall henceforth be and considered as in their possession so as that the said Thomas William Kennard shall not have the right to let the said Workshops, Sheds and Buildings or any part thereof or remove the said Engines, Machinery, Tools, Utensils and Implements or any part thereof until the completion of the said Contract and that the said Company shall have a lieu on the said Engines, Machinery, Tools, Utensils and Implements for any sum or sums of money to be advanced by them to the said Thomas William Kennard under the said Contract or in any other manner however Provided nevertheless that upon completion of the said Contract the right to the said premises chattels and effects shall revert to the said Thomas William Kennard and thereupon this Indenture become of none effect and in lieu hereby created shall cease to all intents and purposes whatsoever. In witness whereof the said Thomas William Kennard hath hereunto set his hand and seal and the said Company have hereunto caused their Common Seal to be affixed the day and year first above written –

Signed sealed and delivered by the above named Thomas William Kennard in the presence of
S. Spofforth.

PLATE A.9: *This decorative glazed plate, with a transfer print of Crumlin Viaduct and some fancy gold edging, is of a type usually sold to be displayed on a sideboard or dresser, or hung on the wall. The base is stamped* 'WITH THE COMPLIMENTS OF BRIGGS & Co, HIGH S^{T}, RISCA', *who described themselves as* 'BOOTERS'. *Presumably they were handed out to suppliers and wholesale buyers as a small promotional gift, and many were clearly treasured as quite a few have survived.* DAVID WESTCOTT COLLECTION

APPENDIX 6 MEMORANDUM, PADDINGTON 1959

Memorandum of Meeting at Paddington on 12th March 1959, in regard to reconstruction of Crumlin Viaduct

PRESENT

Mr L.W. Ibottson (Chairman)
Mr W.R. Stevens (Divisional Traffic Manager, Cardiff)
Operating Department
Commercial Department
Mr C.F.E. Harvey, OOO
Mr G.H. Roper, COO
Mr G.E.R. Penney, OOO
Mr H.V. Milner, COO
Mr K.H. Woodward, OOO
Mr A.P.E. Belcher, COO
Mr W.J. Morris, DOS, Newport
Mr J. Swann, Asst DCM Cardiff.
Mr P.G. Edwards, Asst DOS, Newport
Mr C. Hankins, Asst DOS, Cardiff
Mr L. Bicker, OOO
Mr G.W. Welsh, Asst DCM, Newport.
Engineering Department
Running & Maintenance Department
Mr P.H. Spence, CCEO
Mr H.R. Cox, R&MOO
Signal Department
Mr C.H.D. Read, DR&MO
Mr P.G. Jacobs, SEO

Crumlin Viaduct was opened in 1857, and although the foundations and piers are in good condition, it has been necessary to reconstruct the superstructure. This meeting was called to consider the practicability of dispensing altogether with the Viaduct and diverting the traffic to other routes.

The approximate estimate for reconstruction to carry a single line of railway as now, but with 'red' engine loading and speeds up to 20mph instead of the present 8mph restriction, is £415,000 with a life span of some 50 years. It was stated that the Viaduct can be kept going until 1961 but, owing to the planning work entailed in the reconstruction – in fact a considerable expense is already being incurred in this connection – a decision must be reached very quickly. The Chief Civil engineer had already stated that he could not recommend any short term repair work in order to prolong the life of the present superstructure and such work would in any case be very costly.

The principal alternative route from the Vale of Neath line are Penallta Junction-Caerphilly-Machen and Sirhowy Junction-Risca, the latter being the more practicable, particularly as it is proposed to single the line between Caerphilly and Machen. On the other hand it was stated that, if Crumlin Viaduct remains it would be possible to single the line between Sirhowy Junction and Nine Mile Point, but if the Viaduct is dispensed with the line between Sirhowy Junction and Nine Mile Point would necessarily have to remain as a double line.

A sketch map is attached showing in red the line which might be closed.

Consideration was given to the diversion of freight trains from and to the Swansea District over the South Wales Main Line throughout, but it was pointed out that heavy delays are at times already taking place in the Cardiff District and it had been proposed that five trains should be diverted to the Vale of Neath in order to ease the position.

It was felt that the Swansea District freight trains generally could only be dealt with over the South Wales Main Line, assuming the following:

1. Multiple-aspect signalling between Cardiff and Pyle (not scheduled until about 1966)
2. Upcoding of all freight trains (say 1970)
3. Adjustment of passenger services (subject to TUCC)
4. Completion of multiple-aspect signalling from Cardiff to Severn Tunnel Junction (say 1970)

The question of Pontypool Road Yard and Motive Power Shed was considered in relation to Crumlin Viaduct. It was stated that in any case the construction of the new yards at Gloucester and Shrewsbury would enable considerable economics to be effected at Pontypool Road Yard, while under dieselisation the Shed would disappear as a major depot. Any saving could not properly be credited to the proposal for dispensing with Crumlin Viaduct.

An endeavour had been made to secure the additional annual costs in diverting existing services and the annual savings which could be achieved by elimination of the Viaduct, and these are set out below:

Annual savings	*£*
Charges on the new structure (interest on capital maintenance and renewals)	*22,170*
Savings in charges on recovered portions of the Vale of Neath and certain sections of singling	*15,750*
Signal Department savings – closing of signal boxes, etc.	*5,000*
Staff savings (Operating Department)	*9,715*
Savings in Assisting Engine hours – 225 hours per week at £2 per hour	*23,400*
Total	*76,055*
Annual Additional Costs	
Additional annual mileage for Passenger trains via Newport (assuming they continue to run)	*7,300*
Additional annual mileage for freight trains from Vale of Neath line via Newport	*62,700*
Annual charges in respect of continuance of double line instead of single line between Sirhowy Junction and Nine Mile Point	*5,000*
Total (excluding passenger trains)	*£ 67,700*
Nett approximate annual savings (excluding Passenger trains)	*£ 8,335*

It was realised that the question of the Passenger service over the Vale of Neath line was closely associated with the re-appraisal proposals. The originating revenue for the whole of the Vale of Neath line amounted to some £80,000 per annum, with nearly 700,000 passenger journeys, as illustrated by the following:

Pontypool, Clarence Street	*123,000*
Crumlin (High Level)	*17,000*
Pontllanfraith	*26,000*
Mountain Ash	*56,000*
Aberdare (High Level)	*185,000*

And although it was appreciated that much of this was short-distance traffic, it was felt it would not be easy to convince the TUCC in the matter. Further, it would be difficult to cover all the passenger traffic by buses owing to the peculiar nature of the district, the railway crossing the various valleys, with viaducts and tunnels, while the road routes were in some cases circuitous.

The Commercial Department representatives undertook to ascertain the extent of the passenger traffic actually passing over Crumlin Viaduct, and the approximate cost of alternative facilities which would have to be provided if the through passenger service were discontinued.

Even disregarding any loss of passenger revenue if the viaduct were closed, there would only be a relatively small difference between the estimated annual savings and the additional annual costs.

After making a special review of all the factors, it was agreed to recommend that the Viaduct should be reconstructed, the following being the main considerations:

1. Little difference between the annual savings on the one hand and the additional expenses on the other hand

2. The inability to handle additional traffic over the South Wales Main line until all modernisation is completed in 1970

3. The closing of the Viaduct would leave only one main line route out of South Wales, apart from the Central Wales line. It was appreciated that, with the completion of the Newport MAS scheme, it would be possible to deal with the considerably extra traffic through Newport, but in this connection the new Llanwern Steel Works and its possible subsequent development has to be borne in mind.

4. The value of the Vale of Neath line as an emergency route.

5. Retention of the Vale of Neath line featured in the negotiations for the closing of the MT&A line as affording some measure of alternative communication.

6. The possibility at some future date, even though it may be remote, of major renewal works in connection with the River Usk Bridge at Newport.

7. Further industrial developments in Wales related to Steel Works, Collieries, etc.

8. Longer transits for certain freight traffic, resulting in public complaints and even loss of revenue.

9. The carrying out of MAS schemes at both Port Talbot and Newport, and eventually in the Cardiff District, may well require temporary diversion of freight traffic in order to facilitate the work, when the Vale of Neath line would be essential, especially if the Vale of Glamorgan line had been closed as a result of the recent 're-appraisal' recommendations.

10. The doubtful success in withdrawing the Vale of Neath passenger service, quite apart from any question of loss of revenue.

In concluding the meeting, the chairman remarked that the submission of the scheme to dispense with the Crumlin Viaduct had been amply justified and required considerable breadth of vision, and he expressed to Mr Morris his appreciation of the thought he had given to the whole subject. The chairman also said that, in submitting to the General Manager our recommendation that Crumlin Viaduct be retained it should be made clear that we have not been influenced unduly by the passenger traffic. It was also desired that the necessary preliminary arrangements be taken in hand to deal with the working of traffic during the Engineering Department occupation of the Viaduct.

APPENDIX 7 CRUMLIN VIADUCT TIMELINE

1845
31st July – Monmouthshire Railway & Canal Co. Act passed
4th August – South Wales Railway Act passed
1846
31st August – Newport, Abergavenny & Hereford Railway Act passed
1847
9th July – Taff Vale Extension Railway Act passed
1851
28th April – Charles Liddell appointed engineer in chief to the NA&HR. Liddell also brings his business partner Professor Lewis Dunbar Brodie Gordon to the table
1852
29th April – Liddell recommends to NA&HR Board new site for a viaduct crossing the Ebbw and Kendon valleys and a branch down to Llanhilleth
June – Charles Heard Wild and Thomas William Kennard visit Liddell & Gordon's offices. Wild is joint patentee of the Warren Truss girder design and Kennard has an interest in its use. Kennard's father, Robert William, also has an interest, as a banker and major investor in ironworks at Blaenavon and Falkirk
August – Kennard produces his first design for a viaduct at Crumlin
30th September – An NA&HR appointed committee recommends acceptance of Kennard's tender for the viaduct, over that of William Doyne
October – The NA&HR accepts Kennard's tender of £31,480 to build the viaduct
November – Construction of the viaduct begins with borings in the Ebbw Valley floor for the piers and the search for rock high up on the valley sides for the abutments
1853
March – Surveying of the Kendon Valley underway so drawings of that section could be produced
Early April – NA&HR purchase land at Crumlin on which Kennard will erect his Viaduct Works factory. They are in operation two months later
May – Following modifications to the design, including lengthening of the Ebbw section by 153ft, Liddell's revised tender price of £38,740 accepted by the NA&HR Board
4th August – Amendment to TVE Act obtained, taking into account Liddell's new route
August – Liddell visits Crumlin to inspect progress. Ebbw section abutment foundations reached, foundation for Pier No. 1 reaches 5ft depth
September – Foundations for other piers progressing
20th October – Contract between NA&HR and Kennard for the construction of Crumlin Viaduct finally signed
6th December – The NA&HR run a special train on their main line between Newport and Hereford but public opening is then delayed by a land slip near Llanvihangel
8th December – First column of Pier No. 4 – the 'Isabella Pier', is raised into position. Kennard arranges a commemorative event to coincide with this, the ceremony carried out by Capt. Fitzmaurice, Chairman of the NA&HR, and his niece the Hon. Lady Isabella Fitzmaurice, during which a cup of coins from 1853 is buried beneath the pier. Kennard claims the viaduct will be completed within twelve months
1854
2nd January – NA&HR main line opens to traffic
18th July – Kennard mortgages the Viaduct Works to the NA&HR for £5,000
October – All of the Ebbw section piers are completed. Twenty-five of the forty girders have been fabricated and await lifting into position
December – First girders raised and fixed into position. First fatal accident occurs during the raising of the second girder between piers 1 and 2 but details of exactly when and who was killed are scant
1855
January – Second fatal accident, one man killed when a girder being raised buckled. Work comes to a halt whilst a solution to the buckling is sought
March – Lifting resumes after stiffening of the top chord of each girder with temporary bracing
April – Two girders a week being raised.
18th April – Another serious accident when four girders which had been raised but not fixed toppled and fell after supporting blocks were knocked out. Two men, Ives and Bannister, died as a result, the accident occurring in front of Kennard. An inquest was held on 21st April
May – The Monmouthshire Railway & Canal Co. refuses

permission for a stage to be erected across their Western Valleys line to assist in raising the girders between piers 4 and 5. The problem is resolved at Board level
July – Painting of the ironwork commences
16th August – TVE line opens from Pontypool Road to Crumlin Junction
September – Last girder raised into position. The ironwork for both viaduct sections is now complete
1856
June – Planking of both viaducts completed. Tipping commences on the intermediate hillside to raise its height to track level
Summer – Thomas Kennard poses on the viaduct decking for what has become one of the most iconic photographs of the mid-19th century
31st December – Draft agreement indicating that Kennard had repaid the £5,000 mortgage
1857
January – Viaduct Works bought by Howard Martin Kennard. Henry Maynard appointed as Works Manager. Henry Martyn Kennard later also takes a share
Late February – After numerous delays, track laying over the viaduct finally commences
April – Carr suggests a walkway across the viaduct between the centre girders for inspection and maintenance purposes. After construction, it quickly becomes a local attraction
1st May – Track laying completed, testing with a single engine carried out
8th May – Testing with six of the NA&HR's heaviest engines carried out
15th May – Lt Col. George Wynne carries out an inspection of the viaduct on behalf of the Board of Trade
Late May – Goods traffic commences running over the viaduct
1st June – The TVE line is officially opened to traffic but on this day, numerous special trains run to a temporary station at the east end of the viaduct. Coming from various locations, visitors are able to walk across the viaduct and down into Crumlin for a day of celebration
15th October – Crumlin High Level station opened for passenger traffic. It never had any goods facilities
1859
9th April – Start of litigation between Thomas Kennard and the NA&HR, alleging underpayment for the work carried out
August – Both parties ordered to go to arbitration
4th November – Court of Arbitration sits. After hearing some evidence, court is adjourned until 2nd December
1860
January – Viaduct reopened to traffic after being closed for a few weeks in order that the girders could be strengthened
October & December – Kennard's attorneys request further information for the arbitration hearing
1861
7th January – Arbitration proceedings open at the Law Institution
21st March – West Midland Railway (successors to the NA&HR) Board agrees to a sum of £47,000 in total for Kennard's account, requiring a payment to him of a further £5,592, 3s 7d
5th June – As a result, all proceedings in the action are stayed and the matter of Kennard versus the NA&HR (and their successor) is brought to an end
1865
21st September – BoT testing of the viaduct carried out by Capt. Tyler RE using seven engines with a combined weight of nearly 300 tons, and then with a loaded train of similar weight on the other line as well, indicates that the viaduct is sound. However, following concerns over the rotting decking timbers, the deck is replaced at Capt. Tyler's suggestion with wrought iron sheets and additional girders
1866
November – Strengthening work completed
1871
22nd September – Henry Maynard purchases the Viaduct Works from the Kennard Brothers and incorporates them under a new company, the Crumlin Works Co. Ltd
1875
Unknown date – Further testing of the viaduct by the engineer for the VoN indicates it is in secure condition
1878
January – Crumlin Works Co. Ltd goes into liquidation
August – Works ordered to be sold at public auction
15th October – Date of first auction
1898
December – A derailment at the east end of the Ebbw section damages the railings and rips up a length of track but fortunately with no serious consequences
1902
8th August – The GWR seeks to restrict coal mining activites in the Ebbw Valley within the vicinity of the viaduct but the Act is only partially successful
1903
Single line working is put in place whilst the track is replaced. Electric Train Staff is put in operation between

PLATE A14: This atmospheric photograph, looking south-east from the valley side above Crumlin Navigation Colliery, was taken sometime in the 1930s and shortly after a burst of rain, although the sun now appears to be shining – April perhaps? Smoke from industrial and residential chimneys drifts down the valley and the sidings next to the Western Valleys Brewery (the old Viaduct Works) look busy with wagons, albeit there is very little sign of life in the picture otherwise.
STEPHEN ROWSON COLLECTION

GORDON WOOD

During compilation of this volume, we were always aware that we were in a race against time as Gordon was seriously ill. Sadly, he lost his fight on 26th May 2024, so has not lived to see the results of thirty years of work in print. He did, however, get to see a PDF of the almost completed book a couple of days before he passed. He was absolutely delighted with what we had done to bring his manuscript and drawings to life, recognising that the book would serve as a fitting testimony to the years he had put into his research. His widow, Jean, told us that seeing the book come together had been a great filip and that it had given him several extra months.

Neil Parkhouse & Stephen Rowson

Plate A15: *After stereographs came lantern slides, which could be projected onto the wall. This hand coloured slide (which fortuitously came to light just before the book went to print) appears to date from circa 1895, with a couple of wagons just in view bottom left, at the wharf at the base of the Trinant Colliery incline.* David Westcott collection

This Francis Bedford panoramic study was taken from a very similar spot to the LSC stereo view on page 137 (PLATE 9.7). However, taken some ten or so years later in the mid-1860s, the vegetable plots which occupied the right foreground in that picture now appear to have been abandoned and have become overgrown. The terminus winding hole of the Crumlin Arm of the Monmouthshire Canal can be seen far right, whilst the bed of the Ebbw River running down the centre of the picture is almost dry. Sadly, none of the early photographs of the viaduct show trains crossing over – even at a stately 8mph, the exposure time required would have blurred them completely. STEPHEN ROWSON COLLECTION